Canada and the British World

*Edited by Phillip Buckner
and R. Douglas Francis*

165101

Canada and the British World:
Culture, Migration, and Identity

UBCPress · Vancouver · Toronto

15 14 13 12 11 10 09 08 07 06   5 4 3 2 1

Printed in Canada on ancient-forest-free paper (100% post-consumer recycled)
that is processed chlorine- and acid-free, with vegetable-based inks.

Library and Archives Canada Cataloguing in Publication

Canada and the British world : culture, migration, and identity / edited by
Phillip Buckner and R. Douglas Francis.

Includes bibliographical references and index.
ISBN-13: 978-0-7748-1305-1
ISBN-10: 0-7748-1305-9

1. Nationalism – Canada – History. 2. Canada – History – 19th century. 3. Canada
– History – 20th century. 4. Canada – Relations – Great Britain. 5. Great Britain –
Relations – Canada. I. Buckner, Phillip A. (Phillip Alfred), 1942- II. Francis, R. D.
(R. Douglas), 1944- III. Title.

FC246.N37C35 2006   971.05   C2006-903287-4

Canadä

UBC Press gratefully acknowledges the financial support for our publishing
program of the Government of Canada through the Book Publishing Industry
Development Program (BPIDP), and of the Canada Council for the Arts, and
the British Columbia Arts Council.

This book has been published with the help of grants from the Institute of
Commonwealth Studies and from the Canadian Federation for the Humanities and
Social Sciences, through the Aid to Scholarly Publications Programme, using funds
provided by the Social Sciences and Humanities Research Council of Canada.

UBC Press
The University of British Columbia
2029 West Mall
Vancouver, BC V6T 1Z2
604-822-5959 / Fax: 604-822-6083
www.ubcpress.ca

Contents

Canada and the British World

Introduction

Phillip Buckner and R. Douglas Francis

Since the Second World War a revolution has taken place in Canadian historiography. In the late nineteenth and well into the twentieth century, the majority of English Canadian historians believed that Canada was essentially a "British" nation and that its legal and political institutions and its culture and society could be understood only within the context of its long history as a British colony. Mainly amateurs who wrote history as a hobby, the earliest Canadian historians were proud of their British origins and deeply committed to Canada's participation in the British Empire. They belonged to what J.M.S. Careless once described, ironically but not inaccurately, as the "blood is thicker than water" school.[1] The first generation of professional historians, men such as George Wrong, W.P.M. Kennedy, and Chester Martin, were very similar both in background and in their attitude toward the Empire, even though by the early decades of the twentieth century one can see a growing desire among Canada's small historical community to emphasize that, while Canada was a "British" nation, it was a distinctive British nation with institutions and a cultural identity of its own.[2]

The First World War shook but did not destroy this Britannic vision of Canada. It is a myth that Canadians emerged from the war alienated from, and disillusioned with, the imperial connection. Most Canadians undoubtedly felt that Canada had earned the right to have its own foreign policy and in the interwar period there was a vigorous debate among English Canadian intellectuals about the extent to which Canadians should follow British leadership in international affairs. But few English Canadians wanted to break the imperial tie. They continued to believe that Canada was, and should continue to be, a "British" nation and that it should cooperate with the other members of the British family in the British Commonwealth of Nations. As Wesley Gustavson points out in his chapter in this collection (Chapter 9), even though there were disputes over how Canada's part in the First World War should be interpreted within the British imperial context, these disputes did not imply any fundamental reassessment of Canada's relationship with Britain. In general, most English Canadian historians shared this perspective.

In the interwar years, English Canadian historians began to place greater emphasis on the role of North American environmental factors in the creation of the Canadian identity. But even those historians, such as Frank H. Underhill and A.R.M. Lower, who were increasingly critical of Britain's leadership and who wanted Canada to pursue an independent foreign policy or to become more closely allied to the United States, were, as Douglas Francis argues in his chapter in this collection (Chapter 18), committed to the notion that Canada was essentially a British nation. The Second World War reinforced English Canada's sense of belonging to a family of British nations. In the First World War nearly half the Canadian forces had been British-born but migration from the British Isles dropped dramatically in the interwar years and in the Second World War the Canadian forces were overwhelmingly composed of native-born Canadians. But a majority of those Canadians who served overseas during the Second World War could trace their ancestry to the British Isles. During the war the Canadian forces served alongside the British and other Commonwealth forces, first in defending Britain and then in the invasion of Europe. Both in Britain and in Canada the war was promoted as a "people's" war, and great stress was laid upon the unity of the "British peoples" around the globe in defence of British liberty and British parliamentary institutions against Nazi tyranny and oppression. Even the British monarchy emerged from the war more popular both in Britain and in Canada than ever before. During the war half a million Canadians lived in Britain, and many of them married British women. The war brides, with their children, formed the beginning of a new wave of British immigrants who flooded into Canada in the years after the Second World War.

The Second World War is usually seen as the critical turning point in the creation of Canadian nationalism, and it was. Canadians, whether they had served overseas or on the home front, were proud of the role Canada had played in the war and this pride was reflected in a strong determination in the postwar period that Canada would play an independent role in international relations. In 1947 the Canadian Parliament passed the first Canadian Citizenship Act, and in 1949 it made the Supreme Court of Canada the final court of appeal, ending appeals to the Judicial Committee of the Privy Council. But Canadians were not engaged in a headlong rush to cut their remaining links with Britain. The Canadian Citizenship Act specifically declared that Canadians remained British subjects. When Princess Elizabeth toured Canada in 1951, she received the same warm welcome that her father had received in 1939. In 1949 India became independent and the British Commonwealth of Nations was renamed the Commonwealth of Nations, but most Canadians continued to view the Commonwealth as primarily an association of British nations and as an important instrument of Canadian foreign policy because it promoted solidarity among the British family of nations. The Suez Crisis of 1956 weakened that sentiment but it did not weaken the belief among English Canadians that Canada ought to be a British nation. Indeed, John Diefenbaker's election victory in 1957 was at least partly due to a desire by many English Canadians to reaffirm the importance of the British connection.

In the 1960s, however, Canada underwent two quiet revolutions. The first – and less quiet – took place in Quebec. The Quiet Revolution in Quebec not only modernized and transformed Quebec society but also led to the rise of a viable separatist movement. Of course, French Canadians had never shared English Canadians' enthusiasm for maintaining the imperial connection, particularly when it led to Canadian participation in Britain's wars in South Africa at the end of the nineteenth century and in Europe in the twentieth. But the attitude of the conservative French Canadian elite, from which French Canada's historians were also drawn, had never been entirely negative toward the imperial connection. They saw the connection as a necessary bulwark against American expansionism and even as providing a degree of protection against the English Canadian majority within the Canadian federal system. In the postwar environment, with Canada increasingly integrated into a North American economy and with the removal of appeals to the Judicial Committee of Privy Council (which had often upheld provincial autonomy), these arguments lost their force among Québécois nationalists who had little sympathy for the relics of the imperial past, forgetting (as Serge Courville points out in his chapter in this collection, Chapter 8) how much Quebec's culture had also been shaped and influenced by the imperial connection.

The second quiet revolution took place in English Canada, which also began to redefine its national identity in the 1960s.[3] After a heated debate within English Canada over whether the symbols of empire and Britishness should be retained, Canada adopted its own flag with a new design that did not include the Union Jack. It also made "O Canada" its national anthem. Much of the pressure for these changes came from within English Canada, from those who believed that it was time to abandon the relics of Canada's imperial past. In part, this revolution in English Canada was motivated by a growing fear that Quebec might try to leave the federation. But it was also a response to the heavy postwar migration that came from a much wider range of sources than in the past and that changed the composition of Canada from a predominantly British into a multicultural nation. It was also a response to the increased Americanization of Canada, as Canada was integrated into the American economy and influenced by American popular culture. Younger native-born English-speaking Canadians – even those of British ancestry – no longer felt the strong attachment that previous generations had felt to British institutions and the imperial connection. English Canadian historiography reflected these trends. In the 1950s and even into the 1960s, historians such as Donald Creighton and W.L. Morton continued to insist on the importance of Canada's British and imperial past. But in the 1970s Canadian historians became more interested in the limited identities that Canadians shared – of class, region, ethnicity, and gender. Of course, all of these themes in the past had an imperial dimension, as a number of the essays in this book show, but this dimension was largely ignored in the new Canadian historiography. Even those who disliked the focus on regional identities and called for a return to what they thought of as national history downplayed the importance of imperial history in the shaping of modern Canada. As Doug Owram – a critic of the limited identities approach – notes in the recent *Oxford History of the British Empire*, by the 1960s the study of Canada's place within the Empire had become a specialized field of little interest to most Canadian historians. This, he argues, is as it should be, since the true concern of Canadian historians should be not with imperial history but with "the origin of Canada."[4] British imperial history was now seen as a field that should be left to the British historians – that is to say, to those who focused on the history of the United Kingdom, a subject of less interest to Canadian historians. What had once been a central field in Canadian history was now seen as essentially part of an alien subject: British history.[5] In the other former dominions the same pattern emerged, although more slowly in Australia and New Zealand, where a far greater proportion of the population was of British origin than was the case in Canada.

There were a few voices in the wilderness who protested against this attempt to de-emphasize the British connection in the history of the dominions. The most influential was J.G.A. Pocock, the New Zealand-born historian, whose area of specialization was seventeenth- and eighteenth-century British history. In as early as 1974 Pocock pleaded for a new British history that would include the old dominions (or what he called the neo-Britains overseas) and that would recognize that the history of the dominions was an integral part of imperial history.[6] But the call met with a very limited response from most national historians, who continued to believe that one could be either an Australian, a Canadian, a New Zealander, or a South African or one could be British but one could not hold two national identities at once. In the 1990s, however, historians began to question this simplistic notion, pointing out that in the past, particularly in composite monarchies like the United Kingdom, most people had held multiple national identities.[7] And if it was possible to be Scottish – or even Irish – and British at the same time, why could one not be Australian and British, or Canadian and British, at the same time? Not everyone accepted this conclusion, but the issue of Britishness was slowly put back on the agenda in the writing of the history of the former dominions.

There were other factors at work. A growing number (though undoubtedly a minority) of historians in the older dominions were increasingly disturbed by the marginalization of the dominions within the new imperial historiography that emerged in the period after the Second World War. In the older histories, the creation of a series of self-governing colonies with institutions modelled on that of the mother country had been seen as one of the most significant and lasting contributions of the British Empire and was viewed in wholly positive terms. But in an era of decolonization, British imperial historians could see little that was lasting and less that was positive in the history of the British Empire. They were more concerned with writing a history of British imperialism than with writing a history of the British Empire. The new historiography was metropolitan-centred, focusing on how Britain had managed to acquire and control a vast overseas empire and how this empire had contributed to Britain's wealth and to its status in the world. From this perspective, the division between the parts of the world that were formally part of the Empire and those that simply contributed to the creation of British wealth through trade was not significant. The focus of the new historiography was also on those parts of the world that Britain had exploited most ruthlessly, particularly the impact of imperialism on the African and Asian peoples who had been brought under imperial rule against their wishes. Canadian (and Australian and New Zealand) history was no longer at the front of the new agenda. In fact, it was barely on the agenda of the new imperial history at all. Most historians of the older dominions by and large did not strenuously object to the changes in the way in which imperial history was being written. This was partly because most were nationalists who no longer wished to see their countries as products of the age of imperial expansion. But there were many younger historians, less nationalistic than the previous generation, who felt that the dominions must confront the reality of their own imperial past and the legacies of that past – particularly the exploitation of Native peoples – that remained imbedded within Canada and the other colonies of British settlement.

Gradually, then, there has emerged a renewed interest in Canada's place in what we have called the "British World." The concept of a British World is not a new one. The phrase was frequently used from the late nineteenth century until the 1950s, but its popularity was always overshadowed by the term "Greater Britain," which was coined by Sir Charles Dilke in the late 1860s and quickly became the preferred term for collectively describing the British colonies of settlement overseas. Like the boundaries of Greater Britain, the boundaries of the British World were and are open to interpretation. Dilke originally included the United States as part of his Greater Britain. Obviously, the Thirteen Colonies were at the centre of the first British

Empire. Indeed, although the first British Empire was destroyed when the United States achieved independence in 1783, it could be argued that, during the first half of the nineteenth century, the newly created United States was still to some degree part of a British-dominated cultural and intellectual world. But in the nineteenth century the Americans also created an empire of their own as they expanded across the continent and, in the early twentieth century, even acquired overseas colonies. In the twentieth century British politicians such as Joseph Chamberlain and Winston Churchill talked of the unity of "the English-speaking peoples," but this unity was more imagined than real. Dilke recognized this in as early as 1899 when he declared in his study of *The British Empire* that the pressure to restrict the use of the term to territories that were part of the formal empire was "too strong to resist."[8]

Canada, as the largest and most prominent of the self-governing colonies (or dominions as they came to be called officially in 1907), was clearly part of this British World, a world held together more by a sense of belonging to a shared British culture than by ties of commerce and trade. It was the mass migration of British immigrants to Canada in the nineteenth and early twentieth centuries that ensured that Canada would remain part of a British World until well into the twentieth century. Indeed, most of the chapters in this collection deal – some directly and some indirectly – with the impact of migration from the British Isles on Canada. From the 1960s to the 1990s, there was extensive research on the Scots and the Irish in Canada (particularly in the pre-Confederation era), although only recently have scholars begun to study the impact of Canada's largest immigrant group – the English – on the history of Canada. A variety of factors explain the comparative lack of interest in English immigration to Canada. But clearly one reason is that the descendants of the Irish and Scottish immigrants to Canada have succeeded in disassociating themselves from their British imperial past and in presenting themselves as part of the colonized rather than as the colonizers, thus laying the blame for imperial exploitation on the English and their descendents. This, of course, is a serious distortion of the reality. What existed in Canada was a shared British culture to which all of the various immigrant communities from the British Isles, including the Scots and the Irish, contributed. There are historians who would question whether one can talk about a British diaspora, but this is a question of semantics.[9] What is clear is that the migration of waves of Britons overseas was fundamental in creating a series of new nation-states, which have survived and remain one of the most important and lasting legacies of the British Empire. These new nation-states are no longer as predominantly British as they once were, and Canada and the other former dominions have begun to redefine themselves as multicultural communities with their own distinct national identities, rather than as neo-Britains.

Nonetheless, the legacy of their imperial past cannot easily be wiped away and consigned to the dustbin of history.

Of course, it is important to keep in mind that the dominions never were simple replicas of the "mother country." It is well known that the populations of the dominions were more Scottish and Irish than that of the United Kingdom, although this emphasis on the Scots and the Irish is frequently exaggerated. During the first half of the nineteenth century, Scottish and Irish immigrants did outnumber English immigrants in Canada, but during the even heavier waves of migrations in the late nineteenth and early twentieth century, the English overwhelmingly predominated, though the Scots remained significantly overrepresented.[10] Certainly, it is a myth that the Scots created Canada. Canada drew upon all parts of the British Isles for its immigrants, its institutions, its laws, and its culture. And Canadians frequently rejected aspects of the law or culture of the mother country that they felt were incapable of being transplanted in a new environment or that they felt were undesirable to transplant. Canadians wished to be "British" but on their own terms and in their own way. It was a "Better Britain" – not simply a neo-Britain – that they sought to create. But clearly there remained strong linkages between the British at home and the British immigrants and their descendants in Canada. Hundreds of thousands of Britons in Britain saw relatives, friends, and neighbours migrate to Canada. Some of those who left became return migrants, either because they failed to create a better life for themselves overseas or because they were so successful that they could afford to return in style. During the late nineteenth and early twentieth centuries, as the costs of transport fell and the safety and comfort of travelling by sea improved dramatically, a growing number of British migrants repeatedly moved back and forth between Britain and the colonies. They were joined by many second- or third-generation colonials who were lured to Britain as tourists or for a variety of business, professional, or political reasons. Some of these Canadian migrants never returned to the colony they continued to call home. Indeed, the word "home" had an ambiguous meaning for many English Canadians, who had a sense of having two homes: an ancestral home in Britain and a new home overseas. Over time, loyalty to the new home – to Canada – clearly came to count for more than loyalty to the old. But English Canadians did not perceive any conflict in being loyal both to the Empire and to Canada. In the late nineteenth and the first half of the twentieth century, this loyalty was strengthened by an increasingly complex web of family, cultural, commercial, and professional networks that linked the British in Britain with the British overseas.[11] In the past, Canadian historians have too readily accepted some version of the colony-to-nation thesis. It is as if the Empire existed essentially to create a series of independent nations and that the process of making the transition was simple, uncomplicated, and linear. This teleological approach glosses over the fact that while there was a continual process of renegotiating the status of Canada within the Empire, Canadians were committed to continued participation in the Empire and the preservation of British culture in Canada. Even after the Second World War, the belief in the existence of a British World remained strong for another two decades.

An attempt to explore and interpret the value of the British World as a concept and its meaning to those who were part of it began as an initiative of a small group of historians – John Darwin at Oxford University, Rob Holland at the Institute of Commonwealth Studies at the University of London, and Carl Bridge at the Menzies Centre for Australian Studies at the University of London – who were determined to break the mould in which imperial history was being written and to bring the dominions back into the picture. They recruited Phillip Buckner from Canada (at that time teaching at the University of New Brunswick, although he too would shortly become a senior research fellow at the Institute of Commonwealth Studies), James Belich from New Zealand (shortly to move to the University of Auckland), and Bill Nasson from the University of Cape Town in South Africa. This group formed an informal committee that was responsible for organizing the first British World Conference at the Institute of Commonwealth Studies in June 1998. So successful was the conference that it was decided to hold a series of conferences in the dominions, the first in South Africa, at the University of Cape Town, in 2002.[12]

The third conference was held at the University of Calgary in 2003.[13] Selecting the papers to include in this book on Canada and the British World was a difficult task because of the number of excellent papers from which we could choose. The purpose of resurrecting the concept of a British World is not an exercise in imperial nostalgia, a lament for a world we have lost. Our goal is to re-examine a complex phenomenon and to understand how it shaped the world in which Canadians lived and to some extent still live, and we hope that the chapters that follow give some indication of the quality and complexity of the debate that has been taking place on the issue of the relationships that bound Canada to the wider British World.

Notes

1 See J.M.S. Careless, "Frontierism, Metropolitanism and Canadian History," *Canadian Historical Review* 31 (1950): 105-14.

2 The best overview of English Canadian historiography in the twentieth century remains Carl Berger, *The Writing of Canadian History: Aspects of English-Canadian Historical Writing Since 1900*, 2nd ed. (Toronto: University of Toronto Press, 1986).

3 We have taken the notion of a second quiet revolution from José Igartua. See his "'Ready, Aye, Ready' No more? Canada, Britain, and the Suez Crisis in the Canadian Press," in *Canada and the End of Empire*, ed. Phillip Buckner (Vancouver: UBC Press, 2004), 47-65.

4 D.R. Owram, "Canada and the Empire," in *The Oxford History of the British Empire*, vol. 5, *Historiography*, ed. Robin W. Winks (Oxford: Oxford University Press, 1999), 161. For a critique from a British World perspective of the whole Oxford History project, see Phillip

Buckner, "Was There a 'British' Empire? *The Oxford History of the British Empire* from a Canadian Perspective," *Acadiensis* 32 (2002): 110-28.

5 See Paul T. Phillips, *Britain's Past in Canada: The Teaching and Writing of British History* (Vancouver: UBC Press, 1989).

6 J.G.A. Pocock, "British History: A Plea for a New Subject," *New Zealand Journal of History* 8 (1974): 3-21. See also his "The Limits and Divisions of British History: In Search of the Unknown Subject," *American Historical Review* 87 (1982): 311-36; "History and Sovereignty," *Journal of British Studies* 31 (1992): 358-89; and "The New British History in Atlantic Perspective: An Antipodean Commentary," *American Historical Review* 104 (1999): 490-500. For a Canadian perspective, see Phillip Buckner, "Whatever Happened to the British Empire?" *Journal of the Canadian Historical Association* 3 (1993): 3-32. It was another New Zealander, James Belich, who most consistently sought to examine the extent to which the term "NeoBritain" is a useful description of the dominions. See his "Neo-Britains" (paper presented at the first British World Conference at the Institute of Commonwealth Studies, London, June 1998), and his two-volume history of New Zealand, *Making Peoples: A History of the New Zealanders from Polynesian Settlement to the End of the Nineteenth Century* (Auckland, NZ: Penguin Press, 1996) and *Paradise Reforged: A History of the New Zealanders from the 1880s to the Year 2000* (Auckland, NZ: Penguin Press, 2001).

7 This notion can be found in a host of books written in the 1990s, but the one that had the greatest influence on British scholars was Linda Colley, *Britons: Forging the Nation, 1707-1837* (New Haven, CT: Yale University Press, 1992).

8 Sir Charles W. Dilke, *The British Empire* (London: Macmillan, 1899), 9.

9 For a recent discussion of the usefulness of the concept of a diaspora, see Rosalind McClean, "'How We Prepare Them in India': British Diasporic Imaginings and Migration to New Zealand," *New Zealand Journal of History* 37, 2 (2003): 131-51.

10 For a discussion of why the migration from England has been comparatively neglected, see Phillip Buckner, "Introduction," *British Journal of Canadian Studies* 16, 1 (2003): 1-6. This issue of the journal was devoted to the theme of English migration to Canada.

11 These networks have yet to be properly examined. For a useful start, see Alan Lester, *Imperial Networks: Creating Identities in Nineteenth-Century South Africa and Britain* (London: Routledge, 2001), and Simon J. Potter, *News and the British World: The Emergence of an Imperial Press System* (Oxford: Clarendon Press, 2003).

12 More than fifty papers were given to an audience of at least twice that size and a selection of the papers has subsequently been published in a special issue of the *Journal of Imperial and Commonwealth History,* issued simultaneously as a book under the title *The British World: Diaspora, Culture, and Identity.* See Phillip Buckner and Carl Bridge, "Reinventing the British World," *Round Table* 368 (2003): 77-88, and Carl Bridge and Kent Fedorowich, "Mapping the British World," in *The British World: Diaspora, Culture and Identity,* ed. Carl Bridge and Kent Fedorowich (London: Frank Cass, 2003), 1-15.

13 The Calgary British World Conference attracted more than 120 papers and about twice as many participants. It was decided to publish two collections of papers drawn from those given at the conference – one collection that would focus on the wider British World and a second volume that would examine in greater depth the place of Canada with that world. The first collection has appeared as *Rediscovering the British World,* ed. Phillip Buckner and R. Douglas Francis (Calgary: University of Calgary Press, 2005).

1

"Information Wanted": Women Emigrants in a Transatlantic World

Elizabeth Jane Errington

In June 1827, *Blackwood's Edinburgh Magazine* published one of Mrs. Heman's new poems, "Songs of Emigration":

> There was heard a song on the chiming sea;
> A mingled breathing of grief and glee;
> Man's voice, unbroken by sighs, was there,
> Filling with triumph the sunny air.

The song told "of fresh green lands, and of pastures new," and of "plains whose verdure no foot hath press'd / and whose wealth is all for the first brave guest." There, in the New World, the emigrants sang, "we will rear new homes, under trees that glow / As if gems were their fruitages of every bough ... And watch our herds, as they range at will / Through the green savannas, all bright and still." The exultant strains of this song reflect a good deal of nineteenth-century Britons' rather romantic vision of the New World across the Atlantic and the abundance it promised to all who settled there. Yet even Mrs. Heman, a firm advocate of emigration, recognized that not all shared the vision. While men sang eagerly of new farms in the wilderness, she presented a discordant chorus of women who cried for "the shelter'd garden bower, ... the grey church tower, / And the sound of the Sabbath bell" of home. "But alas!" they sang, "that we should go, / From the homesteads warm and low." Even the soaring triumph of the last verse could not completely drown out the women's lament:

> We will give the names of our fearless race
> To each bright river whose course we trace;
> We will leave our memory with mounds and floods,
> And the path of our daring in boundless woods;
> And our works unto many a lake's green shore,
> Where the Indians grave lay alone before!

But who shall teach the flowers,
Which our children loved, to dwell
In a soil that is not ours?
Home, home, and friends, farewell![1]

"Songs" was but one small part of the discourse of empire and emigration that echoed throughout the British Isles and Ireland and the British American colonies in the first half of the nineteenth century. Drawn by the seemingly limitless possibilities of land and "independence," songs, poems, pamphlets, and emigrant literature celebrated the determination of stalwart young Britons, the very "sinews of the nation," who eagerly went into the wilderness and made it bloom as a rose. Under the hand of British farmers and labourers, the "useless and silent forest" was being "replaced by fields and meadows interspersed with towns and villages, bounding and sparkling with life and enjoyment."[2]

When told in the nineteenth century, the story of the "extraordinary" migration of Britons was of farmers and mechanics, of missionaries and merchants, and of labourers and adventurers who, alone or with their families, made a new life for themselves in the colonies. The heroes of these tales were men. Although it was recognized that to succeed an emigrant needed a wife, and even children could be a real asset, the project of emigration and colonization was decidedly masculine. Like the choruses of Mrs. Heman's song, the thousands of women who went to America, if they were considered at all, were assumed to be only reluctant participants in what many characterized as a great crusade. Recent scholarship has begun to tickle out the complex and diverse roles British women played in creating and defining the British imperial world.[3] There is a growing body of literature that chronicles female migration to the settler colonies, particularly to the Antipodes.[4] With few exceptions, emigration to British America in the first half of the nineteenth century continues to be characterized as the migration of nuclear families and adventurous men. Women's voices and their participation in the process is at best muted or, by implication, of no consequence.

What then, do we make of the notice that appeared in the local Kingston, Upper Canada, newspaper in September 1821: "If JOHN DONEVAN, who left Cork about three years ago, and was last heard of at Mr. Sniders near Point Fortune, about twelve months since, be alive, and will enquire at Mr. Barnhams, Inn Keeper, at Point Fortune, he will find his wife who has come out to this country in search of him."[5] Or the card to the public in York, Upper Canada, printed in the *Colonial Advocate* in 1834 that began, "Where is FRANKY MACHOGAN?" To ensure that there was no doubt to whom the notice was addressed, Mary Jane MacHogan explained that "Franky MacHogan was a native of Ireland, emigrated to Canada from County Armagh between Newtown Hamilton and Keady – by profession a hacker of flax." "His disconsolate companion" had followed him to the colony. Mary Jane, who had recently "delivered a son ... and remains in a very destitute state," asked that editors of newspapers "do an act of humanity" and help her find her husband.[6] And then there was the dilemma that Jane Mayarity found herself in, in early February 1830. She had arrived in York the previous fall to join her brother, Christopher Flinn. Her note to the public explained that although three years before (when she had last heard from him) he had been in Prince Edward Island, he had intended to move "to the upper province." To date, he was not to be found, and Jane was frustrated and did not intend to wait much longer. If she did not hear from Christopher by the end of the winter, she declared that she would return home to Ireland.[7]

Between 1815 and 1845, local newspapers in Upper Canada (and indeed, throughout North America) printed hundreds of similar notices of newly arrived wives looking for husbands, sisters or brothers looking for siblings, and mothers and fathers looking for their children.[8] Newspapers also included cards from "ladies" "lately arrived from England" or Scotland or Ireland, who, either alone or with their sisters, mothers, or husbands, proposed to open a "Seminary of Respectability" for young girls or a hat or dress shop. Some notices were very brief, like that which appeared in the Kingston *Chronicle and Gazette* in March 1834: "If Patrick Brady, from Claremont County, Mayo Ireland be in Kingston, he will confer a favour by making it known to this office."[9] A few told a poignant story. An "Information Wanted" in the *Cobourg Star* in August 1832 addressed to "ALEXANDER CAMERON, late of Glasgow, who came out in March last, by the ship *Nailer*, from Greenock," recounted how his brother, Hugh, and his family had followed Alexander to Upper Canada. "Unfortunately," Hugh had been "seized with the cholera, while coming up the Lake" and had died. His widow and child, who were "totally unprovided for," were "anxiously desirous of hearing from the said ALEXANDER – who is supposed to have settled somewhere in the Township of *Cavan*." Mrs. Cameron's notice concluded: "Any information respecting him, addressed to this *Office*, will be gratefully acknowledged. He has a wife and eight children."[10]

Unfortunately, even the most detailed of these cards offer only a tantalizing glimpse of the lives and expectations of these emigrants and their families. One is left wondering if John Donevan was alive. Were widow Cameron and her child reunited with her brother-in-law, Alexander? Did the growing numbers of "ladies" and craftswomen who established businesses in the colony find economic success? These notices do, nonetheless, offer fleeting details of who these women (and men) were and why they were in Kingston or York or other colonial communities. They also include hints of emigrants' expectations of the New World and suggest that although absent in the imperial discourse, women were actively engaged in the colonial project.

And when these fragmentary stories are read within the context of emigrant correspondence, one can begin to tickle out how at least some Britons regarded the British World in the thirty years after the Napoleonic Wars.

The women and men who placed notices in colonial newspapers and, in most cases, those whom they sought were recent emigrants and all were engaged in what scholars now call the project of empire and colonization.[11] Between 1815 and 1845, hundreds of thousands of Britons left their homes and the British Isles for America, for Australia, for South Africa, and for other colonies around the globe.[12] Contemporaries remarked on the "extraordinary emigration from all quarters of the Old World" and British papers often commented on the "tides" of migrants or "the fever" of emigration that seemed to be infecting the nation.[13] The destiny of choice between 1815 and 1845 was North America, and particularly that "land of promise," the United States.[14] After 1815, however, the new colonies of British North America and particularly Upper Canada began to attract a growing number of English, Irish, and Scottish migrants.[15] By mid-century, many politicians, pamphleteers, colonial promoters, and many of Britain's growing middle classes were extolling the efforts of those "true Britons" who, "by the result of the white man's hard and honest labour,"[16] were creating a new "wondrous Empire" in North America and promoting the spread of the Anglo-Saxon race and "English laws, language," and civilization.[17]

There was nonetheless considerable debate in Britain in the first half of the nineteenth century about the efficacy of emigration. Questions were raised in the British press and in Parliament about whether the population should be "guarded" or if the government should actively promote various emigration schemes to "relieve distress at home." Others proposed that Parliament actively encourage Britons who intended to emigrate anyway to make for the settlement colonies of the Empire.[18] There were also sharp differences as to who should be encouraged to leave the British Isles and what class of people made the best settlers on the imperial frontiers.

There was little debate, however, that emigration and empire were "manly" undertakings. Abandoning one's home for the uncertainties of a new world required individuals with resolve and determination. The imperial frontier and settler colonies needed strong, "true British men" to subdue the wilderness and lay the seeds of civilization. As other scholars have persuasively argued, the project of colonization was a gendered undertaking. And in the first half of the nineteenth century, emigration was certainly a gendered experience.[19] Common sense told Britons that the "emigrant" was male. The growing attention and often heated debates in the British press and in government about the waves of Britons who were packing up and boarding ships bound for America revolved around the need for hardy farmers, questions about whether impoverished peasant labourers would survive, and how to attract "men of capital." The growing body of promotional literature was directed almost exclusively to men of the soil, gentlemen of some means, and craftsmen and mechanics.[20]

Not all men were equally suited for such an enterprise. Certainly, British newspapers and travellers' accounts told stories of young single men who by their ingenuity, determination, and hard work had made their fortune in the colonies.[21] But settlement required families and the discourse privileged married men. "The irregularity of a bachelor's life" should be avoided on the frontier,[22] it was firmly declared. A wife "helped secure [an emigrant's] comfort."[23] An industrious and willing wife could also be a decided economic asset. "Married persons are always more comfortable and succeed sooner in Canada than single men," traveller John Howison advised in 1821. Indeed, "a wife and family, so far from being a burden there always prove sources of wealth."[24] Young men were encouraged to "bring out wives with them ... as generally speaking, a man will find a woman of his own country more congenial to his habits and taste ... than any other."[25]

Some emigrant guides and settlers' accounts did acknowledge that specifically women were "wanted" in British North America.[26] One settler stated, somewhat derisively, that he could readily find husbands for single or young widowed women who had "a snug jointure or disposable fortune."[27] Emigrant guides also pointed out that young, healthy girls would quickly find employment in the colonies as domestic servants, teachers, or farm girls. "And if steady, industrious and deserving," these girls "may probably soon (if they choose) become the mistress of a house of their own."[28] Such encouragement was muted, however. It was "known" that women, by their very nature, were not really suited to such independent action. Indeed, emigrants were periodically warned to expect that their wives would be reluctant to leave home. It was pointed out that women feared the dangerous ocean voyage and that they had a greater attachment to the land of their birth than did their husbands. Emigrants would have to persuade their wives to join them. Most women portrayed in the discourse were, like children, dependants who needed to be directed to acquiesce to their husbands' decision to emigrate.[29]

Those who actually packed up their goods and boarded ships at Greenock, Southampton, and numerous smaller ports to make their way to "America" were certainly not indifferent to the public's growing preoccupation with emigration and empire. Few of those who made their way to Upper Canada between 1815 and 1845 would have recognized themselves in the public discourse, however. The tales of emigration and their implicit assumptions about reluctant women do not seem to have influenced Mrs. Donevan or Mary Jack MacHogan as they negotiated the often difficult world of the transatlantic crossing. And Jane Mayarity was certainly not the only young woman who, either alone or in the company of friends or family, arrived in the colonies in search of kin and economic opportunity.[30]

At the same time, information-wanted notices do illustrate that for many, and perhaps most, women, emigration was a family affair. Most of those who sought the public's help were looking for kin and identified themselves within family relationships. The majority of wives looking for their husbands identified themselves solely by his name, like Mrs. John Donevan or Mrs. Hugh Cameron. As they searched and waited in that liminal space between emigrant and colonist, being a wife, a mother, a sister, or a cousin offered these women at least some sense of certainty and identity. And by characterizing themselves as a wife, mother, or sister of an emigrant, these women may also have been unconsciously asserting their respectability. For in a world that was increasingly concerned about the symbolic role of the "good woman" and the supposed naturalness of women's dependence, this was one way they could gain the public's sympathy and claim the right to support from kin and the wider community.

It is unlikely that Upper Canadians were particularly surprised to read notices of wives and mothers who were looking for their husbands. Although a significant proportion of Britons emigrated to Upper Canada between 1815 and 1845 as part of a nuclear family, the limited shipping lists of the period indicate that adult men outnumbered women by a factor of at least two to one.[31] Some of these men were undoubtedly young, single labourers and artisans who were drawn by the promise of work and land and an opportunity to assert their independence from parental households. But many other apparently unattached men were actually husbands and fathers. Certainly, Mrs. Donevan was not the only woman whose husband had gone ahead, expecting that the rest of the family would follow some time after.[32] Mrs. Comerford, for example, left "the Parish of Guildmore, County of Cavan, Ireland" in 1825, some months after her husband, William, emigrated to Upper Canada. Her notice informed William "that his wife is at York, UC. Information will be obtained of Mr. Ketchum, of that Town, at what place she can be found."[33] Indeed, there were dozens of notices of British wives, often accompanied by children, who were looking for husbands who had gone on ahead.

The practice of heads of households going ahead "to spy out the land" was not unusual. Some men went to the colony to assess the situation for themselves before making a final decision to emigrate. Others, as recommended by a number of emigrant guides and settlers' accounts, went ahead to find work or land and then sent for their families.[34] The decision that the family would be divided, perhaps for an extended period, was not taken lightly. The journey was notoriously dangerous; the colonies were "foreign." And those left behind still had to support themselves until the family could be reunited. The undertaking required careful planning. It must also have prompted lengthy discussions about where "Father" might go and when, how long the family would be divided, and, ideally, how it would be reunited.

The debates in John Gemmill's household may well have been protracted. In 1820-21, John Gemmill, a forty-five-year-old stonemason living just outside Glasgow, had the opportunity to join a local emigration scheme. The proposal included a land grant in Lanark County, Upper Canada, and subsidized passage to the colony. It appears that financial circumstances precluded the family from travelling as a unit. It may also have been that John and his wife, Ann, decided that he should go ahead and begin to make a home for their nine children. Given the local economic situation, John and Ann felt that the opportunity was too good to miss and John boarded the *David of London* at Greenock in May 1821.[35] After he left, Ann and the children, who ranged in age from eighteen to two, went to reside with John's brother, Andrew. In one of his first letters home, John told his wife "to get [herself] entered into some society" and, if need be, have their son Andrew, "entered as head of the family."[36] He also sent detailed instructions on what goods the family should bring and what should be sold, how to pack, and what tools he wanted. John's letter did not arrive, however, until after Ann had set out.[37] We know that, among other things, it was Ann who organized the sale of household items, packed boxes and supplementary food for the voyage, and negotiated the family's passage. And in the end, Ann was obliged to travel alone with the six younger children. To her and John's great disappointment, the three eldest children, daughters Jean and Margaret and son Andrew, decided to remain in Scotland. John and Ann were reunited in 1823, apparently without incident. And all extant records indicate that Ann had shared her husband's commitment to emigrating to the colonies and took an active part in the process.

This was not always the case. In 1832, William Hutton found himself increasingly unable to make a respectable living managing a farm in Ireland. In the spring of 1833, he asked to be released from his lease and, at the same time, wrote his mother that he and his wife, Fanny, and his brother had "been considering the propriety of going out to Canada next month."[38] It seems clear from William's subsequent letters that Fanny was not enamoured by the prospect. Hutton told his mother that "Fanny says she would rather have a situation of £150 per annum than go to Canada; to her the idea of such a trip is odious in the extreme. No wonder, when there are five such helpless little ones about her, but she thinks of two evils 'Canada or idleness' the former is the better."[39] Fanny Hutton's obvious reluctance must have prompted some heated discussions. It was probably not just concerns about the health and welfare of her young children, although this would have been significant. She was also a gentlewoman for whom the colonies offered little but hardship, loneliness, and estrangement from family and friends.

William Hutton travelled to Canada a year later on his own to assess the situation. In June 1834 he wrote to Fanny that he had purchased 165 acres of land within a mile and a quarter of the small village of Belleville in eastern Upper Canada. After describing how he intended to finance the purchase (loans from his father), William then explained: "I have done my very best both in doing and in refraining from doing, and I feel very confident that if my dearest Fanny should think otherwise, she will not reproach me." William was obviously aware that Fanny was still not reconciled to emigrating: "If you feel you cannot be happy at such a distance from home, I would say certainly remain until you can train your mind to it, and send the children forward." But he hoped that her love for him would prevail and, echoing the tropes of the day, he also hoped that "you will endeavour to sooth sorrows which a separation from a beloved country and beloved friends naturally produces in a warm heart. Enough of this, I merely wish to encourage you to hold the mastery over your spirit, to root and ground your love. I know well how grievous, how intensively grievous, your separation from all that you hold dear in Ireland must be."[40] Fanny did have some choice in the matter. She had family members in England willing and financially able to support her and the children. And William would, reluctantly, have accepted her decision. Leaving an ill mother and moving permanently to a new country and a new home that William described as "bare," difficult at best to reach, and surrounded by strangers was almost impossible to conceive. But Fanny too was a gentlewoman of her time. Being separated from her husband and possibly children and refusing to accept those responsibilities of women of her class was, for her, apparently unthinkable. Fanny and the children joined William in Upper Canada in the fall of 1834.[41]

It is perhaps not surprising that Fanny, and a number of other women of her status, did not emigrate until they had a home to go to. Most British families did not have such choices. And even fewer could afford, as the Huttons could, to ship almost all their household goods to Upper Canada. Financial circumstances often forced members of a family to emigrate at different times. And many wives were only too eager to join their husbands. But maintaining contact across the Atlantic was difficult. Not all British emigrants had the ability or could afford to write letters home, and they relied on friends or neighbours to pass on information or to make the necessary arrangements for the family to follow.[42] Even then, letters could take months to reach their intended recipients and they frequently went astray. Although many women, like Fanny Hutton, waited for news and instructions, others, like Ann Gemmill, chose not to wait. Fanny was also fortunate in that William met her and the children at the wharf in New York and took them, together with untold numbers of boxes and furniture, to their new home. For her part, Ann Gemmill had detailed directions to John's location, and she and the children seem to have made their own way there. Many families were probably reunited without significant difficulty. But as notices to the public illustrate, sometimes the family's arrangements went awry; at other times, wives and children, prompted perhaps by desperation or impatience, set out to make the long passage to America to find husbands they had not seen or heard from, sometimes, in years.

John McQueen wrote for his family from a "location near Gananoque," Upper Canada, a year after he left Glasgow. When Mrs. McQueen, with their six children, arrived six months later, she was dismayed that she could not find John. The family was "now in distressed circumstances," she informed the public, and any information of her husband would "receive her grateful thanks."[43] Neil Horkan, "from the neighbourhood of Castleban, Ireland," sent for his family in 1836-37. Upon arrival in Kingston, Mrs. Horkan turned to the local emigrant agent for help to find him.[44] Most information-wanted notices did not include details about what, if any, arrangements the family had made to be reunited. Some, like Irishwoman Mrs. Thomas Wilson and her four children, were "expected" and she seems to have been dismayed that Thomas was not waiting for them.[45] The tenor of other notices only suggests that the family had had news from their husbands before they left home.[46] Some clearly had not. Hannah Cradel from County Clare placed a notice in the *Niagara Herald* in January 1830 that she had come to the colony in search of Michael Power, her husband, "for he never wrote."[47] Fanny Connor was disconsolate when she arrived in Montreal in August 1833 "in search" of her husband, Thomas, who had left home more than two years earlier.[48] Sometimes it was years before the family left at home could make its way to Upper Canada. Mrs. William Banks and her four children had not seen William in more than four years when they arrived in the colony.[49]

Many women and their children appear to have used what limited resources they had just to make the journey and arrived in the colony in dire straits. In 1829, Mary Duffy "arrived at York, UC with five children" and, she informed the public, was "in a distressed situation" and most "anxious to hear from" her husband, John, who had emigrated from County Kerry to Quebec two years before.[50] Mrs. Furgeson Bell announced that she and her three children were now "at the corner of Oak and James Street, New York, destitute of the comfort of life."[51] Mrs. Bell's dilemma was complicated because she did not know where her husband was. Neither did a "dejected" Mrs. William Flia Cooper, who asked that her notice be published "by all the Canadian newspapers" as well as those in the United States as her "last resource."[52] Julia Kain only knew that her husband, Thomas, was "supposed to be living in Upper Canada" when she arrived in York in 1830.[53] When she left home, Julia may have been quite confident that she would be able to find Thomas. One wonders what she thought as she began to realize how large the colony was and, even in 1830, how difficult communications and transportation could be. This was certainly not just another part of Britain, as some at home were claiming.[54] And what, in the end, had prompted her to leave the familiarity of home? Perhaps she did not have family and neighbours, as Ann Gemmill did, to rely on. Or perhaps the promise of a new world and the hope of being reunited with Thomas had greater influence than any regrets about leaving "the sound of the Sabbath bell."

We know next to nothing about how those who were left behind managed while they waited for word from across the Atlantic. Many probably moved in with a close relative – parents or a sibling – and relied on what they and their children could earn and perhaps save for their future departure. A few were delighted when they received remittances from their husbands. Not only did this help defray the cost of the voyage but it was also tangible evidence that he was still alive and waiting for them. A number undoubtedly turned to local charities or depended on the parish poor rates to keep themselves and to pay at least part of their passage to the New World. And when no news arrived, either directly or included in letters sent to neighbours or friends, at least some wives must have wondered if their husbands did not want to be found.

What is startling is these women's determination to join their husbands and reunite their families. As they settled into the steerage of one of the many emigrant ships or, for those fortunate few, took cabin accommodation on a packet, some may, as Mrs. Heman suggested, have sighed with regret, "Home, home and friends farewell." But most would have been too preoccupied with looking after their children, wondering whether they had packed enough or too much, and looking forward to reconstituting their family. Theirs was not an act of particular heroism or of self-effacing dependency. They arrived in the colony as independent and determined women, most of them quite capable of negotiating leaving home and of remaking home and family.

When Jane Grey arrived in Upper Canada in 1831, she had not left home to look for her husband. Rather, she sought news of her sister, Esther Brown, who had left Ireland a year earlier as a member of her employer's household. Jane's notice did not display the urgency that characterized those placed by desperate wives. Although "newly arrived in the colony," Jane and her husband were already "residing in York" when she sought the public's help. Nonetheless, she stated, she "would be happy to hear" from her sister, who was somewhere "in the upper or lower province."[55] Jane may not have needed to find her sister, but having family already in the colony probably had some influence on her destination as an emigrant. And finding her sister would also have provided an element of stability in this new world.

Most information-wanted notices were placed by recently arrived emigrants looking for their siblings.[56] The majority of these were men looking for their brothers or sisters; a significant proportion, however, about 25 percent, were of apparently unattached young women, like Jane Mayarity. Most cards in this category were placed by recently arrived Irish migrants. They included Sarah McCulloch, who put a notice in the *Cobourg Star* in August 1833: "Information is wanting, where Esther McCulloch is to be found." Esther had left the parish of Treshaskin, County Antrim, Ireland, three years earlier. The family must have maintained some contact with Esther, because Sarah knew that when she had first arrived Esther had lived in Belleville and had then moved "on to the Trent." Sarah now thought that Esther had been "seeking service in this village lately." But she could not be found. And Sarah, alone and "in distress," was "most anxious to find her."[57]

An emigrant's choice of destination was, in part at least, often dictated by the whereabouts of other family members or friends. And for many, the pull of kin stretched not just across the Atlantic but over many years. Isabella Stevens must have had a good deal of optimism when she arrived in Upper Canada from Ireland in 1835. She had a brother already living and presumably well settled in the colony and Isabella undoubtedly expected that he and his family would provide her with a home for at least the time it would take her to find employment. Her hopes were dashed, however, when, as she announced to the public, she could not find her brother, whom she had not seen in fifteen years or directly heard of in ten.[58] One wonders what Jane O'Neil had expected when she arrived in York in 1829. Although she found work at Mrs. Methan's, she could not find her brother, Matthew, who had come to the colony only two years before.[59]

Many young women and men arrived to join a sister who was already settled in the colony. Finding a sister could be more difficult than finding a brother. In 1836, for example, a notice in a York paper asked for information of Leticia Ingham. She had emigrated in 1824 and was thought to be "living in or near Montreal." To complicate matters, Leticia had married after she had left home, and her sister, who was looking for her, did not know her married name.[60] Moreover, the family did not seem to have heard from her for a number of years. Many siblings did manage, however, to stay in touch with brothers and sisters on the other side of the Atlantic. When Jane Nelson began to look for her sister, Mary, "the last account" she had had was that Mary was in New York.[61] Before Bridget Drury left home, she had received a letter from her sister Catherine, then in Montreal.[62]

Unlike wives who were going to join their husbands, most siblings did not seem to expect to reconstitute the family of their youth. Rather, they were just trying to establish contact or perhaps to rekindle a relationship. A notice in the *Bytown Gazette* in 1840 was quite typical: "Information wanted of David Chambers, a native of the North of Ireland who came to this country from Liverpool by the ship George Wilkinson in May last. Should this meet his eye, his sister Eliza Chambers who resides in Bytown will be happy to hear from him."[63] A few were rather more urgent. Sarah Palmer wondered if her "brother and sister, Robert and James Palmer," who had left home "some years since," were even alive.[64] For Louise Godfry, it was imperative that she find her brother, William, as she was "in the most heart-rending condition, without money and among strangers."[65] For all newly arrived emigrants, knowing that kin was close at hand must have helped ameliorate the strangeness of the foreign land. Reforging familial relationships helped provide a sense of emotional and, perhaps, financial security.

Many young women were quite capable of coping on their own in the colonies, however. Like four young sisters, aged sixteen, eighteen, nineteen, and twenty-three, who "alone" and having "recently arrived from the neighbourhood of York England"[66] placed advertisements in local newspapers or went door to door looking for work as maids, cooks, governesses, and other domestic help. Some wanted to be taken on as apprentices by a milliner; others offered to become land girls. By the mid-1820s, girls could also register at one of the employment agencies that had been set up by enterprising local shopkeepers and newspaper editors.[67] In communities where servants and "girls" were at a premium, newly arrived emigrant women had little difficulty finding waged work. In this regard, the discourse was right; women were wanted in Upper Canada, not just as wives but as girls of all work and domestic labourers. Many of those usually young women who took on waged work in the colony had probably left home in the company of parents or other siblings. And, as they would have done at home, they entered the labour market when their labour was not needed at home and as a way to supplement their family's income before they married and set up their own households. But the information-wanted notices indicate that, like their brothers, some, at least, left home alone or in the company of siblings, cousins, or friends expecting to join kin already settled in the colonies. And if, on arrival, they could not find their brother or sister, a few, like Jane Mayarity, decided to return home.

Most emigrating women did not have this option. They had used all their resources just to get to the New World. And for some, there was little reason to return. Perhaps the most poignant notices were from widowed women and elderly parents and fathers looking for their sons or daughters. In July 1840, Lucy Chambers, who had "lately arrived in Upper Canada," was "feeling anxious to hear from her sons, Alexander Hughes and Henry Elam."[68] Ten years earlier, Ann Dunlop had been particularly "anxious to hear from" her son, Thomas Wright. She had just arrived from Aughnacky, Ireland, her card stated, and had missed meeting him in Montreal.[69] Ann Crone was in "distressed circumstances" in 1832 when she began to look "desperately" for her sons, Cormick and James.[70] Not all, or likely even most, parents were in such difficulties. Richard Parson's mother was "very anxious that he would join" her and her new husband, William Lane, at their new home in

Ottonabee Township. They were well settled; what Richard's mother wanted was to be reunited with her son.[71] Edward and Mary Moran had followed their daughter Sarah to the colonies. Now that they were settled in York, they were eager to find her. They wrote, "[they will] be thankful to any person giving any account of her and should this meet her eye, they are willing to pay her expenses to York."[72] For the Morans, emigration was an opportunity to reconstitute the family. For Ann Crone and Ann Dunlop, leaving home may have been an act of desperation. They were searching not just for their children but for the financial security that was no longer available to them at home.

The importance of kin in the process of emigration cannot be overstated. As Marjory Harper and others have concluded, "private encouragement and practical assistance from family, friends and community ... were of inestimable and enduring importance in stimulating secondary migration and directing patterns of settlement."[73] This was as true of emigrating women as of emigrating men. Moreover, when British women (and men) left home, they did so, in part at least, within the context of their identities as wives, sisters, and mothers. In many households, the decision to emigrate was cause for considerable family debate and discussion. And once the decision was made and they had arrived in the colony, emigrants consciously asserted kin relationships to gain the public's attention and assistance and to find emotional and often financial support.

A small but significant portion of unattached women emigrants were in quite different circumstances. After 1820, Upper Canadian newspapers included notices from a few women who had "recently arrived from the old country," who announced their intention of setting up a shop in one of the female trades – dressmaking, bonnet making and mantuamaking – or opening a girl's school.[74] Staymaker Jane McBradney was one of a growing number of craftswomen who, having "served a regular apprenticeship" or having been trained in Britain, tried to parlay their status as recent emigrants to gain custom in the colony.[75] Jane Arnold of Brockville, newly arrived from England, made a point of informing the public and potential customers that she was already an "experienced" seamstress.[76] Other women-merchants claimed to have owned or worked in a shop before they emigrated to the colony. Many of those who opened millinery, hat, and bonnet shops, or offered to make ladies' gowns and children's clothes, were widows, often accompanied by their daughters. Others were apparently younger women who, like the Misses Rubergall of Brockville in the early 1830s or the Misses S. & J. Ross of York,[77] hoped to find in the colony greater economic opportunities than existed at home. These women must have had some financial resources to buy supplies and, at the very least, rent a room. They also possessed the confidence that their skills were valuable assets even in this far-flung part of the British World.

After 1815, notices began to appear in colonial newspapers, of that group of women Martha Vicinus has identified as British gentlewomen in distress.[78] Certainly, most of those looking for a situation as a governess in a good home were "local" women who had recently fallen on hard times. But, if their cards to the public are to be believed, a few were "gentlewomen" who had just arrived in the colony and intended to try to take advantage of the growing demand for formal education for both girls and boys. Like their sisters who emigrated to Australia, a number of these self-proclaimed "ladies" stated that they had particular expertise in a specific subject or had themselves had the benefit of a "complete" education at home. Some may have feared "the loss of caste and humiliation which would accompany a wage earning career at home" and thought they could "safely pursue the same career anonymously in the colonies."[79] The "lady," who had "lately arrived from England" and proposed to establish a seminary of respectability in Kingston in the early 1820s,[80] obviously anticipated that she would be able to attain some degree of economic security and personal independence in the colony. Others, with an introduction to a local family and perhaps a little capital, may have relished the move. Mrs. Twigg stated that she had been "induced" to emigrate to Upper Canada. She had "conducted a boarding and day school in the north of Ireland" for many years and brought with her her good name and her "long experience and credentials."[81] Mrs. Twigg and, by the 1830s, dozens of other "independent" women were offering formal instruction to the colony's daughters in reading and writing as well as those "accomplishments" – drawing, languages, dancing, and fancy needlework – so necessary for middle-class wives and mothers. Many of these "seminaries of respectability" were short lived and most seemed to have only a few students. But a few teacher proprietors were very successful. By the mid-1830s, Mrs. Cockburn of York had forty day and boarding students and a full-time staff of three teacher assistants.[82]

A number of these craftswomen and teachers were consciously claiming a place for themselves in the British World. Their skills, their womanhood, and even their "condition" as unattached women filled a need in the burgeoning colonial society. Many newly arrived milliners, bonnet makers, and others who sold their womanly skills found ready markets for their work. Gentlewomen teachers not only met the growing demand for an educated citizenry; in their schools they also actively promoted and embraced the gendered constructions of true womanhood that many in the colony considered essential for civilized society. By emigrating, at least some British "spinster" women who at home were increasingly considered "superfluous" gained status and a new respectability.[83]

Leaving home clearly promised hundreds of thousands of Britons new economic and personal opportunities in the first half of the nineteenth century. But emigration was only one of the options available to those looking for work, for security for themselves and their families, or for a way to escape an untenable situation. The decision to leave home and make the always difficult and often treacherous journey across the Atlantic was not taken lightly. The brief notices of women and men looking for work or asking for the public's assistance to find relatives or friends illustrate some of the complexities of these decisions. They also indicate how integral familial relationships were in who went and where.

It would appear that, in the short term at least, emigration may also have accentuated ethnic and local identities.[84] Information-wanted notices almost always identified the parties by their origin – Scots, Irish, Welsh, or English – and often included details about the particular town, village, or community in which the individual being looked for had lived. This was undoubtedly an attempt to make it easier for the public to help identify and find the husband, sister, or other party sought. And yet, the advertisements of those new arrivals looking for work also frequently included whether they were Scottish or English. And those who placed help-wanted ads often explicitly stated their requirement for an English or a Scottish girl. Although Upper Canada may have been part of a British World, those who arrived to join husbands and reconstitute their families or to find other family members seem to have seen it as an extension of the more immediate and personal world of family and kin relationships, perhaps overladen by ethnic identity.[85] And in their determination to reforge these connections, women created their own stories of emigration.

Acknowledgments
The research for this chapter was supported by grants from Social Science and Humanities Research Council of Canada and from the Royal Military College of Canada.

Notes
1 Originally in *Blackwood's Edinburgh Magazine* 22 (July 1827): 32. This was then picked up in the *Brockville Gazette*, 23 July 1830, and *Farmers Journal* (St. Catharines), 26 September 1827.
2 *Thoughts on Emigration as the Means of Surmounting Our Present Difficulties* (London, 1831), 45.
3 The literature on this has grown exponentially in the last twenty years, and most attention to women and empire was in the latter half of the century. For a recent overview, see the discussion in Lisa Chilton, "A New Class of Women for the Colonies: *The Imperial Colonist* and the Construction of Empire," in *The British World: Diaspora, Culture and Identity*, ed. Carl Bridge and Kent Fedorowich (London: Frank Cass, 2003), 36-56, and R. Kranidis, *Imperial Objects: Essays on Victorian Women's Emigration and the Unauthorized Imperial Experience* (New York: Twayne, 1998).
4 In addition to James Hammerton's classic study, *Emigrant Gentlewomen: Genteel Poverty and Female Emigration, 1830-1914* (London: Croom Helm, 1979), see also Janice Gothard, *Blue China: Single Female Migration to Colonial Australia* (Melbourne: Melbourne University Press, 2001), and Charlotte MacDonald, *A Woman of Good Character: Single Women as Immigrant Settlers in Nineteenth Century New Zealand* (Wellington, NZ: Bridget Williams, 1990).
5 *Kingston Chronicle*, 21 September 1821.
6 *Colonial Advocate* (York), 31 May 1834.
7 Ibid., 4 February 1830.

8 This preliminary study rests on about 360 notices that appeared in Upper Canadian news-papers between 1815 and 1845. This is only a fraction of the information-wanted notices that were printed in these years. Most were placed by "settlers" who appear to have been quite well established, looking for children who had left home or for other relatives or friends who had "disappeared" while looking for work or on a business trip. The notices used here were those that can be clearly identified as having been placed by recently ar-rived emigrants, or those looking for new arrivals.

9 *Chronicle and Gazette* (Kingston), 22 March 1834.

10 *Cobourg Star,* 8 August 1832.

11 For a discussion of this see, among others, Catherine Hall, ed., *Cultures of Empire: Colonizers in Britain and the Empire in the Nineteenth and Twentieth Centuries: A Reader* (New York: Routledge, 2000), and Adele Perry, *On the Edge of Empire: Gender, Race and the Making of British Columbia, 1840-1871* (Toronto: University of Toronto Press, 2001).

12 It is still unclear how many actually emigrated from Britain in this period. P. Cain, "Econom-ics and Empire: The Metropolitan Context," in *The Oxford History of the British Empire*, vol. 3, *The Nineteenth Century*, ed. Andrew Porter (Oxford: Oxford University Press, 1999), 31-52, estimates 600,000 between 1815 and 1859. For a discussion of the problems in determin-ing the volume of emigration and its ethnic composition, see D.H. Akenson, *The Irish in Ontario* (Montreal and Kingston: McGill-Queen's University Press, 1984).

13 This language was particularly evident in the early 1830s. See, among others, articles in *Scots Times,* 26 June 1832; *Chronicle and Gazette* (Kingston), 3 June 1840, taken from *Herald* (London); *Manchester Guardian,* 17 April 1830; *Cobourg Star,* 17 May 1832, taken from *Fife Herald* and *Bell's Messenger; Canadian Emigrant* (London), 6 July 1833; *Christian Guardian* (York), 3 July 1830; *Kingston Chronicle,* 26 June 1830.

14 As many have illustrated, British colonies in America had been attractive to migrants throughout the seventeenth and eighteenth centuries. This persisted after the American Revolution and in the nineteenth century was a growing concern for many in Great Brit-ain. See, among others, David Cressey, *Coming Over: Migration and Communication between England and New England in the Seventeenth Century* (New York: Cambridge University Press, 1987); Bernard Bailyn, *Voyagers to the West: A Passage of the Peopling of America on the Eve of the Revolution* (New York: Vintage Books, 1988); Marilyn C. Baseler, *"Asylum for Mankind" America 1607-1800* (Ithaca, NY: Cornell University Press, 1998); Ronald Hyam, *Britain's Imperial Century, 1815-1914: A Study of Empire and Expansion* (Lantham, MD: Barnes and Noble, 1993).

15 Marjory Harper, "British Migration and the Peopling of the Empire," in *The Oxford History of the British Empire,* vol. 3, *The Nineteenth Century,* 75-87.

16 "Hochelaga," *Blackwood's Edinburgh Magazine* 61 (October 1846): 464.

17 "A Letter of Emigration and Colonization," *Bytown Gazette,* 9 February 1843, in a letter taken from a London pap er. See also *Chronicle and Gazette* (Kingston), 27 December 1834, in an article taken from *Agricultural and Industrial.* This evolving discourse of emigration and empire presages many of the images and themes that would preoccupy travellers and the British public in the second half of the nineteenth century. Although rooted in tradi-tional visions of the New World, the early-nineteenth-century discourse of emigration reinvented British America as an integral part of the global British Empire, and a colony that shared a uniquely Anglo-Saxon vision of the world, whose "children will present at no great distant period, the most glorious family compact man has ever seen [and] they will govern the earth by their influence and example." Robert MacDougall, *The Emigrant's Guide to North America,* ed. Elizabeth Thompson (1841; reprinted Toronto: Natural Heritage Books, 1998), 7. See Mary Louise Pratt, *Imperial Eyes: Travel Writing and Transculturation* (New York: Routledge, 1992), and Peter Hulme, *Colonial Encounters: Europe and the Native Caribbean, 1492-1979* (London: Methuen, 1986).

18 See Michael Vance, "The Politics of Emigration: Scotland and Assisted Emigration to Upper Canada, 1815-26," in *Scottish Emigration and Scottish Society,* ed. T.M. Devine (Edinburgh: John Donald Publishers, 1992), 37-60; Harper, "British Migration."

19 See the discussion in Perry, *On the Edge of Empire,* and Hall, introduction to *Cultures of Empire.*

20 One notable exception, of course, is the work of Catherine Parr Traill, *The Backwoods of Canada* (London, 1836) and her sister Susanna Moodie, *Roughing It in the Bush* (London, 1852). For a good survey of promotional and settler literature about Upper Canada, see Daniel Keon, "The New World Idea of British North America" (PhD thesis, Queen's University, 1984).

21 See for example G.W. Warr, *Canada As It Is* (London, 1847), 99; *Thoughts on Emigration*, 43; *A Few Plain Directions* (London, 1820), 48; John MacGregor, *Observations* (London, 1830), 41; John MacGregor, *British America* (London, 1833), 1, 473.

22 Thomas Radcliffe, *Authentic Letters from Upper Canada* (Dublin, 1833). William Blane, *An Excursion Through the United States and Canada ... 1822-23* (1864; reprinted New York: Negro University Press, 1964) judged that "a Bachelor has no business in the Backwoods," 163.

23 Martin Doyle, *Hints on Emigration* (London, 1832), 66.

24 John Howison, *Sketches of Upper Canada* (Edinburgh, 1821), 239. An article in the *Aberdeen Herald* noted that men who "have sons and daughters old enough to lend them efficient assistance ... let them emigrate by all means and we will answer for their success." Quoted in *Sequel to Counsel to Emigrants* (Edinburgh, 1833), 7. See also *Blackwood's Edinburgh Magazine* 27 (August 1832), where it was noted that the more numerous a man's children, the better he would succeed. *View of Canada* (Edinburgh, 1844), 40-41; Doyle, *Hints on Emigration;* MacGregor, *British America.*

25 *Sequel to Counsel to Emigrants,* 7.

26 Andrew Picken, *The Canadas as They at Present Commend Themselves to the Enterprise of Emigrants, Colonists, and Capitalists ...* (London, 1832), 36.

27 Radcliffe, *Authentic Letters,* 26. See also MacDougall, *The Emigrant's Guide,* 5.

28 Picken, *The Canadas,* 36.

29 Adele Perry also discovered this attitude on the BC frontier; see *On the Edge of Empire,* chap. 6. Joanna de Groot, in "'Sex' and 'Race': The Construction of Language and Image in the Nineteenth Century," in *Cultures of Empire,* 37-60, 38, notes how the cultural dependence of women in the colonial/imperial context and their portrayal as "children in need of protection and care" intersected and reinforced understandings of race.

30 See Hasia Diner, *Erin's Daughters in America: Irish Immigrant Women in the Nineteenth Century* (Baltimore and London: Johns Hopkins University Press, 1983).

31 See Charlotte Erickson, "Emigration from the British Isles to the United States of America in 1831," in *Leaving Home: Essays on British Emigration in the Nineteenth Century* (Ithaca, NY, and New York: Cornell University Press, 1994), 126-66.

32 Ibid.

33 *Niagara Gleaner,* 3 September 1825.

34 See John Matheson, *Counsel for Emigrants* (Aberdeen, 1834), 36-37. The correspondence of those who had been in the colony for some time often remarked on meeting new arrivals who were on a farm-hunting expedition.

35 See John McDonald, *Emigration to Canada* (Edinburgh, 1823).

36 Scottish National Library, John Gemmill Family Papers, MU7424, 2 March 1822.

37 The letter arrived, according to the annotation made on receipt, about six weeks after Ann left. The Gemmill correspondence is quite unusual, as all the letters include the date written and the date received.

38 Gerald E. Boyce, ed., *Hutton of Hastings: The Life and Letters of William Hutton, 1801-1861* (Belleville, ON: Hastings County Council, 1972), 19 April 1833, 32.

39 Ibid.

40 Ibid., 32-33.

41 See Amanda Vickery, *The Gentlemen's Daughter* (New Haven and London: Yale University Press, 1998); Jack Little, ed., *Love Strong as Death: Lucy Peel's Canadian Journal 1833-1836* (Waterloo, ON: Wilfred Laurier University Press, 2001); and discussion in Elizabeth Jane Errington, *Emigrants' Worlds* (Montreal and Kingston: McGill-Queen's University Press, forthcoming).

42 The letters included in Wendy Cameron, Sheila Haines, and Mary McDougall Maude, eds., *English Immigrant Voices: Labourers, Letters from Upper Canada in the 1830s* (Montreal and Kingston: McGill-Queen's University Press, 2000) illustrate this most eloquently.

43 *Kingston Chronicle,* 14 January 1832. A number of women explicitly mentioned that "they had been sent for." *Chronicle and Gazette* (Kingston), 23 August 1837; *Bytown Gazette,* 14 December 1843.

44 *Chronicle and Gazette* (Kingston), 23 August 1837. So too did Mrs. Barker, accompanied by four children. Ibid., 13 June 1840.

45 *Bytown Gazette,* 14 December 1843.

46 Many were like the notice of Mrs. Spright and her children, which stated simply that they were looking for Thomas Spright. "They have just arrived from England," Mrs. Spright informed the public. *Colonial Advocate* (York), 9 July 1829.

47 *Niagara Herald,* 21 January 1830. This also seems to have been the situation of the Donevan family, mentioned earlier. Mrs. Donevan's notice concluded that she "[had] come out to this country in search of him." *Kingston Chronicle,* 21 September 1820. See also notice of Mary White who, with her three children, was looking for Joseph. *Chronicle and Gazette* (Kingston), 19 April 1834.

48 *Chronicle and Gazette* (Kingston), 17 August 1833.

49 *Kingston Chronicle,* 21 September 1821.

50 *Farmers Journal* (St. Catharines), 4 March 1829.

51 Ibid., 9 April 1828.

52 *Chronicle and Gazette* (Kingston), 2 September 1843.

53 *Niagara Herald,* 21 January 1830. She had not seen him in three years. Robert Morris' wife and three children and Mary White of Scotland were two others in this situation. See *Toronto Patriot,* 28 November 1837; *Kingston Chronicle,* 19 July 1834; *Chronicle and Gazette* (Kingston), 1 October 1831, notice of Mrs. William McIndoe.

54 See, among others, accounts in "MacGregor's British America," *Blackwood's Edinburgh Magazine* 27 (June 1832): 927.

55 *Colonial Advocate* (York), 17 November 1831.

56 This category made up almost 60 percent of those placed by emigrants.

57 *Cobourg Star,* 28 August 1833. See also notice of Margaret Graham, looking for her brother Robert, *Canadian Freeman* (York), 3 May 1832; Ann Coyle, looking for her brother and sister-in-law, *Colonial Advocate* (York), 11 June 1834. Most of the information-wanted notices of emigrants were placed by people who identified themselves as Irish. This is not surprising, as long before the famine migrations of 1846-48, Irish immigrants to Upper Canada outnumbered all others.

58 *St. Catharines Journal,* 26 November 1835. See also that of Margaret Young, looking for her brother Thomas, who had left County Derry seventeen years earlier. *Chronicle and Gazette* (Kingston), 28 June 1834.

59 *Colonial Advocate* (York), 24 September 1829.

60 *Christian Guardian* (York), 8 June 1836. See also *Hallowell Free Press,* 24 July 1832, Ann Bleakney looking for Margaret, whom she thought had married a farmer.

61 *Christian Guardian* (York), 15 February 1832. Jane was in York.

62 *Canadian Freeman* (York), 24 May 1832.

63 *Bytown Gazette,* 17 September 1840.

64 *Christian Guardian* (York), 19 February 1834. See also *Chronicle and Gazette* (Kingston), 29 May 1839: Mrs. Phillips of Cobourg looking for Catharine O'Brien, who had not been heard of since her arrival.

65 See notice in *Christian Guardian* (York), 8 March 1837. See also Margaret Scott, looking for brother George, a blacksmith who was a native of Scotland; she had "arrived in this country last summer and [was] anxious to hear from him." *Cobourg Star,* 10 December 1834. A number of notices were from brothers and sisters looking for siblings who had arrived with another family. Mary Hamill was looking for her cousin, Sally, who had come from Ireland in the company of William and James Brown eight years before. *Chronicle and Gazette* (Kingston), 7 April 1832; Ann Sherlock, now Ann Maine, had arrived in Kingston with three women from Ireland in October 1836; "Where is she?" her sister now asked. Ibid., 16 May 1838. In 1837, sisters Eliza, Isabela, and Margaret were looking for their brother, John Taylor, who had left County Donega for York in May 1835, *Christian Guardian* (York), 15 November 1837.

66 *Patriot* (York), 30 June 1831.
67 For a little more detail on this and opportunities for employment generally in the colony, see Elizabeth Jane Errington, *Wives and Mothers, School Mistresses and Scullery Maids* (Montreal and Kingston: McGill-Queen's University Press, 1995), particularly 144 and accompanying notes.
68 *Upper Canada Gazette* (York), 8 July 1840.
69 *Niagara Gleaner,* 14 August 1830. In 1833, Elizabeth Hetherington, who had emigrated from County Fermanagh, Ireland, some months after her son, Adam, had left home, could not find out her son's new place of residence. Her call for assistance stated: "Any person acquainted with him would serve the cause of humanity by letting him know that his mother is at the house of Mr James Botfield, Matilda, UC and wishes him to write or come to her immediately." *Christian Guardian* (York), 31 July 1833. See also Ann Dundoon and her daughter, who were looking for Patrick Dundoon, *Niagara Herald,* 21 January 1830.
70 *Canadian Freeman* (York), 22 November 1832. Widow Fox turned to the emigrant agent for assistance in finding daughters Nancy and Betty. *Christian Guardian* (York), 13 October 1847. See also notice looking for Francis Duffy; his mother and sisters were anxious to find him. *Patriot* (York), 25 September 1840; Michael Carey's "distressed parents" were looking for him. *Chronicle and Gazette* (Kingston), 20 January 1841.
71 *Cobourg Star,* 10 April 1833.
72 *Canadian Freeman* (London), 24 November 1833.
73 Harper, "British Migration," 83.
74 See discussion in Errington, *Wives and Mothers,* chap. 8.
75 *Brockville Recorder,* 21 July 1831. Miss Wilson, recently arrived in Kingston, became an independent dressmaker and milliner only after, she stated, she had had five years' training under Mrs. Kennedy. *Kingston Chronicle,* 22 November 1834. See Sally Alexander, "Women's Work in Nineteenth Century London: A Study of the Years 1820-60s," in *Becoming a Woman and Other Essays in 19th and 20th Century Feminist History,* ed. Sally Alexander (London: Virago Press, 1994).
76 Mrs. Jones and Miss Rose Anne Osborne, *United Empire Loyalist* (York), 24 May 1828; Jane Arnold, *Brockville Recorder,* 6 August 1830; Misses S. and J. Ross, *Brockville Recorder,* 28 July 1831; Mrs. Steward, *Colonial Advocate* (York), 6 June 1834.
77 See *Brockville Recorder,* 28 July 1831; *Colonial Advocate* (York), 21 January 1830.
78 Martha Vicinus, *Independent Women: Work and Community for Single Women, 1850-1920* (Chicago: University of Chicago Press, 1985).
79 Hammerton, *Emigrant Gentlewomen,* 46.
80 *Kingston Chronicle,* 4 January 1822.
81 Ibid., 4 January 1825.
82 See discussion in Errington, *Wives and Mothers,* chap. 9.
83 See Rita Kranidis, *The Victorian Spinster and Colonial Emigration: Contested Subjects* (New York: St. Martin's Press, 1999).
84 Charlotte Erickson notes that European migrations "were not so much national in scope" as "constituted by particular streams from one village or region to a particular county or city elsewhere"; *Leaving Home,* 7.
85 See discussion in Bridge and Fedorowich, "Mapping the British World" and Phillip Buckner and Carl Bridge, "Reinventing the British World," *Round Table* 368 (2003): 77-88 for a discussion of emigrant and colonial "identities."

2

Self-Reflection in the Consolidation of Scottish Identity: A Case Study in Family Correspondence, 1805-50

Sarah Katherine Gibson

> On Saturday morning last one of the oldest most generally known and highly respected Scotch residents of Lower Canada, Mr. Hugh Brodie of Coteau St. Pierre departed this life at the mature age of 72 years, 49 of which he spend in the vicinity of Montreal.

Hugh Brodie's obituary notice, printed in the *Montreal Gazette* on 16 January 1852, gathered the threads of his life into a coherent narrative of Scottish colonial endeavour. He had been "devoted to agricultural pursuits in which he became a pattern to his French Canadian neighbours." Brodie had also helped set other cultural patterns: he had been an elder of the Presbyterian Scottish Church of Montreal, St. Andrew's, a judge at the New York State agricultural exhibition, and a guide to immigrants. This public review of a life represented a complex moment of colonial identification. By linking Brodie's achievements to his Scottish origins, the obituary's author showcased a specifically Scottish contribution to the British colonial project and held it up as an example to the colonized "other," the French Canadians.[1] While Hugh Brodie's death notice seemed designed to demarcate the particularity of Scottish contributions to the colony, it also hinted at the construction of identities that happened within the group so defined. Hugh Brodie's life reflected well on his Scottish community. His relatives in Scotland read the obituary in a Toronto newspaper: it occupied "the forth of a coloum [sic]" they reported proudly, and "was filled with one of the best penned charectors [sic] wrote upon man."[2] Their participation in his achievements folded him into a community of relatives and countrymen and conferred on him a public identity. He was not just any resident of Lower Canada; he was a "Scotch resident."

This chapter looks at how the concept of "a Scottish resident of Lower Canada" carried such self-evident, inherent meaning for colonials. During Hugh Brodie's lifetime, Scots occupied a self-conscious position in Montreal.

Scottish residents formed a St. Andrew's Society in 1835, and churches celebrated the nation's saint day.[3] The minister of St. Andrew's, the church at
which Hugh Brodie and his family worshipped, preached that "attachment
to the land of [their] birth" was "amongst the highest virtues that adorn
humanity." He extolled "the social sympathy" aroused by "national associations" because they preserved "in memory, all that is great and good in
the characteristics of [their country of origin]."[4] The Reverend Mathieson
stoked the hearts of his audience with patriot fervour. Yet, why was remaining in contact with "the characteristics" of Scotland a necessary good for
those Scots who attended the celebration of their nation's saint day?

A large collection of letters received by Hugh Brodie and his wife Ann
provide a window into the operation of a Scottish identity in the colonies.
While no letters sent by Hugh or Ann appear to be extant, the letters they
received from family and friends in Scotland provide a mirror in which to
understand the cultural context of their everyday lives in Canada. This perspective from within the group suggests that Scottishness appeared as an
essential and necessary category because it provided the framework for personal identity and relationships. Between 1805 and 1856, Hugh and Ann
received upward of three hundred letters from friends and family in Scotland, Upper and Lower Canada, and the United States. These letters are the
material remains of an international network of kin and kith. A substantial
proportion came from family members living in the west of Scotland and
Ireland: from Hugh's mother, Mary Gemmel; from his full siblings, Mary,
William, and Jean; from his half-brothers, Andrew and Robert; from his
sister Jean's husband, Archibald, and their two sons, Hugh and James; and
from Ann's cousin, Margaret Brodie Sloan. The Scottish writers appear to
have been of the farming and weaving class.[5] In 1803 Hugh Brodie, two of
his brothers, and his bride, Ann, left behind family and friends to establish
themselves in Montreal. Brodie began his career in Montreal as a farm manager and closed his life a prosperous farmer, having acquired the social status to become a justice of the peace.[6] The careful preservation of the Scottish
letters signals the letters' importance to the Montreal branch of the family.

Their letters are terse in describing the economic and social upheaval of
modernizing Scotland or their Scottish identities. Rather, the letters focus
on retaining affective ties with emigrated relatives. The distance separating
the Scottish and Canadian Brodies intruded into the intimate space of the
family, and the Scottish writers expressed a constant uncertainty about what
to write for their Canadian relatives. This act of correspondence created a
semi-public platform on which the Brodies self-consciously constructed
themselves. A desire to share their feelings, to describe their lives, and to
answer requests for information motivated them to write at least once a year
most years. However, the lack of common reference points in the everyday
lives of the Canadian Brodies and their family and friends in Scotland forced

family members to identify shared core values in order to continue relating to each other. In the process of this self-reflection, the Scottish Brodies drew upon the dominant Scottish discourses of enlightened progress, Presbyterian temperance, and romantic nostalgia to nurture their affective ties. The values distilled out of the dislocating forces of modernity replaced the physical common ground they had once shared with a metaphorical one, a Scottish identity. The content of the Scottish Brodies' letters mirrored Hugh Brodie's legacy to Lower Canada. His was indeed a "Scotch" life.

This case study searches for the public, objective identity of Scottishness in the private and subjective realms, within the family and in the self. Recent studies of the Scottish experience tend to examine it as an objective element of the British colonial world. American and Canadian studies identify the cultural forms and ideologies Scots bequeathed to the United States and Canada. The ideals of the Scottish Enlightenment and of Presbyterian Calvinism, it has been argued, introduced democratic and progressive principles to the nascent nations.[7] Most studies remain focused on the objective facets of the Scots' presence, the structure of church government, temperance and national societies, and cultural products, rather than on the process of change. The everyday experiences of individual Scots are missing. When individuals do appear, they do so as vectors or as representatives of larger cultural forces.[8] The Scottish Brodies' letters allow us to see how individual Scots deployed the dominant discourses to construct their personal identities. The relatives' need to remain in contact, moreover, illustrates how, as others have suggested, Scottishness was constructed in a dialectic between colony and nation; it was not a net cultural export.[9]

Other studies examine Scottishness from the perspective of Scotland's status within the British Empire. The 1707 union with Britain provoked a cultural efflorescence as the literati negotiated a new role for their now provincial nation. First philosophers and then poets defined their homeland's trajectory. David Hume relocated the civic humanist ideal of virtue in material prosperity. In so doing, he tied the interests of all Scots to the nation's economic well-being.[10] A discourse of morality and sensibility, focused on the preservation of community bonds, counterbalanced the competitive effects of commercialism.[11] Poets introduced romantic ideals to the nation and "literally" invented a cultural tradition in order to lend their elites historical legitimacy.[12] The nation's philosophically defined "psychology of improvement" impelled many Scots to take advantage of the opportunities their British identity afforded them in the Empire. The Scots' political identity appears "paradoxical" and "ironic" because Scots moved so easily between positions as colonized Scots and British imperialists.[13] The vantage point of these studies is of the elite and middling ranks of Scottish society. Michael Vance has already demonstrated how the Lowland Scottish weavers deployed, as a group, a civic humanist discourse in the public arena.[14]

The Scottish Brodies' letters reveal the extent to which individual working-class Scots internalized, and drew upon, these public discourses to construct their sense of personal identity.

The Brodie family papers offer a new perspective on the study of Scottish identity in the colonial world – a perspective from the shadowy world of the self. Historians of colonialism have turned to the historical category of the self as another analytical tool with which to describe social and cultural change. A "self" exists only in relationship to something else, another self or selves, and is thus a prism for understanding a culture as a whole.[15] Instances of misrecognition, or the failure to tolerate difference, produce the negative "other" identity constructions of colonial discourse. However, identity and recognition can be mutually constructed between subjects, each subject becoming the other's object.[16] Thus, a self mirrors another self and in the process constructs a common understanding. The Scottish Brodies' responses to the Canadian relatives demonstrate that, at least in part, colonial expectations determined the portrait of Scotland drawn for the Canadian Brodies by their Scottish relatives. Scottishness – the values and ideas distilled out of the emigration process – became the new common ground that allowed the Scottish Brodies to maintain ties of love and friendship with their Canadian relatives. This chapter describes the cultural mirror of self-expression the Scottish Brodies provided for the colonial Brodies, in order to identify how patterns of Scottishness were summoned into objective being and given meaning. What follows is a description of the conditions that challenged the Brodies' self-expression as they sat down to reflect on their lives for the Canadian relatives, and an exploration of how they constructed their identities by deploying the three dominant Scottish discourses. The concluding section suggests that Hugh Brodie's life in Lower Canada embodied the Scotch pattern of values his relatives' letters reinforced by repetition.

The primary object of the Brodie family letters was to maintain personal and emotional contact between friends separated by Hugh and Ann's move to Lower Canada. Many of the writers did not have the time or the skills to reflect on themselves, but they yearned to share their fears, anxieties, experiences, love, and affection. The writing of these letters ensured the continued personal cultivation of Scottish values, and repeated a pattern of sociability.

The decades of rapid industrialization that transformed the west of Scotland defined the lives of Hugh Brodie and his correspondents. The parishes of Kilburnie in Ayrshire and of Lochwinnoch in Renfrewshire where the Scottish Brodies lived underwent significant structural change. Agricultural innovations redefined the countryside, while newly industrializing towns provided markets for the parishes' dairy farms and market gardens. Two cotton mills integrated the small town of Lochwinnoch into an imperial market as dependants of larger mills in Paisley and Glasgow. The parish of Kilburnie and the seaside town of Saltcoats, in Ayrshire, were equally marked by social change. Their respective ministers' contributions to *The New Statistical Account of Scotland* describe communities touched by the reforming attitudes to agriculture and the economic importance of the textile industries.[17] After Hugh and his party left Scotland, his mother and his sister Mary went to live in the town of Lochwinnoch, where Mary earned a living in the weaving industry.[18] Hugh's brother William returned to Scotland and drifted from occupation to occupation and when he became an elderly, indigent man, he had no parish from which to claim support.[19] Hugh's sister Jean also lived in Lochwinnoch, where her husband, Archibald, kept an inn and worked in the weaving trade, employing their two sons, James and Hugh Cameron. Archibald also earned extra income as a sergeant in the militia and eventually emigrated to North America, but failed to establish himself. Both sons also tried their hands at different trades. Hugh emigrated and James acquired the skills of a ploughman. Ann's cousin Margaret was married to a merchant in Lochwinnoch, whose business, though fairly small, was prosperous. Hugh's half-brother Robert was a retired wool-merchant living in Saltcoats in the neighbouring county of Ayrshire. Hugh's other half-brother, Andrew, "labour[ed] against the stream" in Ireland's "stocking business."[20] The letters written by these correspondents represented the taut bonds of love that joined the Scottish Brodies and their Canadian relatives.

The Scots' desire to nurture affectionate contact with their Canadian relatives created the conditions that objectified their relationships. Interactions they had once lived and experienced now had to be thought about, given self-conscious shape and form. Hugh's mother and sister reassuringly wrote that they had filled the gap left by his physical absence with thoughts and love: "Though you be absent in body you are often present in my mind"; "altho we are separated in person yet you are seldom absent from my minde."[21] However, many of the Scottish Brodies experienced difficulties in reflecting on their lives. Mary Brodie's letters were descriptive but scripture filled and sometimes had an aggrieved and admonishing tone. Margaret Brodie Sloan's letters were heavy with unexpressed feelings. The word "dead" appears with hypnotic regularity and she was unable to find new ways of thinking about her world. Her self-expression was very limited, but she continued courageously to put her life into words. William Brodie, in contrast, had a verbal flair, though his letters are often devoid of detail. The purpose of his letters was to evoke an emotional response in his brother, rather than to share thoughts or opinions about his world. Jean appears to have written few letters at all, leaving the correspondence for her husband to maintain. Hugh's other correspondents – his half-brothers, Andrew and Robert, his brother-in-law, Archibald Cameron, and the latter's sons, James and Hugh –

wrote livelier, more expressive letters. Yet their expression too was formulaic, focused on reaffirming their religious beliefs and exchanging useful information.

The lack of common experiences made it difficult for the Scottish Brodies to reflect on their lives for the Canadians, since the details of daily life no longer seemed relevant. Their thoughts seemed to require more paper than they had, and while they could write a book of news, none of it would be of interest. Hugh Brodie's nephews struggled to write interesting narratives, but felt "inadequate" to the task and offered to send newspapers instead. William, Robert, Mary, Andrew, Jean's husband, Archibald Cameron, and their sons, and Cousin Margaret wrote Hugh and Ann every year at considerable pains, yet often found themselves at a loss for words. A constant refrain ran through the Scottish family's letters: "I have nothing in particular to report"; "I have little or no news"; "I have nothing new to inform you of."[22] The Scottish Brodies realized that the passing of time had made them unrecognizable to their colonial relatives.

The emotional strain of the permanent separation between loved ones could also cut both ways. At the end of a short letter entrusting her son to Hugh's care in Canada, Jean Cameron wrote: "I can say No More my heart is full at present no more at present."[23] For the relatives who remained in Scotland, the departure of a loved one was a near equivalent to their death. The Scottish relatives maintained the same hope of seeing their friends again in heaven as they had of reuniting with the deceased.[24]

Economic hardship represented another barrier to self-expression. Mary, William, and Archibald and James Cameron, who all worked in Lochwinnoch's weaving industry, may not have had the leisure to write often.[25] Lack of writing skills also curtailed expression. Margaret, though married to a fairly prosperous shopkeeper in the town of Lochwinnoch, appears to have been functionally illiterate.[26] She depended on the kindness of others to write her letters for her. While she wrote to Ann at least once most years, describing the births and deaths of her children and relating the other accidents and deaths in the parish, she lacked the privacy to express personal feelings.

Yet all the Brodies overcame the practical and emotional difficulties in writing letters to their cousins. Beyond the function served by maintaining personal contact with their relatives, the letters reaffirmed a reality they had once shared. Their point of reference was a social landscape. The Scots reported news of the marriages and deaths from among their "old acquaintances," and pointedly left out information about people they did not know. They described changes in the neighbourhood, confirmed their religious beliefs, and reported the state of the markets and trade in the country. When their environment deprived them of the means to assert their individuality, they borrowed language from other discourses to fill the gaps and absences in their lives. This shared Scottish sensibility became a new deracinated point of reference. The values were integral to the Scottish Brodies' sense of identity because they allowed them to present themselves in a recognizable state to the Canadian relatives. It became the essence of their bonds. Like the tender, conventional address of their letters – "I embrace this opportunity" – the Brodies filled the voids in their lives with tangible letters and objectively sanctioned ideas. The essence of Scottishness was distilled out of this experience.

The modern subject is as much a creation of modernity as the modern nation-state. Scots embodied, as individuals, the cultural patterns of Calvinism, the Enlightenment, and Romanticism because all three ideologies cultivated forms of individual awareness. Calvinism envisaged a social order that radiated outward from the self-disciplined individual while also reminding individuals of their subordination to the will of God.[27] Calvinism's emphasis on individual responsibility made it a crucial factor in promoting the critical inquiry and independence of mind that marked the Scottish Enlightenment.[28] Even when the romantic poets challenged the Enlightenment's rationalism, they rooted nationalist sentiment in the individual, in a person's sincere experience of the local and the particular.[29] In expressing their personal experiences and visions for the future, the Scots drew from these public discourses.

The ideals of the Scottish Enlightenment provided common ground that sustained the transatlantic connection between the branches of the Brodie family. The Brodies, like other Lowlanders of their class, self-consciously employed a civic humanist language – of liberty and independence – to assert their rights to economic security.[30] Hugh Brodie's death announcement celebrated the "independent" way in which he had achieved his economic success and public recognition. When in New York, Hugh's brother-in-law, Archibald Cameron, reported that he had found a "Scotch man's" place "the best place for Work and civility I could have found in New York." The "Scotch" employer did not exploit his workers, but invested his interests with theirs.[31] Scotland, the nation, however, figured little in the Brodies' correspondence. Enlightenment ideals of material and intellectual progress appear in their letters as functions of their everyday familial identities.

On a fundamental level, the Brodie family valued education as a requirement of individual expression and economic advancement. Hugh Brodie's achievements were most remarkable, according to his obituary notice, because he overcame the lack of early education to become a knowledgeable agriculturalist. Cousin Margaret's self-expression was constrained by her lack of education, but she promoted the education of her children, especially of her youngest daughter. If Margaret could not write, her daughter could.[32] Access to literacy was also an improving strategy of those in Scotland intending to emigrate. Hugh's nephew Hugh went to school to prepare himself for emigration to Canada.[33] Kinswoman Jean Buchanan prepared for her intended emigration by "going to the writing skool to take some learning."[34]

Besides drawing upon the educational resources available in Scotland, the Brodies wrote and thought in the terms set out by the Scottish Enlightenment. Hugh and his brother, Robert, engaged in a serious exchange of "Domistick" news, "useful information," and details of "improvements" made. Market prices and political news were duly shared.[35] But the report also had a metaphoric quality and served as a shorthand description of the overall quality of life in Scotland. This was Adam Smith's Scotland of integrated markets, and the price of peas conveyed a wealth of information about a cousin's real income and financial stability. Awareness of market conditions was also embedded in women's descriptions of their social environment and a regular feature of Mary's and her mother's letters.[36] The last sentence of one of Mary's letters to Hugh began with a friend's singlehood and ended: "Trade is very dull markets are now high, remains till death, your loving Sister Mary Brodie."[37]

Hugh Brodie and his brother Robert chose as the basis of their relatedness the promotion of innovation in agriculture. Hugh and Robert exchanged seeds and produce and experimented with new plants. Robert was delighted with the pumpkin seeds Hugh sent him, though they yielded only two apple-sized gourds, and he requested tobacco seeds as an experiment. In return, Robert sent Hugh a strain of bean that he hoped would be useful. Robert took a lively interest in Hugh's welfare and asked him to send "useful information" and details of the "improvements" Hugh was making.[38] With the help of his cousin in Scotland, Hugh also introduced a strain of new milk cow into the province. William Caldwell bought and sent over "a fine Bull" to Lower Canada. The animal's bloodlines united the cousins in a bond of shared interest: "I am glad to hear that the Bull is agreeing with the climate and seems to please in your country we have a fine Guery calf of him by a young heifer which took him when at Beltrees, the calf is his very picture both in collour [sic] and shape."[39] The brown and white cow, bred as a high-producing dairy cow, was itself the product of Scotland's agricultural revolution. Hugh also helped import new farming equipment to the province – the metal-covered plough, another innovation of the Lowland's agricultural revolution.[40] One Scot, in Scotland briefly, forwarded an iron plough for himself to be taken into Hugh's care until he could make further arrangements. On the letter accompanying the plough, the words "with an iron plough" are linked by a bracket with Brodie's name; Brodie's identity was visually tied to this instrument of progress and self-determination.[41]

However, not all the Brodies were able to express their identity through an instrumental relationship with nature. William, Robert, Mary, and Margaret couched their concerns in Calvinism's language of submission to the will and grace of God.[42] This older vision preserved an alternative value system – one that valued continuity and regarded the individual agency of commerce and improvement with skepticism. Nevertheless, the Brodies were united in their belief in Presbyterian church-government, with its democratic principles of representation and emphasis on community leadership.[43] Hugh Brodie became an elder of St. Andrew's Church in Montreal, which began as a secessionist church connected to the Associate Reformed Synod of Scotland of the Burgher Succession promoting the democratic government by the congregation, but in later years sought to establish institutional connections with the Church of Scotland.[44] St. Andrew's created a common tie between Hugh and Ann and their relatives in Scotland. In 1853, the St. Andrew's minister, Alexander Mathieson, paid a visit to Margaret and her husband while he was in Scotland.[45] Such connections were tenuous. More enduring was the faith they shared.

The Presbyterian theology of tempering desires preserved an alternative value system and helped individuals express themselves. All of Hugh and Ann's correspondents reflected on the dangers inherent in fixing their thoughts on vain temporal objects: children, people, and riches. William, Mary, Margaret, and Robert, for example, all used scriptural metaphors and repeated theology to help them reflect on their experiences. The tenets allowed them to imagine a future that they could share with the departed family and with the deceased. Margaret was united with Ann in a shared conversation about the pain of life. In 1817, Margaret sent these words to Ann:

> But I may take up my Theme where you left off on the instability of Human happiness for experience has taught me the sincerity of this short advice Lean not on earth it will peirce thee to the heart A broken reed at best but of a spear on its sharp point peace bleads and hope expires. Since I wrote to you last we had the Measles in our Family at which time it pleased God to take of Elizabeth which makes it the Sixth time that the arrow of Death hath wounded my peace by cutting of my own offspring ere they had ripened to any great maturity but we ought not to repine it is Gods hand let him do what he will though he slay me yet will I trust in him for the Lord giveth and the Lord taketh away blessed be the name of the Lord.[46]

This Christian language of submission was ballast against the uncertainty of life.

Robert Brodie also drew upon this language – not to mourn the death of children but to restore a sense of balance and order in his life. While Robert shared Hugh's quest for improvement and progress, themes of vanity and of the ephemeral nature of the material world intruded in his forward-looking view. Robert was reportedly prosperous, but he was careful not to invest too much of his identity in his worldly prosperity.[47] He cogitated on his certain death, and on the ultimate meaninglessness of his temporal concerns.[48] William and Mary also drew upon scripture to express themselves in similar ways.

Shared religious beliefs in the ultimate inconsequence of earthly goods kept material squabble from rending the family apart when they divided into warring camps over the disposition of their mother's effects. William made unwelcome financial decisions in disposing of the estate; Mary was incensed by the number of her mother's things Jean and Archibald claimed. In sorting out the web of entitlement and justifications, however, William and Mary evaluated their actions and the actions of others in religious terms. If William had erred and given into greed, he could expect his brother to abide by the biblical edict for brotherly forgiveness.[49] Mary's reaction was more complicated, for she felt victimized. She adopted an admonishing, protective attitude toward her brothers and worried about the state of their souls. This gave her an identity and a role in the family and created the conditions for an exchange of support and loyalty from Hugh over the division of their mother's estate.[50] The tenets of Presbyterianism and Calvinist theology were important aspects of the Brodies' individual identities because these tenets allowed them to maintain perspective and to make claims on the family.

The Brodies' nostalgic attachment to the landscape of Scotland represents a third strand of typically Scottish thought available for their self-expression. The Brodies located and understood themselves in their shifting, uncertain world by relating to their neighbourhoods with a mixture of pragmatism and nostalgia. The works of Robbie Burns are credited with rooting Scottish identity in the physical land of Scotland.[51] However, the Brodies' letters reveal the practical ways in which they located identity in the landscape by describing their social grid in geographical terms. The social relationships of the neighbourhood – of daily contact and knowledge, rather than strict kinship relationships – defined the reach of their benevolence and concern.[52] The family's letters also reveal the ways in which Scotland's rural transformation not only destroyed a known social order but also temporarily deprived the Brodies of a sense of identity. The letters invoked memories of a neighbourhood and a shared childhood as the common ground that helped the Scottish Brodies relate to their Canadian brother and sister-in-law.

Reflexive, terse descriptions of Lochwinnoch's and Kilburnie's changing neighbourhood played a crucial role in assisting the Brodies in self-reflection. The neighbourhood, the properties and their owners, customers of shops, and servants of houses served as the grid for the Brodies' network as much as the bonds of kinship. The bonds of neighbourliness impelled Ross Robertson to write to Hugh asking him to assist Hugh's distant relative who had been Ross' neighbour "for forty years." Margaret sent Ann a letter introducing a family whose members were "excelent costomers" in her husband's shop. When William Dunsmore introduced a man to Hugh's notice, he located the prospective emigrant in a landscape that William and Hugh had once shared: he was a grandson of "old James Carswell that kept the corner house at the crose." The lives and deaths of old neighbours were a regular feature of the Scottish Brodies' correspondence, particularly that of Mary and Margaret. Also a regular feature of the correspondence was the alteration to the old landscape. In 1809 Mary wrote to Hugh, referring him to William for public news, but adding that there "is a new road to Greenock and a new toll house built where you used to delve [dig] in." Longing and nostalgia touched Mary's description to her brother of the changes taking place in the neigbourhood. She wrote: "I often think with grief on the place we used to cast peats where you and me were want to be together [now] it is a field of corn." The older order of things provided the referents for describing the new.[53]

The physical grid of the neighbourhood and of the landscape was an important facet of identity. The full names of adults conveyed little individuality unless associated with a place name. When William introduced his nephew, Hugh Steels, to Hugh, he was sure to clarify that he was not one of the Steels of Makes Mill, who were "all dead," but the son of a cousin.[54] Thus, we can understand the depths of William's grief when he considered that the family name was almost gone from the place, Langcroft, where it had "once stood high." The dissolution of the place that had anchored his name deprived him of an identity: "I am now like a stranger in the land of our Fathers." Yet William rallied, and continued to cogitate upon his certain death and his anonymity for another twenty years. Sadly, though, he lost his mental faculties in his final days. Perhaps this was his body's final attempt to articulate his sense of alienation. In the end, he literally lost himself, his mind, and a parish to support him.[55] While able, though, William drew upon a romantic language and sentiment to reflect on the course his life had taken.

In particular, William drew from the romantic genre of poetry and sentimentality to reflect on his situation. He mourned the loss of friends, family, and youth: "Now I stand almost alone like some solitary tree upon the mountain's brow with growing symptoms that long I cannot here remain but must in turn yield to nature and become pray to worms." He speculated that a privately printed copy of their father's poetry had never reached Hugh because the vessel carrying it had sunk and it therefore "numbered among those who have been swallowed up by the mighty deep." William equated the loss of the publication to the loss of a human life; their father was embodied in his poetic expression. William also adopted sentimentality as an aspect of his identity. By echoing his father's voice, he lent legitimacy to his life and created a role for himself in the family. Never having prospered in temporal concerns, he became custodian of the family's sentimentality. It was he who caused their father's "elegy composed ... on the death of [a] friend" to be printed. It was he who made sure Hugh received a copy of it.[56]

Mary too reminisced about her childhood days at Langcroft as the touch-stone of her social identity. The family home represented a pattern of socia-bility, stability, and parental protection that united her concerns with Hugh's. Her nostalgic retreat into this world allowed her to voice her longing for Hugh and for protection in terms she knew Hugh would understand. In March 1811, Mary reflected on the changes and instability in her life. Trade was "so low" in the country that work was scarce, though she was getting by. Eighty-five people had drowned in the new canal at Paisley. She felt used by her sister Jean's husband, Archibald, after the death of their mother, and blamed him for "taking away and keeping up what was our mothers [sic]." After reflecting on the fact that her mother's effects would be of little use in the future eternal world, she began remembering Langcroft: "I was lately up at Langcroft where you and me spent our early days I could not help taking a view of the place where our dear Father often poured out his soul to God." Perhaps she took solace in remembering a time when she had not faced the uncertainties of life alone. Perhaps she was uniting herself with Hugh in bereavement and in the expectation of meeting their father again in heaven.[57] All the Brodies required the emotional support of their relatives. Hugh's and Ann's views are reflected in the responses of the rela-tives, while their needs are more visible. Each group mirrors the other, cre-ating a community of the like-minded – a stable source of identity in their changing world.

Scottish values replaced the Scottish countryside as the grid in which individuals located their identity. The Brodie siblings invoked all three strands of thought – enlightened progress, Presbyterian temperance, and romantic nostalgia – to express their personal experiences during a period of revolu-tionary change. These typically Scottish ideas and words filled the voids in their lives. The ideals of the Scottish Enlightenment articulated the means by which they met economic deprivation. The warmth and common sense of their Presbyterian values shielded them from an uncaring world. A poetic language of nostalgia helped them maintain bonds of commonality. The letters flow from Scotland to Lower Canada, one after the other, in a sooth-ing pattern of repetition: markets are fluctuating, the neighbourhood is changing, the only certainty in life is death, and we love you.

Hugh Brodie's life embodied these concerns. He strove to be a "good man" after the Calvinist ideal and in so doing recreated in Lower Canada the patterns of sociability that he had learned in Scotland.[58] He was a progres-sive agriculturalist, adapting to a changing environment. He became a guide and counsellor to many, as a friend and as an elder of the Presbyterian

Church. His new home he named after the old: Langcroft. But his innovations also affected his environment and other people. The new strains of fruit and livestock he introduced would change the ecology of Lower Canada. The pattern he evolved to meet the challenges of modernity tended to extol his own culture, and he regarded himself as an example to his French Canadian neighbours. Historian Colin Coates has demonstrated in *Metamorphoses of Landscape and Community in Early Quebec* the subtle but aggressive way in which English colonists painted French Canada out of picturesque representations of the province. Their value system literally obliterated the previous order.[59] Perhaps the vision of Scottishness outlined here will help humanize the impersonal forces of colonialism by identifying the personal stake individuals had in national identities.

Notes

1 Robert Blair St. George, introduction to *Possible Pasts: Becoming Colonial in Early America,* ed. Robert Blair St. George (Ithaca, NY: Cornell University Press, 2000), 6; Nicholas Thomas, *Colonialism's Culture: Anthropology, Travel and Government* (Princeton, NJ: Princeton University Press, 1994), 143.

2 "Obituary of Hugh Brodie," *Quebec Gazette,* 16 January 1852; McCord Museum of Canadian History, PO21, Brodie Family Papers, file 15, no name, 12 August 1856; file 11, Margaret Brodie Sloan to Ann Brodie, 20 March 1852. Hereafter, all references introduced by a file number will refer to this collection.

3 The society ordered transparencies of Sir William Wallace, John Knox, Sir Walter Scott, Robert Burns, and a Highland chief in full costume, flags bearing the royal arms and the royal standard of Scotland, and banners reading "Caledonia" and "an ancient Caledonian." See *Narrative of the Proceedings of the St. Andrew's Society of Montreal* (Montreal: J.C. Becket, 1855), 6-7.

4 Alexander Mathieson, *A Sermon Preached in St. Andrew's Church on the Thirtieth day of November, 1836 (St. Andrew's Day)* (Montreal: James Starke, 1837), 15, 19.

5 Hugh Brodie's father was a portioner (very minor landowner) of a property called Langcraft in Lochwinnoch. The family lost the farm to creditors, likely prompting Hugh and his brothers to emigrate. Family members who stayed in Scotland did not achieve the same economic stability as Hugh Brodie did in Montreal and were vulnerable to the changes in the textile industry. George Crawford, *A History of the Shire of Renfrew* (Paisley, UK: Alex. Weir, 1782), 167. Andrew Crawfurd, "The Cairn of Lochwinnoch," 46 vols, Paisley Central Local Studies Library, PC 1407-52, vol. 7, p. 472 4/4.

6 William Wood, ed., "The Brodie Family," in *The Storied Province of Quebec: Past and Present* (Toronto: Dominion Publishing, 1932), 5:642; Robert Campbell, *A History of the Scotch Presbyterian Church, St. Gabriel Street, Montreal* (Montreal: W. Drysdale, 1887), 98; Archives nationales de Québec (ANQ), CN601, S192, mf 2626, 29 August 1842, Last Will and Testament of Hugh Brodie; ANQ, TL32, S31, January 1842, List of Justices of the Peace for the District of Montreal.

7 Ned C. Landsman, "Introduction: The Context and Functions of Scottish Involvement with the Americas," in *Nation and Province in the First British Empire: Scotland and the Americas, 1600-1800,* ed. Ned C. Landsman (Lewisburg, PA: Bucknell University Press, 2001), 15-35.

8 For articles relating to individual and group contributions to the United States, see Richard B. Sher and Jeffrey R. Smitten, *Scotland and America in the Age of Enlightenment* (Princeton, NJ: Princeton University Press, 1990), and Landsman, ed., *Nation and Province in the First British Empire.* For essays exploring similar contributions to Canada, see Charles H. Scobie and G.A. Rawlyk, eds., *The Contribution of Presbyterianism to the Maritime Provinces of Canada* (Montreal and Kingston, McGill-Queen's University Press, 1997), and Marjory Harper and

Michael E. Vance, eds., *Myth, Migration and the Making of Memory: Scotia and Nova Scotia 1700-1990* (Halifax: Fernwood, 1999).

9 See for example Edward J. Cowan, "The Myth of Scotch Canada," in *Myth, Migration and the Making of Memory*, 62.

10 Istvan Hont, "The Rich Country-Poor Country Debate," in *Wealth and Virtue: The Shaping of Political Economy in the Scottish Enlightenment*, ed. Istvan Hont and Michael Ignatieff (Cambridge: Cambridge University Press, 1983), 292; T.C. Smout, "Problems of Nationalism, Identity and Improvement in Later Eighteenth-Century Scotland," in *Improvement and Enlightenment: Proceedings of the Scottish Historical Studies Seminar, University of Strathclyde, 1987-88*, ed. T.M. Devine (Edinburgh: John Donald Publishers, 1989), 15.

11 John Dwyer, *Virtuous Discourse: Sensibility and Community in Late Eighteenth-Century Scotland* (Edinburgh: John Donald Publishers, 1987).

12 Hugh Trevor-Roper, "The Invention of Tradition: The Highland Tradition in Scotland," in *The Invention of Tradition*, ed. Eric Hobsbawm and T. Ranger (Cambridge: Cambridge University Press, 1984), 15-41.

13 Eric Richards, "Scotland and the Uses of the Atlantic Empire," in *Strangers within the Realm: Cultural Margins of the First British Empire*, ed. Bernard Bailyn and Philip D. Morgan (Chapel Hill: University of North Carolina Press, 1991), 80; Ned C. Landsman, "Nation, Migration, and the Province in the First British Empire: Scotland and the Americas, 1600-1800," *American Historical Review* 104 (1999): 463-75.

14 Michael E. Vance, "Advancement, Moral Worth, and Freedom: The Meaning of Independence for Early Nineteenth-Century Lowland Emigrants to Upper Canada," in *Nation and Province*, 151-80.

15 Greg Dening, "Introduction: In Search of Metaphor," and "Histories of Self" in *Through a Glass Darkly: Reflections on Personal Identity in Early America*, ed. Ronald Hoffman, Mechal Sobel, and Fredrika J. Teute (Chapel Hill: University of North Carolina Press, 1997), 1-12.

16 Many theories of identity formation in the British Empire posit a negative self-definition against a different other. That is, people know themselves by who they are not. See for example Edward Said, *Orientalism* (New York: Vintage, 1979), and Linda Colley, *Britons Forging the Nation: 1707-1837* (New Haven, CT: Yale University Press, 1992). A failure of recognition and mutuality is the root of this lopsided and destructive creation of identity between a colonizer and a people colonized. This chapter, however, focuses on identity construction within a group motivated by economic and emotional ties to maintain recognizing links. Charles Taylor, "The Politics of Recognition," in *Multiculturalism: Examining the Politics of Recognition*, ed. Amy Gutmann (Princeton, NJ: Princeton University Press, 1994); Jessica Benjamin, *The Bonds of Love: Psychoanalysis, Feminism and the Problem of Domination* (New York: Pantheon, 1988).

17 Anthony Slaven, *The Development of the West of Scotland: 1750-1960* (London and Boston: Routledge and Kegan Paul, 1975), 4-7; T.M. Devine, *The Transformation of Rural Scotland: Social Change and the Agrarian Economy, 1660-1815* (Edinburgh: Edinburgh University Press, 1994), 131; George Robertson, *A General Description of the Shire of Renfrew, including an Account ...* (Paisley, UK: J. Neilson, 1818), 355-56, 432; *The New Statistical Account of Scotland by the Ministers of Their Respective Parishes ...* (Edinburgh and London: William Blackwood and Sons, 1845), vol. 5, 689-717, vol. 6, 80-112.

18 Mary reported that she had not been to Langcroft since she left it, five weeks after Hugh departed. File 6, Mary Brodie to Hugh Brodie, 17 March 1808, 19 March 1811.

19 File 3, William Dunsmore to Ann Brodie, 15 December 1856.

20 File 7, Robert Brodie to Hugh Brodie, 26 July 1816; file 5, James Cameron to Hugh Brodie, 21 March 1825, 8 August 1829; file 3, Hugh Steel to Hugh Brodie, 30 July 1856, 4 December 1856; file 6, Mary Brodie to Hugh Brodie, 19 March 1811; file 5, Archibald Cameron to Hugh Brodie, n.d., 27 May 1806, 22 April 1816; file 7, Robert Brodie to Hugh Brodie, 4 April 1814; file 3, William Brodie to Hugh Brodie, 12 June 1829; file 7, Robert Brodie to Hugh Brodie, 27 March 1815, 26 March 1816, 26 July 1816, 18 March 1819; file 2, Mary Gemmel to her sons, 4 March 1805; file 6a, Andrew Brodie to Hugh Brodie, September 1818, 5 July 1818; National Archives of Scotland, Ayr Sheriff Court Inventories, Robert Brodie, 25/6/1839, SC6/44/9, p. 985; Andrew Crawfurd, "The Cairn of Lochwinnoch," vol. 7, p. 473 1/4.

21 File 6, Mary Brodie to John Brodie, n.d.; file 2, Mary Gemmel to her sons, 4 March 1805.
22 "I have nothing very particular to inform you of; I have little or no news of any great importance to inform you off, Were I to Mention all the Vieissitudes [sic] and Casualties within the sphere of My Own knowledge it would take more Paper than I am at present possessed off and even when done would require to be sent to the Book Binders in order to get Bound; you mentioned in your letter that you received no News from me but this I feel myself uqualified [sic] to do but I will endeavour if ever I am favoured with another opportunity [of] writing you to send you some News Papers; I thought when I sat down that I would [...] Require a Ream of Paper to have held all I wis[hed] to say & I Still believe so, but for the present I shall conclude." File 7, Robert Brodie to Hugh Brodie, 26 March 1816; file 2, Mary Gemmel to her sons, 4 March 1805; file 5, Archibald Cameron to Hugh Brodie, n.d.; file 5, James Cameron to Hugh Brodie, 21 March 1825; file 10, Elizabeth Miller to Hugh Brodie, 21 March 1830.
23 File 5, Jean Brodie Cameron to Hugh Brodie, 28 March 1817.
24 This is a common refrain through out the papers. See for example file 3, William Brodie to Hugh Brodie, 28 April 1816; file 5, Jean Cameron to Hugh Brodie, 2 April 1823; file 6, Mary Brodie to Hugh Brodie, 19 March 1811.
25 Those engaged in factory weaving worked between sixty and sixty-nine hours a week, while the handloom weavers worked twelve-hour days, from 5 a.m. to 10 p.m. *The New Statistical Account of Scotland*, vol. 5, 715-17.
26 File 11, Jean Lairde to Ann Brodie, 5 August 1845.
27 This is the general thesis of Charles Taylor, *Sources of the Self: The Making of Modern Identity* (Cambridge, MA: Harvard University Press, 1989). For his discussion of Calvinism, see 227-30. Charles Camic, *Experience and Enlightenment: Socialization for Cultural Change in Eighteenth-Century Scotland* (Chicago: University of Chicago Press, 1983), 18-19, 24-25.
28 James K. Cameron, "Theological Controversy: A Factor in the Origins of the Scottish Enlightenment," in *The Origins and Nature of the Scottish Enlightenment*, ed. R.H. Campbell and Andrew S. Skinner (Edinburgh: John Donald Publishers, 1982), 116-30.
29 Smout, "Problems of Nationalism," 7.
30 Ibid.; Vance, "Advancement, Moral Worth, and Freedom," 151-80.
31 File 5, Archibald Cameron to Hugh Brodie, 9 September 1830.
32 File 4, Margaret Brodie Sloan to Ann Brodie, 31 March 1827.
33 File 5, Archibald Cameron to Hugh Brodie, 22 April 1816.
34 File 4, William Dunsmore to Ann Brodie, 5 August 1850.
35 File 7, Robert Brodie to Hugh Brodie, 27 March 1815, 26 July 1816.
36 File 4, Margaret Brodie Sloan to Ann Brodie, 21 May 1832; File 2, Mary Gemmel to her sons, 4 March 1805.
37 File 6, Mary Brodie to Hugh and John Brodie, 17 March 1808, 9 August 1809.
38 File 7, Robert Brodie to Hugh Brodie, 4 April 1814, 27 March 1815, 26 March 1816, 26 July 1816.
39 File 8a, William Caldwell to Hugh Brodie, 21 March 1831.
40 Slaven, *The Development of the West of Scotland: 1750-1960*, 71-72.
41 File 2, Andrew Lindsay to Hugh Brodie, 15 April 1820.
42 Camic, *Experience and Enlightenment*, 18-19, 24-25.
43 William Klempa, "Scottish Presbyterianism Transplanted to the Canadian Wilderness," in *The Contribution of Presbyterianism to the Maritime Provinces of Canada*, 6.
44 J.S.S. Armour, *Saints, Sinners and Scots: A History of the Church of St. Andrew and St. Paul, Montreal, 1803-2003* (Montreal: Church of St. Andrew and St. Paul, 2003), 19, 23, 31, 67, 238.
45 File 11, Margaret Brodie Sloan to Ann Brodie, 12 August 1853.
46 File 4, Margaret Brodie Sloan to Ann Brodie, 1 April 1817.
47 File 5, James Cameron to Hugh Brodie, 8 August 1829.
48 Examples are littered throughout letters of Robert Brodie to Hugh Brodie, file 7.
49 File 3, William Brodie to Hugh Brodie, 3 April 1831, 26 March 1839.
50 File 6, Mary Brodie to Hugh Brodie, 11 August (no year).
51 Marjory Harper and Michael E. Vance, "Myth, Migration and the Making of Memory: An Introduction," in *Myth, Migration and the Making of Memory*, 32; Smout, "Problems of Nationalism," 7.

52 Barry Real explores a similar phenomenon in "Kinship and the Neighborhood in 19th Century Rural England: The Myth of the Autonomous Nuclear Family," *Journal of Family History* 21 (1996): 87-104.
53 File 11, Ross Robertson to Hugh Brodie, 31 March 1834; file 4, Margaret Brodie Sloan to Ann Brodie, 29 March 1825; file 11, William Dunsmore to Hugh Brodie, 29 March 1849; file 6, Mary Brodie to Hugh Brodie, 11 August (no year), 9 August 1809.
54 File 3, William Brodie to Hugh Brodie, 26 March 1839.
55 File 3, William Brodie to Hugh Brodie, 26 February 1836, Hugh Steel to Ann Brodie, 4 December 1856.
56 File 3, William Brodie to Hugh Brodie, 3 April 1851, 11 June 1842.
57 File 6, Mary Brodie to Hugh Brodie, 19 March 1811.
58 Alexander Matheson, *A Sermon, Preached in St. Andrew's Church Montreal. On the Occasion of the Death of Hugh Brodie Esq. Late, One of the Elders of that Church* (Montreal: J. Stracke, 1852).
59 William Cronon, *Changes in the Land: Indians, Colonists and the Ecology of New England* (New York: Hill and Wang, 1983); Colin Coates, *The Metamorphoses of Landscape and Community in Early Quebec* (Montreal and Kingston: McGill-Queen's University Press, 2000).

3
Entering the Christian World: Indigenous Missionaries in Rupert's Land
Andy A. den Otter

In the waning years of the eighteenth century, a revival of Protestant Christianity, mainly British and North American, unleashed an unparalleled expansionist missionary movement that spread the gospel to every continent of the globe.[1] Rivalling earlier Roman Catholic proselytizing efforts, this new missionary activity reached the shores of British North America and penetrated the western interior, then called Rupert's Land. These northwestern territories had experienced commercial imperialism in the form of the Hudson's Bay Company, a London based enterprise enjoying a fur trade monopoly granted under a 1670 royal charter. The company did little to advance the cause of Christianity in Rupert's Land but in the 1820s, partly in response to settlement along the Red River valley on the southern edge of its empire and partly in reaction to pressures from missionary societies, it reluctantly permitted both Anglicans and Roman Catholics to establish missionary fields in the valley and immediate environs. That situation remained until 1840, when continued humanitarian and evangelical pressures forced the company to admit more aggressive missionary activity among the region's Aboriginal peoples.

In 1840, two British Protestant denominations, Anglican and Wesleyan Methodist, sent missionaries into Rupert's Land's interior to work among its Native peoples. Among the new missionaries were two indigenous men – Henry Budd, an Anglican, and Henry Bird Steinhauer, a Wesleyan Methodist. Both men appeared to have fitted themselves well into the British World.[2] Taken voluntarily from their Native communities at a relatively young age and educated by the Anglican and Wesleyan-Methodist churches respectively, they gradually replaced their oral, hunter-gatherer, North American tradition with an imported European culture, literate and agrarian. Simultaneously, they abandoned most of their Aboriginal spirituality and adopted the Christian faith. In fact, their newly embraced religion most strongly defined their identity. In other words, residing virtually all their lives in British North America, both associated themselves most explicitly with the spiritual aspect of the British World, and to a lesser extent with its literate and agrarian basis. The wilful process by which they arrived at that position was gradual and complex but owed most to their education.[3]

Born probably in 1812, possibly near York Factory on Hudson Bay, Henry Budd grew up in a traditional Native family whose primary means of survival was hunting and gathering.[4] His parents named him Sakacewescam (Going-up-the-Hill) after the arduous upriver journeys they often made from York Factory to Norway House on the tip of Lake Winnipeg. Despite regular contact with Europeans working for the Hudson's Bay Company, the parents provided a traditional upbringing, which allowed the youngster considerable freedom to develop self-worth and respect for his mental and physical abilities. Education was mainly through stories that memorialized humorous, valorous, and other notable deeds. The oral introduction to his heritage introduced the boy to a world in which there was strong agreement between people, spirits, plants, animals, and the landscape. Unfortunately, the father died while the boy was still young and the remaining family of a brother, sister, and mother relied on their extended family and the Hudson's Bay Company for their survival.[5]

In many ways, Henry Steinhauer's early years are uncannily similar to those of Henry Budd. Born sometime between 1818 and 1820 near Lake Simcoe in Upper Canada, Shahwanegezhick, as he was originally named, spent the first decade of his life among his people.[6] Parents, grandparents, and elders taught him the hunting, fishing, and other skills needed to survive in the North American environment. They also instructed him in the essentials of Ojibwa culture, especially its religious underpinnings. In other words, Shahwanegezhick appeared destined to grow up like hundreds of his fellow Ojibwas and like Sakacewescam among the Cree.

Early in their childhood, Budd and Steinhauer came into contact with Christian missionaries. The transformation of their personal identities that this meeting provoked, although radical, was likely not traumatic.[7] In the first place, both were relatively young and their personalities were still malleable. As well, their peoples had for generations lived alongside Euro-North Americans and thus their way of life would not have been entirely unfamiliar to them, their parents, or their elders. Moreover, the Christianity, taught to them as children, embodied many of the same basic values as the religion of their ancestors. The profound spirituality of their Native religion; the belief in a Supreme Being and a world filled with spirits, some good and some malevolent; the expectation of an afterlife; the visions, fasting, prayer, and the emotional ceremonies that often led to ecstasy prepared them for the teachings of evangelical Protestant Christianity.[8]

Their introduction to Christianity was similar. In Budd's case, the initial instrument of conversion was Rev. John West, a Church of England priest. West had been appointed by the Hudson's Bay Company as its chaplain and by the British-based Church Missionary Society (CMS) as missionary to Rupert's Land. In keeping with contemporary missionary thinking, he held that real progress in converting Natives to Christianity and a settled agricultural life was possible only if children were educated in isolation from their parents. With the permission of a York Factory chief, in 1819 West took Budd and another youth to Red River to be educated.[9] In all likelihood, the fatherless lad was not reluctant to go with the missionary; the promise of regular meals and adequate clothing was probably a sufficient incentive. Fortunately, West treated him well and with respect; in his home, Budd eventually absorbed the generally accepted notion among Europeans that the hunter-gatherer economy was a symptom of inherent laziness and indolence and that an agricultural or industrial economy was a sign of innate drive and enterprise. During this time, likely at his baptism, West renamed Sakacewescam "Henry Budd." Peremptory and paternalistic, the renaming designated a weaning from the child's pagan past and the start of a new spiritual life.[10]

While Budd's introduction to Christianity was externally motivated, Steinhauer, according to his account, had an internally inspired life-altering experience. One day, attracted by the sound of children chanting, he approached a Methodist schoolhouse and lingered in the open door, captivated by the sight of students reading from books. The teacher invited him in and thus launched Steinhauer's career.[11] In 1828, he was baptized in a mass ceremony.[12]

Extrapolating from Steinhauer's narrative, then, a compelling explanation for the adoption of Christianity emerges. He and Henry Budd moved from (what Gerald Friesen has labelled) an oral-traditional to a textual-settler society.[13] Steinhauer, in particular, was first lured to European culture and religion by the written word. Even as a preteenager, he understood that the book not only recorded dreams and wisdom more accurately and enduringly than word of mouth but it could duplicate exactly what had been recorded, a feat that only the greatest of shamans could accomplish. For Steinhauer, as for many Native people, the Christian missionaries were more powerful than the indigenous priests because their Bible contained direct references to the deity. Moreover, they willingly shared the printed word with all who appeared receptive to Christianity and thus permitted them to obtain for themselves the tangible, preserved, and apparently constant truth. Driven mainly by the desire to acquire the power of the written word, Steinhauer gradually shed his Ojibwa identity and slowly but relentlessly accepted the religious doctrines that were integral to the Methodist curriculum.

The churches, then, assumed responsibility for the education of the two boys. For Budd, the facilities were quite primitive. When he and West arrived at Red River in October 1819, the pastor was disappointed that the settlement consisted of only a few widely scattered huts. "In vain did I look for a cluster of cottages, where the hum of a small population at least might be heard as in a village," he complained. "I saw but few marks of human industry in the cultivation of the soil."[14] West was especially chagrined to find no Protestant church or manse in the settlement; he had to lodge at the Hudson's Bay Company's Fort Douglas. Eventually, he and a number of Scottish settlers repaired a log house located about five kilometres below the fort. Here the schoolmaster, George Harbridge, who had accompanied West to Red River, took up residence and taught about twenty children. In contrast, Steinhauer probably began his education in 1828 at the just estab-lished but relatively well-furnished mission school on Grape Island in Lake Ontario, near Belleville, which consisted of nearly two dozen neatly white-washed log cabins and a variety of buildings and shops, including a chapel and a hospital.[15]

Despite the different levels of furnishings, the curriculum at both schools was relatively similar. Their purpose was moralistic, that is, to teach stu-dents to worship God and love humanity. In addition, they had a strong practical theme, reflecting the evangelical foundation common to both faiths. Material success in life was a noble goal, as was awareness of justice, equality, and the need for political reform. The Methodist leader Egerton Ryerson fought relentlessly for a system of nonsectarian, public, universal education, while the founders of the CMS were closely tied to the Clapham Sect, which sought the abolition of the slave trade.[16] Consequently, the boys received instruction not only in the basics of Christianity but also in read-ing, writing, and arithmetic, as well as in gardening, carpentry, and con-struction. In other words, the children born into an oral, hunter-gatherer society were taught the rudiments of a literate, settled agricultural economy.[17]

Despite the practical objectives, the schools' main purpose was to arm the children to fight evil, corrupting spirits. They adopted the principle, common in Upper Canada, the United States, and Great Britain, that the child needed corporal punishment in order to tame the evil tendencies of the human will and to establish uniformity of behaviour and discipline in the classroom.[18] Parents and educators often employed severe physical pun-ishment, rooted in the Bible and deeply embedded in the early-nineteenth-century Christian psyche, to instill in children a sense of honour and responsibility as well as devotion to duty.[19] At Grape Island, bells and whistles regulated the students' activities and, following contemporary practices, corporal punishment was common and harsh. Consequently, Steinhauer and Budd experienced, or at least witnessed, the methods that Methodist and Anglican missionaries employed to transform supposedly undisciplined children, attached to their Native heritage, into obedient students receptive to European culture.[20]

Over the years, the two boys absorbed the religious milieu of their respec-tive denominations. In other words, by embracing Christianity they also accepted the doctrine of one transcendent God, who did not dwell in either plants or animals, and of the salvation of their souls, not solely by good conduct but by abstractly receiving Jesus Christ as their personal saviour. They learned these basic principles through rote memorization of scripture texts, Catechism lessons, and hymns. Very influential in this regard were the catechism and hymns of Isaac Watts. Although an eighteenth-century dissenting clergyman, Watts' work was still popular in the early nineteenth century. His hymns, initially published in 1715 for the moral improvement of children, had been reissued well over five hundred times with more than 6 million copies printed. In keeping with the ethos of the time, the hymns touched on positive aspects of praise and worship, but most often deliberately frightened children by emphasizing the horror of eternal punishment for continued bad behaviour such as lying, quarrelling, swearing, idleness, and disobedience. Direct, and written in simple, blunt language, the songs were sung so often that they were imprinted on the minds of the students.

Song eleven is typical of the genre. Like the vast majority of his hymns, Watts painted the stark reality of eternal damnation and pointed to pious behaviour as the only means of avoiding it:

> There is beyond the sky
> A heaven of joy and love,
> And holy children when they die
> Go to that world above.
>
> There is a dreadful hell,
> And everlasting pains;
> There sinners must with devils dwell
> In darkness, fire, and chains.
>
> Can such a wretch as I
> Escape this cursed end?
> And may I hope whene'er I die
> I shall to heaven ascend?
>
> Then I will read and pray,
> While I have life and breath;
> Lest I should be cut off today
> And sent to eternal death.[1]

Victorian children, then, were from birth exposed to this stark dichotomy of eternal reward and punishment, as parents and teachers used not only Watts' hymns but also his catechism as the foundation of Christian education. The second set, for example, written for eight to twelve year olds, contained a catalogue of sins, including swearing, cursing, lying, scoffing, gluttony, drunkenness, and quarrelling. With evangelical fervour, it encouraged a mindset of industry, piety, obedience, honesty, sobriety, and politeness.[2] In addition to the hymns and catechism, teachers and ministers used exhortations, admonitions, and sermons to inculcate good behaviour. Undoubtedly harsh, and not necessarily effective, their overriding and usually genuine concern was the eternal welfare of the child's soul.

Despite the similarity of curriculum, the tenor at the two schools differed in degree. The Grape Island School adopted some of the educational principles of Johann Heinrich Pestalozzi, who taught that children learned through their senses rather than by abstraction. Pestalozzi suggested teachers cultivate students' sensory skills through observation and communication. Rather than learning by rote memorization, they should, for example, study vegetation, animals, and insects by direct observation.[3] While the Wesleyan Methodists rejected his Rousseau-inspired belief that children were born innocent and pure, they embraced his assumption that they were constantly bombarded by evil, corrupting forces and therefore needed to be taught faith in God as the best moral defence against temptation.[4] Unlike Grape Island, the Red River school did not embrace Pestalozzian pedagogy and therefore its discipline may have been harsher. At the same time, it concentrated more on biblical and doctrinal knowledge.[5] This emphasis was partly intentional, but it was also dictated by the scarcity of textbooks in secular subjects. In the main, however, the thrusts of both programs were similar: to prepare the children for life in a settled, literate, and Christian society.

After their elementary education, the lives of the two youths appeared to move in very different directions. First, after he left home, Steinhauer seldom made contact with his family, likely did not write them, and never referred to them in any of his correspondence. It was as if his entrance into the Methodist world closed the door to any further relations with his people. In contrast, Budd remained closely attached to his mother and sister. In 1822 the two moved to Red River and bought a farm in Lower Church (later St. Andrew's) parish.

Second, although Budd was a superior student and fluently bilingual, his academic career seems to have ended. The CMS did not need him and, consequently, he drifted in and out of various jobs, including stints on his mother's farm. In the early 1830s he signed on with the Hudson's Bay Company as a tripman, but when he completed his three-year contract, he returned to the farm.[6] Meanwhile, Steinhauer continued his education. In 1832, he studied classical languages for one year at New York's Cazenovia Seminary. Next, he taught for three years at the Credit Mission School. In 1836, when the Wesleyan Methodist conference perceived a need for more translators, it enrolled Steinhauer in the Upper Canada Academy, which had just opened at Cobourg. The coeducational academy intended to provide secondary education to Methodist and other students. The school's spiritual aim was to train youth "in the knowledge and obedience of God," and it exposed Steinhauer to an in-depth study of Protestant evangelical theology.[7] In addition, he studied mathematics, English grammar, algebra, geometry, and trigonometry, as well as French, logic, rhetoric, history, and natural philosophy. In the classics, he read *Roman History, Caesar's Commentaries,* and Horace in Latin, and *Jacob's Greek Reader, Idylls of Moscus,* and *Oedipus Tyrranus of Sophocles* in Greek. At the 1838 annual public examination, Steinhauer recited a segment in Latin, supposedly "with ease, fluency, and appropriate emphasis." He also spoke "On the Diffusion of Wisdom and Religion." The oration "delineated in an interesting manner the signs of the times," wrote the *Christian Guardian,* and it "averted to the bloodless conquests of revealed truth and closed with a glowing anticipation of its approaching universal triumph."[8] After graduating from Upper Canada Academy, Steinhauer taught for one year at the Alderville Mission.[9]

Two educators especially influenced Steinhauer. While at Grape Island, he lived in the home of Rev. William Case and developed a deep relationship of mutual respect. A persuasive preacher, tender and deeply religious, Case served superbly as a model of Wesleyan Christianity. Sensitive to the importance of cultural differences and language, his school was bilingual, opening to its graduates the opportunity to become translators. Moreover, he had an abiding faith in the intellectual abilities of Native children, encouraging both genders to become teachers or, alternatively, for boys to train as preachers and girls as homemakers. At times, however, Case displayed the young Steinhauer at public meetings where he belittled Aboriginal culture and religion and aggrandized Christianity, embedded in a supposedly superior culture. Moreover, it may have been Case who renamed Shahwanegezhick "Henry Bird Steinhauer," a name Steinhauer assumed slowly, using his birth name for another twenty years, albeit gradually less frequently, demonstrating that neither the conversion from the ancestral to Christian religion nor the shift from an aboriginal to a European culture was instantaneous or complete but incremental and lifelong.[10]

The denigration of Steinhauer's Native culture was accentuated by Rev. Peter Jones, a convert to Christianity whose mother was Ojibwa and whose father was European. An ordained Methodist missionary, Jones believed his former Native spirituality to be false and also felt that the Aboriginal hunter-gatherer economy would soon give way to a settled, agrarian society. Relentlessly, he preached that the only way for his people to survive the new order was to adopt the ways of the newcomers.[11] In the face of considerable opposition at his Credit Mission, he concentrated his attention on the children. For example, he put students to work on the mission farm to prepare them for the rigours of work and to instill in them a sense of duty and virtue. Moreover, he offended his critics by insisting that children be taught only in English and with an authoritarian European-driven pedagogy that clashed with the traditional practice that no one, not even parents, should command a child to do anything.[12] To thwart the influence of parents and elders, Jones proposed, albeit unsuccessfully, that "all the children be placed entirely under the charge and management of the teachers and missionaries, so that their parents shall have no control over them."[13] On the other hand, Jones' translations of hymns into the Ojibwa language and idiom demonstrated a sensitive accommodation to Native religion.[14]

In the early summer of 1840, the careers of Steinhauer and Budd once again professionally converged. The Wesleyan Methodist Conference sent Steinhauer to Rupert's Land. He was to assist Rev. William Mason, a British-born missionary at Lac La Pluie as interpreter, translator, and schoolmaster. The two did not make much headway in their mandate and, in 1844, James Evans, the field's supervisor, requested Steinhauer to come to Norway House, located at the northern tip of Lake Manitoba.[15] At this well-established mission, Steinhauer worked mainly as Bible translator and schoolmaster.[16] In 1850 he was transferred to Jackson Bay Station, near Oxford House, which was located more than two hundred kilometres from Norway House, on the Hayes River. Here he experienced considerable difficulty with the Hudson's Bay Company postmaster, who opposed the mission as a perceived threat to the fur trade. Steinhauer also had to cope with poor agricultural land and failed fisheries, suffering extreme hunger and misery. In 1854-55 he made a publicity trip in England and, on his return to Canada, he was ordained a minister in the Methodist Church.[17] He was posted to Lac La Biche (in today's northeastern Alberta) but, facing stiff competition from Roman Catholic missionaries, he moved southward in 1858 to Whitefish Lake, where the land was arable and the fish plentiful. Within years, he and his converts had built a small village surrounded by cultivated fields. Although never entirely independent from the nearby buffalo herds and fishery, the Whitefish mission was relatively successful. Steinhauer tended the community until his death in 1884.

Meanwhile, the CMS posted Henry Budd to Cumberland House, where he experienced considerable difficulty. The Hudson's Bay officer in charge was not especially receptive to a mission station so close to his post, nor was the locality well suited for agriculture. As a result, Budd moved some kilometres downriver to The Pas, where the land was relatively dry and supported substantial woodlands and where a semi-settled mixed band of Cree and Ojibwa was receptive to a missionary station.[18] By 1845, when Rev. James Hunter took charge of the mission station, Budd and an assistant were teaching more than sixty-five children in day classes and an additional thirty adults and six children in Sunday school. The arrival of the ordained missionary meant that Budd, who was a charismatic preacher as well as teacher, was relegated to the job of schoolmaster. Much to his chagrin, he often had to leave teaching in order to work in the fields or to supervise the cutting of lumber for the various buildings that Hunter wanted constructed.[19] Although disgruntled by Hunter's strict, often unkind and dictatorial orders, as well as by the incessant demands for hard physical labour, Budd remained at The Pas until 1849.[20]

That year, the CMS appointed David Anderson as the first Anglican bishop of Rupert's Land. The society's secretary, Henry Venn, ordered Anderson to bring Budd to Red River where he was to instruct him in preparation for ordination. Venn's intent was to create a self-supporting Native church and thus he directed the Europeans to train and educate willing indigenous men to completely take over the missions and in effect make the Anglican mission field in Rupert's Land totally self-supporting and independent from the CMS.[21] Accordingly, Anderson began to tutor Budd extensively in Anglican doctrine and biblical knowledge in preparation for ordination to the deaconate.[22]

Considered the best translator in the region, and familiar with indigenous customs, Budd was very useful to Anderson. He often addressed Native members of St. Andrew's after the regular services, and in late December 1850, shortly after his ordination, he preached the first completely Cree sermon in Red River. A magnetic speaker, Budd was well liked by all segments of the settlement but, in typical evangelical humbling introspection, he felt unworthy to be a deacon, promising he would do his utmost to "win my poor Countrymen to the knowledge of Christ and his great Salvation."[23]

After his ordination, Budd returned to The Pas and conducted services there and at the outstations of Moose Lake and Shoal River. In 1853, after he was ordained, Budd opened a mission at Nepowewin (Nipawin, Saskatchewan), which he served alone until 1867. He then returned to Christ Church at The Pas, which had been renamed Devon Mission and had been given parochial status. Budd, therefore, was minister at the first Anglican parish north of Red River, but he was not happy in the new charge. He was disappointed at having to leave Nepowewin. Moreover, with the introduction of liquor, the village and surrounding fields had deteriorated. But ever energetic and resilient, Budd accepted the challenge and by 1870, with the cooperation of the villagers, managed to restore the mission to its former status. The unpredictable climate, however, mitigated against farming and the mission continued to rely on hunting and fishing. Unfortunately, in the mid-1870s, Budd's health declined rapidly. Accustomed to activity, he found physical limitations difficult to accept and, in April 1875, he died of flu complications.[24]

Henry Steinhauer and Henry Budd's lives also coincided in that they married Native women resident in Rupert's Land. Steinhauer married Mamenawatum (Jessie Joyful) during his tenure at Norway House and subsequently parented five daughters and five sons.[25] Budd married Betsy Work, the daughter of Chief Factor John Work and his Métis wife, Jocette Legacé;

together, they reared four sons and a daughter. While Budd already had a support network of friends and relatives in the region, Steinhauer, who migrated into the Territories, established a more limited yet valuable one through Jessie.[26] Moreover, the two women were extremely helpful to their husbands, assisting them in their teaching and translating work by keeping house and rearing the children. In fact, the CMS preferred to hire married missionaries precisely for their essential supportive roles.[27]

While their wives tied the men into the society of Rupert's Land, their education firmly entrenched them in the culture of the British World. Steinhauer, for example, had a strong command of English and the classical languages and, armed with the techniques of rhetoric, logic, and dialectics, was an accomplished speaker. Meanwhile, through geography, he had experienced traditions other than his own; through astronomy, he had encountered a new cosmology; and through biblical and doctrinal studies, he had embraced a different spirituality than his Native creed. He had passed through the intersection of two cultures, two ways of life. After ten or more years in the education system of Upper Canada and New York, he emerged a young Victorian gentleman – at least in demeanour if not in social status. Moreover, he had accepted the virtues inculcated in all British schoolboys: politeness, disinterestedness, and the ability to use one's time usefully and productively. He had deeply imbibed from the well of contemporary European knowledge. He had witnessed first-hand the standard of living among the newcomers. In the end, as a realist, he accepted the new order as the most likely victor in the clash of cultures, and he accepted it willingly and eagerly. But above all, he embraced the imported religion as better than his own and its God as overwhelmingly powerful. To him, the most important difference in religions was that the European one was a religion of the book and that the associated literacy had made its followers powerful and able to control the continent.[28]

While Budd's education had not been as broad and formal as Steinhauer's, his experience with the Hudson's Bay Company had also made him aware of the enormous power of the British Empire. As for Steinhauer, when he had hesitantly approached the mission schoolhouse, he had recognized the authority of the religion of the book. Naively and still dimly, the youth had perceived the nexus of literacy, language, religion, power, and empire. He dearly wanted to learn to read the English language and acquire the newcomers' religion.[29] Both men linked the Empire's power directly to its religious basis. How often had they lustily and voluntarily intoned the words written in Watts' hymn book, "Praise for Birth and Education in a Christian Land":

Tis to thy sovereign grace I owe
  That I was born on British ground;

Where streams of heavenly mercy flow,
  And words of sweet salvation sound.

How do I pity those that dwell
  Where ignorance and darkness reign,
They know no heaven, they fear no hell,
  Those endless joys, those endless pains.[30]

Perhaps those words – that so bluntly connected Christianity with the superiority of British culture – jarred when they sang it the first time but repetition assured them that they had become members of a select community within the powerful British Empire.

By 1840, when both men began their missionary careers in Rupert's Land, they were products of two societies. One was based on oral communication, mobility, hunting, fishing, and gathering; the other was founded on literate intercourse, stability, agriculture, manufacturing, and accumulation. One survived directly from the land; the other lived indirectly from it, cultivating it and exploiting its resources. One was energized by many spirits immanent in the environment; the other served a monotheistic God, transcendent from nature. Born in tents, they had survived for the first decade of their lives on what their people gathered directly from the land. Their basic social values were continuity, tradition, and a sense of place. Time was measured by the changing seasons – mainly the heat of summer and the cold of winter – and by passing generations as well as cataclysmic events. Seasons also dictated the timing of religious ceremonies because the people experienced an intimate connection between the real and the sacred worlds. Thus, Steinhauer and Budd were born into a society of ecological time and religion. The knowledge and secrets that explained the natural and spiritual worlds were passed by word of mouth from person to person and from generation to generation.[31] In stark contrast, at the end of their education, the young adult men were able to read and write and their sense of time, history, and place were different. Time was linear, progressive, and marked by clocks and calendars. Religious ceremonies were still observed in annual cycles but the times rigorously set by specific dates.[32] Nature, while it still had secrets yet to be uncovered by the scientific method, was no longer considered sacred. Most importantly, perhaps, they were learning from a cumulative written record. Over time, Budd and Steinhauer abandoned their traditional heritage and willingly pursued the curriculum offered to their privileged European and Canadian contemporaries. They had entered the British World.

Steinhauer's and Budd's life journeys into the British World and adoption of its religious beliefs and idioms of faith came at some cost. In the first place, their non-Native co-workers did not treat them as equal partners.

Theoretically, the evangelical mission-minded institutions that trained them encouraged the employment of indigenous personnel in the field; practically, however, their Euro-American colleagues were slow to grant them complete equality and full responsibilities.[33] Steinhauer's extended apprenticeship for the ordained ministry – labouring as translator and schoolmaster for sixteen years after graduation from Upper Canada Academy – clearly demonstrated his superiors' prejudice against Native missionaries. Subsequently, despite his training in Methodist educational institutions, completion of a prolonged assistantship under the supervision of British and Canadian missionaries, and his proficiency in the Cree language, the conference preferred Euro-Canadians with less education and local experience as supervisors of the western mission field.[34] Moreover, even after the church ordained Steinhauer, it stationed him in relatively isolated posts. Henry Budd's case may have been slightly different in that Rupert's Land did not have the formal educational facilities to train missionaries, yet the CMS never contemplated sending him to an Upper Canadian or English college. Instead, it waited for the arrival of Bishop Anderson to advance his education.[35] In the meantime, for many years, Budd laboured in classrooms, fields, and woods before receiving his own mission assignment. Neither of these keen students, then, were granted full recognition of their superior talents and abilities.

Second, both men, Steinhauer more explicitly than Budd, distanced themselves from the Aboriginal inhabitants of Rupert's Land. In his 1867 report, Steinhauer noted that his devoted and zealous congregation gave him "much consolation in [his] lonely toils among them."[36] That this statement was partly a lament for being isolated from his fellow missionaries and the church is clear. "Separated far away from the fellowship and kindly counsel of maturer Christians," he noted in the *Christian Guardian*, "I often feel keenly the loneliness of my position in this far-off land."[37] But the suggestion that he was lonesome while working among First Nations people appears also to suggest a certain aloofness from not only the unconverted but also the converted Natives. Rhetorically, he articulated his belief that his uneducated indigenous peers, although Christian, were inferior to him. His 1867 report also noted that he hoped the gospel would prevail "throughout the length and breadth of this dark land," and that "the heathen around us are looking with astonishment at the transition of their brethren of the White Fish Lake from a wretched degradation to our improved, happy condition, clothed and in their right minds; raised, in some small degree, in the scale of being."[38] In other words, he implicitly echoed in this statement a generally held European belief that humanity progressed in stages from savage to civilized, and he expressly articulated his assumption that conversion to Christianity had moved the Aboriginal converts of Whitefish Lake only one step toward civilization.[39] Obviously, Steinhauer had absorbed, from a then current assumption in anthropology and Linnaean science, the supposition that North American Natives had to completely adopt the economics and science, as well as religion, of the European settlers.

Henry Budd, too, detached himself from his fellow Natives. He believed that being chosen by John West for special treatment distinguished him from his people. "The more I meditate on the Sovereign mercy and love of our Heavenly Father in singling me from the race of Pagan countrymen," he asserted, "and in honouring me with the message of love and mercy to the heathen, the more I feel I cannot do enough for Him; and the more I see the importance of the work before me."[40] Highly significant, this statement also implicitly relegated his countrymen to inferior status. Like Steinhauer, Budd believed that those who survived primarily by hunting, fishing, and gathering were inferior to those who cultivated the land. Commenting on the unwillingness of the Plains Cree to accept the gospel, Budd noted that they had "few opportunities of learning the civilized life," adding, "They are *truly heathen* and *truly barbarous*. They live among the Buffalo, eat the flesh of that animal and clothe themselves with its skin." This hunting lifestyle, he judged, made them unsuitable for conversion to Christianity and training for civilization.[41] And lastly, like Steinhauer, the educated Budd, who had lived in Red River in the comparative comfort of the parsonage, often missed the communion of like-minded Christian believers. "Shut up as [he was] in this isolated spot," he lamented, "where nothing but darkness, barbarism and heathenism reign,"[1] he felt desperately alone, even among people of a familiar culture and the same mother tongue.

Budd's loneliness was often accompanied by mild but long-lasting depressions. In part, these were the result of a feeling of inferiority occasioned by his lack of full training and his Aboriginal status. Although relatively successful as a proselytizer, a gifted, charismatic teacher and preacher, as well as a talented translator, Budd never felt totally adequate and needed constant reassurances from his supervisors.[2] The frequent bouts of despondency were also provoked by the loss of his wife and several children, all to illness, some within a few months of each other.[3] Unlike his fellow non-Native missionaries, in his deep mourning he could not muster the adulatory rhetoric of God's loving kindness so common of the era. Instead, on at least one occasion, he wrote of quiet resignation and peace. Then, distancing himself from his heritage, he asked: What if he had not accepted Christianity? "What would I not have done to torture my body in every possible way, according to the custom of my Tribe, cutting myself with knives and lancets until the blood would gush out profusely; cutting my hair and going about barefoot and bare legs; and ready to go into fire and into water, courting death rather than life. Thus would I have been mourning for my dear Son just departed."[4]

Both these Aboriginal missionaries, then, while products of two cultures, were fully at home in neither. On one hand, they remained sympathetic to the heritage of their birth. Both maintained the importance of the local language and actively promoted the translation of documents of Christian faith. Although both established boarding schools in order to continue teaching children while parents were absent on hunts, residence was not compulsory and students lived with their parents when they were nearby. Lastly, both men throughout their entire careers enjoyed the hunt and the fellowship of camping – two activities also necessary for their survival. On the other hand, their strongest affinity was with the approaching society and they believed that the best way for the First Nations of Rupert's Land to survive the onslaught of European settlers onto the plains was to adopt a literate culture and an agrarian economy, as well as the religion of the book. Both matured in an evangelical religious culture that viewed the whole world as its parish, and that bore a burden for the welfare of all humanity. Both faiths actively sought elimination of the sins of slavery and cheap gin, the dark excesses of prisons, and mind-numbing factory assembly lines. Just as John Wesley had sought to ameliorate the darkness of industrial and urbanized British society, so Henry Steinhauer aspired to ameliorate the poverty of the British North American Native. Just as the Clapham Sect had fought against slavery and laboured for prison reform, religious instruction in Sunday schools, self-improvement training for the poor, and dissemination of the Bible, and worked for domestic and foreign missions, so Henry Budd sought to educate his Native charges.[5] Steinhauer and Budd inherited a rich humanitarian compassion for their fellow humans and translated that into a life's work. A profound concern for the material well-being of their wards motivated them. "These poor people have no settled place where they might make their houses and farms," Budd wrote in 1870. "They [the Native peoples] have all embraced the Christian religion from the first that the Gospel reached them, but they are to this day without a settled place and without any one to teach even their children."[6]

Despite their passionate concern for the material welfare of their charges, Budd and Steinhauer always placed the spiritual mandate above the secular humanitarian or economic objective.[7] However much they may have absorbed the understanding of British culture and knowledge and accepted the notion that the prairie soils had to be cultivated, they were much more concerned with the salvation of their peoples' souls. In all their formal education and later in their own private studies, the central message was always focused on life after death. Although troubled about the material welfare of North America's Aboriginal people, they worried immeasurably more about their spiritual health. As missionaries, they unwittingly facilitated the colonizing purposes of imperial expansionists, but that was only a secondary corollary to their evangelistic mandate. Steinhauer and Budd, like their Methodist, Anglican, and also their Roman Catholic counterparts, took Christ's injunction, to bring the gospel to all the world, literally. "I have preached the Gospel of our blessed Lord to those who have never heard of a Saviour's love," Budd asserted; "I have carried the standard of the Cross into the Interior, even where Satan's seat is and have planted it in the midst of barbarism, of ignorance and of superstition."[8] Formal learning, informal experience, and observation had taught them that central message. But it had also imparted to them the understanding that it was their duty to bring British culture – or as the nineteenth century put it, civilization – to all the world.[9]

Henry Budd and Henry Steinhauer can be viewed as successful converts to Christianity and a European and Euro-American way of life. Their passage from the oral-traditional to the literate-settler society was eased to some extent by their youth, their education, the promise of economic security, and the absence of significant numbers of settlers in Rupert's Land, but largely by their affinity for the new religion. The Christian gospel represented to them a new Truth, a literate religion better suited to what was to come. Steinhauer chose, and Budd consented, to enter into the new religion. In the process, they absorbed much of the accumulated knowledge of the newcomers and shared it with their fellow Aboriginal peoples. At the same time, they remembered their Native roots, held dear their language, and retained or synthesized contradictory notions into the new religion. As active agents in their own destiny, they facilitated the introduction of the British World to Rupert's Land. That they remained a tiny minority, and that Venn's vision of a self-supporting, independent Native church was not realized owes its primary cause to the rapid settlement of western Canada at the turn of the nineteenth century, an advance so quick and large that it turned the original inhabitants of the Northwest into a disadvantaged minority and largely silenced the voices of those who chose Christianity as well as of those who did not.[10]

Notes

1 Philip Jenkins, *The Next Christendom: The Coming of Global Christianity* (Oxford: Oxford University Press, 2002), in noting this Protestant revivalist movement, observes that the new missionary imperialism was but the continuation of a movement that began at the dawn of the Christian era and spread first from Palestine southward to Africa, then eastward to Asia, and only centuries later westward to Europe.

2 The term "British World" essentially refers to the global British Empire bonded not only by trade and military power but also by a shared identity that thrived on the flow of peoples, information, and ideas. See Phillip Buckner and Carl Bridge, "Reinventing the British World," *Round Table* 368 (2003): 82.

3 Michael D. McNally, *Ojibwe Singers: Hymns, Grief, and a Native Culture in Motion* (New York: Oxford University Press, 2000) views religious systems as dynamic and conversion a lifelong active process.

4 There is a surprising disagreement among Budd's biographers about the details of Budd's youth. Katherine Pettipas, "A History of the Work of the Reverend Henry Budd Conducted under the Auspices of the Church Missionary Society 1840-1875" (MA thesis, University of

Manitoba, 1972) is the most detailed study. The *Journal of the Canadian Church Historical Society* 33 (April 1991) devoted the entire issue to Henry Budd. See Pettipas, "'The Praying Chief': Reverend Henry Budd," 41-50; Frank A. Peake, "Henry Budd and His Colleagues," 23-39, which has only minor factual differences from Pettipas; and the useful psycho-historical analysis of George van der Goes Ladd, "Going-up-the-Hill: The Journey of Henry Budd," 108-9. The standard biography entry of T.C.B. Boon, "Henry Budd," *Dictionary of Canadian Biography*, vol. 10 (Toronto: University of Toronto Press, 1972), 108-9, presents many factual differences from the other biographers.

5   Van der Goes Ladd, "Going-up-the-Hill," 7-9.

6   Isaac Kholisile Mabindisa, "The Praying Man: The Life and Times of Henry Bird Steinhauer" (PhD thesis, University of Alberta, 1984). Mabindisa's dissertation is the most comprehensive biography of Steinhauer. An admirer of Steinhauer's fortitude and sincerity, he lambastes the Hudson's Bay Company for its obstructionist policies in Rupert's Land and chides the Missionary Society for keeping the Native-born missionary in relatively obscure positions. In the end, Mabindisa concludes that Steinhauer formed a valuable buffer between the Native peoples of western Canada and the encroaching settlers, preparing the former for the latter's lifestyle. Not surprisingly, the brief account of Krystyna Z. Sieciechowicz, "Henry Bird Steinhauer," *Dictionary of Canadian Biography*, vol. 11 (Toronto: University of Toronto Press, 1982), 848, is a relatively dispassionate version that does not evaluate the role of Aboriginal preachers in Rupert's Land. The name Shahwanegezhick may have meant "southern sky" while Bird, Steinhauer's middle name, may have been a mistranslation from the Ojibwa words meaning "fastest boat" or "big sail." See, Mabindisa, "Praying Man," 73-74.

7   Raymond M. Beaumont, "Origins and Influences: The Family Ties of the Reverend Henry Budd," *Prairie Forum* 17, 2 (1992): 167-68.

8   Benjamin Slight, *Indian Researches or Facts Concerning North American Indians* (Montreal: Miller, 1844), 88-90. Slight, a Wesleyan Methodist missionary who described the customs, manners, and traditions of Upper Canada's Natives, viewed their religious ceremonies sympathetically and on at least one occasion drew instructive parallels. Donald B. Smith, *Sacred Feathers: The Reverend Peter Jones (Kahkewaquonaby) and the Mississauga Indians* (Toronto: University of Toronto Press, 1987) provides an account of Jones' childhood that can be applied to Steinhauer's. Incidentally, Smith's thesis argues that Jones, by converting to Christianity, was able to save some of his own people, the Mississauga, from extinction by settling them on farms. Steinhauer held many of Jones' ideas. Catherine Stoehr, "Kahkewaquonaby (Peter Jones) and the Great Spirit (Jesus)" (paper presented at the eighty-first annual meeting of the Canadian Historical Association, Toronto, May 2002) suggests that Jones built his Methodist doctrines on the kernel beliefs of his Aboriginal ancestors. See also McNally, *Ojibwe Singers*.

9   John West, *The Substance of a Journal during a Residence at the Red River Colony* (1824; reprinted New York: Johnson Reprint, 1966), 14. The other lad, son of Withaweecapo, did not take to life in Red River and soon returned to his father.

10 Pettipas, "Praying Chief," 43; Van der Goes Ladd, "Going-up-the-Hill," 10-13. West dedicated his published journal, *Substance of a Journal*, to Rev. Henry Budd, MA, a rector at White Roothing, Essex, a former mentor and friend who promised to underwrite the young Swampy Cree's education. The bishop of Montreal, George J. Mountain, opposed giving converted Natives only a Christian name. His rationale was not a critique of inherent high-handed paternalism but a regret that the loss of Native names sacrificed the aura of mystique that financial supporters of missions appreciated. "The retention of their original names, with the Christian name as a prefix in each case, would have served as a constant mark and of their memento of their having been gathered, with their posterity as a consequence, into the bosom of the Church of God from a state of heathenism," he wrote, "and wherever an individual is made prominent as a Clergyman, a Catechist, or a Schoolmaster, or a helper, in any way, of the cause, an increased interest would be communicated to the report of his proceedings at home – as in the case of some Oriental converts – if he were noticed under his Indian appellation." George J. Mountain, *The Journal of the Bishop of Montreal during a Visit to the Church Missionary Society's North-West*

America Mission (London: Seeley, Burnside, and Seeley; Hatchard and Son; Nisbet and Company, 1845), 73-74. There are interesting references to a new name in Isaiah 62:2 and Revelation 2:17.

11 *Christian Guardian* (Toronto), 10 May 1854.

12 Mabindisa, "Praying Man," 73.

13 Gerald Friesen, *Citizens and Nation: An Essay on History, Communication, and Canada* (Toronto: University of Toronto Press, 2000).

14 West, *The Substance of a Journal,* 21-22.

15 Smith, *Sacred Feathers,* 119-21; Neil Semple, *The Lord's Dominion: The History of Canadian Methodism* (Montreal and Kingston: McGill-Queen's University Press, 1996), 121.

16 Semple, *Lord's Dominion,* 239-40; Michael Hennell, *John Venn and the Clapham Sect* (London: Lutterworth Press, 1958); Earnest Marshall Howse, *Saints in Politics: The "Clapham Sect" and the Growth of Freedom* (Toronto: Allen and Unwin, 1952).

17 Mabindisa, "Praying Man," 77-80.

18 Donald R. Raichle, "School Discipline and Corporal Punishment: An American Retrospect" in *Children's Rights: Legal and Educational Issues,* ed. Heather Berkeley, Chad Gaffield, and W. Gordon West (Toronto: Ontario Institute for Studies in Education, 1978), 108-20.

19 Alice Miller, *For Your Own Good: Hidden Cruelty in Child-Rearing and the Roots of Violence,* trans. Hildegarde Hannum and Hunter Hannum (Toronto: McGraw-Hill Ryerson, 1983), 3-91, takes an extreme position, calling nineteenth-century discipline "poisonous pedagogy." The use of strong physical and psychological measures, Miller argues, resulted in the suppression of emotion and any sort of self-will in children. Priscilla Robertson, "Home as a Nest: Middle Class Childhood in Nineteenth-Century Europe" in *The History of Childhood,* ed. Lloyd deMause (New York: Psychohistory Press, 1974), 407-8, 421, disagrees, suggesting that educators were interested more in changing than replacing personalities. References to physical punishment are common in the Bible, for example, Proverbs 13:24: "He who spares the rod hates his son, but he who loves him is careful to discipline him," and Proverbs 29:15: "The rod of correction imparts wisdom, but a child left to himself disgraces his mother." Scriptures also repeatedly refer to God physically punishing those who disobey his injunctions.

20 Peter Jones, *History of the Ojebway Indians; with Special Reference to Their Conversion to Christianity* (1861; reprinted Freeport, NY: Books for Libraries, 1970), 67, 277.

21 Isaac Watts, *Divine Songs Attempted in Easy Language for the Use of Children,* with an introduction by J.H.P. Pafford (1715; reprinted London: Oxford University Press, 1971), 225-26.

22 Isaac Watts, *The Second Set of Catechisms and Prayers or Some Helps to the Religion of Children* ... (London: J. Buckland and T. Longman, 1768).

23 George Boas, *The Cult of Childhood* (London: Warburg Institute, 1966), 36-41; Richard Gravil, "'Knowledge Not Purchased with the Loss of Power': Wordsworth, Pestalozzi, and 'the Spots of Time,'" *European Romantic Review* 8 (1997): 233-34, 239; William J. Reese, "The Origins of Progressive Education," *History of Education Quarterly* 41 (2001): 1-24; and Clem Adelman, "Over Two Years, What Did Froebel Say to Pestalozzi?" *History of Education* 29 (2000): 104-7.

24 Boas, *The Cult of Childhood,* 36-41.

25 George van der Goes Ladd, "Father Cockran and His Children: Poisonous Pedagogy on the Banks of the Red," in *The Anglican Church and the World of Western Canada, 1820-1970,* ed. Barry Ferguson (Regina: Canadian Plains Research Center, University of Regina, 1991), completely accepts the "poisonous pedagogy" concept articulated by Miller, *For Your Own Good.* While discipline in early-nineteenth-century schools certainly was harsh, the subsequent lives of Budd and Steinhauer suggest that their individual wills and personalities were not broken.

26 Van der Goes Ladd, "Going-up-the-Hill," 18-19.

27 Semple, *Lord's Dominion,* 241-45.

28 *Christian Guardian* (Toronto), 9 May 1838.

29 Steinhauer had interrupted his studies at the academy in 1837 for one year to help Case re-establish the faltering Grape Island mission at Alderville. Within years, Alderville became the first Canadian Methodist residential school.

30   McNally, *Ojibwe Singers,* contends that religion is more than a system of belief; it is a prac-
      tice, a useful notion for understanding conversion as a process that may never be com-
      pleted. Steinhauer may have been named after a wealthy Philadelphia businessman who
      underwrote the youth's education.
31   Jones, *History of the Ojebway;* Smith, *Sacred Feathers.*
32   Smith, *Sacred Feathers,* 154-60. Ironically, George Copway, another Mississauga preacher,
      held a romantic view of Ojibwa culture. I am indebted to Robin Jarvis Brownlie, who
      persuasively argued this point in "Discourses of Cooperation: Ojibwe Self-Representation
      in Mid-Nineteenth Century Upper Canada" (paper presented at the eighty-second annual
      meeting of the Canadian Historical Association, Halifax, May 2003). Copway also valued
      English instruction but for more sophisticated reasons than Jones. He believed that knowl-
      edge of English provided an entry into the riches of English literature. G. Copway, *The
      Traditional History and Characteristic Sketches of the Ojibwa Nation* (Boston: Benjamin B. Mussey,
      1851), 245-46.
33   Victoria University Library, Peter Jones Collection, Sermons and Addresses, "Memoran-
      dum, Thoughts on Indian Schools, delivered at Toronto – February 1835."
34   Peter Jones, trans., *A Collection of Chippeway and English Hymns for the Use of the Native
      Indians* (to which are added a few hymns translated by James Evans and George Henry)
      (Toronto: Conference Office, 1840). See, McNally, *Ojibwe Singers,* for an analysis of Jones'
      work. Stoehr, "Kahkewaquonaby and the Great Spirit," suggests that Jones built his Meth-
      odist doctrines on the kernel beliefs of his Aboriginal ancestors.
35   United Church of Canada Archives (UCCA), Wesleyan Methodist Missionary Society Col-
      lection, Steinhauer to Evans, 19 December 1840; Jacobs to Alder, 23 May 1844; Mason to
      Secretaries, 20 August 1844; Jacobs to Alder, 20 August 1844. See also Peers, *Ojibwa of
      Western Canada.*
36   UCCA, Mason to Fathers, 22 December 1845; Mason to Fathers, 29 August 1850.
37   UCCA, Steinhauer to Mason, 25 June 1851, 5, 21, and 22 July 1851, 25 June 1852; and
      extracts from Mason's journal, 1852-53, 29 April 1853; Thomas H.B. Symons, "John Ryerson,"
      Dictionary of Canadian Biography, vol. 10 (Toronto: University of Toronto Press, 1972), 638;
      Mabindisa, "Praying Man," 371-400.
38   Pettipas, "Praying Chief," 44-46.
39   University of Birmingham, Church Missionary Society Archive (CMSA), Hunter's Report
      for the year ending 1 August 1846.
40   CMSA, Rev. William Cockran to Secretaries, 5 August 1847; Budd to Cockran, 31 December
      1847; Hunter's report, July 1848.
41   CMSA, Venn and Smith to Rev. John Smithurst and Rev. Robert James, 4 June 1849. Useful
      studies of the notion of an indigenous church are C. Peter Williams, *The Ideal of the
      Self-Governing Church: A Study in Victorian Missionary Strategy* (New York: E.J. Brill, 1990),
      and Jehu Hanciles, *Euthanasia of a Mission: African Church Autonomy in a Colonial Context*
      (Westport, CT: Praeger, 2002).
42   CMSA, Bishop of Rupert's Land to Venn, n.d., likely 22 November 1849. Budd was to re-
      ceive a £10 fellowship. Although Venn had not yet officially stated his Native church policy,
      he made frequent references to the subject. See Wilbert R. Shenk, *Henry Venn: Missionary
      Statesman* (Maryknoll, NY: Orbis Books, 1983) and T.E. Yates, *Venn and Victorian Bishops
      Abroad: The Missionary Policies of Henry Venn and Their Repercussions upon the Anglican Epis-
      copate of the Colonial Period, 1841-1872* (Upsalla: Swedish Institute of Missionary Research,
      1978).
43   CMSA, Budd's journal, 22 December 1850; Anderson to Venn, 7 August and 27 November
      1850; Budd's journal, 25, 29, and 30 December 1850.
44   Peake, "Henry Budd," and Pettipas, "Praying Chief."
45   Beaumont, "Origins and Influences," 181, spells her name as Muninawatum and suggests
      she likely was the daughter of Budd's niece. In other words, Steinhauer married into Budd's
      family network.
46   Beaumont, "Origins and Influences."
47   Derek Whitehouse-Strong, "'Because I Happen to Be a Native Clergyman': The Impact of
      Race, Ethnicity, Status, and Gender on Native Agents of the Church Missionary Society in

the Nineteenth Century Canadian North-West" (PhD thesis, University of Manitoba, 2004), 268, 286.

48 Friesen, *Citizens and Nation*.
49 Copway, *Traditional History*, 246.
50 Watts, *Divine Songs*, 215-16.
51 Friesen, *Citizens and Nation*.
52 Clark Blaise, *Time Lord: The Remarkable Canadian Who Missed His Train and Changed the World* (Toronto: Alfred A. Knopf, 2000). Easter is the exception in that it is set by the lunar as well as the solar calendar.
53 Whitehouse-Strong, "Native Clergyman."
54 Mabindisa, "Praying Man," 575.
55 In one instance, a British-born deacon was ordained a priest somewhat prematurely to ensure he would not be outranked by Budd when working in the same place. CMSA, Bishop of Rupert's Land to Venn, 7 January 1856.
56 Wesleyan-Methodist Church in Canada, Missionary Society, annual report 1866-67, xiv.
57 *Christian Guardian* (Toronto), 3 April 1867.
58 Wesleyan-Methodist Church in Canada, xiv.
59 John G. Burke, "The Wild Man's Pedigree: Scientific Method and Racial Anthropology," in *The Wild Man Within: An Image in Western Thought from the Renaissance to Romanticism*, ed. Edward Dudley and Maximilian E. Novak (Pittsburgh: University of Pittsburgh Press, 1972).
60 CMSA, Budd to Secretary Knight, 4 August 1851.
61 CMSA, Budd to Secretaries, 13 January 1853.
62 CMSA, Budd to Maj. Hector Straith, 1 August 1859.
63 CMSA, Budd's journal, 10 July 1853; Budd to Knight, 12 January 1854.
64 A daughter died in 1856, a son in 1857, and another daughter in 1860 (CMSA, Budd to Secretary John Chapman, 30 July 1857; Budd to Secretary, 8 August 1860). Two sons, a daughter, and his wife died in the fall and early winter of 1864. Among the dead was his eldest son and namesake, who had been trained in England for the ministry (CMSA, Budd to Straith and to Secretary, 18 January 1865).
65 CMSA, 7 September 1864. Quoted in Peake, "Henry Budd," 34.
66 Hennell, *John Venn and the Clapham Sect;* Howse, *Saints in Politics;* Yates, *Venn and Victorian Bishops*.
67 CMSA, Budd to Secretary, 15 August 1870.
68 For three randomly selected examples, see *Christian Guardian* (Toronto), 10 May 1854; *Wesleyan Missionary Notices*, 1 May 1869; and *Missionary Outlook*, vol. 1, 3 April 1883.
69 CMSA, Budd to Straith, 2 August 1853.
70 Jenkins, *New Christianity*, argues that European Christianity has played only a minor role in world history compared to its impact in pre-1400 Christendom in the Middle East, Asia, and Africa. He discounts the popular notion of a European-centred Christian spiritual imperialism. Similarly, Andrew Porter, "Religion and Empire" in *The Oxford History of the British Empire*, vol. 3, *The Nineteenth Century* (Oxford: Oxford University Press, 1999), 244, argues that it is "impossible to speak in any straightforward way of 'religious,' 'ecclesiastical' or 'missionary' imperialism." However, much as they wanted to, neither the missionary societies nor its agents, he argued, could duplicate the metropolitan religious institutions.
71 Sarah Carter, *Lost Harvests: Prairie Indian Reserve Farmers and Government Policy* (Montreal and Kingston: McGill-Queen's University Press, 1990), convincingly demonstrates that government policy rather than Native attitudes to agriculture led to the failure of the reserve policy.

4

Law and British Culture in the Creation of British North America

David Murray

English law travelled as an essential part of the baggage of the British Empire everywhere that Britain created colonies, and it remains a living imperial legacy in the nations that emerged from that colonial experience. Both the law and the legal institutions in which it functioned were slowly but steadily evolving, so that the law that established itself in South Australia in 1836 had changed perceptibly from the law that had been transmitted to Upper Canada in 1792. The most striking example of this change can be found in the criminal law, since the number of offences that could result in hanging dramatically declined between 1792 and 1836. The changes in the criminal law that steadily reduced the more than 200 capital offences of the "Bloody Code" of the late eighteenth century occurred sooner in nineteenth-century England than they did in Upper Canada, but even Upper Canada dutifully followed in England's wake. In 1833, Upper Canada passed a statute dramatically reducing the number of capital crimes from more than 150 to 12 and effectively eliminated the system of discretionary justice that had determined the ultimate fate of those sentenced to be hanged.[1] John Beattie reminds us, however, that we must resist the notion that significant changes in English criminal law occurred only after 1770; change had been evident throughout the period he examined, from 1660 to 1800 and beyond.[2]

Upper Canada inherited as its own law all prior English law as of 17 September 1792, the date of the opening of the first legislature of the colony. This enormous body of inherited law would establish precedents for the new colony until its legislature modified them by passing laws of its own. Along with this formal body of law came principles, both legal and moral, to guide the legislators and the jurists of Upper Canada. Since a similar process occurred in other British settlement colonies, what happened in Upper Canada can be examined as one example to illustrate how all-encompassing this legal implantation was. Because both the law itself and the legal institutions were constantly evolving, and each was also adapting to the colonial circumstances of the particular colony, the evolution and implantation of English law occurred in different patterns across the extended British Empire.

How important was this process for the nature and character of the Empire? Phillip Buckner has ably illuminated the historiographical issues of the Empire in an article in *Acadiensis,* contrasting the historical approach to empire found in the nine volumes of *The Cambridge History of the British Empire,* published over a thirty-year period from 1929 to 1959, with the historical approach taken by the authors in the more recent *Oxford History of the British Empire,* published in five volumes in 1998-99.[3] Buckner argues that in the new *Oxford History,* "the assumption that there was something distinctive about the British Empire has been largely abandoned."[4] We are left therefore with the question of whether there was anything distinctive about the British Empire or, as he phrases it, of what really was British in the British Empire.

Buckner does not mention the law or legal institutions in his review and indeed the subject receives only limited coverage in both sets of histories. Yet the idea of the British exporting their system of law, along with other essential British items – from language to political institutions – underscores the positive benefits of British imperialism praised in the earlier Cambridge histories. One example will suffice: "Peace, order and the rule of law came as benefits to many troubled lands; hopes and ideas were stirred, a spirit of freedom roused, and there was a pattern of material and intellectual progress."[5] This is one extract of what Buckner correctly labels a "romanticized, triumphant, Whiggish version of Imperial history" requiring a modern historical corrective.[6] We might well agree that this rhetoric is outdated, but is there a case to be made for the transmission of a uniquely English system of law to its empire, part of what we might label a distinctively British Empire? If so, how should we make the case? In order to do this we need to know more about how these transplanted English institutions actually worked on the ground and what effects they had. This will come from both local and comparative studies.

The reception of English law in each part of the Empire had wide-ranging ramifications, as Tina Loo and Lorna McLean stress, using the example of Canada in their book, *Historical Perspectives on Law and Society in Canada.* They argue that since colonial order was constructed, and constructed through law that created and enforced "certain relationships among people and between people and governments," the nature of the law as implanted helped to determine the nature of that constructed colonial order. They also point out that "the law's institutions and officers were the outposts and liegemen of empires, establishing the boundaries of sovereign power as well as symbolizing it."[7] A recent book on the impact of law in New South Wales, Australia, reiterates that English law was "an important part" of the "cultural baggage" carried to the penal colony by all the colonists, convicts, and others alike. Its author, David Neal, states that "the rule of law ... played a prime role in changing New South Wales from a penal colony to a free society."[8] Greg Marquis, a Canadian historian, has written that "the law and its administration were not remote for nineteenth-century British North Americans but part of their orientation towards local affairs, government, and the Empire. Justice, in the form of the constable, the alderman, the justice of the peace, or the stipendiary magistrate, was a highly visible if decentralized sign of the state."[9]

A view of the process from the imperial centre, that is, from London, might emphasize the unity of English law to go along with the unity of the Empire. My approach in my recent book, *Colonial Justice,* was to examine how criminal law actually worked from the bottom up in one district of Upper Canada. The Niagara district revealed less unity and more diversity in the actual application of English law in a colonial situation, and my study showed how British institutions were adapted to new colonial circumstances.[10] I also hope that it might stimulate other local studies that, in turn, will provide the material for larger comparative projects. I want to draw on my book to illustrate how the colonial culture of British Upper Canada was permeated by English law and legal institutions from the bottom up as well as from the top down, but also that the local circumstances of the district helped to shape the way both the law and the legal institutions evolved. If, as Peter Marshall tells us in his chapter called "British North America, 1760-1815" in *The Oxford History of the British Empire,* "Upper Canada was to become the model North American colony of settlement," knowledge of how British law actually worked in this colony should provide a point of comparison for studies in other parts of the Empire.[11]

Another example to illustrate how this evolving British law took root in various parts of the Empire, leaving behind identifiable footprints, comes from the history of one of the most pervasive courts in the Canadas, as well as in England and other parts of its empire: the court of quarter sessions, also known as the court of general sessions of the peace. This court has its roots in late medieval England in the latter part of the fourteenth century, and in England it continued until its abolition in 1971. The importance of the court steadily increased through the sixteenth and seventeenth centuries, as did the range of its activities. Small wonder, then, that it was one of the pieces of legal luggage accompanying the British colonial authorities as they created settlement colonies in North America and in other territories around the globe.

Among the colonies that later combined to form Canada, we can find five eighteenth-century examples of the court of quarter sessions in operation: Nova Scotia, founded in 1749; Quebec, where the court was created in 1764; Upper Canada, in 1792; and Newfoundland and New Brunswick, both of which had courts of quarter sessions operating in the eighteenth century. The local justices of the peace were empowered to hold a court with broad jurisdiction every three months. In Upper Canada the courts of quarter sessions also functioned as the local government. Although elected representative legislative assemblies existed at the colonial level in each of the Canadas from 1792, local government was carried out by a non-elected group of justices of the peace. Far from being an anomaly, this was simply following the English example and utilizing the same institutions. Empowering local magistrates with the power to enforce laws and carry out local government was a cheap way of extending the sway of empire over vast regions and it was also familiar to all British colonists, who were therefore more likely to accept it.

Courts of quarter sessions functioned at the county level in England with larger populations and smaller territory to cover than was the case in the Canadas, where they were created for each district. When the districts of Upper Canada were disbanded in 1849, the courts reverted to being county courts as they were in England.[12] As new districts were added, new courts of quarter sessions came along with them. In Quebec, the court of quarter sessions held civil jurisdiction from 1764 to 1770, when it was removed because of the distress it was causing.[13] In Upper Canada, unlike New South Wales after 1823, the quarter sessions court was not a circuit court. It was held in the district capital just as in England, where the court met in the county town. Also, in New South Wales the courts of quarter sessions, introduced into the colony after the passage of the New South Wales Act of 1823, possessed summary jurisdiction over the convicts with the power to extend a convict's time of punishment or order transportation to another penal settlement.[14] The courts in Upper Canada did not possess this characteristic either, because of Canada's status as a penal colony.

What sort of colonial order was constructed through this system of intertwined local government and law, carried out by magistrates who were themselves not trained lawyers? Not until after the Act of Union of 1840 brought Upper and Lower Canada together did the government appoint trained lawyers as district judges who would chair the court of quarter sessions, bringing the professionalism of their legal training to bear on the district courts. The first lieutenant-governor of Upper Canada, John Graves Simcoe, wanted Upper Canada to be a model of England overseas, where it would be possible to show off the superiority of English institutions to the upstart American republicans who had dared to create their own separate republic. He wanted "to inculcate the principles of eighteenth-century English government along with its hierarchical stratification to secure the foundation for this new British colony and an antidote to the seductive influences of American republicanism."[15] What actually occurred was a little different. Upper Canada did not establish a landed aristocracy in imitation of Britain, although

Simcoe certainly tried to lay the foundations for this. But with the primary district court and local government in the hands of magistrates appointed by the governor, the basic purpose of the English justice system, defined by John Beattie as the preservation of order and the protection of property, also became the raison d'être of the colonial justice system in Upper Canada as well as in the other colonies of British North America.[16] The new colony was neither seduced nor conquered by American republicanism, although it would be hard to conclude that it succeeded in showing off the superiority of British institutions to the Americans, who remained convinced that their republican versions were better.

The local magistrates in Upper Canada were really the district rulers, just as in England magistrates were rulers of the county.[17] I have stated that they "were at once accountable to the representative of the Crown who had appointed them and deeply imbedded in their local communities, creating a tension which often manifested itself as they carried out their myriad functions."[18] They were appointed primarily because they were persons of substance within their communities, meaning particularly that they had substantial property or wealth. The act of 1842 setting out the qualifications for magistrates in Upper Canada declared that "they shall be of the most sufficient persons in the District," having a minimum property qualification of £300 a year.[19] In effect, the magistrates in Upper Canada were the Canadian equivalent of the British gentry.

Magistrates in the Niagara district tended to serve for lengthy periods, adding to their power and influence, and many were linked to each other through family connections as well as through business. They were in reality local oligarchs, often with interconnecting nexuses of influence.[20] There was an elaborate but informal process of screening whereby names were carefully sifted by the lieutenant-governor's trusted advisers, and certainly not everyone who sought the office received it. Being a magistrate in the new colony was seen as a desirable office not just for the prestige it conferred but also for the economic opportunities it opened up. Acting collectively as the court of quarter sessions for their district, the magistrates exercised great local power, whether in granting or withholding licences, setting assessment rates, making appointments, or approving petitions for social assistance, just as they exercised the full extent of their legal powers in the criminal law cases that came before them. They were the people the government called upon when it wanted special tasks undertaken, especially in times of war, emergency, or feared rebellion. They were not subject to recall by the elected legislature. Only the lieutenant-governor could revoke their appointment, and this happened very rarely. More likely was the possibility of a man finding himself left off a new commission of the peace, issued usually at the beginning of a new reign, either because his economic circumstances had changed or because he was out of favour with the lieutenant-governor. That the reign of a king or queen determined the timing of these appointments indicates how closely tied the positions were to the monarchical cycles of empire.

The role and power of the magistrates, certainly as exemplified by the experience of those in the Niagara district, illustrates how effectively the English system of magistrates and quarter sessions courts adapted to this colonial environment, and how well rooted the system became in Upper Canada during the first half of the nineteenth century. It was not just these institutions of magistrates and courts, along with the law they represented, that Britain planted in its settlement colonies. Along with them came a legal culture that shaped the lives of the colonists as firmly as did the institutions that nurtured the culture. To understand how local government actually worked in Upper Canada and in the Niagara district, it is necessary for us to know, for example, what a presentment was, what it contained, and how it was used. Through this knowledge we can gain some insight into the workings of this British colonial legal culture.

This can be illustrated again using the example of the Niagara district. A presentment as used in early-nineteenth-century Upper Canada was a written bill of particulars of an offence, produced by a grand jury and used to form a bill of indictment. If the bill was then found by the grand jury to be a true bill, the offence would go forward to trial. In its broader meaning, a presentment could mean a formal statement of a legal matter, usually prepared by a grand jury. The trial process inherited from England relied on grand juries at both the quarter sessions courts and the assize courts, although the composition of the juries would vary depending on the court level. To demonstrate how pervasive the legal culture was, grand jury presentments were used not just in criminal cases but also in cases of poor relief, which in the Niagara district were decided by the court of quarter sessions.

English law and its institutions, once introduced into new colonies, began to adapt to the circumstances of each colony and, indeed, to the particular areas, such as districts, in which they functioned. In Upper Canada poor relief illustrated how English law procedure had to be adapted to colonial needs. Upper Canada had consciously rejected the English Poor Laws for reasons that historians have speculated about but, lacking clear evidence, have not been able to pronounce theories on with any sense of certainty.[21] Having explicitly rejected the English model, the Upper Canadian legislators then left the various localities to deal with the problems on their own until well into the nineteenth century. The court of quarter sessions in the Niagara district thus spent a large amount of time from the 1820s into the 1840s wrestling with the question of whether or not to grant petitions for poor relief, and, if the answer was yes, on what grounds they would grant them.

Supplicants wanting relief in the Niagara district either approached the court of quarter sessions in person or, more often, given their distance from the court, sent a petition, usually supported by neighbours and often written on their behalf. These petitions and requests were turned over to the quarter sessions grand jury, which would examine the evidence produced and write a presentment setting out the facts of the case and the jury's recommendation. Thus the same legal document used to determine whether or not a person charged with a crime should be formally indicted for trial was also used to determine an individual's eligibility for poor relief. By subsuming poor relief under the criminal process, Upper Canadians helped to reinforce the image of the pauper as little different from that of the criminal.[77] Each of the grand jurors at the Niagara district court of quarter sessions in the first half of the nineteenth century knew and absorbed the legal culture surrounding not only criminal trials but also local government issues, including poor relief. For them, presentments also became vehicles for transmitting the collective opinion of the grand jury to the magistrates. Given the lack of any representative institutions at the local level, the grand jury presentment was often the only voice of collective district public opinion.

This role of the quarter sessions grand jury also had a long and strong English pedigree, and it can be found as well in a variety of English colonies. John Beattie portrayed the grand jury in eighteenth-century England as "the one authentic and legitimate voice of county opinion," a view echoed by Norma Landau.[23] As I point out in my study of the Niagara district, the grand jury in Upper Canada and in the other colonies of British North America derived from the English tradition of the "Grand Inquest," in which the jury voiced the opinion of the district (in England, the county) on any matters of local public concern through its presentments, as well as determining whether the charges brought before it should proceed to trial or, certainly in the Niagara district, whether the petitions for relief should be granted.[24] Thus the grand jury of the court of quarter sessions was an integral element of local government in the Niagara district, as it was in other parts of British North America, becoming on occasion as much a political institution as a legal one even if in the British colonies it was not a centrepiece of local democracy. This tradition began to decline in England in the early nineteenth century, but it continued in Upper Canada until the latter part of the century before it faded out.[25]

Behind the grand jury presentment and the political role of the grand jury in local government lay the larger question of the jury trial. In 1792 the second act passed by the new legislature of Upper Canada proclaimed jury trials throughout the colony, stating this to be "one of the chief benefits to be attained by a free Constitution."[26] In order to possess the rights and privileges of freeborn Englishmen, these eighteenth-century colonists deemed it essential to enshrine the right to jury trials throughout their colony. This symbolic importance of the jury trial endured throughout the history of Upper Canada down to the Union of 1840, and it has continued into the modern period even as the number of jury trials has steadily declined. The government of the colony also believed that it was important to the functioning of justice in the colony to adhere as closely as possible to English precedents. Defending the methods used to select jurymen, the legislative council of Upper Canada stated in 1836: "Nor has usage here varied in any one respect from the Law and practice followed in the Mother Country."[27] By extending the right to and obligation of jury duty to all inhabitant householders in the colony, the colonial government helped ensure that a larger proportion of the male population of the colony was eligible for jury duty than was the case in Britain at the same time. Even though many indictments at the court of quarter sessions never reached the stage of a jury trial, it is still the case that jury trials were far more prevalent during these early colonial days than they have become more recently. I have also stressed that "the jury helped to legitimate legal processes for the local community" and, at the same time, the grand jury, especially, acted "as a voice for that community."[28]

I have also explored the importance of local jury cultures in rural colonial Nova Scotia, as has Jim Phillips for eighteenth-century Halifax, and both of us have stressed the importance of the jury in each locale.[29] In Shelburne, the Barrington men certainly paid lip service to the importance of the jury, but they did not always hasten to answer the summons to serve on colonial juries; "some even went to great length to avoid what were seen as tiresome, expensive and annoying calls upon their time."[30] Yet jury service was a constant fact of life, especially for qualified adult males in underpopulated rural areas, and many faced repeated demands on their time. Jim Phillips reiterates the fact that although the basic structure of the jury system in Halifax, as elsewhere in Nova Scotia and British North America, reflected the English criminal law heritage, local factors "subtly altered the ways in which juries were constituted and in which they operated."[31] The decline of the jury system in Canada meant a diminution in lay participation as the criminal justice system became increasingly professionalized. Over time, law reform embraced economy and efficiency, and the rights of Englishmen symbolized in the jury trial began to fade into historical oblivion.[32]

We can contrast the experience of Upper Canada, indeed all of British North America, with that of New South Wales, where a long struggle was required to persuade the British government to permit trials by jury. Here it was the colonists, especially the emancipists, who appealed to well-known English traditions to support their demands for jury trials. David Neal claims that for these colonists, "the right to serve on juries symbolized citizenship"; it certainly carried with it a sense of possessing the full rights and powers of free Englishmen.[33] Although the right to jury trials in criminal cases was not conceded partially until 1833 and fully in 1839, the struggle over jury trials in New South Wales highlights the variations in the transmission of key English legal institutions to different parts of the Empire.

I have also argued that the transmission of English law to Upper Canada in the late eighteenth century embraced a Christian moral order. W.C. Keele's handbook compiled for magistrates in Upper Canada in 1835 stated that "the Christian religion, according to high authority, is part and parcel of the laws of England. To reproach or blaspheme it, therefore, is to speak in subversion of the law."[34] This legal culture, with its imbedded Christian moral order, was reinforced by laws and by royal proclamations issued at the beginning of each reign; basically they were imperial codes of conduct for the monarch's subjects wherever they lived. The one issued at the beginning of William IV's reign in 1830, like its earlier predecessors, was to be read four times a year in all churches and chapels, as well as at the opening of all courts of quarter sessions or assize courts, to ensure that the colonists were well aware of its provisions. Even though no specific laws against Sabbath-breaking were passed in the Upper Canadian legislature before 1845, charges were brought against Sabbath-breakers in the Niagara district with the force of the royal proclamation behind them. The monarch had commanded all his officials "to be very vigilant and strict in the discovery and effectual prosecution and punishment" of anyone guilty of "dissolute, immoral or disorderly practices," including "profanation of the Lord's Day."[35] There was a large gap between the orders issued on behalf of the monarch and successful prosecutions brought at the district level, as was evident in the Niagara district, suggesting again the complexity of the legal culture transmitted to the new colony. If we are to understand more fully the nature of the colonial environment, it is important to acknowledge not just its legal culture imported from Britain but also the moral and religious components wrapped within it.

In asking whether there was a case to be made for the transmission of a uniquely English system of law to its colonial empire, part of what might be termed the distinctive "Britishness" of that empire, I also raised the question of how that case should be made. One of the ways the case has been made occurs in the second volume of the new *Oxford History of the British Empire.* Jack Greene tells us that in the eighteenth century, "liberty, as it had been from the beginnings of English overseas expansion, was the single most important ingredient of an Imperial identity in Britain and the British Empire." Liberty for British colonists consisted of enjoying "all the rights and privileges of freeborn Englishmen."[36] Essential to those rights and privileges was the right to live in a society governed by the rule of law, and laws to which they through their elected representatives had consented. P.J. Marshall points out later in the same volume how controversial the definition of British liberty had become even by the mid-eighteenth century and certainly by the time of the American Revolution, yet the export of English law continued unabated to colonies such as Upper Canada and those founded in Australia and New Zealand following the Revolution.[37] Greg Marquis has confirmed that the concepts of British justice and British liberty became "deeply enshrined in [British North American] popular culture" despite the obvious class inequalities of the society.[38]

The law as transmitted was itself evolving over time and it adapted to the different circumstances of each of the colonies. By examining how both the legal institutions and the legal culture that surrounded them actually worked from the bottom up in the various localities of the Empire, we can see diverse patterns of accommodation, as well as the way in which these institutions and the culture shaped varying structures of colonial order. A number of other Canadian legal historians have ably illustrated how the continuous adaptation of English law to the local conditions of British North American colonies has taken place.[39]

Whether we are discussing courts of quarter sessions, the role of grand juries, the influence of legal documents such as presentments, or the pervasive influence of English legal forms in colonial local government, we can see that while each of these permeates British colonies, whether in British North America or in the Antipodes, their role and function differ from colony to colony and possibly across the individual colonies as well. These institutions, such as the court of quarter sessions or the grand jury and its presentments, even the jury trial, all of which were such bulwarks of empire in the late eighteenth and early nineteenth centuries, are now historical artefacts in many cases, since the evolution of legal institutions and culture, certainly in Canada, has all but left them behind. Even if some of the institutions that characterized early British North American justice have now disappeared, British traditions have had a profound effect in shaping the contours of the Canadian legal system.[40] In his book illustrating this, Boris Laskin, one of Canada's most influential judges of the twentieth century, states with assurance that the English tradition "remains a vital and omnipresent force in Canadian law."[41] What lies behind this tradition, the rule of law, emerges as a powerful component of the British imperialism responsible for the colonies in British North America, as well as in other areas of the world, even if historians continue to find the concept of the rule of law as complex and elusive in definition as the idea of British liberty.

Notes
1 Peter Oliver, *"Terror to Evil-Doers": Prisons and Punishments in Nineteenth Century Ontario* (Toronto: Osgoode Society, 1998), 97-100.
2 John Beattie, *Crime and the Courts in England, 1660-1800* (Princeton, NJ: Princeton University Press, 1986), 13.
3 Phillip A. Buckner, "Was There a 'British' Empire? The Oxford History of the British Empire from a Canadian Perspective," *Acadiensis* 32, 1 (Autumn 2002): 110-28.

4 Ibid., 111.
5 *The Cambridge History of the British Empire,* vol. 2, *The Growth of the New Empire, 1783-1870* (Cambridge: Cambridge University Press, 1940), vii.
6 Buckner, "Was There a 'British' Empire?" 114.
7 Tina Loo and Lorna R. McLean, *Historical Perspectives on Law and Society in Canada* (Toronto: Copp Clark Longman, 1994), 2-4.
8 David Neal, *The Rule of Law in a Penal Colony: Law and Power in Early New South Wales* (Cambridge: Cambridge University Press, 1991), xii.
9 Greg Marquis, "Doing Justice to 'British' Justice: Law, Ideology and Canadian Historiography," in *Canadian Perspectives on Law and Society. Issues in Legal History,* ed. W. Wesley Pue and Barry Wright (Ottawa: Carleton University Press, 1988), 44.
10 David Murray, *Colonial Justice: Justice, Morality and Crime in the Niagara District, 1791-1849* (Toronto: Osgoode Society, 2002). Susan Lewthwaite has carried out another recent local study of how the law operated in a particular district of Upper Canada in her doctoral dissertation, "Law and Authority in Upper Canada: The Justices of the Peace in the Newcastle District, 1803-1846" (PhD thesis, University of Toronto, 2000). See also her "The Pre-trial Examination in Upper Canada," in *Criminal Justice in the Old World and the New,* ed. Greg Smith, Allyson May, and Simon Devereaux (Toronto: Centre of Criminology, University of Toronto, 1998), 85-103, and "Violence, Law and Community in Rural Upper Canada," in *Crime and Criminal Justice: Essays in the History of Canadian Law,* vol. 5, ed. Jim Phillips, Tina Loo, and Susan Lewthwaite (Toronto: Osgoode Society, 1994), 353-86.
11 Peter Marshall, "British North America, 1760-1815," in *The Oxford History of the British Empire,* vol. 2, *The Eighteenth Century,* ed. P.J. Marshall (Oxford: Oxford University Press, 1998), 385.
12 Margaret Banks, "The Evolution of the Ontario Courts, 1788-1981," in *Essays in the History of Canadian Law,* vol. 2, ed. David H. Flaherty (Toronto: The Osgoode Society, 1983), 492-572.
13 Donald Fyson, with the assistance of Evelyn Kolish and Virginia Schweitzer, *The Court Structure of Quebec and Lower Canada, 1764-1830* (Montreal: Montreal History Group, 1994/97).
14 See the website for the quarter sessions records in New South Wales, http://www.records.nsw.gov.au.
15 Murray, *Colonial Justice,* 4.
16 Beattie, *Crime and the Courts in England,* 15.
17 The term "district ruler" was first used by James Aitchison in his doctoral thesis, "The Development of Local Government in Upper Canada, 1783-1850" (PhD thesis, University of Toronto, 1953), 28. Sydney and Beatrice Webb described the magistrates as "rulers of the county" in their magisterial work, *English Local Government,* vol. 1, *The Parish and the County* (North Haven, CT: Archon Books, 1963), 319-86.
18 Murray, *Colonial Justice,* 29.
19 *An Act for the Qualifications of Justices of the Peace* (UK), 1842, 6 Vict. c. 3.
20 See Murray, *Colonial Justice,* 28-42, for a discussion of the role and powers of the magistrates in the Niagara district.
21 Russell C. Smandych, "Upper Canadian Considerations about Rejecting the English Poor Law, 1817-1837: A Comparative Study of the Reception of Law" (Canadian Legal History Project, University of Manitoba, 1991), 1-59; J.C. Levy, "The Poor Laws in Early Upper Canada," in *Law and Society in Canada in Historical Perspective,* ed. D.J. Bercuson and L. Knafla (Calgary: University of Calgary Studies in History, no. 2, 1979), 23-44.
22 Murray, *Colonial Justice,* 107-9.
23 Beattie, *Crime and the Courts in England,* 320; Norma Landau, *The Justices of the Peace, 1679-1760* (Berkeley and Los Angeles: University of California Press, 1984), 50-54.
24 Murray, *Colonial Justice,* 55.
25 Ibid.
26 *An Act to Establish Trials by Jury* (UK), (1792), 32 Geo. III, c. 2.
27 Murray, *Colonial Justice,* 53.
28 Ibid., 64.

29 David Murray, "Just Excuses: Jury Culture in Barrington Township, Nova Scotia, 1795-1837," in *Planter Links: Community and Culture in Colonial Nova Scotia,* ed. Margaret Conrad and Barry Moody (Fredericton, NB: Acadiensis Press, 2001), 36-57; Jim Phillips, "Halifax Juries in the Eighteenth Century," in *Criminal Justice in the Old World and the New,* 135-82.
30 Murray, "Just Excuses," 56.
31 Phillips, "Halifax Juries in the Eighteenth Century," 138.
32 On this, see Nancy Parker, "Swift Justice and the Decline of the Criminal Trial Jury: The Dynamics of Law and Authority in Victoria, B.C., 1858-1905," in *Essays in the History of Canadian Law,* vol. 6, *British Columbia and the Yukon,* ed. Hamar Foster and John McLaren (Toronto: Osgoode Society, 1995), 171-203.
33 Neal, *The Rule of Law in a Penal Colony,* 169.
34 Quoted in Murray, *Colonial Justice,* 73.
35 Ibid., 77.
36 Jack P. Greene, "Empire and Identity from the Glorious Revolution to the American Revolution," in *The Oxford History of the British Empire,* vol. 2, *The Eighteenth Century,* 228.
37 P.J. Marshall, "Britain without America – A Second Empire?" in *The Oxford History of the British Empire,* vol. 2, *The Eighteenth Century,* 590-91.
38 Marquis, "Doing Justice to 'British' Justice," 60.
39 See for example Philip Gerard and Jim Phillips, eds., *Essays in the History of Canadian Law: Nova Scotia* (Toronto: Osgoode Society, 1990), Louis Knafla, ed., *Law and Justice in a New Land: Essays in Western Canadian Legal History* (Calgary: Carswell, 1986); W. Wesley Pue and Barry Wright, eds., *Canadian Perspectives on Law and Society: Issues in Legal History* (Ottawa: Carleton University Press, 1988); Tina Loo and Lorna McLean, eds., *Historical Perspectives on Law and Society in Canada* (Toronto: Copp Clark Longman, 1994); Foster and McLaren, eds., *Essays in the History of Canadian Law;* Smith, May, and Devereaux, eds., *Criminal Justice in the Old World and the New.*
40 Bora Laskin, *The British Tradition in Canadian Law* (Toronto: Carswell, 1969).
41 Ibid., 1.

5

New Brunswick Women Travellers and the British Connection, 1845-1905

Gail G. Campbell

Travel accounts remind us that life in the nineteenth century was far from static. This was especially true in Maritime communities, which included significant numbers of quite ordinary people who had the opportunity to broaden their horizons by travelling to distant places. Many young men went to sea for a few years before settling down to life on a coastal farm or in a coastal town. And a surprising number of young women, particularly wives and daughters of sea captains, also went on sea voyages. For those relatives and friends who remained ashore, these travellers opened a window to a wider world. Thus, Kate Loggie, for example, a young schoolteacher in rural New Brunswick, noted in an 1881 diary entry the receipt of a letter from her older sister, Maggie, who regularly accompanied her sea-captain husband on his voyages: "The letter contained some very interesting information about the Chinese." Unfortunately for us, Kate does not record the nature of the information, offering only the cryptic, yet suggestive, comment, "We have great reason to be thankful for the gospel."[1] Visiting home later that month, Kate learned more about her sister's adventures when she had a chance to read her log.[2] As a schoolteacher, Kate no doubt disseminated the "information" she received well beyond her family and home community. But what kind of information were women travellers sending home, and what version of reality did it reflect?

Throughout the great age of sail and well beyond, many Maritime women travelled the world. Like Maggie Loggie Valentine, some of those women kept a record of their journeys. Yet while there has been a good deal of interest in British women travellers, their Canadian counterparts have received little attention. To what extent did British North American women travellers share the values, perceptions, and prejudices of their British counterparts? This chapter addresses this question through the medium of a case study of thirteen white Anglo-Saxon Protestant women from a single province. Although most analyses of British women travellers have focused on accounts written for publication, this study is based on an analysis of travel accounts in diaries and letters that were never meant for publication.[3] In their private commentaries on life in other countries, New Brunswick women travellers produced a useful source for historians interested in the ways British values and attitudes were refracted through the eyes of cosmopolitan colonials. As they watched the New Brunswick coastline recede in the distance, sailing away on ships bound for the United States or England, and then as they moved beyond the familiar boundaries of the English-speaking world into continental Europe and on to more exotic destinations, what cultural baggage did such New Brunswick travellers carry with them? Did they, like British travellers, view the world through imperial eyes, identifying their interests with British interests and themselves in the context of the wider Empire? How strong was the British connection, how clear the imperial gaze?

New Brunswick, established as a separate province in 1784 as a result of the influx of the Loyalists, is, in many ways, the ideal setting for such a case study. By the mid-nineteenth century, most New Brunswickers were native-born and most immigrants were from the British Isles. Yet even as immigration strengthened the imperial connection, emigration renewed family and business connections with the United States. Thus, for New Brunswickers, the question of whether the American or the British connection has been stronger in shaping the Canadian identity is a very real one. Because Canadians have recently tended to define themselves in relation to the United States rather than to Britain, in considering that elusive concept "the Canadian identity" as a possible exemplar of Britishness, an analysis of travellers and sojourners in the United States can offer a useful point of departure.

During the nineteenth century, New Brunswickers moved back and forth across the American border in a very casual way. Parents sent their children to school in the United States, young men and women migrated there to work as sojourners or as lifetime residents, and many people had relatives across the line. On many levels, New Brunswickers of that earlier era seemed to draw no distinction between themselves and their American friends and relatives. And yet, evidence in letters and diaries indicates that they did see themselves as different. When, in 1845, Achsah Upton, feeling out of place among the more sophisticated American girls at her boarding school in Maine, longed to come home, her older sister responded with a mixture of exasperation and reassurance. Offering to send Achsah "some trifles ... some lace I could get cheap, and pretty if you would like it," Margaret Upton noted disparagingly, "as for dress I should not care, as the Americans are proverbial for show, and the English for plainness."[4] A generation later, Annie Trueman, writing to her mother from Sommerville, Massachusetts, where she was visiting her brother and cousins, commented on the negative effect of living in America on some of their female relatives: "Mrs Charles Wood & Carrie have returned from Maine. Mrs W. is quite ill – a confirmed invalid,

I was going to say, *like all the American* women. How early they fade, & become invalid." American men, on the other hand, were consumed by the profit motive. Her brother "Al wakens up every morning at 5 o'clock, gets dressed, has breakfast & is off at 6 ½ to the city. – People work so much harder here. Businessmen are so much more wide awake & active here than the provincial fraternity."[5]

Such stereotypical views were not ubiquitous. Mary Hill thoroughly enjoyed her experience in a boarding school near Boston in the 1840s, and in the 1860s, Ann Eliza Rogers Gallacher, who followed her husband to Boston, where he had found work, enjoyed the city and its suburbs, where she had both family and friends.[6] Just the same, Ann Gallacher clearly saw herself and other sojourners as outsiders during the Civil War: in her diary she drew clear distinctions between the Americans and the British and British North Americans among her friends and relatives. Her American relatives' participation in the war was almost taken for granted: on 1 November 1861, for example, she reported that "Aunt Emeline has three sons at the war." A year and a half later, when the draft was instituted, Ann, still living in Boston, noted with equanimity that "my Cousin Liberty Packard has been drafted."[7] In contrast, when her friend Sam Curren's name appeared on a list of those drafted, her response was quite different. Although Sam was, like Ann and her husband John, a long-time resident in the United States, she reported that "he has a British protection and he hopes to get clear. He belongs to Albert County, New Brunswick."[8] Similarly, she expected her husband, a transplanted Scot who had spent more time in the United States than he had in New Brunswick, to escape the draft. The Civil War was an internal matter, and even long-time sojourners remained aloof from it. Perhaps the distinctions New Brunswick women drew between themselves and their American counterparts emerged in reaction to the popular notion of American exceptionalism. One recent study of American women travellers argues that their "travel writing is as much about American exceptionalism and the romance of America as about home and abroad."[9] Or perhaps New Brunswick women chose to position themselves within the wider world of the British Empire.

Certainly the Maritime colony's links with Britain were strong and varied. Travellers to England usually had connections – relatives or friends – to visit, although, of course, a trip to England was a more unusual undertaking than a trip to the United States. By the mid- to late 1880s, those who could afford to travel to Europe as tourists travelled in style. Jessie Loggie described one such trip in 1887: "Friday morning, July 29th, finds me comfortably seated in the music room of the *Parisian*. On coming out from Rimouski last evening in the tender, this boat looked almost like a little town, all lit up as it was. It is very comfortably fitted up and possesses every convenience for travellers."[10] Arriving in Liverpool, Jessie and her sister Maggie took a cab to their apartments. Jessie wrote, "We have two nice large bedrooms, drawing room with piano and use of dining room, and are altogether very comfortable."[11] But although the Loggie sisters' log of their transatlantic crossing on the *Parisian* provides insight into the typical tourist experience, these were no ordinary tourists. Maggie Loggie Valentine was comfortable not only in her spacious apartments but in the city of Liverpool itself. Maggie's sea-captain husband, William Valentine, regularly sailed out of that port. During their short stay in Liverpool, before joining William on his ship, the *Muncaster Castle,* en route to India, the sisters visited friends and took advantage of the opportunity to do some shopping: "We ... saw through some of the swell shops, purchased a bonnet, jacket and parasol. Maggie got a white embroidered dress and made several other purchases."[12]

The experience of the Loggie sisters was far from unique. As the long-established entrepôt for overseas trade with the Americas, Africa, the Far East, Australia, and New Zealand, Liverpool served as home port to half a dozen major New Brunswick shipping firms.[13] Members of the prominent New Brunswick shipping families who owned these firms cemented their business ties with Liverpool by relocating one or more of their members in that city,[14] a practice so common that the area on the outskirts of Liverpool where many of the best-known seafaring families lived became known as "the New Brunswick settlement."[15] A good many New Brunswick sea captains and their families, including diarist Anne Parker of Tynemouth Creek, her husband, Capt. Dan Cochrane of St. Martins, and their two small children, also settled in Liverpool.[16] Thus, while in England, the Loggie sisters, like many other seafaring New Brunswick women, remained part of a colonial community, transplanted families of sea captains and shipping agents.

Canadian visitors to England who lacked such a community often felt the tug of divided loyalties, manifested as a tension between imperialist pride in the British heritage and the desire to be recognized as more than "an ignorant country cousin from the colonies."[17] Mrs. R. Wilmot's response to the Great International Exhibition, which she attended in London in 1862, exemplifies this tension. Although she was impressed with both the industrial and fine arts exhibits, she remained a true colonial, reporting: "We visited the Nova Scotian department & as is natural I thought everything in it beautiful. More especially was my attention directed towards some wax fruit & flowers which were done by an Aunt of mine & they certainly were most beautiful so very natural – we also saw some Pianos made of native wood, also some beautiful jewelry, preserved fruits, & maple sugar."[18] Returning to the exhibition two days later to visit the Foreign Apartment of Paintings, she "saw a great many very beautiful pictures & liked them much better than the English paintings for they seemed to have a much softer appearance."[19]

Other diarists reflected this same ambivalence and were often similarly critical of things British. Violet Goldsmith, visiting relatives in England with her Aunt Maggie in 1901, reported that "on Sunday I went to Church morning and evening, and to Sunday School in the afternoon. I do not like the service as well as our own. They have chants, like they have in the Church of England."[20] But if the English Methodist Church was too formal, Violet proved even less pleased with the Congregationalists' approach to ceremony, recording on 1 June that "on Thursday the crowning of the May Queen took place. That part of it was very good, but they had wire-walkers & a trick-cyclist afterwards. I thought their performances very vulgar. It was got up by the Congregational Church." Such judgments may have been a reflection of her loyalty to her father, a Methodist minister. Yet her critique extended beyond church practice and included her own relatives. Following a visit to her Cousin Annie's classroom, she noted: "I do not think that she is as good a teacher as most of the N[ew]. B[runswick]. teachers are. She teaches the Infant School."[21] But as an aspiring teacher herself, Violet remained interested in visiting schools and took note of their different methods. On 18 July she recorded that she had met Miss Davies, "a teacher in Hanover St. School, and I intend to go to her school tomorrow." The following day, she wrote, "[I] spent most of the morning in Miss Davies' room. I met two teachers from Belfast who were visiting the school, and we went through it together. Miss Davies gets the children to stand back to back to work their sums."[22] In visiting British schools, Violet was, after all, seeking a model for her own practice.

Like their American counterparts, the New Brunswick women travellers commented on being accosted by beggars on the streets of European cities.[23] Yet New Brunswick diarists and letter writers did not complain, as the American women regularly did, about the accommodations, thieves, or filth.[24] And, in Britain at least, their critique often took on a sympathetic tone. Laura Trueman Wood was appalled by the poverty in British cities. While visiting Glasgow with her politician husband in 1883, she "picked up a number of the *Contemporary Review* here in the Library, which I found intensely interesting." As she reported to her sister, back in Sackville, New Brunswick, "most of all I was taken with an article called 'Social Wreckage,' which deals with the alarming increase of pauperism." She went on to comment, "I have been so struck with the poverty & degradation here, that I suppose it struck a chord responsive in my heart."[25]

In the end, pride in the British heritage and identity with things British prevailed. As members of the British Empire, the diarists took a proprietorial pride in Britain and British history.[26] Visiting France in 1863, Mrs. Wilmot no longer made comparisons with the colonies but, rather, with England, and the English became "we." Thus, she reported, upon arrival in Rouen, that "it is the chief seat of the cotton manufacture in France and may be called the French Manchester."[27] Of the Abbey of St. Denis, she reported, "The edifice itself is most grand and when it is restored as they are now doing will be exquisitely magnificent ... We have nothing like this in England though Westminster Abbey has far more splendid monuments. The streets put me in mind of some old picture and look very, very unEnglish."[28] Casting the French as "other," following visits to several churches, she noted: "We were much interested in looking at the people entering, how they crossed themselves and bowing to the Virgin Mary, &c. In the midst of their praying how they rose to light a taper &c. They all seemed very devout."[29] Mrs. Wilmot approved of the sidewalk cafés, which, though apparently unknown in England or New Brunswick, were common enough in Paris in 1863.[30] Yet, noting that "one great feature of the streets of Paris is the great number of seats you see all around," she could not resist commenting that "it is a pity that they have not the fountains with cups attached to them as we have in England, where every one could drink of the water when thirsty. It would be a vast improvement."[31]

For diarists who visited other European countries, English guidebooks were *de rigueur* and when they were without them the lack was sorely felt.[32] Although travelling with a Norwegian companion, Margaret Loggie Valentine, heading into the interior of Norway, noted in a journal-letter to her mother that as "the train whistled & off we went ... we settled down to reconsider our route as I must admit I had not the remotest idea of not being able to procure an English guide book. Miss Shultz had to be interpreter then, as all through our jaunt."[33] Although Mrs. Wilmot does not mention a guidebook, her descriptions of the famous historic sites in Paris offer compelling evidence that she had one in hand.[34] The guidebooks most often used by Canadians were Baedeker and Murray, favoured by the British but popular with American tourists as well. The young Amelia Holder's description of the Lipari Islands and the volcanic island of Stromboli also seems to have been copied from a guidebook or, more probable in the case of this sea-captain's daughter, a geography.[35] Amelia usually provided her own youthful descriptions, however. Especially on her first voyage, she was awed by the scenery, noting, as they neared the Straits of Messina, that "the land is very high and one mountain with its top covered with snow is away up in the clouds. I was frightened almost when I first saw it." Making the awesome familiar, she added, "The snow on the top reminds me of home. I have been looking at it with my glasses very much."[36] A year later, in Tarragona, Spain, waiting for a charter, Edwin Holder and his children became tourists for an afternoon, taking a ride out to see the Devil's Bridge, which, according to their coachman, was more than a thousand years old. Because there was no longer any river for it to span, they were able to go "down underneath it. It looked dreadfully high and it has a great many arches." Following a practice associated with the rise of tourism, and with the search for the picturesque, Amelia reported, "We got a piece off of it."[37]

The search for the picturesque had begun to emerge as an aesthetic movement around the middle of the eighteenth century. In her analysis of women travellers in colonial India, Indira Ghose points to the acquisitive connotations of the search for the picturesque: "William Marshall in his 1795 history of landscape painting sees 'something of the big-game hunter' in these tourists, boasting of their encounters with savage landscapes, 'capturing' wild scenes, and 'fixing' them as pictorial trophies in order to sell them or hang them up in frames on their drawing room walls."[38] The association of "an eye for the picturesque" with the imperial gaze may seem incongruous when applied to travellers who found the picturesque in places as disparate as the Straits of Messina, the landscape of India, and the western interior of North America. Yet in each case, the trace of Marshall's "big-game hunter" – or of what Mary Louise Pratt has referred to as the "monarch of all I survey" – trope remains, suggesting the underlying "dynamics of power and appropriation" that characterize the imperial gaze.[39] The interior of Norway, where Maggie Loggie Valentine sought the picturesque, seemed as potentially threatening and thrilling to her as did the western interior of North America to European travellers. The trip was challenging, up such a path as Maggie "had never trod before," but the destination fully met her expectations. As she described it to her mother, "Kavenuset ... is an immense ravine 180 feet deep, we cautiously went close up there, laid down on the overhanging rocks & looked down into the narrow rushing waters below. I can not explain the grandeur of this sight. It was *awfully* grand. The high mountains on each side, & far down the narrow seething waters below." Something of "the monarch of all I survey" outlook is evident not only in this description but also in her pride and amusement at the reaction of a "young [Norwegian] gent with bycicle ... He burst forth with so many exclamations, went into ecstasy over it saying I *never!* No, I never! I have travelled all over. I have been here, I have been there, & I have never seen anything to compare with this. He admired us for our perseverance in coming up at that hour of the evening after our long day's travelling. He sometimes wrote for a paper & would mention meeting two so courageous ladies." Amused as she was by "the young gent," Maggie and her companion rather agreed with his characterization, for at the end of the trip, "the conclusion we came to between ourselves was that we were two very courageous & clever women to have undertaken & planned this route ourselves without the help of any of the sterner sex to assist – or rather to make a fuss & jumble matters."[40]

The diarists who visited exotic places were not tourists in the same sense that Mrs. Wilmot was a tourist. Rather, they were seagoing women, travelling with sea-captain husbands, fathers, brothers-in-law, and brothers. When sea captains and their families went ashore, they fraternized mainly with other sea captains and their families.[41] Yet while they were in port loading and unloading cargoes, they often took in the sights. It was largely through the seagoing women that families and communities back home gained their understanding of the broader world. Whenever Maggie Loggie Valentine accompanied her sea-captain husband, William, on voyages, she continued to keep a log, sending it home in instalments, along with her letters, to be passed around among her parents and siblings. In 1887, her sister, Jessie, accompanying Maggie and William on a voyage to India, kept a diary of the entire trip and a kind of journal-letter for their family at home, in which she reported her observations of this exotic world: "26th December 1887. Just wish you could see the natives in the tugboat. I think they are real nice looking. Not at all like I imagined they would be ... Three boats came down to us this evening full of natives ... They are small boned and featured and quite nice looking and the poor wretches have nothing on but a diaper, while some have a piece of cotton they draw over their shoulders ... It was amusement enough for me to watch them for awhile."[42]

In recording her observations for her family back home, Jessie adopts the voice of disinterested observer. It is clear from her report that Jessie Loggie had "imagined" what natives of India would be like. She found the reality quite different. Yet, as Ghose points out, "the texts produced by travellers do not simply reflect a pre-given reality, but create the world they purport to describe." The information that Jessie was passing along to her family was "a product of social and 'sensuous interaction.'"[43] Through her journal-letter she was revising her family's view of India to conform with her own perceived new reality, gained through personal observation. At the same time, she was articulating a view of India that, according to Saree Makdisi, had emerged in England in the late eighteenth century. According to this view, the Orient was "a space defined by its 'backwardness,' its retardation; no longer a region or a field offering materials for extraction, exploitation, and exchange, it became a field to be rewritten and transformed; it became 'undeveloped,' a region whose 'development' suddenly became the European's burden."[44] With her refracted imperial gaze, Jessie reflected the colonialist discourse, identifying herself with the British imperial power by identifying the people of this exotic land as the colonized other. Her process of othering was fairly typical. She tended to homogenize the natives "into a collective they." She further portrayed them as inadequately clothed, generally childlike, and in all ways inferior to herself:[45]

> The native houses or huts are built of mud divided into two apartments, one of which is occupied by the Buffalow which is their cow. I picked a bunch of flowers but they were not much to look at. We were followed by a body guard of natives and which made some of us feel ten inches taller. We

got back in time for tea and which we were all ready for ... There are lots of natives on board now. You can't form any idea of how they look, some are all rolled in rags always displaying a back view of bare legs ... I followed them round this morning trying to get a sketch of them, but just as soon as I would get the back of a head done he would turn his face round, and as it was particularly a back view I wanted t'was no go. Eventually I captured one old man on a spar and seating myself immediately in front proceeded to reproduce him on paper much to the interest of the others who gathered round.[46]

Thus did Jessie "capture" the exotic locals, who were unable to escape her imperial gaze.[47]

In Calcutta, however, Jessie found a different India. Here, too, she found herself revising her previously imagined vision of the country and its people. Upon arrival in Calcutta on 29 December, "Will, Maggie and I went ashore ... and had a drive away up the miadan up to the Eden Gardens, and past the Government House. I did not imagine Calcutta was half as grand a place as it is."[48] A few days later, she noted: "I never get used to the native dresses. You see so many different kinds. Saw a native Prince Sat. evening who was dressed in a green changeable silk robe. They are quite good look-ing and as straight as arrows. Calcutta is a very showy place."[49] William Valentine's ship remained in Calcutta for more than two months, and, usu-ally in the company of other ship-captains' families turned tourist, Jessie and Maggie visited the sights. Jessie described the grandeur of the Raj for her family in almost guidebook terms:

Capt. Pattman, Maggie, Edin Baker and I drove out to the Seven Tanks to-day – a most magnificent place. It is a Rajah's residence, but he does not reside there, therefore it is open to public inspection ... The rooms are all immense. Very large and lofty. There are several pieces of statuary with little or no clothing on. The paintings are something fine and the Rajah's picture is also among the number and her Majesty in royal robes. There are mag-nificent tables, some inlaid with every kind of marble, all colours. Mirrors reaching almost to the ceiling in every room and that is saying a good deal for I never saw such lofty ones ... In one room there was a row of huge bolsters round, with little pillows in between for reclining on. Quite our ideas of old Eastern life.[50]

In contrast to her descriptions of the previously unimaginable natives she had observed with amazement and amusement upon her arrival in India the bustling and surprisingly "grand" city of Calcutta, in her portrayal of the rajah's residence, Jessie could at last provide some support for her own

– and, presumably, her family's – previously imagined version of life in India. But it was a life without Indians, for the rajah no longer resided there.

Other women created quite a different world for their friends and relatives to view, for, as Ghose has argued, "there was not *the* woman traveller in India, but a variety of different women – there is no overarching story to be told ... different discourses are always co-present at the same point in time and intersect ... colonialism was at all times an ambivalent and not a monolithic project."[51] Anne Parker Cochrane, in Bombay with her sea-captain husband and small daughter, Annie, in 1878, was able to introduce her family to individual natives:

We were invited to Jehanisfee's day before yesterday, which was their New Year's Day, to see the grand ceremony of opening the new books. Six sheets of paper wouldent half hold it all, so I can't begin to tell you about it. I will only say Jehanisfee was flying around in a new pair of yellow satin trousers and scarlet slippers and all his children were there with 30 others, all relatives. He gave everyone a rupee for luck and a daub of red stuff like red paint on their forehead. Annie wouldn't keep it on. I don't think the old fellow noticed it though. We had champagne icecreams and enjoyed it all vastly. I haven't seen such a grand performance before and never expect to again.[52]

Yet, sympathetic as this construction of reality may appear, it, too, reflected a "colonial construction of India."[53] Anne Cochrane offered her family the exotic flavour of the ceremony she had attended, without a meaningful explanation of it. Like Jessie Loggie, she saw India through imperial eyes.

When in port, seagoing women, often confined to socializing with other captains and their families either on board ship or in the office and warehouse district close to the shore, were sometimes bored even when they found themselves in quite exotic locations.[54] Fifteen-year-old Clara Winifred Fritz, writing to her mother from Tourane (now Da Nang, Vietnam) in 1904, reported that "there is nothing much to see, except the life of the natives." Like many of her contemporaries, she evinced more interest in the search for the picturesque than in the people, noting, "There are marble mts. a short way from the town, which I should like to go to see."[55] She was even less impressed with Haiphong, in French Indochina: "Haiphong is not much of a place ... We have been on board all day. There is no place to go ... I really have not a thing to tell you, for we do about the same thing every day, just go ashore and around to the offices at which papa has business."[56] Clara's imperial gaze was a dismissive one. In contrast, Amelia Holder, though similarly bored when confined to the ship, never complained of boredom when allowed to go ashore.

In some ways, the young Amelia Holder, who was just eleven years old when she first accompanied her father on a sea voyage, was the most generous observer, reserving judgment even as she drew clear distinctions between "them" and "us." Thus she observed the women in Spain "making sails like men."[57] A few years later, on a trip to Buenos Aires, her family took advantage of the opportunity to attend a carnival, despite the threat of yellow fever, which was said to be "in the low and poor parts but they fear it will spread all over the town." In the midst of crowds, "push[ing] along all of the time," Amelia watched as a "masker threw a kiss to a lady on a balcony." Reporting the incident in her diary, she commented, "I suppose young ladies in our country would be offended but the ladies do not get offended here because it is the custom of the place."[58] The Holders left two days later, escaping the yellow fever that soon spread not only "all over the town" but into the harbour and onto the ships there as well.[59] Yet, like her older counterparts, Amelia Holder, too, reflected an innate racism. In Bridgetown, Barbados, in April 1871, she commented that "it amuses us very much to hear the negroes talk" and, in recording her father's conversation with two men he had taken on board to help them get the anchor up, provided further evidence that he regarded these men as childlike, if not lesser, beings.[60] Amelia no doubt learned by example, and that example included the imperial gaze.

Josephine Turner's imperial gaze may have reflected a more mature social conscience rather than a less generous outlook. Having spent several days observing the loading of vessels in the port of Santander, Spain, in 1881, this young sea-captain's wife wrote to her sister: "The work is mostly done by the women, they even load the vessels with iron ore which they carry in baskets on their heads about a hundred weight at a time and it is surprising to see how quick they will go up the stage with it. They work all day this way for about one Peseta (equal to about 20 cents) while their husbands are loafing around the streets ready to receive their money when it is so hardly earned. It is too bad isn't it, but there are strange people in the world."[61] In that same year, she had described similar activities in Antwerp, Belgium: "It is amusing to watch the Belgians in their red or blue jackets, working away jabbering in Flemish all the time. The women come on board and work as well as the men, indeed they are the bosses here. The men let them look after the business affairs and they – the men – do the light work in the house, such as washing potatoes, dishes, etc. The women here are a hardy looking crowd, and their looks do not deceive them, they nearly all go bareheaded on the streets, except on Sunday. They are the queerest lot I ever saw."[62] Josephine Turner reveals herself clearly as a *British* North American: by characterizing the Spanish as "strange people" and the Belgians as a "queer lot," she was not only defining them as other but was implicitly defining herself as a member of a "superior" culture.

While New Brunswick women travellers mirrored British outlooks and attitudes in many ways, those outlooks and attitudes were refracted through a colonial lens. Nowhere was this clearer than in their attitudes toward religion and religious practice. They missed their colonial homes most on Sundays, and especially the young among them regularly commented on what they saw as a failure to "keep the Sabbath." In Barcelona, on Sunday, 29 December 1867, Amelia Holder concluded that "they do not have much Sunday here I guess," for they were able to buy oranges and apples and vessels were loading and unloading. It did not, apparently, occur to twelve-year-old Amelia that the chiming bell, "just like the one in Havana," might be calling people to mass.[63] Similarly, fifteen-year-old Clara Fritz, writing from Haiphong in 1904, reported to her mother that "they do not seem to recognise Sunday at all. There is a church but, of course the service is in French, so we should not be able to understand it."[64] Mrs. Wilmot, who among all the New Brunswick diarists identified most clearly with England, would have sympathized. In Paris in 1863 she had attended a service in an English chapel "which was conducted in French, so was in a very great measure quite unintelligible to me. The singing sounded very peculiar the tunes were so very unlike any we have in England." And, like other diarists in Catholic countries, she noted that "all the shops being opened and altogether the working aspect of the people made it have an appearance very unlike Sunday, however when we did reach the little chapel we found that the congregation seemed quite serious and devout." Attending a Catholic mass that afternoon, she described it as quite foreign. Apparently, she had no idea that similar services were held in her own province.[65]

Firm in her own British Protestant values, Mrs. Wilmot further concluded that the French, particularly those of "the poorer class," did not exhibit a proper reverence for the dead. While visiting France, she had seen "a number of funerals" and had been struck by "the quantity of people who followed the body apparently seeming to have nothing to do with it. The conduct of the people seemed so cold not as if they were following a body to its last resting place. They seemed so engaged talking to each other, were not dressed in mourning and all together gave me a sad impression of how very little they were thinking of what they were doing." Nor did she approve of the famous Père-Lachaise cemetery. Although it was "a very pretty place and from the hill we got a very fine view of Paris," she found it "very unlike any English Cemetery," giving "a very gay appearance in my idea, for nearly all the tombs are covered with what they call memorials which are crowns of different sizes made of different coloured paper and beads ... I think the cemetery looks very much gayer than such a place should be."[66] In her Paris diary, Mrs. Wilmot thus definitively identified herself with the English. Yet her London diary entries had just as clearly reflected the tension inherent in colonial status. Angela Woollacott argues that Australians felt a similar tension. As she puts it, "Like other white colonial women, women from the Australian colonies, or post-1901 the Australian Commonwealth, were insiders in the empire because of their whiteness, but simultaneously outsiders in England due to their colonial origins and often subordinated because of their sex."[67]

Nonetheless, both inside and outside England, the British connection for New Brunswick world travellers remained strong. Like their Australian counterparts, they saw themselves as insiders in the British Empire and participants in the British imperial project. Theirs was the romance of empire rather than the romance of America. Particularly in their portrayal of the "other," they reflected a clear imperial bias. Writing home, these seagoing women, more than their husbands, fathers, and brothers (who wrote fewer and shorter letters), shaped their families' and communities' perceptions of the wider world.[68] For New Brunswick women, seeing for oneself led to a revision of their understanding of the world. At the same time, that revisioning was grounded in a British-Canadian world view conditioned as much by their own experience of time and place as by the British connection. Gerald Friesen has reminded us that nationality is "acquired by social interaction and education." In stressing the importance of communication – ordinary people talking and writing to one another – in the transmission of the ideas and values that make up our shared understanding of nation, he points to "the remarkable capacity of cultures to absorb change" while at the same time preserving continuity.[69] The experience of the Loggie family exemplifies this process. Through their letters and logs, Maggie and Jessie took their family with them on their travels. Sailing the oceans of the world, they revised and expanded the horizons of the parents and siblings they left behind. But the view they provided was one informed and constructed by the imperial gaze. This perspective is implicit even in the lighthearted title Maggie gave her 1885 journal-letter to her mother: "A few remarks on a ten days trip into the interior of Norway – Dedicated to her Highness Lady Alex Loggie of the City of B[urnt]. Church."[70] Through that letter, Maggie expanded the homefolks' ideas about Norway to include the picturesque grandeur of the interior. Three years later, the Loggie family's ideas about India were revised and that country re-envisioned as a result of Jessie's ocean voyage. At home in Burnt Church, New Brunswick, schoolteacher Kate no doubt drew on the "interesting information" she gained from her sisters in transmitting "knowledge" to her young charges. But whether at home or abroad, the Loggie sisters' perspective was conditioned by their own North American experience. Together with other New Brunswick women travellers and their families, they adapted and changed, even as they provided the continuity that would ensure that Canada maintained a British connection, a shared British World view, filtered through Canadian eyes.

Notes

1 University of New Brunswick Archives (UNBA), MG H 128, Kate Loggie Diary, 16 March 1881. Original spelling has been preserved throughout.
2 Ibid., 30 March 1881.
3 For analyses of published British women travellers, see for example Dea Birkett, *Spinsters Abroad: Victorian Lady Explorers* (Oxford: Basil Blackwell, 1989); Alison Blunt, *Travel, Gender, and Imperialism: Mary Kingsley and West Africa* (New York: Guilford Press, 1994); Shirley Foster, *Across New Worlds: Nineteenth-Century Women Travellers and Their Writings* (Hemel Hempstead, UK: Harvester Wheatsheaf, 1990); Billie Melman, *Women's Orients: English Women and the Middle East, 1718-1918* (Ann Arbor: University of Michigan Press, 1992). Sara Mills emphasizes the significance of the distinction between women's public and private writing: in the latter, women were freer to express their opinions on even taboo subjects. Quoted in Cheryl McEwan, *Gender, Geography and Empire: Victorian Women Travellers in West Africa* (Aldershot, UK: Ashgate, 2000), 44.
4 Provincial Archives of New Brunswick (PANB), MC1001 MS6, Hill Family Papers, Margaret Upton to Achsah Upton, 14 June 1845.
5 PANB, MC218, MS8/68, Wood Family Papers, Annie Trueman to Rebecca Trueman, 8 August 1862.
6 PANB, MC1001, MS6/4, Hill Family Papers, correspondence, MS6/1, Mary to friends at home, n.d. [1846], 2 December 1846; MS6/4, Mary to parents and sisters, 26 March [1846], 28 July 1846, 28 May 1847, 20 July 1847, 4 August 1847, 15 December 1847; MS6/6, Mary to Achsah Upton and George S. Hill (father), 11 August 1847; MS6/12, Mary to Upton Hill (brother), December [1845]. PANB, MC260, Ann Eliza Rogers Diary, July 1860-June 1862; May-August 1863.
7 PANB, MC260, Ann Eliza Rogers Diary, 14 July 1863.
8 Ibid., 10 July 1863.
9 Mary Suzanne Schriber, *Writing Home: American Women Abroad, 1830-1920* (Charlottesville: University Press of Virginia, 1997), 9.
10 UNBA, MG H 128, Jessie Loggie Diary, 29 July 1887.
11 Ibid., 6 August 1887.
12 Ibid., 9 August 1887.
13 Alan Gregg Finley, "Shipbuilding in St. Martins, 1840-1880: A Case Study of Family Enterprise on the Fundy Shore" (MA thesis, University of New Brunswick, 1979), 15; Esther Clark Wright, *Saint John Ships and Their Builders* (Wolfville, NS: E.C. Wright, 1976), 17. As T.W. Acheson has pointed out, the great merchants of Saint John, who were involved not only in the shipping industry but also in buying, selling, and contracting for the construction of vessels, had been forging links between the harbours of Saint John and Liverpool since the early years of the nineteenth century. T.W. Acheson, "The Great Merchant and Economic Development in St. John, 1820-1850," *Acadiensis* 8, 2 (Spring 1979), 10.
14 Finley, "Shipbuilding in St. Martins," 21.
15 Donal Baird, *Women at Sea in the Age of Sail* (Halifax: Nimbus, 2001), 43.
16 Baird, *Women at Sea*, 54-55.
17 Eva-Marie Kröller, *Canadian Travellers in Europe, 1851-1900* (Vancouver: UBC Press, 1987), 12-14.
18 PANB, MC300, MS23/3, Mrs. R. Wilmot Travel Diary, 8 July 1862.
19 Ibid., 10 July 1862.
20 UNBA, MG H 133, Violet Goldsmith Diary, 22 May 1901.
21 Ibid., 17 June 1901.
22 Ibid., 18-19 July 1901.
23 See for example PANB, MC665, F569, Amelia Holder Diary, and PANB, MC218, MS5, Wood Family Papers, Laura Trueman Wood Correspondence.
24 Schriber, *Writing Home*, 18.
25 PANB, MC218, MS5/74, Wood Family Papers, Laura Trueman Wood to Annie Trueman, July 1883.
26 For similar examples of Canadian pride in Britain and the imperial connection, see Kröller, *Canadian Travellers in Europe*, 14-15.

27   PANB, MC300, MS23/3, Mrs. R. Wilmot Travel Diary, 22 June 1863.

28   Ibid., 24 June 1863.

29   Ibid., 26 June 1863.

30   Ibid.

31   Ibid., 28 June 1863.

32   The dependence on, and almost tyranny of, guidebooks during this period is effectively dealt with in Kröller, *Canadian Travellers in Europe*, chap. 3; and Schriber, *Writing Home*, 17.

33   UNBA, MG H 128, Margaret (Loggie) Valentine to Mrs. Alexander Loggie, 1885.

34   See especially her descriptions of the Tuileries, the Pantheon, and the Place de la Concorde. PANB, MC300, MS23/3, Mrs. R. Wilmot Travel Diary, 28 June, 8 and 16 July 1863.

35   PANB, MC665, F569, Amelia Holder Diary, 19 January 1868.

36   Ibid., 20 January 1868. Cheryl McEwan, *Gender, Geography and Empire*, 78-79, also notes this tendency among British women travellers of the period to want to make the unfamiliar familiar, to provide a frame of reference for the exotic or wild.

37   PANB, MC225, F569, Amelia Holder Diary, 4 February 1869.

38   Indira Ghose, *Women Travellers in Colonial India: The Power of the Female Gaze* (New Delhi: Oxford University Press, 1998), 42.

39   Mary Louise Pratt, *Imperial Eyes: Travel Writing and Transculturation* (London and New York: Routledge, 1992), 10, 201-8. Ghose, *Women Travellers in Colonial India*, asserts that "like so many other superior attributes, an eye for the picturesque remains firmly the prerogative of the colonial rulers" (49).

40   UNBA, MG H 128, Margaret (Loggie) Valentine to Mrs. Alexander Loggie, 1885.

41   See for example New Brunswick Museum Archives (NBMA), F46 S208-1, Turner Family Papers, Josephine (Reid) Turner Diary, February-March 1884.

42   UNBA, MG H 128, Jessie Loggie Diary, 26 December 1887.

43   Ghose, *Women Travellers in Colonial India*, 7.

44   Saree Makdisi, *Romantic Imperialism: Universal Empire and the Culture of Modernity* (Cambridge: Cambridge University Press, 1998), 113.

45   These and other features of othering that make up the discourse of imperialism are effectively developed in Sara Mills, *Discourses of Difference: An Analysis of Women's Travel Writing and Colonialism* (London: Routledge, 1991), 87-94.

46   UNBA, MG H 128, Jessie Loggie Diary, 28 December 1887.

47   Cheryl McEwan, *Gender, Geography and Empire*, 157, notes that this type of detailed physical description was "a form of appropriation typical in many imperialist discourses."

48   UNBA, MG H 128, Jessie Loggie Diary, 30 December 1887.

49   Ibid., 2 January 1888.

50   Ibid., 16 February 1888.

51   Ghose, *Women Travellers in Colonial India*, 10.

52   Quoted in Baird, *Women at Sea*, 51.

53   Ghose, *Women Travellers in Colonial India*, 139. Like British women travellers in India and Africa, Jessie Loggie and Anne Cochrane were "empowered by the fact that within the empire status was determined by skin colour rather than gender"; McEwan, *Gender, Geography and Empire*, 32.

54   A similar kind of boredom is discussed with reference to British women in India in Margaret MacMillan, *Women of the Raj* (New York: Thames and Hudson, 1988).

55   Clara Winifred Fritz to Mama, 3 February 1904, quoted in Elizabeth W. McGahan, *Whispers from the Past: Selections from the Writings of New Brunswick Women* (Fredericton, NB: Goose Lane, 1986), 69.

56   Clara Winifred Fritz to Mama, 21 February 1904, quoted in *Whispers from the Past*, 73.

57   PANB, MC665, F569, Amelia Holder Diary, 10 January 1868.

58   Ibid., 24 February 1871. When she visited Buenos Aires more than a decade later, Josephine Turner also joined in the carnival celebrations, getting "pretty well sprinkled too, it being the custom ... during ... Carnival to throw water on anyone who goes on the street ... There is no distinction of persons, all are served alike." NBMA, F46 S208-1, Turner Family Papers, Josephine (Reid) Turner Diary, 27 February 1884. The more famous traveller, Flora Tristan,

had her interest "aroused ... by local spectacles like Holy Week processions, a mystery play, carnival celebration, and ... a civil war." Pratt, *Imperial Eyes,* 160.

59 Jenny Clayton, "'A Long Voyage Before Us': New Brunswick's Holder Family and the Nineteenth-Century Seafaring Experience" (MA thesis, University of New Brunswick, 2001).

60 PANB, MC665, F569, Amelia Holder Diary, 18 April 1871.

61 NBMA, F46 S208-1, Turner Family Papers, Josephine (Reid) Turner to Charlotte Reid, 11 December 1881.

62 Ibid., Josephine (Reid) Turner to Charlotte Reid, 15 March 1881.

63 PANB, MC665, F569, Amelia Holder Diary, 29 December 1867.

64 Clara Winifred Fritz to Mama, 14 February 1904, quoted in McGahan, *Whispers from the Past,* 72. See also NBMA, F46 S208-1, Turner Family Papers, Josephine (Reid) Turner to Charlotte Reid, 15 March 1881.

65 PANB, MC300, MS23/3, Mrs. R. Wilmot Travel Diary, 28 June 1863. Of the Catholic mass, she reported: "They said a great deal but it being in Latin was of course quite unintelligible to us. After a short time the priests kept going to & fro changing their gowns and at last they began throwing the incense about which was in my opinion anything but nice."

66 Ibid., 8 July 1863.

67 Angela Woollacott, "'All This Is the Empire, I Told Myself': Australian Women's Voyages 'Home' and the Articulation of Colonial Whiteness," *American Historical Review* 102, 4 (October 1997): 1007.

68 The Victorian British traveller and writer Elizabeth Eastlake suggested that women made better tourists than men "by way of their superior, detailed gaze." Janice Schroeder, "Strangers in Every Port: Stereotypes of Victorian Women Travellers," *Victorian Review* 24, 2 (Winter 1998): 120-21.

69 Gerald Friesen, *Citizens and Nation: An Essay on History, Communication, and Canada* (Toronto: University of Toronto Press, 2000), 225 and 229.

70 UNBA, MG H 128, Margaret (Loggie) Valentine to Mrs. Alexander Loggie, 1885.

6

"Our Glorious Anglo-Saxon Race Shall Ever Fill Earth's Highest Place": *The Anglo-Saxon* and the Construction of Identity in Late-Nineteenth-Century Canada

Paula Hastings

Articulations of British identity in the late-nineteenth-century British World varied widely and were often ambiguous, fluid, and contradictory. The Canadian context was no exception. English Canadians continuously negotiated their position within the British Empire and their constructions of British identity were often inspired by domestic circumstances. *The Anglo-Saxon*, a monthly periodical published in Ottawa from 1887 to 1900, provides an illuminating example of the complexities of this negotiation.[1] In the pages of the *Anglo-Saxon*, constructions of British identity were inextricably connected to the reaction against French Canadian culture, especially Roman Catholicism and the French language. The journal was, however, hopelessly inconsistent in defining this identity. According to its subtitle, the journal was "devoted to the interests of Englishmen and their descendants," but the identity promoted was often more British than exclusively English, and the term "Anglo-Saxon" was never clearly defined in its pages. While the English "race" was most often exalted in cultural and historical terms, it was the British race that promised to further the political objectives advocated in the journal, primarily by addressing the growing tension between French and English Canadians.

By the 1880s, many Protestant Canadians of British descent firmly believed that the survival of Canada would require a singularity of race, religion, and language among its peoples, and they sought to strengthen Canada's British identity through a variety of race-orientated organizations and journals, like the *Anglo-Saxon*. The purpose of the journal was to preserve, strengthen, and promote the Anglo-Saxon identity in Canada by emphasizing the importance of Canada's ideological and political connection with Britain and by advocating the international confederation of the Anglo-Saxon race.[2] The journal had a heavily political, racial, and anti-Roman Catholic focus and it consistently sought affiliations with organizations that shared the same goals and interests, although it failed to cement a permanent relationship with any one particular organization.

Owned and operated by Edwin J. Reynolds, an Ottawa-based printer and publisher, the *Anglo-Saxon* was distributed in Canada, the United States, and to various parts of Britain and its empire, including Australia, New Zealand, India, and South Africa.[3] The founding editor was Richard John Wicksteed, an assistant law clerk and English translator in the House of Commons.[4] In March 1888 the *Anglo-Saxon* announced that Wicksteed would no longer edit the *Anglo-Saxon* because of pressing work obligations, although Wicksteed did continue to contribute to the journal throughout the next decade. Atkins Spencer Jones wrote the announcement about Wicksteed's departure and periodically assumed editorial responsibilities during the 1890s, but it is not clear whether he was Wicksteed's official replacement. The articles that appeared in the *Anglo-Saxon* were signed by a wide variety of authors, including Wicksteed and Jones, but in some cases the articles were unsigned. The format of the journal was similar to that of a newspaper and was typically eight to ten pages in length. Most issues included editorials on the political climate in Canada and Britain, "colonial news items," serial fiction, popular poetry, and advertisements. The journal was circulated to various clubs, emigration societies, and more than four hundred reading rooms throughout Great Britain. It was distributed to mechanics' institutes and farmers' associations in England, Scotland, and Ireland and was available in the Royal Colonial Institute's reading room, the Imperial Institute's reading room, and in several public libraries in England. It was also on a number of newspaper exchanges throughout the British Empire and was cited in a number of newspapers in Britain, including *Imperial Federation,* the *Pall Mall Gazette,* and the *Manchester Examiner.*[5]

This chapter approaches the question of identity from the ethnic studies framework that emphasizes how groups construct ethnic identities as a means to achieve their political and ideological objectives. It conceptualizes ethnicity "as a reaction to social context, a dimension of social participation." In this interpretive frame, "ethnicity is instrumental; individuals consciously adopt a group identity to promote their collective self-interest." This chapter also takes from Benedict Anderson the idea that nations are "imagined political communities," artificial constructs whose characteristics are both historically and culturally specific. Constructions of British identity in the *Anglo-Saxon* and their relation to ideas about the Canadian nation were intimately bound to the English Canadian reaction to French Canadian culture at the end of the nineteenth century.[6]

When the *Anglo-Saxon* commenced publication in September 1887, Richard Wicksteed asserted that the purpose of the journal was to "speak for the Anglo-Saxon race, – the nation formed by the union of the Angles, Saxons and other early Teutonic settlers in Britain, from whom the English, the Lowland Scotch, a great proportion of the present inhabitants of Ulster, and the mass of the population in the United States and the various British

Colonies have sprung."[7] Wicksteed's observation that descendants of the
Anglo-Saxon race could be found in various parts of the British Empire provides an explanation, albeit somewhat unsatisfactory, for the often synony-
mous use of the terms "Anglo-Saxon" and "British." The journal wrote
favourably about the Protestant Irish, the Welsh, and the Scots, but its main
interest was in promoting the interests of Englishmen and their descendants. Although all the British peoples were respected for their place within
the Empire, the English were perceived as the core, superior race of the
Empire, the superlative personification of "Anglo-Saxoness."[8] One contribu-
tor to the journal, Thomas C. Andrews, voiced his dissatisfaction with the
term "Anglo-Saxon" in July 1899. Insisting on the term "Briton" rather than
"Anglo-Saxon," he argued:

> Why Anglo-Saxon? ... there is another name known even ages before a Saxon
> had put foot on the British Isles. That name is Briton ... It is usually ac-
> cepted that the ancient Briton proper, was a Celt, that we yet find his de-
> scendants in the mountains of Wales, the Highlands of Scotland, and almost
> universally in Ireland ...
>
> The English language is itself more assimulative [sic] to Danish and Low
> Dutch, than to Teutonic German. Why, then, shall we call ourselves and
> submit to be called Anglo-Saxons, otherwise English-Germans.
>
> Britons should surely be the name, it is the oldest of all, it does justice to
> all alike. Anglo-Saxon is an insult to the Celt. Let us of the British race
> whether originating in the old world or the new, ever remember that many
> of the brightest leaders in arts of both war and peace, are true Britons of
> undoubted Celtic origin.[9]

Andrews had a point. But the *Anglo-Saxon* persisted in its use of the term;
it changed its title four times during its thirteen-year existence, but each
new title included the term "Anglo-Saxon." When it commenced publication in September 1887, the full title read: *The Anglo-Saxon, A Journal Devoted to the Interests of the Anglo-Saxon Race in Canada*. By 1889, this had
been replaced with *The Anglo-Saxon, Devoted to the Interests of the Loyal and
Protestant Anglo-Saxons of British America and to the Sons of England Society*. In
1891 it became *United Empire Anglo-Saxon, Devoted to the Interests of Englishmen and Their Descendants*. This was accompanied by an illustration of a
banner that listed the various regions of the Empire: Canada, British Africa,
India, England, Ireland, Wales, Scotland, the West Indies, New Zealand, and
Australia. The banner was draped across an illustration of the British crown
and a globe of the world, both of which appeared beneath the slogan "United
We Stand." By the end of the 1890s, the journal had been retitled *The Anglo-
Saxon, The British Advocate*. These changes certainly complicate any attempt
to understand the identity promoted in the journal, although the often inter-

changeable use of the terms "British" and "Anglo-Saxon" does imply a much wider, and perhaps more cultural than genetic, understanding of the concept of an Anglo-Saxon race. As Robert Page has argued, "there was no common definition of the term race in Victorian Canada. Some used the phrase 'Anglo-Saxon race' as a synonym for total culture which they understood to be a product of history not of blood. They did not necessarily presume a determinism based upon inherited characteristics."[10] By the middle of the nineteenth century, the term had come to characterize English-speaking peoples throughout the world.[11]

One of the most frequently cited characteristics of the Anglo-Saxon race in the journal was its superiority to all other races, and divine Providence was the most common explanation given for this superiority. Anglo-Saxons were often referred to as the "chosen people," for whom the "Almighty stands pledged to ... [their] prosperity," and the journal accepted that it was England's mission to lead civilization.[12] The concepts of Providence, mission, and superiority were inextricably connected to the notion of progress. Imperialists in Canada viewed the Empire as "the vehicle and embodiment of a progressive civilization which was designated by Providence to spread its culture, religion, and political institutions across the face of the earth."[13] As a poem published in May 1891 declared:

Oh may that Fatherland be still
Safeguarded by th' Almighty's will!
May Heaven prolong our times of peace,
Our commerce bless, our trade increase,
And wider yet the bounds expand
Of our Imperial Fatherland!

Our glorious Anglo-Saxon race
Shall ever fill earth's highest place;
The sun shall never more go down
On English temple, tower, and town;
And, wander where a Briton will,
His Fatherland shall hold him still.[14]

On several occasions the *Anglo-Saxon* published statistics in an effort to prove the superiority of the English race. In March 1890, for example, an article pointed out that the ratio of illegitimate to legitimate births in England was only 4:100, while it was much higher in other countries: 48:100 in Paris, 91:100 in Munich, 118:100 in Vienna, and 243:100 in Rome. The article also claimed that a person living in Rome was 237 times more likely to be murdered than a person living in England.[15] A comment in May 1890 noted that the "illiterate people in civilized countries are mostly of the

Romanist population," which suggests that the purpose of the statistics was to demonstrate the inferiority of Roman Catholics as well as to prove the superiority of the English.[16] In September 1888 the *Anglo-Saxon* reported the research findings of an English physician, Arthur Conan Doyle (better known as the creator of the fictional detective Sherlock Holmes), in an article entitled "Geography and Intellect." Measuring intellect by the number of "distinguished citizens" in different geographical regions, Doyle marvelled at how "fertile" the British intellect was: "In the group of islands that constitutes Great Britain there has been going on ever since the Norman conquest a mixing up of brains that has made it on the whole the most virile country in the world. To-day it is simply a wonder to outsiders that the British intellect is so fertile as it is. In every branch of activity, where the mind shoots forward, there is an Englishman at the front."[17]

The myth that the Anglo-Saxon race possessed unique qualities that allowed it to persevere in the face of difficult circumstances was a common theme in the journal. References were frequently made to "plucky little England fighting her way through a host of difficulties."[18] In constructing this myth, a historical narrative was created that emphasized not only the obstacles the English had surmounted in the past but also the continuity of this struggle up to the present. This narrative is evident in the stories of the experience of English emigrants, as well as in articles describing the difficult circumstances Englishmen encountered as a result of their relations with French Canadian Roman Catholics. In describing the English emigrant experience in Manitoba, the editor wrote that they "came by hundreds, many with but little or no capital. Suffering, hardship and privation ... [had] been the lot of not a few, but in the end, indomitable pluck, determination and perseverance" allowed them to overcome the difficulties they encountered.[19] According to the journal, the English were similarly challenged by the "oppression" they faced by other groups in Canada: "The bondage these Anglo-Israelites are laboring under – the whips and scorns they are enduring from their Franco-Egyptian and Hiberno-Egyptian taskmasters."[20]

The *Anglo-Saxon* frequently appealed to history to provide legitimacy for its notion of the superiority of the Anglo-Saxon race. In drawing attention to the work of George L. Craik's *Manual of English Literature,* the editor argued that, with the exception of some Celtic dialects, the English language could be traced further back in history than any other language. According to Craik, the English language had its origins in the fifth century, when it was spoken by both the Angles and the Saxons. Drawing on the work of philologist Jakob Ludwig Grimm, the editor also insisted that the English language was progressive, that it had a power of expression unparalleled by other languages, and that it would inevitably replace all other languages throughout the world. Other languages "should yield willingly and gracefully to their fate of being elbowed out of existence."[21] A poem in the journal, entitled "The Anglo-Saxon Tongue," emphasized this theme:

Tis going east, tis travelling west
'Tis sweeping south and north;
Where'er its strident footsteps rest,
Intelligence bursts forth,
... Science, Art and Chivalry
Are sitting at its feet,
The past, the present, the to be,
Around its footstool meet –
It gazes with prophetic eye
Into the coming gloom;
And through its vistas can descry
Its future triumphs bloom![22]

This poem and the various "expert" opinions regarding the origin and development of the English language with which it was coupled were clearly efforts to further validate the claim that the English race was superior, but they also served a more immediate, political purpose. The idea that all other languages would inevitably submit to the English language gave weight to the anti-French, anti-bilingual argument in Canada.

History was also used to foster an increased appreciation for England's greatness. In an article entitled "The Englishman's Birthright," the author argued that, given England's history, the English should be more proud of their native land than any other race: "The deep love of the Englishman for the land of his birth is paramount. Who, after a perusal of English history, can wonder at this? Hoary with antiquity, laden with illustrious deeds, her past comes floating down to us across the gulf of time. Her history is bright with the names of warriors, statesmen, philosophers, and poets. She has been the bright star of hope twinkling before the tired gaze of a down trodden world crushed under the burden of ignorance, superstition and doubt."[23] In drawing attention to the greatness of England over several centuries, the *Anglo-Saxon* was constructing a memory of the nation that was exceedingly one-sided. Britain's military victories were cast in a positive light, while the less admirable aspects of English conquests were ignored. The *Anglo-Saxon* highlighted the positive features of English history to promote Canada's closer connection with the Empire, including a more integrated imperial defence system. Furthermore, in promoting a memory of England's distinguished military history, the *Anglo-Saxon* was providing legitimacy for the belief that the Anglo-Saxon race should assume a pre-eminent position throughout the world.

Stories and poems were often employed to draw attention to the heroism of Englishmen, their loyalty to Britain, and their military contribution in the history of England and British North America. Most issues of the *Anglo-Saxon* included an article that recounted the heroic events of one of England's many historic battles, with frequent references to the "fighting blood of Englishmen" and the uniquely English brand of bravery. When Capt. H. Murrell of Yorkshire rescued passengers from the troubled Atlantic vessel *Denmark* in the spring of 1889, the *Anglo-Saxon* made much of his heroic feat, but quoted Murrell's self-effacing comment that he had simply done what "any other Englishmen would have done." Lest any reader miss the implication, the editor noted:

> The English race blossoms and blooms with perennial vigour and fruitfulness. Acts of gallantry on sea or land, heroism in new and glorious forms of self-sacrifice ... it comes to pass that some deed brilliant enough to set all the world wondering, if done by an Englishmen only elicits a half growling recognition which could be expressed by the words "of course!" The sun shines, what of that? England wearies us with her glory, her triumphs are monotonous, if we blew forth the story of her victories we should blister our lips, for the trumpet would never be silent![24]

The emphases on heroism, military prowess, and loyalty to Britain reinforced the manliness of the identity promoted in the journal. With few exceptions, the *Anglo-Saxon* carried no stories dealing with women and few written by women. A woman's column did appear in the *Anglo-Saxon* in April 1888 and the author, Lizzie Lyle, appears to have been under the impression that her column would become a regular feature in the journal, but the column did not reappear in subsequent issues. This is not to suggest that the journal did not appeal to women or that there were no women among its readership, but that the identity it constructed was a masculine one.[25]

According to the journal, the Anglo-Saxon man embodied the political and ecclesiastical principles necessary for the survival of Canada. These principles were not only gendered but implicitly antithetical to French culture. As the editor wrote in September 1887: "The Anglo-Saxon man is the representative of two ideas, great ideas which are closely related – one of them is civil liberty. The other ... is that of a pure spiritual Christianity."[26] The journal similarly identified the failure of Canadian political authorities to pursue initiatives designed to eradicate French culture with failed masculinity. It was the "obnoxious preferences for the Roman Catholic French [that] had been continued and increased under the short-sighted, temporizing ... conduct of Canadian Ministries; a policy almost compulsory and necessary owing to the legacy left by British official timidity, and the unmanly – even childish action of the British Protestants in the Dominion Legislatures."[27]

Politicians who demonstrated a tolerance of French Canadian culture failed to act manly and, in so doing, undermined the cause of Britishness.

The *Anglo-Saxon* was incessantly critical of those groups in Canada that disagreed with the political ideas advocated in the journal. Roman Catholics and French Canadians were the journal's favourite targets and were considered a threat to the development of Canada. Roman Catholicism, Quebec civil law, and the French language were the three major issues of irritation raised in the journal. The *Anglo-Saxon* advocated that they should be replaced with Protestantism, English common law, and the English language. The aversion toward civil law in Quebec was primarily because it was not based on British constitutional principles but had instead been imported from France. The *Anglo-Saxon* insisted that having two different legal systems in operation in Canada was inconsistent and confused the appeal progress.[28] British constitutional principles were believed to represent progress and liberty, and the adoption of these principles in Canada was not only necessary for the development of Canada but an inevitable outcome of the Anglo-Saxon presence. Similarly, the journal argued that one language was necessary if national unity was to be assured. Frequent arguments were presented against the use of two languages, including an insistence that it was too costly to print laws in both French and English and that language was the "badge" of a nationality.[29]

The most frequent argument presented against Roman Catholicism was that it was superstitious and archaic, and thus thwarted progress and liberty. As a result of the prevalence of Roman Catholicism in Quebec, the journal referred to the province "as an example of the survival of the mental and moral darkness of the middle ages."[30] Roman Catholicism was viewed as a major threat to both national development and English political authority in Canada. Once again, the journal appealed to history to validate its concerns. In announcing the 284th anniversary of the Gunpowder Plot, an early-seventeenth-century conspiracy among English Catholics to blow up the Parliament of England in protest against the laws imposed on their religion, the *Anglo-Saxon* argued that there were many papist conspirators in Canada, like those whose

> intrigues and mischievous meddling lost the crown of Britain to James II., and the empire of France to Napoleon III.; they fanned the flames of persecution against the Huguenots; they prompted the revocation of the edict of Nantes and inspired the massacre of St. Bartholomew; they were responsible for the plots against Queen Elizabeth; for the murder of Henry III. of France; for the thirty years' war and the Franco-German war; they were at the bottom of the two rebellions in our own North-West. They now fully control the entire legislation of the Province of Quebec, and a very large share in our Ontario and Dominion Parliaments. If we as Canadians do not

throttle them, and that very soon, they will, before long, put us in such a position that they will be our entire masters.[31]

The journal sought to situate French Canadians in a "papist conspiracy" historical narrative to provide evidence why Protestants in Canada should fight Roman Catholicism.

The journal also insisted that too many French Canadians were being appointed to positions of political authority. In January 1900 the *Anglo-Saxon* condemned the Liberal government for appointing French Canadians to government positions to please Quebec, rather than on the basis of their merit.[32] The Liberals, according to the *Anglo-Saxon*, "preferred to build up a strong party to creating a powerful and united State."[33] In opposing the appointment of French Canadians to political office, the journal again raised the issue of Anglo-Saxon racial superiority. The editor stated that it was wrong for the "lords of the universe" to be "made hewers of wood and drawers of water to the Irish and French." He later asked, "What is the reason why the less fitting and less worthy of Canada's population are placed in high lucrative positions, in places of power, influence and trust; thus reversing nature's own decrees?"[34]

Increased immigration of "desirable races" to Canada was advocated as the means by which the influence of the French could be contained. After 1892 the *Anglo-Saxon* became increasingly focused on promoting immigration, especially from England. In an article entitled "The Canadian Northwest – Englishmen Will Soon Outnumber All Others," the editor wrote that the "continuous influx of English immigrants proves for itself that this nationality must soon outnumber all others."[35] Despite this preference for English immigrants, however, the journal recognized that its political objectives could be achieved only with the support of the wider British community. The development of an English-speaking, Protestant nation would require increased immigration of Protestant Welsh, Irish, and Scots as well as the English. Thus, in promoting immigration to Canada, the *Anglo-Saxon* emphasized the unique qualities of the British race, qualities that made this race well suited for the task of national development. The journal's advertisements promoting immigration made the connection between nation-building and race implicit. As Mariana Valverde has shown, there was a strong belief in the relationship between nation-building and "racial character" in late-nineteenth-century Canada, and Canadians of British descent were believed to have the strongest character.[36]

The *Anglo-Saxon* also pursued its objectives through affiliation with a series of organizations that seemed to share its views. Politically, the journal criticized both the Conservative and Liberal Parties of Canada, but favoured the Conservatives, believing them to be more loyal to Britain. This preference often prompted the journal to "urge all true English-men ... to cast their votes and exercise their influence on behalf of the Conservative Party."[37] Although Prime Minister John A. Macdonald was often criticized for not taking a harder line against the French language and Roman Catholicism in Canada, the Liberals were believed to be particularly accommodating to the French fact.[38] But the *Anglo-Saxon* preferred the more extreme anti-French Canadian wing of the Conservative party led by D'Alton McCarthy.[39] This support for McCarthy was not surprising, given his promotion of imperialism and his disdain for French Canadian nationalism. McCarthy considered French Canadian nationalism a "bastard nationality" and argued that "assimilation to an Anglo-Saxon norm" was necessary for national unity.[40] Although the *Anglo-Saxon* shared McCarthy's political viewpoint in many respects, the journal's conception of imperialism appears to have differed somewhat from his. James Miller has argued that McCarthy's imperialism was based on "prosaic considerations of strategic advantage, commercial opportunity, and diplomatic assistance" and had "little connection [with] ... Anglo-Saxon racism."[41] The *Anglo-Saxon* did place a great deal of importance on the commercial and military aspects of imperialism, but it also strongly promoted the idea of Anglo-Saxon racial superiority. Its concept of imperialism not only was commercial or defensive in form but also included the belief that all English-speaking states of Anglo-Saxon blood should (and indeed would) eventually be consolidated under one government.[42] As a poem published in the journal in July 1888 read:

> It is coming, Anglo-Saxons, it is coming, sure and fast,
> The birth-day of the future world – the death day of the Past.
> The day when One, to judgment, the race of man shall beckon –
> How think you, Anglo-Saxons, are you prepared to reckon?[43]

The United States was often included in this idea of an Anglo-Saxon confederation. An article published in October 1887 referred to the United States as "an old Anglo-Saxon colony." The editor asked, "Why call one man a Yankee and another a Britisher? We speak the same tongue, we are proud of the same history."[44] With the exception of the occasional article that was critical of US society or politics, the journal normally sought to illustrate the similarities between the United States and Canada. Significantly, one of the *Anglo-Saxon*'s professed objectives was "to remove all causes of irritation between Canada and the United States of America."[45] Americans were, according to the journal, part of "a great racial family."[46] This interest in the United States is striking when one considers that pro-British and pro-American sentiments during this period were, in general, mutually exclusive.

From October 1890 to June 1891, the *Anglo-Saxon* published a series of essays on imperial federation, written by Thomas MacFarlane. Many of MacFarlane's essays were primarily concerned with commercial union and, to a lesser extent, imperial defence, but he did address the question of how imperial federation would affect "nationalities." He argued that imperial federation would not "seek and could not accomplish the national oblitera-tion of any of the races of the Empire. The Canadians, Australians, Africaners, West Indians and East Indians would, each of them, still have their separate national existence, which Federation would tend far more to preserve than to destroy."[47] The racial heterogeneity implicit in the concept of imperial federation explains why the *Anglo-Saxon* was, according to its 1888 New Year's address, more concerned with consolidating the "Empire of English-speaking peoples" than consolidating the "mighty British Empire."[48] Impe-rial federation promised to strengthen Canada's connection with the Empire, which was an important aspect of the identity promoted in the journal, but it would do little to recognize the more important aspect of that identity, the supremacy of the Anglo-Saxon race. The belief in the supremacy of the Anglo-Saxon race, and the corresponding belief in the superiority of the English language, formed the basis for the idea of a confederation of English-speaking peoples. In allowing for the preservation of distinct "nationali-ties" within the British Empire, imperial federation would not facilitate the "elbowing out of existence"[49] of other languages.

The *Anglo-Saxon's* principal aim was to unite the "English nationality" in Canada, and it pursued this objective through its association with various ethnic organizations.[50] The journal's first affiliation was with the League of the Rose and, in September 1887, the editor, Richard Wicksteed, announced that the *Anglo-Saxon* would be the official organ of the league. Both organi-zations were based in Ottawa and many people involved in the operation of the journal were also on the League of the Rose's grand council; Wicksteed was the grand master of the league, and the journal's printer-publisher, Edwin J. Reynolds, was the league's grand councillor. Highly political in its focus, the league's purpose was "to redress grievancés under which the Brit-ish Protestants labored" in Canada. The league declared that it would at-tempt to eradicate papal influence and anglicize everyone in Canada: "It is by no means rash prophecy that, if the League of the Rose is well manned, there will not be a papist left in any position where he, (the Pope, or King of the Estates of the Church) or he (the blind and ignorant follower of his Kingly Holiness) can do any further injury to the Canadian state." The ob-jectives of the *Anglo-Saxon* were to shape public opinion and to place mem-bers of the league in Parliament and in provincial legislatures.[51] Initially, the journal called for the formation of a party that would cater exclusively to the interests of Anglo-Saxons in Canada: "Let them act at once, muster their forces, and in Legislative halls and in Municipal council chambers fight out the English Reformation and Revolution over again."[52] But the appeal for an Anglo-Saxon party (also referred to as an Anglo-Canadian party) failed to gain sufficient support and was gradually abandoned.

The League of the Rose was based on principles similar to those of the Primrose League of England, a constitutional organization which, according to the editor of the *Anglo-Saxon,* had done "excellent work in opposing the further degradation of England through the spread of the blasphemous all-men-are-born-equal doctrine of radical democracy." However, when the League of the Rose sought a closer relationship with its counterpart in England, it was refused because the Primrose League welcomed all religious denominations, while the League of the Rose welcomed only Protestants.[53] The editor of the *Anglo-Saxon* explained the refusal of the Primrose League to form a relationship with the League of the Rose by observing the distinction between Catholics in England and Catholics in Canada. Catholics in England, he asserted, were extreme Conservatives, while French Catholics in Canada "care nothing about the Empire" and Irish Catholics "want to break it up."[54] In fact, the Primrose League and the League of the Rose were unique responses to very different political circumstances in England and Canada. For the League of the Rose, it was not radical democracy that posed a serious threat to the English identity in Canada but, rather, Roman Catholic political power. Within the British Empire of the late nineteenth century, animosity toward French Catholics was, in large part, a uniquely Canadian sentiment.

The League of the Rose did not long survive the founding of the *Anglo-Saxon* and, as early as October 1887, the journal began to nurture a relationship with the Sons of England Benevolent Society; its affiliation with the organization would prove to be the strongest the *Anglo-Saxon* would maintain throughout the greater part of its run. In 1874 the society opened its first lodge in Toronto and by 1890 had 103 lodges, with approximately 9,500 members. The purpose of the Sons of England was to unite healthy Englishmen between the ages of eighteen and sixty for their mutual benefit and support, foster a feeling of loyalty toward England, and educate them in the "true principles of manhood."[55] As a mutual insurance organization, the society provided financial and moral assistance to those members in need, including the families of deceased members. The Sons of England did not identify their organization as a charitable society because it was believed that the solicitation of charity could be a humiliating experience for those in need of assistance.[56] The grand secretary of the society, John W. Carter, stated: "Whatever benefits you receive ... are not charity but your right, and paid to you by the proper officers without explanations or apologies, and all that is required of you is a small initiation fee, and prompt payment of your dues."[57] Membership was restricted to Protestant English, Welsh, and their descendants. Catholics were not welcome in the society because it was believed that their loyalty was to the pope rather than to the Crown of England.[58] This strong anti-Catholic sentiment in the Sons of England was likely the characteristic that most attracted the *Anglo-Saxon* and led the editor to seek affiliation with the society. The *Anglo-Saxon's* role in promoting the Sons of England was to provide communication among lodges, and to inform the society of the activities of its members. Most issues contained a statement of the "Aims, Objects and Benefits of the Sons of England Benefit Society," lodge news and communications, and a complete list of lodge directories, including the dates and locations of regular meetings at each lodge. The journal also had representatives at many lodges throughout Canada.

In 1892 the *Anglo-Saxon* also became affiliated with the Daughters and Maids of England Benevolent Society. Established in Hamilton in 1892, this society welcomed all healthy Protestant English and Welsh women between the ages of sixteen and fifty. The organization's object was to educate women in charitable practices and "true principles of womanhood," maintain and nurture a memory of England, and care for fellow members. Each lodge was required to have no more than twelve members, and each lodge could have no more than eight male "financial members," who were required to be members of the Sons of England.[59] The society established lodges across Canada following its announcement in 1895 that it would offer health benefits.[60] As was the case with the Sons of England, the *Anglo-Saxon* published the Daughters and Maids of England Society's lodge directories.

One issue on which the Sons of England and the *Anglo-Saxon* were not fully aligned was politics. The members of that society shared many of the political viewpoints expressed in the *Anglo-Saxon* and, according to the editor, many of those joining the Sons of England did so as a result of the "aggressiveness of the Roman Catholic Church in matters political and educational," but discussion of politics was not permitted in the lodges.[61] This prompted the editor of the *Anglo-Saxon* to note in September 1891: "We have ... at times ventured to criticize adversely the society's *inaction* on matters that should be of vital concern to this society, having such aims and objects as are set forth in its constitution and ritual, and in doing so it is just possible some simile or adjective might wisely have been politely toned down or omitted to suit the tastes of some; but all we can say is, we wrote as we thought and felt, and it is for those in authority to know that such thoughts and feelings do exist."[62]

Ross McCormack has written that "the Sons of England contributed substantially to the maintenance of aesthetic cultural forms." The society's Sunday evening gatherings had the atmosphere of an English music hall. During the evening, members sang along to jingoistic songs, drank English-style dark ale, spoke regional dialects, and "wept at evocations of England's green and pleasant land."[63] In so doing, society members were engaging in a process of "self-mythologization." Myth in this context has been defined as a "codification of historical experience, real or imagined, past, present or yet to come, an essential construct which people feel compelled to devise for themselves for the sake of self-preservation."[64] Indeed, the purpose of the Sons of England and the *Anglo-Saxon,* whether it was often articulated or not, was to preserve the English identity in Canada. But the *Anglo-Saxon's* pursuit of this objective differed from that of the Sons of England in that the journal gave little attention to old English custom. This was because the identity promoted in the journal was fundamentally a political-racial identity, one constructed with the express purpose of effecting change in the Canadian political environment.

The third major organization with which the *Anglo-Saxon* was affiliated was the St. George's Society of Toronto. The objective of the Toronto society, established in 1834, was to foster a patriotic sentiment among Englishmen and provide assistance to all those in need. St. George's welcomed the membership of Englishmen, Welshmen, and their descendants, and was a non-partisan organization.[65] By-law VIII of the St. George's constitution of 1855 stated: "The introduction of political or religious subjects, or their discussion, shall never be allowed at any meeting of the Society."[66] Lectures and discussions relating to the Empire often took place during society meetings, but more often the management committee simply discussed the activities of the society and how its resources would be distributed.[67] The St. George's Society of Toronto differed from the Sons of England in that it was a charitable organization rather than a mutual insurance association.[68] Persons seeking assistance were not required to be members. St. George's provided assistance to all members of society in need and "especially to the underdog."[69] Society members believed there was something unique about the English race that suited it for charitable work. "St. George's Societies are the agencies through which the charitable feelings of our race finds both objects and means of action."[70]

In 1877 a North American Union of St. George's Societies was established in Philadelphia and, following the union's 1899 convention in Hamilton,[71] the *Anglo-Saxon* was declared the "official organ of St. George's union of North America."[72] St. George's Societies were concerned with promoting a loyalty and affection for England and an appreciation of English culture. According to a 1908 Royal Society of St. George's publication, one of the purposes of the society was "to cultivate an interest in English literature, history, folk-lore, and antiquities."[73] Given the Sons of England and St. George's Society's emphases on the importance of preserving aspects of English tradition and culture, it would seem to follow that the *Anglo-Saxon* would also be concerned with promoting these interests. But while the journal did place an emphasis on English history and tradition, it was less inclined to promote an affection for literature and antiquities. To the *Anglo-Saxon,* history and tradition served a political purpose. High culture was given slight attention because it contributed little to the accomplishment of the journal's political objectives.

The *Anglo-Saxon* appears to have abruptly ceased publication in January 1900.[74] In a period when many race-oriented periodicals were short-lived and limited in circulation, the *Anglo-Saxon's* longevity and its diverse international readership are significant. A major factor in the journal's success was obviously the way in which it was managed; it was distributed across Canada, in various parts of the British Empire, and in the United States. There were clearly many readers in Canada and elsewhere who shared the principles advocated in the journal. Animosity toward Roman Catholicism and the French language was rampant during this period and was not confined to the English population. Indeed, a main reason for the journal's success was that it appealed not only to Englishmen but to other ethnic identities as well. As the editor declared as early as January 1888, "men of all creeds and nationalities" could be found on the journal's subscription list: "the sturdy Englishman, the canny Scot, the witty Irishmen, [and] the patient German."[75]

The identity promoted in the journal was both English and British, and was Protestant, male, and heavily racial. The superiority myth constructed in the journal was designed to legitimate the racial superiority of Anglo-Saxons. But it was this extreme racial and anti-Roman Catholic outlook that was responsible for the journal's inability to have any great political influence. It could not consistently endorse either the Conservative or Liberal Party of Canada, both of which sought a base in Quebec. D'Alton McCarthy represented a more extreme view that was appealing to the *Anglo-Saxon,* but even he was too moderate in his racial views. The journal at first hoped to pursue its objectives through the formation of an exclusively Anglo-Saxon political party, but the party never materialized, and with the collapse of the League of the Rose, the *Anglo-Saxon* was forced to create new alliances with the Sons of England and the St. George's Society. But the aims of these organizations were not entirely compatible with the more politically focused objectives of the journal.

To a large extent, the journal's emphasis on the superiority of the Anglo-Saxon race may have impeded it from gaining the support to accomplish its political goals. Protestant Irish, Scots, and Welsh clearly supported many of the principles promoted in the journal, but most of them were unlikely to have raced to the newsstand to learn of the most recent activities in which the English race had "blossomed and bloomed with perennial vigour and fruitfulness."[76] The journal included the wider British population in its designs for the development of Canada, but the not-so-subtle expression of Anglo-Saxon racial superiority may have been unpalatable to the wider British community in Canada. The boundary between "British" and "Anglo-Saxon," however, was not clear in the journal. This ambiguity may have contributed to the *Anglo-Saxon's* longevity, but it may also have been responsible for the journal's end. Politically, the identity it promoted was British, but culturally and historically it was English, and heavily infused with notions of racial superiority. The conflict between the attempt to strengthen the British presence in Canada and the promotion of Anglo-Saxon racial superiority was never reconciled in the journal. In a period when ideas about race were essential to the articulation of identity, the journal's failure to work out these conflicting interests may have marked its demise. The *Anglo-Saxon* was attempting to construct an identity even it could not define.

Acknowledgments
I would like to thank Kerry Abel, Norman Hillmer, Andrew Horrall, Mark Inglis, Brian McKillop, James Opp, and John Herd Thompson, who kindly commented on earlier drafts of this chapter. I am also grateful to Phillip Buckner and Doug Francis, who provided helpful comments on a more recent version. A special thank you is due to Bruce Elliott, who introduced me to *The Anglo-Saxon* and offered ongoing and insightful feedback.

Notes
1 From January 1892 to August 1894, two issues were published per month, with the exception of March and April 1892.
2 See Douglas Cole, "Canada's 'Nationalistic' Imperialists," *Journal of Canadian Studies* 5, 3 (1970): 47.
3 "Think of It?" *Anglo-Saxon* 7, 21 (July 1893): 5.
4 Born in Kingston in 1842, Richard Wicksteed was the eldest son of Gustavus W. Wicksteed, a prominent officer of the House of Assembly and the House of Commons. Richard Wicksteed studied in the Faculty of Arts at McGill College in Montreal, where he obtained a BA in 1863 and an MA in 1866. In 1868 he graduated from McGill with a degree in law. He was admitted to the bar of Lower Canada in 1867 and was subsequently called to the Ontario bar in 1872, the same year he was appointed assistant law clerk and English translator in the House of Commons. Throughout his life he was involved with various organizations, including the Upper Canada College Debating Society, Burnside Literary Society of Montreal, Young Men's Christian Association, Royal Society of St. George's, Church of England Young Men's Association, Temperance Coffee House Company, Field Naturalists' Society, Society for the Prevention of Cruelty to Animals, and the Royal Canadian Academy. He died in Ottawa in 1912. Wicksteed's journals indicate that he met with Prime Minister John A. Macdonald on a fairly regular basis. See for example entry 17, 5 September 1887, Richard J. Wicksteed Papers, Rare Books and Special Collections Division, McGill University Libraries. A useful summary of Wicksteed's activities can also be found in George Maclean Rose, *A Cyclopaedia of Canadian Biography* (Toronto: Rose Publishing, 1886), 698-99.
5 See "Notice to Readers" and "Think of It?" *Anglo-Saxon* 6, 21 (July 1893): 4, 5. In April 1889 the editor announced that eight thousand copies would be circulated the following month. See "Editorial Notes," *Anglo-Saxon* 2, 8: 210.
6 Ross McCormack, "Cloth Caps and Jobs: The Ethnicity of English Immigrants in Canada, 1900-1914," in *Ethnicity, Power and Politics in Canada,* ed. Jorgen Dahlie and Tissa Fernando (Toronto: Methuen Publications, 1981), 48. Although somewhat dated, this framework continues to prove useful for its emphasis on the instrumentality of ethnicity. Benedict Anderson, *Imagined Communities: Reflections on the Origin and Spread of Nationalism* (London: Verso, 1983), 5-6. On the protean nature of nations and nationalism, see also Eric Hobsbawm and Terence Ranger, *The Invention of Tradition* (Cambridge: Cambridge University Press, 1983), and Eric Hobsbawm, *Nations and Nationalism Since 1780: Programme, Myth, Reality* (Cambridge: Cambridge University Press, 1990).
7 "Prologue," *Anglo-Saxon* 1, 1 (September 1887): 2.
8 J. Saxon Mills of the Royal Society of St. George asserted that the English race was the "central and solar stock" of the Empire. See *The English Race: The Journal of the Royal Society of St. George* 1, 1 (February 1908): 3. On the dominance of the English in Britain, see also

Phillip Buckner, "Whatever Happened to the British Empire?" *Journal of the Canadian Historical Association* 4 (1993): 9.

9   "Why Anglo-Saxon?" *Anglo-Saxon* 13, 10 (July 1899): 5.

10 Robert Page, "Carl Berger and the Intellectual Origins of Canadian Imperialist Thought, 1867-1914," *Journal of Canadian Studies* 5, 3 (1970): 42. Page added that Victorian Canadians used the term "race" in the same way "ethnic" is used today. Lawrence James, *The Rise and Fall of the British Empire* (London: Abacus, 1998), 205, has suggested that the British were the "assumed progeny" of the Anglo-Saxons.

11 See Reginald Horsman, *Race and Manifest Destiny: The Origins of American Racial Anglo-Saxonism* (Cambridge, MA: Harvard University Press, 1981), 4.

12 See for example "Prologue," *Anglo-Saxon* 1, 1 (September 1887): 2-3; and "Anglo-Saxon Confederation," *Anglo-Saxon* 1, 2 (October 1887): 13-14.

13 Carl Berger, *The Sense of Power: Studies in the Ideas of Canadian Imperialism, 1867-1914* (Toronto: University of Toronto Press, 1970), 217.

14 Verses nine and ten of "Where Is Britain's Fatherland?" *Anglo-Saxon* 5, 9 (May 1891): 6. The author noted is Davaar. On the idea that Providence had brought victory to England in her military campaigns, see also John R. Gray, "Characteristics of Englishmen Discussed," *Anglo-Saxon* 9, 4 (December 1895): 8.

15 "Important Figures," *Anglo-Saxon* 3, 7 (March 1890): 2.

16 Taken from the Boston publication *The Christian* and published in *Anglo-Saxon* under the heading "Illiterate People," 3, 9 (May 1890): 1.

17 *Anglo-Saxon* 2, 1 (September 1888): 130.

18 "St. George's Day Banquet in British Columbia," *Anglo-Saxon* 2, 10 (June 1889): 3.

19 "Englishmen in the Canadian West," *Anglo-Saxon* 12, 8 (May 1899): 3.

20 "The League of the Rose," *Anglo-Saxon* 1, 3 (November 1887): 19.

21 "Articles of Our Political Faith," *Anglo-Saxon* 1, 3 (November 1887): 19-22. See also "English Rather Than French," *Anglo-Saxon* 2, 11 (July 1889): 2.

22 Taken from the fourth verse of William Pittman Lett's poem, "The Anglo-Saxon Tongue," as quoted in *Anglo-Saxon* 1, 5 (January 1888): 42-43.

23 *Anglo-Saxon* 3, 7 (March 1890): 4.

24 "An Heroic Englishmen," *Anglo-Saxon* 2, 10 (June 1889): 1.

25 See "Woman's Welfare," *Anglo-Saxon* 1, 8 (April 1888): 72.

26 "Prologue," *Anglo-Saxon* 1, 1 (September 1887): 3.

27 "The League of the Rose," *Anglo-Saxon* 1, 5 (January 1888): 43.

28 See "Articles of Our Political Faith," *Anglo-Saxon* 1, 4 (December 1887): 29-32.

29 "Prologue," *Anglo-Saxon* 1, 1 (September 1887): 2-4.

30 Ibid., 6.

31 "The Jesuits and the Gunpowder Plot," *Anglo-Saxon* 3, 2 (October 1889): 2.

32 "The Grafters," *Anglo-Saxon* 13, 4 (January 1900): 6.

33 "The League of the Rose," *Anglo-Saxon* 1, 5 (January 1888): 43.

34 "Prologue," *Anglo-Saxon* 1, 1 (September 1887): 2.

35 *Anglo-Saxon* 6, 20 (June 1893): 1. For additional articles on immigration, see "New from the Prairies – Foreigners Coming in Fast Taking Up the Land," and "The Wondrous Prairies," *Anglo-Saxon* 6, 5 (November 1892): 5; "Filling up the Country – Prospective Condition of Farmers in the North-West," *Anglo-Saxon* 6, 11 (February 1893): 5; "Wealth of the North-West – A Vivid Description of Slocan and Lardeau Districts," *Anglo-Saxon* 6, 12 (February 1893): 4; "Homesteads for Everyone – What the Canadian North-West Offers to Farmers" and "Glories of Southern Alberta – A Rich Inheritance for Incoming Settlers," *Anglo-Saxon* 6, 13 (March 1893): 4; "The Season's Immigration – Suggested Arrangement to Provide for Prepaid Passages," *Anglo-Saxon* 6, 13 (March 1893): 5; "Great Ranching Possibilities," *Anglo-Saxon* 6, 21 (July 1893): 5; "Nebraska Farmers Testify – to the Canadian Northwest and Its Resources," *Anglo-Saxon* 7, 10 (January 1894): 5; "Manitoba and the Northwest – Englishmen Who Give Their Testimony for the Benefit of the English Farmer – Lots of Land and a Grand Farming Country," *Anglo-Saxon* 7, 19 (June 1894): 4-5; and "Immigration," *Anglo-Saxon* 10, 10 (June 1897): 5.

36 Mariana Valverde, *The Age of Light, Soap and Water: Moral Reform in English Canada: 1885-1925* (Toronto: McClelland and Stewart, 1991), 104.

37 "The General Election," *Anglo-Saxon* 4, 6 (February 1891): 4.

38 See "The Political Situation" and "Editorial Notes," *Anglo-Saxon* 4, 7 (March 1891): 4.

39 On McCarthy's political ideas, see James R. Miller, "As Politician He Is a Great Enigma: The Social and Political Ideas of D'Alton McCarthy," *Canadian Historical Review* 58 (1977): 399-422. See also James R. Miller, *Equal Rights: The Jesuits' Estates Act Controversy* (Montreal and Kingston: McGill-Queen's University Press, 1979).

40 Miller, "As Politician He Is a Great Enigma," 412-13. The phrase "bastard nationality" is quoted in Miller, and taken from the *Toronto Daily Mail*, 13 July 1889.

41 Miller, "As Politician He Is a Great Enigma," 416-18.

42 See "Prologue," *Anglo-Saxon* 1, 1 (September 1887): 2-3; and "Anglo-Saxon Confederation," *Anglo-Saxon* 1, 2 (October 1887): 13-14. Interest in an Anglo-Saxon confederation also inspired a particular brand of nationalism in the journal. In an article in June 1888 on the subject of nationalism, Richard Wicksteed declared: "The modern dogma of Nationalism is the assumption that a nation in the sense of being an aggregate mass of persons connected by ties of blood and lineage and sometimes of language ought necessarily to be a nation in the sense of being a state or independent society united by common political institutions. In fewer words, Nationalism is the doctrine that people of the same origin and race should be united under the same government." Wicksteed's assessment of nationalism was based on a political-racial connection to Britain rather than a sentimental or affectionate one. The function of this nationalism was to unite the British population in Canada to build a stronger dominion; the importance of an official or political connection, therefore, was of principal concern. See "Nationalism," *Anglo-Saxon* 1, 10 (June 1888): 90.

43 First and final verses from a poem entitled "That Day!" *Anglo-Saxon* 1, 11 (July 1888): 3.

44 "Anglo-Saxon Confederation," *Anglo-Saxon* 1, 2 (October 1887): 14.

45 "New Year's Address," *Anglo-Saxon* 1, 5 (January 1888): 39.

46 "The Possibility of a Permanent Alliance between Great Britain and the United States," *Anglo-Saxon* 12, 11 (August 1899): 8. See also "The British-American League, in the United States," *Anglo-Saxon* 1, 5 (January 1888): 4; and "Comments and Criticisms," *Anglo-Saxon* 2, 11 (July 1888): 105.

47 "Within the Empire; An Essay on Imperial Federation by Thomas MacFarlane," *Anglo-Saxon* 4, 3 (November 1890): 2.

48 "New Year's Address," *Anglo-Saxon* 1, 5 (January 1888): 39.

49 "Articles of Our Political Faith," *Anglo-Saxon* 1, 3 (November 1887): 22.

50 See "Our 'Tenth' Year," *Anglo-Saxon* 10, 1 (September 1896): 4. By forming alliances with various organizations the *Anglo-Saxon* was also able to attract more subscribers and thus increase its revenue.

51 "The League of the Rose," *Anglo-Saxon* 1, 3 (November 1887): 19.

52 "Prospectus," *Anglo-Saxon* 1, 1 (September 1887): 3.

53 "The League of the Rose," *Anglo-Saxon* 1, 3 (November 1887): 19. For more on the Primrose League, see Martin Pugh, *The Tories and the People, 1880-1935* (Oxford: Basil Blackwell, 1985), and for the involvement of women in the Primrose League, see Jane Rendall, *Equal or Different: Women's Politics 1800-1914* (Oxford: Basil Blackwell, 1987), and Beatrix Campbell, *The Iron Ladies: Why Do Women Vote Tory?* (London: Virago Press, 1987).

54 "The League of the Rose," *Anglo-Saxon* 1, 5 (January 1888): 43. In the same issue, the editor announced the creation in Hamilton, Ontario, of a counter organization to the League of the Rose, called the League of the Cross. It was an organization of Irish Roman Catholics (44).

55 "Sons of England Benevolent Society," *Anglo-Saxon* 1, 8 (April 1888): 74.

56 D.A. MacKinnon and A.B. Warburton, *Past and Present of Prince Edward Island* (Charlottetown, PEI: B.F. Bowen, 1906), 209-10.

57 "Sons of England Benevolent Society," *Anglo-Saxon* 1, 8 (April 1888): 74. The government of the Sons of England comprised a Grand Lodge and subordinate lodges; the Grand Lodge was made up of delegates elected by subordinate lodges to represent their interests and was

financed by the fees paid by its members, while subordinate lodges elected their own officers and required weekly dues in addition to an initial membership fee. See also "Some
Statistics," *Anglo-Saxon* 4, 12 (August 1890): 2.

58   "The Order of the Sons of England and Friendly Societies," *Anglo-Saxon* 1, 9 (May 1888): 80.

59   "Daughters and Maids of England Benevolent Society," *Anglo-Saxon* 7, 19 (June 1894): 3.

60   Bruce Elliott, "English," in *Encyclopedia of Canada's Peoples,* ed. Paul Robert Magosci (Toronto:
University of Toronto Press, 1999), 483.

61   "The Progress of the Order," *Anglo-Saxon* 3, 7 (March 1890): 2; and "Sons of England Benevolent Society," *Anglo-Saxon* 1, 8 (April 1888): 74.

62   "Our Fifth Anniversary," *Anglo-Saxon* 5, 1 (September 1891): 1.

63   McCormack, "Cloth Caps and Jobs," 47.

64   Edward J. Cowan, "The Myth of Scotch Canada," in *Myth, Migration and the Making of
Memory,* ed. Michael Vance (Halifax: Fernwood, 1999), 56.

65   See *Anglo-Saxon* 7, 9 (May 1899): 4.

66   Quoted in Anne Storey, *The St. George's Society of Toronto: A History and List of Members 1834-
1967* (Agincourt, ON: Generation Press, 1987), 1.

67   *Anglo-Saxon* 7, 9 (May 1899): 4. The Society's management committee consisted of a president, vice-president, chaplains, doctors, stewards, and other officers.

68   See Elliott, "English," 483.

69   Storey, *St. George's Society of Toronto,* 1.

70   "To Englishmen and Their Descendants in Canada, and Especially to the Sons of England
and St. George's Societies" (emphasis removed), *Anglo-Saxon* 1, 8 (April 1888): 67.

71   See Elliott, "English," 483. Conventions of the North American Union were often held in
Canada.

72   "The Anglo-Saxon – Official Organ of St. George's Union of North America," *Anglo-Saxon*
13, 1 (September 1899): 6.

73   *The English Race: The Journal of the Royal Society of St. George* 1, 1 (February 1908): 3.

74   Since no announcement was made, the date of the journal's demise remains an open question. The Canadian libraries that hold the *Anglo-Saxon* in their collections list the journal's
publication date as uncertain. Library and Archives Canada holds the last available issue,
but it is not clear whether this was the final issue.

75   "New Year's Address," *Anglo-Saxon* 1, 5 (January 1888): 39.

76   "An Heroic Englishman," *Anglo-Saxon* 2, 10 (June 1889): 1.

7

Canada's Boys – An Imperial or National Asset? Responses to Baden-Powell's Boy Scout Movement in Pre-War Canada

Patricia Dirks

Turning adolescent boys into loyal citizens with "proper" values became a primary concern in early-twentieth-century Canada, and Anglo-Canadians looked beyond their country's borders to both Britain and the United States for citizenship training schemes. Different interpretations of what it meant to be Canadian within the British World had a direct effect on the search for the best boys' training program in the years leading up to the First World War. The importation into Canada of Lord Baden-Powell's Boy Scout movement was followed quickly by the introduction of Canadian Standard Efficiency Tests for Boys (CSET), an alternative citizenship training program designed by boys' workers in the nation's Young Men's Christian Association (YMCA). Religious beliefs and nationalist aspirations as well as personal ambitions played a part in convincing Canadian YMCA boys' workers that the British-run Boy Scout movement was unsuitable for training Canada's adolescent males. Without questioning Canada's continued membership in the Empire, the evangelical Protestant designers of CSET promised that this program of Christian leadership training would turn the nation's male adolescents into "masterful men of powerful influence" capable of meeting "the outstanding needs of Canada in her task of nation-building" and of determining what role Canada should "play in the future history of the world."[1] Baden-Powell, to the contrary, sought Canadian support for Boy Scouts by arguing that the scheme would ensure Canada's future "as one of the greatest and strongest units" of the British Empire.[2]

The simultaneous growth of Boy Scouts and CSET in Canada occurred in the context of differences over the place of religion in citizenship training and debates within the British World about how to reconcile the growth of colonial nationalism with an increasing sense of imperial unity.[3] The widespread popularity of Boy Scouts attested to the strength of, and reinforced, an imperial Canadian identity. The successful launch of CSET reflected both the continuing influence of evangelical Protestantism in Canada and acceptance of the idea that support for the national aspirations of one of the separate units within the Empire was compatible with loyalty to the British World.[4] The complexity of the British World concept explains the popularity of both Boy Scouts and its Canadian-made rival in the era of the First World War.[5]

Canadians of British origin, thousands of whom were recent immigrants, ensured that Baden-Powell's Boy Scout movement entered Canada on the heels of its launch in the mother country. In communities throughout Canada, boys learned about the scouting program developed by Baden-Powell from British publications such as the *Boy's Own Paper* and *The Boys' Herald* and were eager to join troops. Links with England meant that Scout troops began springing up in centres across the country well in advance of Lord Baden-Powell's official introduction of his movement during a cross-country tour in 1910.[6] Taylor Statten, Boys' Work Secretary of Toronto's Central YMCA, for example, recalled being given a copy of *Scouting for Boys* in 1908 when the physical director of Upper Canada College, A.L. Cochrane, returned from a summer visit to England.[7]

Scouting's reinforcement of traditional values, including the tie to the Empire and Baden-Powell's promise that the movement would instill much-needed discipline into Canadian boys who, in his view, already had enough self-reliance and assertiveness, appealed to many adults. While becoming Scouts provided boys with opportunities to have fun while acquiring interesting new skills and camping out, it also involved "plenty of work that look[ed] like play," parents were assured, and taught their sons how to apply and discipline themselves so as to reach attainable goals. The nation's boys who had been brought up on tales about Baden-Powell, hero of the Boer War, clamoured for the opportunity to don uniforms and learn to do all the things his Army Scouts had done to enable them to withstand the siege of Mafeking. The patriotic instincts inherent in every boy were central to Scouting's early success, according to the Toronto Scout council, which went on to explain that Boy Scouts were "taught that their Empire [was] a heritage left to them by their forefathers to keep and guard."[8]

Involvement in Scouting was also presented as an antidote to the debilitating effects of city life. Instead of getting into trouble in their spare time, urban schoolboys could be learning to perform a variety of tasks and participating in games that would foster physical and mental development and teach the value and importance of teamwork. That the Scout program left religious training entirely to parents and churches appealed to many Canadians, but the movement's military overtones disturbed many others. In an October 1910 report on the Boy Scout movement, B.K. Sandwell drew attention to the fact that Scout leaders were often "militia men, usually of the engineering or signaling corps." To bolster his claim that military men had played a key role in the introduction of scouting across Canada, Sandwell singled out Capt. Richard John Birdwhistle, who served as the first Dominion secretary; Lt. Col. J.C. Gardiner, who did the initial organization work in Montreal; and Col. S.B. Steele of the Royal North West Mounted Police, whom he identified as the most ardent backer of Boy Scouts in the Canadian west.[9]

Ties to England were central to the spread of Scouting across Canada, as illustrated by the origins of Boy Scouts in Calgary. The introduction of Scouting in this western city also demonstrates the important role clergymen, especially Anglicans, played in the movement's dissemination. Boy Scouts came to Calgary following the arrival of Rev. C.W.E. Horne at the cathedral, the Church of the Redeemer, in 1909. As superintendent of the Sunday school, Reverend Horne soon found out that nothing was being done for the city's boys and he wrote back to England to find out if there was anything new in the way of boys' organizations. When friends in England sent him back a copy of *Scouting for Boys*, Horne read it and passed the book on to several men at the cathedral who were interested in the welfare of boys. By February 1910 a decision had been made to bring Scouting to Calgary and an organizing committee was formed to promote the movement. The only committee member with any experience with Boy Scouts was Alfred T. Jewitt, whose son had been a Scout in England.[10] Calgary's first three Scout troops were all church-related: the first and second were at the cathedral, and the third was at St. Stephen's Church. Troop number four was on the North Hill at the school where Jewitt was the principal.

There are many examples of the close link between heavy British immigration to Canada in the years following the Boer War and the rapid establishment of Boy Scout troops from Ontario westward in the years immediately following publication of *Scouting for Boys*. Connections to the mother country provided organizers far removed from Scouting headquarters with opportunities to organize and outfit Boy Scout troops. In Calgary, for instance, Scouts got their first uniforms through a man who, although not connected with the movement, was going on a trip to England and volunteered to bring back $300 worth of uniforms, to be paid for as they were purchased by Scouts and officers.[11]

In Ituna, Saskatchewan, the introduction of Scouting can be traced to the arrival of J.B. Hardinge, who had met Baden-Powell while at school in England and taken part in a guinea pig camp before Scouting officially started. When Hardinge moved to Raymore, Saskatchewan, in 1913, the Boy Scouts spread to yet another western community. Decades later Hardinge remained active in the Scout movement in Vancouver.[12] Farther west another British immigrant, Rev. T.R. Heneage, was responsible for bringing Scouting to Victoria. Noting that he had worked with the poorest boys in England for years until ill health had brought him to Canada in 1906, Heneage linked his introduction of Boy Scouts to finding no organizations for boys in Victoria. His search for an appropriate organization ended in

1909 when he was given a copy of *Scouting for Boys* and, in his words, "away we went." With Victoria boys flocking to the movement, Heneage's friends were prevailed upon to take charge of troops, and the movement soon appeared wherever leaders could be found.[13]

While ties to the mother country account for the appearance of Boy Scout troops in many communities across Canada, expansion of the movement in Canada, as in other parts of the British Empire, was not left to chance. Baden-Powell took steps from the outset to build an Empire-wide organizational structure from the top down. As soon as *Scouting for Boys* appeared in book form in 1908, copies were sent to governors general of the dominions with a letter from Baden-Powell seeking support for his movement. When it became apparent less than two years later that Scouting in Canada was suffering from the lack of a central governing body, Baden-Powell asked Canada's governor general, Lord Grey, "to interest himself in the formation of a central Council or Committee, with Headquarters at Ottawa, ... which would serve as a Boy Scout Council for the whole of the Dominion."[14] Lord Grey, in turn, asked Col. Percy Sherwood, his military secretary, to look into this matter, and through his efforts a temporary national council was in place by the time of Baden-Powell's visit in August 1910, and Richard John Birdwhistle, a captain in the 43rd Regiment, the Duke of Cornwall's Own Rifles, had been appointed as honorary dominion secretary.[15]

At this juncture, leadership of the Canadian movement was drawn largely from men with military connections, supplemented by a sprinkling of members from politics, the professions, and the church. The temporary dominion council of thirty members that ran Boy Scouts on the national level in 1911-12 had twenty-two members with military titles, one of whom was also a clergyman. Three others, for a total of four out of thirty, had religious titles. Of the remaining five, two were Members of Parliament and one was a doctor. Saskatchewan and New Brunswick were not represented on this committee. Of the seven Boy Scout commissioners, all but the one from Prince Edward Island had military titles.[16] The men chosen to promote Boy Scouts in pre-war Canada and those who took it upon themselves to found troops were likely to perpetuate and spread a pro-imperial sense of Canadian identity. The welcome accorded Baden-Powell on his first Canadian tour in 1910 indicates that the adults and boys drawn to the movement shared the view that Canada's national destiny lay within the British Empire.

Baden-Powell's cross-country tour in August and September 1910 was a pivotal event in the pre-war spread of Boy Scouts. In an effort to explain the Boy Scout scheme to as many Canadians as possible, Baden-Powell travelled over 13,500 kilometres by train, visiting fifteen Scouting centres, where local branches of the Canadian Club organized seventeen meetings of interested people. The Chief Scout was impressed by "the keenness with which the public entered into consideration of the scheme and backed it up." He also reported that the country's "leading educational, religious, military and business authorities [were] very sympathetic" to Boy Scouts and remarked on "the fitness and good class" of the men volunteering as scoutmasters in Canada. The movement, he concluded, was poised for rapid expansion and would soon be training the Dominion's "rising generation in the theory and practice of good citizenship." And, as Baden-Powell made very clear, this training was designed to turn all of Canada's boys – French Canadians, those of British descent, and the sons of "foreigners" – into useful citizens of the great empire within which the Dominion of Canada was "a rising nation." In an address to a special joint meeting of the Canadian and Empire Clubs in Toronto, Baden-Powell explained why Boy Scouts offered loyal citizens more than the cadet movement did. Scouting not only could reach boys in communities too small and remote to support cadets but it also had a much broader appeal:

A great many religious denominations and parents have conscientiously objected to boys belonging to a military organization ... therefore, to avoid military training we find many of these denominations and parents send their boys to join the Scouts simply for the training of good citizenship which they receive. At the same time, of course, we do not neglect patriotism but encourage it as much as we can, so that eventually when they take up the idea of their duty to their country and join a defence force, as many of them will, with the experience they have gained in campaigning and woodcraft – knowing how to cross rivers, signal, find their way in a strange place day or night – all these traits of good soldiers which are scarcely touched upon in the training of Cadets, will make the Scout a far superior soldier than if he received merely the usual Cadet Training.

Baden-Powell also directly linked Canada's future as an imperial nation to the success of Boy Scouts. Urging Canadians to support and encourage the movement, he promised that the scheme would "build up character in the rising generation, so that your nation in the future will be a nation of character, and therefore one of the greatest and strongest units in our great Empire."[17]

Wherever Baden-Powell went in Canada, boys, their parents, and community leaders responded enthusiastically. In the far west Baden-Powell was given such an eager welcome on his arrival at the Canadian Pacific Railway dock in Victoria that "the police had a time keeping back the people who wished to catch a glimpse of the hero." In addition to members of the local establishment and ordinary citizens, many veterans of the Boer War had donned their medals and gathered on the wharf to shake "B.P.'s" right hand. Here as elsewhere the reception committee consisted of a cross-section of the city's elite, and the Canadian Club had arranged for Baden-Powell to address a public meeting in the Victoria theatre.[18] In Vancouver Baden-Powell was hailed as the "man who has done and is perhaps doing more ... today for the youth of England and Canada."[19]

Calgary, where a hundred Scouts paraded to the Mounted Police barracks to be inspected by Baden-Powell, gave an equally warm reception to the "hero of Mafeking and leader in the empire-wide scout movement."[20] While in the city, Baden-Powell singled out the West's "frontiersmen," "backwoodsmen," and "Royal North West Mounted policemen" as "splendid examples to hold up to boys" and argued that what Canada's boys needed most was "a strong sense of discipline."[21] While pointing out that Boy Scouts had no military ties and was not a cadet movement, Baden-Powell argued that scout training would produce better soldiers. In discussing the German naval threat to Britain while in Edmonton, he expressed approval of Canada's establishment of a navy and the hope that "some day some of his boy scouts in Canada [would] be trained in the new Canadian naval service."[22]

In Winnipeg, where the Canadian Club luncheon was chaired by Col. S.B. Steele of the Royal North West Mounted Police, who had served under Baden-Powell in the Boer War and had assisted in the organization of the South African Constabulary, clear connections were drawn between Baden-Powell's reception and imperial unity. According to the *Manitoba Free Press*, "the whole function was a demonstration of the bond of loyalty between the mother country and Canada." The article went on to argue that Winnipeg's response to Baden-Powell's visit demonstrated the "innate love and admiration of Canadians for the men who have upheld the prestige of the flag of the Empire." A desire "to pay tribute to 'B-P of Mafeking'" had brought almost every prominent business and professional man in the city to the Canadian Club's luncheon at which, it was claimed, "memories were revived of the roar of jubilation which went up throughout the entire British Empire when the relief of Mafeking was announced."[23]

Baden-Powell's reception in Toronto, where he opened the 1910 Canadian National Exhibition, was particularly important in generating widespread publicity for the Boy Scout movement. Troops from across Ontario flocked to the provincial capital to camp on the Exhibition grounds and be reviewed by the "Hero of Mafeking." The Chief Scout's grand review of over two thousand Boy Scouts was seen both as "a wonderful incentive to the growth of the organization" and as "a demonstration of boy patriotism that [would] stir the heart of every British subject."[24]

The performance of the troop of British Scouts that visited Canada at the same time as Baden-Powell added to the interest in Scouting. The sixteen members of the Wolf and Beaver patrols who had competed for the privilege of accompanying Baden-Powell to Canada gave Scouting demonstrations while aboard the *Empress of Ireland* and in the towns and cities they visited between Quebec City and Banff. Their skills and demeanour brought Scouting favourable publicity and taught Canadian Boy Scout leaders much about the movement.[25] In Cochrane, Alberta, for example, the local newspaper remarked on "their good set up and bearing, and their quiet and courteous manners," as well as their eagerness to move on to their camping ground in Grand Valley. Formed up around their transport wagon after an early lunch, the British Scouts reportedly arrived at camp "between five and six o'clock in good shape after their walk."[26] In Toronto the British Scouts joined their Canadian brothers in camp on the Exhibition grounds, where they took part in Scout demonstrations and in Baden-Powell's review of over two thousand Scouts.

In his report to the Boy Scout movement's Imperial Headquarters in Britain on his 1910 tour, Baden-Powell began by paying tribute to Earl Grey's initiative and "personal interest in the movement," which had given Canada a dominion council prior to his arrival. Baden-Powell's task, therefore, had been to explain the movement to the public and this he had done with the help of the Canadian Club, "a patriotic Association with a branch in almost every city." Although "shortness of time" and "long distances" had prevented him from visiting as many centres as he would have liked, Baden-Powell reported that he had left Canada convinced that "the leading educational, religious, military and business authorities [were] very sympathetic" to the Boy Scout movement and that there would be "a rapid development of the movement in each Province."[27] There is evidence that Baden-Powell's first Canadian tour did indeed stimulate both the creation of new Boy Scout troops in many communities and efforts to expand Scouting's organizational structure. On the organizational front, the dominion council's honorary secretary, Capt. Birdwhistle, travelled across the country in 1911 helping the lieutenant-governors set up provincial councils everywhere except in Ontario and Quebec, where they already existed.[28] In British Columbia Baden-Powell's visit of August 1910 led directly to Rev. T.R. Heneage's appointment as provincial organizer and to Lt. Col. J.H. Hall's agreement to serve as provincial commissioner. According to his own account, Heneage subsequently resigned his parish and gave all his "time to organizing the Scout Movement in B.C. (unpaid)." Interest in the movement was so great that troops were founded "here, there and everywhere."[29]

In British Columbia, as elsewhere, the increased interest in Boy Scouts generated by Baden-Powell's tour put great pressure on the movement's Canadian organizers, who faced mounting demands for help in the establishment of troops whose survival they could not always ensure. Following the Chief Scout's visit to Calgary, Scout leaders there were asked to send representatives to various parts of the province and even to eastern British Columbia to assist with the setting up of Scouting troops.[30] In Ontario, the home of more than half of Canada's pre-war Scouts, the movement mushroomed in 1911 and more than a hundred troops were founded in small villages as well as in major urban centres across the province.[31] The Chief Scout's South African connections contributed directly to the expansion of the Boy Scout movement. When his train passed through Red Deer, Alberta, in 1910, the chief of police, George Rothnie, who had served under Baden-Powell in South Africa, accompanied by A.R. Gibson, a school vice-principal, was invited on board to visit his former commander. Baden-Powell's encouragement led to the immediate creation of two Boy Scout troops with three patrols.[32]

Scouting in Canada received another boost in 1911 when a Canadian contingent was sent to be part of Boy Scout activities planned around George V's coronation.[33] In spite of seemingly insurmountable impediments, several provincial councils managed to make the necessary transportation arrangements, and the dominion council, with the approval of Canada's Chief Scout, Lord Grey, appointed Lt. Col. F. Minden Cole, chairman of the Montreal council, to command the Canadian contingent in England. The contingent included four commissioners, eleven scoutmasters, and 125 Scouts, representing six provinces.[34] Just over one hundred members of the contingent, including the Scouts from Ontario, Quebec, and Saskatchewan, gathered in Montreal and were inspected by the governor general before sailing to England with Lt. Col. Cole. After being greeted by British Scout officials, the Canadian Scouts were taken to Roehampton House, the home of Capt. Arthur Grenfell, who had provided space for a large Scout camp. While the Canadians formed but "an infinitesimal part" of the great camp, a lot of interest was taken in those who had come so far to participate in the post-coronation Scout rally.[35] Just after noon on the appointed day, the Canadians took their place on the parade ground at Windsor Park as part of the 1st Division, numbering about 2,500. In mid-afternoon, after being inspected by King George, about 30,000 Scouts participated in "The Rally." The patrol leaders, followed by the other Scouts, rushed forward, shouting their patrol calls. After running nearly two hundred yards at top speed, the Scouts came to an abrupt halt and remained silent until the bands struck up the Ingonyama Chorus, followed by "Be Prepared" and three cheers for the King. As the monarch took his leave, "some enthusiastic patrols started a cheer for the King" and within seconds the 30,000 Scouts and thousands of spectators "were together raising their voices in honor of His Majesty."[36] This unprogrammed finale was an appropriate end to an event that Boy Scout organizers had hoped would meld together Scouts throughout the Empire in recognition of their common imperial citizenship.

On the eve of their return to Canada, Baden-Powell expressed his great pleasure at having had Canadian Scouts "in the Old Country on the auspicious occasion of our King's Coronation, and, especially at his public recognition of our Common Brotherhood at the Rally." Commenting on Canada's ability to send such a large and "smart and efficient" contingent, the Chief Scout hoped that they would "carry away with them pleasing recollections of the Motherland, and of the comradeship which their brother-scouts in Great Britain feel towards them."[37] As a parting gift, Baden-Powell sent the Canadian Scouts signed photographs of himself and gave voice to his wish that they would further the spread of the Boy Scout movement and "continue to practice the patriotism, the discipline, and the helpfulness to others" that they had learned as Scouts. In reply, Lt. Col. Cole, the leader of Canada's contingent, assured the Chief Scout that his parting wish to the overseas Scouts would "bear fruit" in the various dominions to which they were returning. Cole singled out the opportunity of "joining with the Scouts from other parts of the Empire" as one of the greatest pleasures of their visit. The weeks they spent together in the Roehampton Camp, he declared, "gave the boys chances of forming friendships which may go a long way towards settling the difficult questions of Imperial unity which the coming generation will be called upon to deal with." Cole concluded by promising that on returning home the members of Canada's contingent would try to convey to their "brother scouts ... our sense of gratitude that we as their representatives have been privileged to participate in events of historic import, not the least of which was the great review at Windsor Park, in which we from overseas joined with our brother scouts of the British Isles in doing honor to our newly crowned Sovereign."[38]

Farewell letters between Capt. Arthur Grenfell and Lt. Col. Cole underline that the organizers of the Boy Scout participation in the celebrations surrounding George V's coronation hoped to use these events to ensure that Scouts throughout the British Empire shared a sense of imperial identity. As the camp at Roehampton broke up, Capt. Grenfell expressed pride at having had "such fine young Britons amongst us and if, as is possible, the future of the Empire is in the hands of the overseas dominions it only remains for the young generation in the Dominion to be determined to play the game for the side and all will be well with the Empire." Lt. Col. Cole, for his part, provided all the Canadian boys with copies of Grenfell's farewell letter to take home and assured their British host that all his kind acts and considerate words had "endeared [him] to everyone of our youthful but representative band," who would, he felt sure, "grow up better men, better citizens – and more loyal subjects of the King if that were possible – for having met you."[39]

The impact of sending this contingent of Canadian Scouts to the coronation spread far beyond the relatively few boys who actually attended.

Communities, large and small, were involved in finding the means to send Canada's representatives, and the press kept everyone well informed about their experiences before, during, and after their trip. Alberta, for example, sent twenty-five Scouts, nine each from Calgary and Edmonton, and the remaining seven from centres throughout the province. The selected Scouts who gathered in Calgary before their departure had on the Sunday a big church parade to the cathedral, headed by the Calgary Citizens' Band. Later the 103rd Regimental Band escorted the boys to the CPR station, where they embarked on "their trip to the Old Country."[40] In Toronto the selection process for the city's "coronation contingent" added to the publicity. In April 1911 scoutmasters from all over the province attended a demonstration at Massey Hall during which Scouts competed to win a place in the coronation contingent. The competition was still going on a month later, and tests were scheduled at Hogg's Hollow for 20 May.[41] The decision to send Canada's Boy Scout contingent to George V's coronation also enabled newspapers across the country to draw attention to the nation's place within the British Empire. In its report on 22 July 1911 entitled "Forty Thousand Boy Scouts Cheering King George," the *Montreal Daily Witness* commented that it was almost impossible to believe that so little time had passed since the first troop of Scouts had been formed in January 1908.[42]

While Scouting enjoyed great popularity in the two years during which Capt. Birdwhistle served as honorary dominion secretary, the movement was suffering reverses by 1912-13. Serious organizational weaknesses had surfaced, and these may well be the reason that none of Canada's provincial councils sent Scouts to the international Boy Scout rally held in England in July 1913.[43] By late September 1913 Capt. Birdwhistle's replacement, Gerald Brown, had to report to the governor general, the Duke of Connaught, that the "machinery of management" had failed to keep up with the demands of the growing movement in Canada.[44] The organization had broken down so completely that some provinces had not even submitted the results of the required annual census of Scouts. The information he did have led Brown to conclude that there had been no growth in total Boy Scout membership during the 1912-13 season. Contending that this stagnation was not due to any loss of support among parents nor to waning interest among boys, Brown argued for the creation of a more efficient Boy Scout organization, especially since the governor general's recent appeal for funds to support the Boy Scout movement had met with great success. With promises of subscriptions amounting to $35,000, hopes for an additional $10,000, and a $15,000 gift from the late Lord Strathcona, the Boy Scout movement was clearly in a position to consider the appointment of a full-time dominion secretary who would be able to assist the provincial councils. In thanking those who had responded to his appeal, the governor general singled out three of Canada's most prominent businessmen, Sir Henry Pellatt, Sir

Edmund Osler, and William Price, each of whom had donated at least $3,000 to the national Scout association. The backing of the country's political and business elite made it possible for Scouting's advocates to set up the organization necessary to capitalize on "widespread sympathy for the movement."[45] The first step in this process, federal incorporation of the Boy Scout movement, was completed in mid-June 1914.

The makeup of the first Canadian general council of the newly incorporated Boy Scout Association read like a who's who of the political, religious, military, and educational elite of the dominion.[46] Each of the council's seventy-four members had a network that would be of immeasurable use in the spread of the Boy Scouts. With this new organization in place there was every reason to expect that there would soon be many more than the 13,565 Scouts counted in the September 1914 census.[47] By 1914, however, the Boy Scout movement faced competition within the Anglo-Canadian Protestant community from CSET, the boys' training program developed in Canada's YMCAs.

Members of Canada's early-twentieth-century YMCAs were drawn largely from the rising numbers of urbanized middle-class Protestant males, and they had a clear sense of the political, religious, and social values that they wanted the nation's Protestant adolescents to share. These young men saw themselves as manly, efficient achievers to whom boys could, and should, look up. The YMCA provided the expanding ranks of male white-collar employees with the recreational and social activities they desired, as well as an opportunity to help mould future leaders for Canada. Younger and less established than the men recruited for leadership positions in the Boy Scout movement, the men who shaped the CSET were convinced that their nation on its own had something unique, and superior, to contribute to the twentieth century.

Based on an image of a liberal democratic Canada in which a homogeneous social order rested firmly on British political institutions and Protestantism, CSET challenged Canada's male adolescents to strive for improvement physically, intellectually, spiritually, and socially. Taylor Statten, Canada's pre-eminent YMCA boys' worker of the early twentieth century, had been developing this fourfold training program for several years before the arrival in Canada of Baden-Powell's Boy Scout movement. Statten's success as a volunteer in boys' work at Toronto's Central YMCA had earned him the appointment as the association's first full-time boys' work secretary in 1905.[48] At this time Canada's rapidly expanding YMCAs remained part of the New York-based North American YMCA. Thus, the growing field of boys' work in the YMCAs in Canada's burgeoning urban centres was linked to developments in the United States. Statten, for example, attended a YMCA Older Boys' Conference in upstate New York during the summer of 1907 and heard the secretary of the Chicago Central YMCA expound on "the four-fold development of boys," and the secretary of a boys' work department in Cleveland explain a system of tests and badges based on the Y triangle.[49] In the following season at Toronto Central, Statten set out to combine the merits he saw in each of these American schemes in a training program that suited Canadian needs. On the organizational level, meanwhile, YMCA resources were increasingly being used to expand the boys' work field. In 1908 the North American YMCA's International Committee acted on a request from the Ontario and Quebec Boys' Work Committee and gave Canada its own boys' work secretary.[50] Arguing that the country's "greatest crop [was] not her wheat, but her boys," Canada's YMCA boys' workers sought to play a pivotal role in meeting the challenge the half-million adolescent boys presented to the nation.[51]

It was in this context that Baden-Powell's Boy Scout scheme was introduced into Canada and YMCAs were called upon to incorporate *Scouting for Boys* into their programming. Many did so, including Toronto's Central YMCA, where Taylor Statten remained boys' work secretary.[52] But, although some YMCAs continued to sponsor Boy Scout troops, the YMCA's boys' work leadership objected to several aspects of Baden-Powell's plan. In particular, they balked at the lack of initiative allowed adult leaders and the boys involved. While they supported many of the methods used in *Scouting for Boys,* the YMCA's boys' work leadership believed that Canada's adolescent males needed a training program that encouraged individual initiative, rather than one that stressed obedience to authority. Moreover, as religious educators, YMCA boys' workers believed that religion had to be an integral part of any training program. This belief and the conviction that Boy Scouting would not provide the leaders Canada needed to fulfil its national and international destiny justified continued development of the YMCA's Canadian-made boys' program. The complex mix of personal, religious, and political reasons behind this decision did not include a rejection of Canada's membership in the British Empire. It did, however, mean that the Boy Scout movement would face competition from a boys' program designed and directed by Canadians.

The YMCA's determination to assume a leadership role in the boys' work movement across Canada is evident in the invitation the YMCA of Ontario and Quebec issued to organizations serving boys – such as Sunday schools, high schools, and Boy Scouts – to send delegates to a boys' work conference in Ottawa over New Year's 1910. As a result of the YMCA's initiative, 433 delegates from thirty-two places met to discuss how to meet the perceived needs of the estimated 270,000 teenaged boys in Ontario and Quebec.[53] Taylor Statten remained at the centre of this effort when he became the YMCA's first provincial boys' work secretary for Ontario and Quebec in March 1911 and after his appointment, the following year, to the position of national boys' work secretary in the recently created Canadian YMCA.[54] Statten arrived to take up his national position armed with the draft of CSET, the first version of which was published in October 1912.[55] The ideas and methods of CSET were international in origin and drew heavily on the latest American and European child development and education theories, as well as on the experiences of lay and clerical boys' workers in Britain and the United States. Over the opening decade of the twentieth century these ideas had been packaged into a training program that its Canadian creators hoped would further Canada's development as a nation distinct from and superior to both Great Britain and the United States.

By the middle of 1913, Canada's national YMCA council had a special subcommittee at work on the development and promotion of CSET.[56] Under the chairmanship of H.H. Love, president of the book publisher W.J. Gage Company, the YMCA's Standard Efficiency Tests Sub-Committee, into which Love had drawn a group of prominent young businessmen, endeavoured to ensure that its boys' work program would be widely adopted, especially by Canada's major Protestant churches. To this end the YMCA took steps to involve these churches in the operation and promotion of CSET.[57] And, as war clouds gathered over Europe in July 1914, Canada's major Protestant churches agreed to join forces with the YMCA in the National Advisory Committee for Cooperation in Boys' Work, a body created to promote the CSET scheme. By the time war broke out, a potentially powerful coalition had been put in place in Canada for the purpose of increasing CSET's influence by making the program acceptable not only to the YMCA but to the nation's Sunday schools and other boys' organizations.[58] While supporting Canada's participation in the imperial war effort, CSET's promoters spent the war years planning how best to attract more of the nation's Protestant boys into their program. Scout memberships of 17,423 by war's end far exceeded CSET's less than 14,000 registrations, but given the latter program's mid-war launch, these statistics suggest that CSET was an attractive option for many Protestants.[59]

CSET was offered to Canadians as a means of transforming the nation's teenagers into well-rounded men who would rise to leadership positions in whatever segment of Canadian society their respective talents led them to specialize. As in Scouts, boys following the fourfold CSET program did so in small groups that came to be called Trail Rangers for those aged twelve to fourteen and Tuxis Squares for boys fifteen to seventeen. Those over eighteen were to be involved in leadership training.[60] In contrast to the top-down nature of the Boy Scout organization, CSET was organized "so as to put the task of self-government progressively in the hands of the boys," and leaders were expected to involve boys in the planning of every aspect of their group's program. Under the guidance of manly Christian mentors, boys enrolled in CSET were to be inspired to become self-motivated and self-regulated adults trained "in the art of directing ... others."[61] The adult creators of CSET, however, determined the content of the scheme's training program. The three-year course on Nation Study prescribed for boys from seventeen to twenty years of age in the 1916 program thus provides insights into CSET leaders' views on Canada's relationship to and role within the British Empire. After a year spent studying "the outstanding needs of Canada in her task of nation-building," CSET boys were given the task of stating their thoughts on "the permanent relationship between the two nations, Canada and India, as parts of the Empire." In the final year of the course they were required to develop a position on what role the nation of Canada would "play in the future of the world."[62] While CSET taught boys about Canada's imperial ties and did not question Canada's continued membership in the British Empire, the requirements of the Nation Study course indicate that its designers expected relations between Canada and other nations within that empire to change and foresaw a day when Canada would play a role on the world stage in its own right.

Under the leadership of Baden-Powell, the epitome of the British World's virtues and glories, the Boy Scout movement helped to perpetuate and popularize a pro-imperial sense of Canadian identity in the years leading up to the outbreak of the First World War. The Chief Scout's ideals, fame, and connections won the movement broad public support and the endorsement of the upper echelons of government, the church, business, and the military. This support, combined with high levels of British immigration in pre-war Canada, contributed to the rapid spread of the Boy Scouts across the country. Ties to Britain and the imperial loyalties of many native-born Canadians provided the Boy Scout movement with an excellent opportunity to teach its brand of imperial citizenship to thousands of the nation's boys in the First World War era. As several of the papers delivered at the British World II conference demonstrated, the work of a number of voluntary associations, including the Boy Scouts, reinforced efforts by Canada's schools to teach the nation's youngsters what it meant to be British and why they should want to remain so. The widespread popularity of Boy Scouts significantly contributed to the persistence of widespread support in Canada of the British World concept well into the twentieth century.[63]

The Scout movement's failure to be endorsed by Canada's emerging class of professional boys' workers and religious educators stemmed from the desire of these evangelical Protestant groups to shape citizenship and leadership training in what they hoped would be "Canada's century." A belief in the central importance of religion in citizenship training and the conviction that they, as evangelical Protestant Canadians, knew best what training the nation's boys needed was behind their decision to reject Scouting in favour of CSET. While they accepted Canada's imperial ties, the men behind CSET set out to produce Canadian leaders who would be capable of ensuring that their nation fulfilled its destiny at home, within the Empire, and on the world stage. The steady growth in the number of Boy Scout troops and CSET groups in the years following the First World War demonstrates that the citizenship training provided by both programs continued to enjoy widespread support among Canadians. After reverses caused by the loss of significant YMCA backing due to that association's postwar financial crisis, CSET enrolments grew dramatically, reaching 28,152 by 1926, closely rivalling Boy Scout registrations of 28,817 for the same year.[64] The persistent popularity of both programs reflects, in part, the ongoing debate over what it meant to be Canadian in the British World.

Notes

1 National Historical Library, YMCA (NHL, YMCA), International Committee Records, file: Canada – Boys' Work Publications, *The Canadian Standard Efficiency Tests for Boys*, proof ed., 1913, 3, and 8th ed., 1916, 76.

2 Scouts Canada Archives, Ottawa (SCA), file: Baden Powell's Tour of Canada – 1910, "THE BOY SCOUT MOVEMENT, An address delivered in Toronto by Lieut.-General Sir R.S.S. Baden-Powell, at a joint special meeting of the Canadian and Empire Clubs – with Mr. J.F. MacKay, President of the Canadian Club, in the Chair – on August 31st, 1910."

3 For a discussion of the meaning of the British World concept and of the relationship between loyalty to the Empire and to one of the member nations, see Carl Bridge and Kent Fedorowich, "Mapping the British World," *Journal of Imperial and Commonwealth History* 31 (2003): 1-15, and Phillip Buckner and Carl Bridge, "Reinventing the British World," *Round Table* 368 (2003): 77-88.

4 Simon J. Potter, "Communication and Integration: The British and Dominions Press and the British World, c. 1876-1914," *Journal of Imperial and Commonwealth History* 31 (2003): 190-92, 199.

5 Bridge and Fedorowich, "Mapping the British World," 6, and Buckner and Bridge, "Reinventing the British World," 79-81.

6 SCA, file: Letters from and to John Stiles re Early Days of Scouting in Canada, 1908-1914, George Matheson Murray, MP, Cariboo, in an article on early days of Scouting in Canada. See also R.H. MacDonald, *Sons of the Empire: The Frontier and the Boy Scout Movement, 1890-1918* (Toronto: University of Toronto Press, 1993), 193-95; Bridge and Fedorowich, "Mapping the British World," 3-6; Potter, "Communication and Integration: The British and Dominions Press and the British World, c.1876-1914," 191.

7 SCA, file: Letters from and to John Stiles re Early Days of Scouting in Canada, 1908-1914, Taylor Statten to John Stiles, 14 November 1951.

8 Ontario Scout Council Records, Toronto (OSCR), "'The Boy Scout Movement,' Issued by Authority of the Publication Committee, Toronto Scout Council and Prepared by Frederick Tod, Joint Secretary and Warrant Scout Master," n.d.

9 *Ottawa Evening Journal*, 1 October 1910.

10 SCA, file: Origins and Early Years of Boy Scouts, Alberta, "The Early History of Scouting in Calgary, by Mr. E.V. Spiller, as told to Mr. J. Scott," Calgary, 2 February 1953. Mr. Spiller, who was seventy-four at the time of this interview, was honorary district commissioner and had been present at the beginning of Scouting in Calgary. According to Mr. Spiller, the committee that brought Scouting to Calgary was composed of Rev. C.W.E. Horne, Maj. De Cann, and misters Jewitt, Clarke, Hole, Northcott, and himself.

11 Ibid. See also Bridge and Fedorowich, "Mapping the British World," 3-6.

12 SCA, file: Letters from and to John Stiles re Early Days of Scouting in Canada, 1908-1914, J.B. Hardinge to John Stiles, 19 June 1953; F.B. Hathaway to John Stiles, 22 December 1952, identified Lt. Col. J.B. Hardinge as the current president of the Dunbar-Point Grey Area Scout Council.

13 Ibid., the Rev. and Hon. T.R. Heneage to John Stiles, 6 January 1953.

14   SCA, file: John Stiles Notebook, Copy of a Letter from Government House, Ottawa, re Headquarters' Council for Canada, Boy Scouts, 12 March 1910.

15   *Ottawa Citizen,* 13 October 1953. In an article on Col. John Birtwhistle, who had recently died, it was noted that at the request of the governor general, Earl Grey, and Col. Sir Percy Sherwood, he had served as honorary secretary of the Dominion Scouting Association for two years. After retiring from this position in 1912, Col. Birtwhistle remained on the council of the Boy Scout association and was the movement's longest-serving member in Canada. (The spelling of Col. Birtwhistle's name was changed from Birdwhistle sometime after he served as honorary Dominion secretary of the first Canadian Boy Scout Association.)

16   Library and Archives Canada (LAC), MG 28 I73, Boy Scouts of Canada Records, vol. 14, file 1, Minutes of Canadian General Council, First General Meeting, 31 October 1914, Report of the Acting Secretary, Gerald Brown. See also SCA, file: Letters from and to John Stiles, 1951, re Early Days of Scouting in Canada, 1908-1914, copy of John Stiles to Col. R.J. Birtwhistle, 18 October 1951, setting out Birtwhistle's answers to Stiles' questions in an interview the previous day and asking for any corrections.

17   SCA, file: Baden-Powell's Tour of Canada – 1910, "THE BOY SCOUT MOVEMENT, An address delivered in Toronto by Lieut.-General Sir R.S.S. Baden-Powell, at a joint special meeting of the Canadian and Empire Clubs – with Mr. J.F. MacKay, President of the Canadian Club, in the chair – on August 31st, 1910."

18   *Victoria Daily Times,* 12 August 1910.

19   SCA, scrapbook #2, 1909-10, Baden-Powell's Canadian Tour, untitled newspaper clipping labelled Vancouver, British Columbia, 15 August 1910.

20   Ibid., file: Origins and Early Years of Boy Scouts, Alberta, "The early history of Scouting in Calgary, by Mr. E.V. Spiller as told to Mr. J. Scott," 2 February 1953. See also *Calgary Daily Herald,* 24 August 1910.

21   *Calgary Daily Herald,* 24 August 1910.

22   *Edmonton Daily Bulletin,* 22 August 1910.

23   *Manitoba Free Press,* 27 August 1910.

24   SCA, scrapbook #2, 1909-10, Baden-Powell's Canadian Tour, untitled, undated newspaper clipping from Baden-Powell's scrapbook of his 1910 tour of Canada. See also *Toronto Daily Star,* 30 August 1910, and *Toronto Star Weekly,* 3 September 1910.

25   SCA, file: Origins and Early Years of Boy Scouts, Alberta, "The Early History of Scouting in Calgary by Mr. E.V. Spiller as told to Mr. J. Scott," 2 February 1953.

26   SCA, file: Letters from and to John Stiles re Early Days of Scouting in Canada, 1908-1914. The collection of clippings sent in by Frank Helmn, a member of the British Scout contingent that accompanied Baden-Powell to Canada in 1910 included an undated excerpt from the local newspaper in Cochrane, Alberta, describing the visit of the British Scouts.

27   SCA, file: Baden-Powell's Tour of Canada, 1910, Baden-Powell, "The Boy Scout Movement in Canada," extract from the annual report of the Boy Scouts Association for 1911.

28   SCA, file: Letters from and to John Stiles re Early Days of Scouting in Canada, 1908-1914, John Stiles to Colonel Birtwhistle, 16 October 1951.

29   Ibid., the Rev. and Hon. T.R. Heneage to John Stiles, 6 January 1953.

30   SCA, file: Origins and Early Years of Boy Scouts, Alberta, "The Early History of Scouting in Calgary by Mr. E.V. Spiller as told to Mr. J. Scott," 2 February 1953.

31   OSCR, file: Boy Scouts, Province of Ontario, Early Records of Registration. There were approximately 109 troops with registration dates in 1911, compared to 27 in 1912, 20 in 1913, and 22 in 1914. See also LAC, MG 28 I73, Boy Scouts of Canada Records, vol. 14, file 1, Minutes of Canadian General Council, 1914-20, "Minutes of the Second Meeting of the Executive Committee, 12 December 1914." The census at the end of September 1914 indicated that there were 13,565 Scouts in Canada, of whom 6,979 were in Ontario.

32   SCA, file: Letters from and to John Stiles re Early Days of Scouting in Canada, 1908-1914. A.R. Gibson, retired school inspector, to John Stiles, n.d.

33   SCA, file: Reports re Boy Scout Contingent to the Coronation, June and July 1911, "Report of the Officer Commanding the Canadian Boy Scouts' Contingent to England, 1911, Introductory Remarks by Gerald H. Brown, Hon. Secretary Dominion Council."

34 Ibid., List of Members of the Canadian Contingent. All but two members of the Canadian Contingent came from four provinces, Ontario (fifty-nine), Quebec (twelve), Saskatchewan (thirty-three), and Alberta (twenty-six); only two Scouts from Manitoba went, and British Columbia's representation consisted of one scoutmaster.

35 Ibid., "Reports re Boy Scout Contingent," 22. By the eve of the rally, the overseas contingent numbered 160 with the addition of Scoutmaster Bramble and his seven Gibraltar Scouts.

36 Ibid.

37 Ibid., copy of letter from Sir Robert Baden-Powell to Lieutenant Colonel Cole, 11 July 1911.

38 Ibid., copy of letter from Lt. Col. Cole to Sir Robert (Baden-Powell), 19 July 1911.

39 Ibid., copy of letters from Capt. Arthur M. Grenfell to Lieutenant Colonel Cole, 7 July 1911, and Lt. Col. Cole to Captain Grenfell, 15 July 1911.

40 SCA, file: Origins and Early Years of Boy Scouts, Alberta, "The Early History of Scouting in Calgary by Mr. E.V. Spiller as told to Mr. J. Scott," 2 February 1953.

41 SCA, scrapbook #.1, 1911, undated clipping. "A Nation in Miniature. Of Boys, for Boys, by Boys," and C.J. Atkinson, chairman, examining board, to A. Jarvis, 2nd Toronto Troop, Baden-Powell Boy Scouts, 16 May 1911.

42 Ibid., *Montreal Daily Witness*, 22 July 1911.

43 SCA, file: Extracts from Minute Books Furnished by the Quebec Provincial Council, "Minutes, Quebec Provincial Council, April 15th, 1913 and May 14th, 1913."

44 LAC, MG 28 I73, Boy Scouts of Canada Records, vol. 12, Canadian Boy Scout History, 1914, Minutes of the Annual Meeting of the Dominion Council, 27 February 1914, report submitted by Gerald Brown, honorary secretary, Dominion Council, to Field Marshal His Royal Highness the Duke of Connaught, Chief Scout, Canadian Boy Scouts, Ottawa.

45 Ibid., Address by the Chief Scout, His Royal Highness the Duke of Connaught.

46 Ibid., vol. 14, file 1, Minutes of the Canadian General Council, 1914-1920; Minutes of the First Meeting of the Elected Executive Committee, Dominion Council, Canadian Boy Scouts, 31 October 1914.

47 Ibid., Minutes of the Second Meeting of the Executive Committee, 12 December 1914.

48 C.A.M. Edwards, *Taylor Statten: A Biography* (Toronto: Ryerson Press, 1960), 24-27, 43-44.

49 Bibliothèque, Comité Universel Chrétien de Jeunes Gens, Genève. Pamphlet 21246, "Young Men's Christian Association: Boy's [sic] Work in Canada – May 1923," n.d., 2.

50 LAC, MG 28 I75, YMCA of Canada Records, vol. 299, YMCAs of Ontario and Quebec, Provincial Committee Minutes: Advisory Committee Minutes, 7 November 1907; and NHL, YMCA, New York, International Committee Records, file: Boys' Work History: pamphlet, "Leadership for the Boys' Work of Canada."

51 NHL, YMCA, International Committee Records, file: Boys' Work History: pamphlet, "Leadership for the Boys' Work of Canada"; F.H.T. Ritchie, "A Challenge to a Christian Nation," *Association Boys* 9, 5 (October 1910): 176-80.

52 SCA, file: Letters to and from John Stiles re Early Days of Scouting in Canada, 1908-1914, Taylor Statten to John Stiles, 14 November 1951.

53 NHL, YMCA, International Committee Records, file: Canada – Boys' Work Publications: Report/Proceedings, Fifth Annual Boys' Work Conference of the Provinces of Ontario and Quebec ... Under the Auspices of the Ontario Sunday School Association and the Ontario and Quebec Provincial Committee of the YMCA, 55.

54 LAC, MG 28 I75, YMCA of Canada Records, vol. 47, minutes, Ontario and Quebec Executive Committee, 23 March 1911.

55 Edwards, *Taylor Statten*, 47.

56 LAC, MG 28 I75, YMCA of Canada Records, vol. 234, minutes, National Council Executive Committee, 3 July 1913.

57 United Church Archives, Toronto (UCA), National Advisory Committee for Cooperation in Boys' Work, 1914-1915, Minutes of Conference of Representatives of Provincial Sunday School Associations, Denominational Sunday School Committees with the Boys' Work Committee of the National Council Young Men's Christian Association, 13 May 1914.

58 Ibid., minutes, 10 July 1914.

59 SCA, Annual Report of the Executive Committee of the Canadian General Council of the Boy Scout Association, for the Period Ending 31 December 1918, "Comparative Census Returns, Boy Scouts 1914-1918," 3; D. MacLeod, "'A Live Vaccine': The YMCA and Male Adolescence in the United States and Canada, 1870-1920," *Social History* 11, 2 (May 1978): 22, where CSET membership for 1919 is reported to have been 13,421.

60 NHL, YMCA, International Committee Records, file: Canada – Boys' Work Publications: *The Canadian Standard Efficiency Training for Trail Rangers and Tuxis Boys,* Committee on Canadian Standard Efficiency Training, Toronto, 1918, vi, vii.

61 Ibid., file: Canadian YMCA, Canada, National Council, Maj. Wallace Forgie, *Comrades to Canadian Boys and the Four Square Program,* Canadian Citizenship Series #9, Military Service Department, 3.

62 Ibid., file: Canada – Boys' Work Publications: *The Canadian Standard Efficiency Tests for Boys,* 8th ed., Committee on Canadian Standard Efficiency Training, Toronto, 1916, 76.

63 For an analysis of the longevity of the imperial Canadian identity, see Phillip Buckner, "The Long Goodbye: Canadians and the British Connection" in *Redefining the British World,* ed. Phillip Buckner and R. Douglas Francis (Calgary: University of Calgary Press, 2005).

64 LAC, MG 28 I327, National Boys' Work Board Records, Minutes of the Annual Meeting, the National Boys' Work Board, March 1926, Statistical Report by Provinces: As at April 1st, 1923; 1924; 1925; 1926; SCA, Annual Reports of the Canadian General Council of the Boy Scouts Association, Annual Report for the year ending 31 December 1926, Comparative Statement of Census Returns, 1914-1926.

8

Part of the British Empire, Too: French Canada and Colonization Propaganda
Serge Courville

"If the French Canadians wish to survive in North America, they must imitate the English ... that nation of small shopkeepers who dared to face Napoleon," wrote Étienne Parent in the 1840s.[1] Parent was not the first French Canadian intellectual of his time – nor would he be the last – to admire the British. Many did so, claiming that there was nothing greater than to be both part of Canada and part of the most powerful empire in the world. As the French Canadian clerico-nationalist Antoine Labelle stated in 1880: "Because God placed us here in the cherished country of Canada, in the British Empire, He made it our land to live in."[2] How were such laudatory comments possible in nineteenth-century Quebec, given our present understanding of French Canadian nationalism?

To address this issue, one has to question the nature of colonization propaganda in Quebec, and compare it with contemporary ideas on emigration and colonization, not only in Canada but in the rest of the British Empire. This can be done using diverse sources. One such source is the numerous brochures, emigrants' guides, immigrants' manuals, and other writings that were published throughout the century in Quebec and in the British Empire, as well as in the United States, to convince the emigrant to come and settle in the areas recently opened to colonization. Although this documentation is well known to national scholars, few have seen its content in the light of a comparative study.

From 1815 to 1930, between 50 and 60 million Europeans, probably more, left their native land for the European colonies overseas, hoping for a better life, as promised by every propagandist of the period. This fever was not specific to Europe. Even in the New World there was such a movement. More than 2.3 million people left Canada for the United States between 1870 and 1930. From Quebec, more than 720,000 people immigrated to the United States during the same period.[3] This exodus posed a major threat to the French Canadian national identity. In the late nineteenth century, many French Canadian intellectuals thought that Quebec would lose its political weight and place in the Canadian Confederation because of this large French Canadian outmigration from the province.[4] Moreover, because Manitoba and Ontario had just gained part of the northern lands that had once belonged to the Hudson Bay's Company, the French Canadian elite believed that the province also should extend its jurisdiction to the north, by colonizing the Laurentian Plateau, where some valleys offered good potential for agriculture. Colonization would sustain and improve the economy of the south and create new opportunities for the people who were shifting from agriculture to other sectors of activity, or leaving for the cities or, worse, for the United States.

Hence the idea came about of launching large colonization programs supported by propaganda in order to convince the farmers, the unemployed, and even the European emigrant to move to the new colonization regions. According to most clerical and political leaders, these programs would be the best means of increasing the population in the province and bringing to Quebec respect and revenue. Since this was a time of free trade and economic laissez-faire, it was the Catholic Church that had to become the leading institution in these projects, helped by the local colonization societies. As for the government of Quebec, it would be responsible only for surveying the townships and building roads and railroads with the help of private companies. Only in the last decades of the nineteenth century did the government itself get involved in these projects, under pressure from the Catholic Church and its colonization allies.

To most scholars, the colonization propaganda in Quebec was a reactionary discourse, aiming to create in the mountainous plateaus of the province a semi-feudal and theocratic society living apart from capitalist America. Well governed by its priests and political elite, this society would be agricultural, remaining French and Catholic. In reaction to such an interpretation, other scholars argued that the propaganda was a variation of the American Dream, full of the same utopian promises of success and happiness told of the American West.[5] Were not the Laurentians "Our true California?" many French Canadian propagandists asked potential colonists.[6] The problem with these theories is that they do not adequately take into account the place Quebec held both in Canada and, more generally, in the British Empire.

This is not to deny French or American influences on Quebec; numerous examples prove such influences were important.[7] Nor is it to deny the power of attraction of the United States, since there was a strong French Canadian immigration movement to that country.[8] However, it would be an error to believe that Quebec somehow evolved apart from the rest of the British Empire. On the contrary, because the province was part of Canada, it had numerous relationships with Britain (financial, commercial, institutional). Moreover, the common references in political economy and colonization were British – a fact not only true in Canada but in the United States and continental Europe, including France, where theorists like A. Bordier frequently referred to British authors in their works.[9] British ideas therefore played an undeniable role in defining the French Canadian colonization propaganda.

However, as the English were said to be responsible for the Conquest (1759-60), the failure of the 1837-38 Rebellions and, through their Canadian heirs, the hanging of Louis Riel (1885), it was through subtle processes that these ideas came to Quebec. Many came through the writings of the French Canadian propagandists themselves, who learned about the themes and rhetoric of the colonization propaganda by reading Canadian and British brochures while working for the Canadian Department of Immigration. Among these propagandists were Father J.B. Proulx and Stanislas Drapeau, both of whom would later become active colonization propagandists in Quebec, along with Antoine Labelle, a nationalist priest who already was promoting the Laurentians north and west of Montreal, and who eventually became an emigration agent for Canada in Europe.[10]

Like their Canadian counterparts, the Quebec propagandists presented the land to be colonized as the best "poor man's country," worthy of immigrants capable of farming. At the same time, the French Canadian propagandists called for immigrants with some financial means, and made special appeals to capitalists, seeking to attract the necessary capital to develop mining and forestry in order to assist the colonists in gaining some money for their own establishments. The Quebec propagandists also promoted the building of railroads as a means of accelerating colonization and attracting European emigrants, and, like English Canadian nationalists, they vigorously condemned immigration to the United States. To counteract this movement, the French Canadian propagandists emphasized the low price of land in Quebec, the government services available, the help given by colonization societies in the province, the presence of agronomists and agricultural societies, the possibilities of finding work, and the close proximity of urban markets in which to sell agricultural surpluses. As to the suitability of northern land for colonization, the Quebec propagandists echoed the Canadian Pacific experiments on the Prairies and the Ontario propagandists on behalf of New Ontario, claiming the land was as fit for agriculture as that in the southern climes of the province.[11]

As a wide reading of the propaganda literature reveals, even the idea of launching interior colonization programs directed by the Church and state was not original to Quebec. It was inspired by the British home colonization propaganda, which came to Britain by way of Holland and Java, where the Dutch general Van den Bosch learned new agricultural techniques from Chinese immigrants living near his plantation. Impressed by the yields the

Chinese immigrants were obtaining on their small tracks of land, he asked them to join his staff. The changes they wrought were so efficient that, when the general's plantation was sold, he netted a profit of over 600 percent on his initial investment.[12] Back in Holland, Van den Bosch became active in creating inner colonies for the poor on the marginal lands of the kingdom, where small agriculture could feed hundreds of people. From Holland, the idea quickly reached Britain, where philanthropist organizations began promoting such colonies as a national remedy to poverty.[13] Even the Church of England engaged in the movement, planning the creation of self-sufficient villages in which hundreds of poor families could be established in cottages specially built for them on heretofore marginal lands that would be worked in common.[14]

In the New World, this plan took a different path, one that can be traced through its influence on the utopian projects of New Harmony, founded by Robert Owen on the Wabash River in Indiana, and the community of Icarie, created by Étienne Cabet at Nauvoo in Illinois, and in the practices of certain speculators (for example, Morris Birkbeck in Illinois) and some land companies that built houses and cleared land for emigrants (for example, the Holland Land Company in the United States and the Canada Land Company in Upper Canada). However, most of the utopian projects ended in a forlorn state, being replaced by the idea of a more systematic approach to Church and state aid for emigrants. This was the case with J.F. Boyd, who suggested in 1883 a program that could bring some two hundred thousand British emigrants on lands set aside by the Canadian government for its British counterpart in the great Canadian North-West. Most would be poor families that would be obliged to repay the British government after their successful re-establishment.[15] Ultimately, the project did not work, but it tells us much about British imperialism in the late nineteenth century.

As for Quebec, it would engage in a similar form of internal colonization. But, as in Great Britain, it would allow the initiative to pass to private interests, specifically the Catholic Church and the colonization societies. Launched in the last quarter of the nineteenth century, the internal colonization projects would transform the Laurentian Plateau into "colonies" of southern Quebec. To these colonies would go the redundant population of the St. Lawrence lowlands, although, ironically, demographical pressure was actually lowering at this time in the valley.[16] In return, from these colonies would come the raw materials needed by the growing urban centres and markets of the St. Lawrence valley. In that function, the French Canadian colonies actually had much in common with the British overseas colonies. However, being internal colonies, the French Canadian colonies were never granted a regional autonomy sufficient to manage their own affairs. Not until the 1930s would the Quebec government take a more supportive role in colonization, using the themes and arguments of earlier propagandists.[17]

Finally, even the Quebec government tried to attract British emigrants.[18] To oppose the federal propaganda and that of the Canadian Pacific Railway on behalf of Manitoba and the Canadian North-West, and not merely as a reaction to the drawing power of the American West, as is often thought, the Quebec propagandists promoted certain areas of the Laurentian Plateau. Some of these areas, such as the Ottawa Valley, became "Our Grand Provincial North-West";[19] others, such as Lake St. John, "The Great North-East of Canada."[20] In these cases, inspiration came from Ontario and the Atlantic provinces, also struggling against western propaganda, which diverted numerous colonists away from eastern Canada. This competition was not particular to Quebec or Canada. In the United States, New England had similar problems.[21] As for the southern states, they too tried to persuade the railway companies to divert the newcomers away from northern and western destinations in order to bring them to the South.[22] In other words, similar problems called for analogous responses, except that in Quebec the reference was the Canadian Prairies, and for the southern states, it was the promised lands of Oregon and California.

All these facts suggest that, if there were different ways to present colonization in the nineteenth century, there was only one general matrix around which elements could be arranged according to time, place, and prospective readership. The attributes of this discourse remained sufficiently similar so that most can be traced back to the same origin and sources. In other words, external elements of colonization propaganda permeated the local colonization literature everywhere that open land, people, and colonization ambitions were present. In this light, it is much easier to explain the strong presence of British ideas in Quebec, besides those of English Canada, United States, and France: it was due to the power of British propaganda, which was everywhere influential. This can be easily seen in the guiding principles of the emigrants' guides, immigrants' manuals, and other propaganda brochures that were published in the nineteenth and early twentieth centuries to bring people to the New World, and was the same philosophy that filled the treatises periodically published after 1840. No matter the author or the place of publication, in Europe or in the New World, all emphasized the same theories and proposals about emigration and colonization, some of which were defined as early as the sixteenth and seventeenth centuries.

Although Britain entered into the colonization process later than other European countries, it engaged rapidly in the project, thanks to the writings of its explorers, cartographers, and theoreticians who made early Spanish discoveries known in England, and who were sometimes part of the French Huguenot expeditions overseas.[23] The main contribution of these individuals, however, was less to promote active colonization, which they did with great enthusiasm, than to define its principles. They created a literature of action and persuasion whose goal was to present in simple terms the details of New World expeditions, and the necessary arguments to promote emigration and colonization.

Howard Mumford Jones provided a considerable analysis of this literature, whose rationale can be summarized in five main thrusts.[24] The first argued that England had a providential mission, that of bringing God and civilization to the unknown and still heathen segments of humanity revealed by the Great Discoveries. The second theme emphasized the manifest destiny of the English "race" to grasp the riches God had placed on earth and make them accessible to other nations through commerce and trade. The third thrust provided virtuous and patriotic attributes to emigration and colonization, arguing that these projects could be carried out only by men of honour who would find therein happiness, fame, and glory. The fourth argument promised that the founding of colonies would be a means of alleviating poverty and vagrancy, as well as religious tensions at home, and of helping ordinary men to rear their families. The fifth thrust morally justified the taking of "unoccupied" lands and making commerce with nomadic Indians, who only "passed" over the land. All these initiatives would bring the motherland respect and increased revenues. Hence the repeated appeals to the wealthy segment of English society, including the merchant class, and the interminable lists of trees, fruits, animals, and minerals that were often added to these writings – and the ubiquitous promises of success, which served as a means to fight the negative rumours about the colonies and prove that colonization was a profitable endeavour, worthy of state protection.

The arguments of the seventeenth- and eighteenth-century French propagandists were similar, concerning themselves with the riches of the New World, the need to curb Spanish expansion, and the benefits of colonization for emigrant, seigneur, and king. They too insisted on the virtuousness of colonization, asking for men of good character, hard workers confident in God and the future. However, when France finally succeeded in establishing a durable colony in the St. Lawrence valley, the English colonies were already significantly peopled.[25]

From the debut of European colonization until the nineteenth century, the discourse of colonization changed little over the course of nearly two hundred years. It was only after 1815, and more specifically after 1830, that it became increasingly systematic and heavily influenced by late-eighteenth-century and early-nineteenth-century economic theories. These theories lent significant weight to those who viewed emigration as a solution to the problems of poverty and unemployment created by unheralded population growth and cyclical economic crises. Thanks to the departure of emigrants, most propagandists argued, it was possible to maintain the existing social order while constructing a new economy. Furthermore, they began to associate human happiness with free trade, a positive morale, scientific discoveries, and British values and traditions. Such conditions could be best maintained, they continued, through the creation of markets and trading partners – in this case the new colonies. And, since the mass movement of thousands of emigrants was in itself a market in need of many services, propagandists enthusiastically tried to convince the population to emigrate.

Along with those active in lobbying Parliament and British society about the benefits of colonizing emigration was a rising group of theorists who supported a scientific approach to emigration, based on new understandings about free trade and economic laissez-faire. One of the most passionate supporters of this stance was Edward Gibbon Wakefield, who, it is said, greatly influenced British emigration and colonization policies in the nineteenth century. Although his role has been somewhat exaggerated,[26] Wakefield did significantly influence colonization propagandists, who used his ideas to promote their own goals.

Wakefield's views were made known to the public in the 1820s, and were formalized by the 1830s in a series of writings emphasizing the idea that successful colonization policies must balance the weight of three interrelated factors: land, capital, and employment.[27] His ideas were praised by all those who sought systematic programs of emigration and colonization. These new propagandists did much to promulgate the concept of a promised land, wherever Britain was establishing new settlements. At the same time, they revived the sixteenth- and seventeenth-century themes of virtue, fame, glory, providential mission, and manifest destiny, and applied them to the ordinary man. They then grafted those themes with the new Victorian celebration of scientific progress and morality, the republican ideals of liberty and independence, and the new economic theories relating to happiness through free trade and prosperity.

In doing so, the propagandists couched these complex and often competing themes in religious, moral, or philanthropic undertones (ubiquity of the human race, evangelization, obligations toward the poor, the youth and the family, virtue, fame, and sense of duty). They also supplied a steady stream of material that played on the adventurous dreams of the emigrant, promising vast fertile areas of land where all the benefits of British civilization and society would be recreated from the wilderness (sense of honour, respect of the law, religious worship, and community life). This recreation of British society was important, and propagandists continually emphasized this when counselling and trying to persuade emigrants to avoid the United States – where more than half (and soon 70 percent) of those who embarked from British ports were emigrating[28] – and instead go to the British colonies where they would contribute to the strength and expansion of the Empire and British civilization. "Greater England, but England all the same," wrote a distinguished Cambridge professor. "Greater Britain, but Britain all the same," most British propagandists would soon repeat on the prompting of Sir Charles Dilke.[29]

These themes and arguments greatly influenced the propagandists of the New World, as revealed in their own promotional literature. For example, despite local particularities, most colonial propagandists continued to favour science and agriculture without neglecting commerce and industry. They presented colonization as beneficial to the emigrant, the dominion, and the motherland, and promised that, by coming to the colonies, British capitalists would gain access to new markets and useful economic resources. As for the riches of these colonies, they were everywhere alike. All colonial propagandists promoted the quality of the land (fertile soil, good for cereals, hay, vegetables, and even fruits), the suitability of the climate for human health (seen as a factor of longevity), the diversity of the natural resources (namely gold, silver, iron, and coal, and, in many places, other useful minerals and forests), the "civilization" and the security of the country, which was always well developed, well policed, and where Natives were peaceful and well controlled by missionaries. These advantages, according to the colonial propagandists, made the New World a perfect destination for the European capitalists and emigrants. Even in the early-nineteenth-century United States, where colonization was still dominated by British interests and propaganda, American propagandists valued the same issues, portraying the rich states of the Northeast as the metropolis of the still undeveloped western hinterlands.[30]

One of the reasons for this mimetic behaviour is that most colonial propagandists were themselves British-born or of British culture. In addition, most were writing with their British fellow citizens in mind. Furthermore, many published their brochures in Britain, where they had to adopt a presentation style familiar to their readers. Even when they were from a non-British origin – French or American, for example – such propagandists often could not escape the permeating influence of the British propagandists, for whom some non-British colonials even worked. In the end, all came to adopt a similar discourse, proclaiming their sincerity and disinterest, and trying to dissipate any negative rumours previously said about their colony.

Because the attraction of the United States was so powerful, competition to lure prospective colonists was everywhere vigorous. Another reason for this competition was that only the southern colonies (in Australia, New Zealand, and South Africa) benefited from state-aided programs. Since Canada was closer to the British Isles, most initiatives were left to local governments and land or transportation companies, hence the numerous brochures published in the Canadian colonies, in comparison with the other British colonies.

As a consequence of this competition, all colonization areas were presented as a second Eden, equal to any other country but without their faults.[31] For example, if the Canadian Prairies were "gently undulated," Quebec's Laurentian Plateau was no less so; if Australia was in some places a "desert," there was no fog as in England; in Georgia and in Quebec's Eastern Townships, the temperature was comparable to that of southern France; in Texas, one was reminded of Italy. And to those who believed that the hot summers of Australia, the United States, and South Africa were unsuitable to the British and European constitution, or that it brought fevers, others answered that the colonies were much more diversified than that. For while it was true that some places could be hot and humid, other nearby places had air perfectly fit for persons suffering from lung diseases. As for the Canadian winter, it was invigorating. Of course, it was true that near Quebec the air was rigorous, but according to Charles F. Grece, "the mother country has adopted [Quebec City] for the seat of government; which, most assuredly, would not have been the case, had the winters been as severe as some interested writers have asserted."[32]

In this context, time delays were of no importance. As the colonization discourse followed the pioneer front into the interior, it happened that some themes became more popular with the progress of colonization or the arrival of the first land speculators. One can find numerous examples of this process in the propaganda brochures. For example, numerous were the nineteenth-century propagandists who portrayed the English countryside as a garden. This garden theme appeared as early as the turn of the nineteenth century in Canada, in the 1840s in central United States, and at the end of the nineteenth and the beginning of the twentieth centuries in Australasia, South Africa, and French Canada. The same use was made of the word "granary" for good wheat and grain-producing regions. One can trace its use back to the 1840s in the Upper Mississippi Valley, in the 1880s in the Canadian Prairies, and in the early twentieth century to describe the Lac-Saint-Jean area of Quebec, which was presented as the great granary of eastern Canada. Numerous also were the authors who made reference to fruit culture, especially the melon, to prove the quality of the soil and the climate either in the United States, the British colonies, or northern Quebec. Finally, most if not all propagandists praised the noble and patriotic character of those immigrating to a British colony. As many repeated, it was only by valuing the ideals and institutions of the motherland, and by keeping faith in progress and the future, that the emigrant would build the New World. Betraying this obligation would result in failure or, worse, degeneration and rejection – hence the high personal qualities requested from emigrants, who were expected to remain loyal to the Crown. In the United States this theme would be modified to upholding the honour of the constitution;

later, in French Canada, emigrants would be reminded of their patriotic duty to pre-Revolutionary Catholic and civilizing France.

In other words, the references and geopolitical context could change from place to place, but the principles of allegiance remained the same. This explains why the French Canadian colonization propaganda so closely mimicked that of the others. It was part of the same world, and, in many ways, of the same dream. It would present the new areas of settlement in Quebec not only as a promised land sufficient to assure the physical and spiritual regeneration of French Canadians but also as places for a new beginning, perfectly fit to those who dreamed of liberty, success, and happiness. It also presented colonization as a remedy against the evils of the time, beneficial to the colonist as well as to the entire province and, ultimately, as a means (a manifest destiny) of preserving the French race in North America.

That the French Canadian propagandists took such examples from other propagandists in composing their materials does not lessen their originality. However, it would be an error to believe that in achieving these goals the partisans of colonization in Quebec could invent a discourse free of external influences. On the contrary, because they were aware of similar colonization experiences, and because many of them first worked as immigration propagandists for the Canadian federal government, they used the then current discourse as a model, adapting it to their own views and interests.

This explains the similarities of their proposals with those of the anglophone propagandists of Quebec, many of whom were British officials or clergymen. These anglophone propagandists had a telling influence on their French Canadian counterparts, one that permitted the external Anglo-American discourse to penetrate more easily the French Canadian discourse, and offered a matrix for the French references that would later be used by the French Canadian propagandists.

This same process was ongoing in the other colonial societies of the epoch. By relying as they did on British models, their elite gave form to a discourse full of reference to a metropolitan view of immigration. As the Cormaroffs have pointed out,[33] colonialism in the nineteenth century took many forms. It seems that one of its most prominent attributes was the projection of metropolitan preoccupations onto colonial societies. Eventually, those same preoccupations were integrated by the colonial societies into their own discourse of colonization and development. But is such not the essence of history and even identity – to owe one's origins to many different influences?[34] In the particular case of Quebec (but was it really so particular?), it would give birth to new internal colonies in areas that were to be useful to the cities of the St. Lawrence lowlands: Greater Quebec, but Quebec all the same. This in turn would give birth to a discourse that portrayed the new colonies as lands of happiness and rebirth for a population that wished to remain faithful to its ethnic and religious origins. Furthermore, it would give rise to new places of identity for a society charged with a providential mission in North America.

Far from making the Quebec experience common, this mimetic behaviour is at the roots of what has come to be called "Québécitude": the ability to integrate external influences in order to tame the territory and make it a place of survival as well as a place for new beginnings. This is the heart of the colonization propaganda literature of the nineteenth century. It shows that far from being turned inward on itself, nostalgic about its past and anxious to renew its traditions, Quebec society was, on the contrary, well embedded in the international currents of its epoch, criss-crossed by the same desires and the same utopian ideas as the other colonial societies, viewing its hinterlands as places to create and build its own promised lands. It also shows that the history of Quebec was not a simple continuation of the French colonial experience on the shores of the St. Lawrence. It was influenced by the many changes that took place in the nineteenth century. And so hence the dichotomy between the search for new promised lands that would become new places of national identity and the actual popular response, which preferred city life and industrial work to self-sufficient agriculture in these new Edens.[35]

Acknowledgments

This chapter was made possible thanks to financial support of the British Academy and the Canada Council for the Arts. I am grateful to Professor Alan Baker (Emmanuel College, Cambridge) for his kind cooperation in launching the research project. I also thank Professor Matthew Hatvany (Université Laval) and Professor Aidan McQuillan (University of Toronto) for their kind and attentive reading of this chapter.

Notes

1 Quoted in Robert Major, *Jean Rivard ou l'art de réussir: idéologies et utopie dans l'œuvre d'Antoine Gérin-Lajoie* (Sainte-Foy, QC: Les Presses de l'Université Laval, 1991), 47.
2 Antoine Labelle, *Pamphlet sur la colonisation dans la vallée d'Ottawa au nord de Montréal, et règlements et avantages de la Société de colonisation du diocèse de Montréal* (Montreal: John Lovell and Son, 1880), 18-19.
3 Yolande Lavoie, *L'émigration des Canadiens aux États-Unis avant 1930: mesure du phénomène* (Montreal: Les Presses de l'Université de Montréal, 1972).
4 Yvan Lamonde, *Histoire sociale des idées au Québec, 1760-1896* (Montreal: Fides, 2000); Paul-André Linteau, René Durocher, and Jean-Claude Robert, *Histoire du Québec contemporain: de la Confédération à la Crise,* vol. 1 (Montreal: Boréal Compact, 1989).
5 On this American influence, see Christian Morissonneau, *La terre promise: Le mythe du Nord québécois* (Montreal: Hurtubise HMH, 1978). See also Major, *Jean Rivard ou l'art de réussir.*
6 Sociétés de colonisation des diocèses de Montréal et d'Ottawa, *Au nord. Brochure accompagnée d'une carte géographique des cantons à coloniser dans les vallées de la Rivière Rouge et du Lièvre, et dans partie des vallées de la Mattawin et de la Gatineau. Publiée sous les auspices des Sociétés de colonisation des diocèses de Montréal et d'Ottawa* (Saint-Jérôme, QC; 1883), 10.
7 Yvan Lamonde, "Le lion, le coq et la fleur de lys: l'Angleterre et la France dans la culture politique du Québec (1760-1920)," in *La nation dans tous ses états: le Québec en comparaison,* ed. Gérard Bouchard and Yvan Lamonde (Montreal: L'Harmattan, 1997), 161-82; Lamonde, *Histoire sociale des idées.*

8   Yolande Lavoie, *L'émigration des Canadiens*. Paul-André Linteau, "Les migrants américains et franco-américains au Québec, 1792-1940: un état de la question," *Revue d'Histoire de l'Amérique française* 53 (2000): 561-602.

9   A. Bordier, *La colonisation scientifique et les colonies françaises* (Paris: C. Reinwald, 1884).

10   Jean-Baptiste Proulx, *Le guide du colon français au Canada* (Ottawa: Department of Agriculture, 1886); Jean-Baptiste Proulx, *Cinq mois en Europe, ou voyage du curé Labelle en France en faveur de la colonisation* (Montreal: Beauchemin, 1888); Stanislas Drapeau, *Canada. Le guide du colon français, belge et suisse, etc. avec illustrations, contenant des informations générales pour tous ceux qui veulent s'établir au Canada, tant pour la culture de la terre que pour l'exploitation forestière et minérale* (Ottawa: Department of Agriculture, 1887); Labelle, *Pamphlet sur la colonisation dans la vallée d'Ottawa au nord de Montréal*.

11   On the similarities between the English and French Canadian propaganda in Canada and elsewhere in the world, see Serge Courville, *Immigration, colonisation et propagande: du rêve américain au rêve colonial* (Sainte-Foy, QC: Éditions MultiMondes, 2002).

12   *Poor Colonies at Home! Shewing How the Whole of Our Pauper Population May Be Profitably Employed in England* (Chichester/London: P. Binstead/Simpkine Marshall, 1831), 8ff.

13   John Thomas Law, *The Poor Man's Garden; or a Few Brief Rules for Regulating Allotments of Land to the Poor, for Potato Gardens, with Remarks Addressed to Mr. Malthus, Mr. Sedler, and the Political Economists: and a Response to the Opinions of Dr Adam Smith in His Wealth of Nation* (London: C.J.G. and F. Rivington, 1830).

14   On this, see for example Church of England, *The Church of England Self-Supporting Village, for Promoting the Religious, Moral, and General Improvement of the Working Classes, by Forming Establishments of Three Hundred Families on the Land, and Combining Agricultural with Manufacturing Employment, for Their Own Benefit* (London: Petter, Duff, 1850).

15   J.F. Boyd, *State-Directed Emigration. With a Preparatory Letter from His Excellency the Right Hon. the Earl of Dufferin* (Manchester: John Heywood, 1883), 25-33.

16   Serge Courville, Jean-Claude Robert, and Normand Séguin, *Le pays laurentien au XIXe siècle, les morphologies de base* (Sainte-Foy, QC: Les Presses de l'Université Laval, 1995), 13-14.

17   Courville, *Immigration, colonisation et propagande*, chap. 10.

18   Two examples can be provided of this propaganda: Quebec, *The Province of Quebec and European Emigration* (Quebec, Department of Agriculture, 1870), and Quebec, *Happy Homes in the Province of Quebec for European Settlers in Canada* (Quebec: Ministère de la Colonisation, des Mines et des Pêcheries, 1915).

19   G.A. Nantel, *Notre Nord-Ouest provincial: Étude sur la vallée de l'Ottawa, accompagnée de cartes géographiques* (Montreal: Eusèbe Sénécal et fils, 1887).

20   Quebec and Lake St. John Railway, *Lake St. John and the Great North-East* (Quebec, 1883).

21   On this issue, see for example Calvin Colton, *Manual for Emigrants to America* (London: F. Westley and A.H. Davis, 1832).

22   This was a clear issue in Frank J. Warne et al., *Immigration and the Southern States, from a Railway Standpoint* (Philadelphia: Railway World Publishing, 1905).

23   D.W. Meinig, *The Shaping of America*, vol. 1, *Atlantic America, 1492-1800* (New Haven and London: Yale University Press, 1986), 29.

24   Howard Mumford Jones, "The Colonial Impulse. An Analysis of the 'Promotion' Literature of Colonization," *Proceedings of the American Philosophical Society* 90 (1946): 131-61.

25   Courville, *Immigration, colonisation et propagande*, chap. 3.

26   Ngatata Love, "Edward Gibbon Wakefield: A Maori Perspective," in *The Friends of the Turnbull Library, Edward Gibbon Wakefield and the Colonial Dream: A Reconsideration* (Wellington, NZ: GP Publications, 1997), 3-10. Ged Martin, "Wakefield and Australia," in *Friends of the Turnbull Library*, 20-44.

27   Edward Gibbon Wakefield, *Sketch of a Proposal for Colonizing Australasia* (London: J.F. Dove, 1829); *A Letter from Sydney, the Principal Town of Australasia* (London: J.F. Dove, 1829); Edward Gibbon Wakefield, *A Statement of the Principles and Objects of a Proposed National Society for the Cure and Prevention of Pauperism, by Means of Systematic Colonization* (London: James Ridgway, 1830); Edward Gibbon Wakefield, *England and America: A Comparison of the Social and Political State of Both Nations* (London and New York, 1834); Edward Gibbon Wakefield, *A View of the Art of Colonization in Present Reference to the British Empire in Letters*

between a Statesman and a Colonist (London: John W. Parker, 1849); Fred H. Hitchins, *The Colonial Land and Emigration Commission* (Philadelphia/London: University of Pennsylvania Press/Humphrey Milford, Oxford University Press, 1931); Lillian F. Gates, *Land Policies of Upper Canada* (Toronto: University of Toronto Press, 1968); Marjorie Harper, "Emigration from North-East Scotland," in *Willing Exiles*, vol. 1 (Aberdeen: Aberdeen University Press, 1988).

28 Stanley C. Johnson, *A History of Emigration from the United Kingdom to North America, 1763-1912* (London: George Routledge and Sons, 1913). Marcus Lee Hansen, *The Atlantic Migration 1607-1860: A History of the Continuing Settlement of the United States*, 3rd ed. (Cambridge, MA: Harvard University Press, 1945). Helen I. Cowan, *British Emigration to British North America: The First Hundred Years* (Toronto: University of Toronto Press, 1961). Dudley Baines, *Emigration from Europe, 1815-1930* (Cambridge: Cambridge University Press, 1995).

29 Quoted in Hugh Edward Egerton, *A Short History of British Colonial Policy, 1606-1909*, 12th ed., revised by A.P. Newton (London: Methuen, 1950), 11-12.

30 Courville, *Immigration, colonisation et propagande*, chap. 7.

31 Serge Courville, *Rêves d'empire. le Québec et le rêve colonial* (Ottawa: Institut d'études canadiennes and Les Presses de l'Université d'Ottawa, 2000); Serge Courville, "The Colonial Dream: Empire, Quebec and Colonial Discourse in the Nineteenth Century," in *Place, Culture and Identity: Essays in Honour of Alan R.H. Baker*, ed. Iain Black and Robin Butlin (Sainte-Foy, QC: Les Presses de l'Université Laval, 2001), 289-309; Courville, *Immigration, colonisation et propagande*.

32 Charles F. Grece, *Facts and Observations Respecting Canada and the United States of America Apporting a Comparative View of the Inducements to Immigration Presented in Those Countries. To Which Is Added an Appendix of Practical Instructions to Emigrant Settlers in the British Colonies* (London: J. Harding, 1819), 9-10.

33 Jean and John Cormaroff, *Of Revelation and Revolution*, vol. 1, *Christianity, Colonialism and Consciousness in South Africa* (Chicago and London: University of Chicago Press, 1991).

34 Rosalind O'Hanlon, "Recovering the Subject. Subaltern Studies and Histories of Resistance in Colonial South Asia," in *Modern Asian Studies* 22 (1988): 189-224.

35 Courville, Robert, and Séguin, *Le pays laurentien au XIXe siècle*.

9

Competing Visions: Canada, Britain, and the Writing of the First World War

Wesley C. Gustavson

In February 1917, Maj. Talbot Papineau delivered an address entitled "The war and its influences upon Canada" to the Canadian Corps School in Pernes, France. The postwar era, Papineau maintained, would see the emergence of a "strong, self-reliant spirit of Canadian Nationality" forged from the sacrifices and achievements of war. He also predicted a rise in what he deemed "Imperial patriotism" as Canadians took pride in their association with the British Empire for which they had gone to war. For Papineau these identities were not contradictory or irreconcilable, but he shrewdly noted the possibility of friction should either position be taken to its extreme. Concessions from both sides were therefore necessary to maintain union and harmony within Canada and throughout the Empire.[1]

The writing of the British and dominion official histories of the Great War would seem to be an obvious source of the imperial-national tension to which Papineau referred. The Australian official historian C.E.W. Bean was consciously writing a national history to chronicle and commemorate how "the Australian nation came to know itself" and resented implications by his British counterpart, Brig. Gen. Sir James Edmonds, that the Australian account was only a parochial "corps history." It was, Bean responded, much more than that.[2] Faced with the cancellation of the Canadian official history in 1947, Col. A.F. Duguid expressed similar views, and lamented that the history's absence would deprive Canadians of their "only national epic" and even mused about the "60,000 dead who bought the Statute of Westminster."[3] Equally skeptical of British intentions, Duguid reported to his superiors that Edmonds and the British Historical Section (the branch of the Committee of Imperial Defence charged with compiling the British official histories) required careful monitoring. For his part, Edmonds complained that the dominion historians had their own agendas and remarked that "if the Canadian Historical Section wants a vainglorious account it better write its own as the Australians have done. I am afraid nothing I can write will satisfy them."[4]

These disputes occasionally spilled over into the public sphere. Australian objections to early drafts of the British official history of Gallipoli resulted in front-page headlines in 1927. Veterans, politicians, and the public deplored Brig. Gen. Cecil Aspinall-Oglander's statements that Anzac troops had "straggled" back to the beach during the initial Gallipoli landings in April 1915 and had only narrowly avoided disaster. The British account, it seemed, challenged Australian heroism and unfairly sought to tarnish the Anzac legacy and the reputation of the humble digger. Former Australian prime minister Billy Hughes even questioned if Australians could fight along side the British in future conflicts after such an injustice. Anxious to reestablish good relations and diffuse this minor imperial crisis, Edmonds and Bean quietly worked toward a settlement. Under pressure from Edmonds, Aspinall agreed to omit or rework the offending passages, and his subsequent account followed Bean's earlier interpretation that very little "straggling" had occurred.[5]

An Anglo-Canadian clash over interpretations of the second Battle of Ypres (coincidentally also in April 1915) managed to stay out of the limelight but nonetheless generated strong feelings among those involved. At issue, the Canadian Sir Andrew Macphail declared, was the "whole Imperial relation and future cooperation in war." He noted that Edmonds' treatment of later battles was upsetting as well. Macphail was perhaps overstating the risk to the imperial relationship but his reaction illustrates the seriousness with which contemporaries viewed the affair. Neither side prevailed and in the end a compromise was reached that avoided the "wrath and recrimination" that Macphail feared a public quarrel would engender.[6] However, according to Tim Travers, the dispute exposed "the mutually suspicious relationship between British and Canadian officers both during the war and after."[7]

It is tempting to view this row over an official history and other disagreements as the inevitable product of the emergence of a confident new Canadian nationalism and the weakening of imperial sentiment. After all, as early as 1918, Prime Minister Sir Robert Borden had remarked to David Lloyd George that "the idea of nationhood has developed wonderfully of late in my own Dominion: I believe the same is true of all the Dominions."[8] English Canadian historians have generally agreed with Borden and have perpetuated the notion that the First World War led Canadians to reject the imperial relationship and seek independence. Today, for instance, it is almost an article of faith that soldiers like Private Gad Terence Neale jettisoned their British identity atop Vimy Ridge in favour of a Canadian one.[9] However neat and tidy or desirable an explanation, these incidents cannot be solely attributed to the development of Canadian nationalism at the expense of the imperial or British connection. Battlefield success did contribute to a sense of a separate Canadian national identity and the war certainly made Canadians wary of imperial ventures. Nevertheless, this new Canadianness and the increased autonomy that Canada achieved in the postwar era did not necessarily "contradict or undermine imperial Britishness," as Carl Bridge and Kent Fedorowich have noted.[10] Nor does this approach fully consider the complexities of the official history process or the possibility that matters other than nationality could influence the attitudes and biases of those involved.

Much of the tension between Duguid and Edmonds stemmed from their very different approaches to the official history process and not from Papineau's imperial-national tension. This difference, Duguid explained, could be attributed

> to the fact that the first British line of defence is the regular army, professionals, while ours is the militia, citizens. Another difference is that I work on a main axis running from the recruiting office in Canada through the caps in England and the Canadian Corps area – another comparatively narrow strip – to a restricted section of the front line. The point of origin to which I automatically return is somewhere in the O.P. line in touch with Infantry Brigade Headquarters, for that is the point of contact with the enemy, towards which all Canadian effort was directed ... Edmonds, on the other hand, works, I think, on a different main axis, as it seems to me, and the point to which he always returns, and very properly, is British G.H.Q. Very properly also, he addresses himself primarily to the professional soldier, I to the citizen.[11]

These structural or organizational distinctions, however, mask Duguid's very specific vision of the purpose of an official history and history itself. In the preface to the official history, Duguid stated that he hoped it would provide "a memorial to participants, a source for historians, a manual for soldiers, and a guide to the future."[12] It was not an accident that providing a memorial was foremost on Duguid's list of objectives, as he believed that accurately documenting the Canadian experience was "a duty to the dead and to generations yet unborn."[13] Key to any understanding of Duguid is this conviction that history's primary purpose was commemoration. Like Bean, Duguid saw no contradiction between historical accuracy and nationalist commemoration. An "old original" of the Canadian Expeditionary Force (CEF), Duguid also had a personal interest in commemorating the fallen and ensuring that their deeds would not be forgotten. As he explained to the Canadian Historical Association in 1935: "Not the least of the functions of history is the preservation of the tradition of self-sacrifice and the transmission to posterity of that precious heritage so dearly bought in battle overseas during the most momentous years in Canadian history."[14] He therefore attempted to write history that he thought would be understood "100, 200, 1000 years hence."[15]

Duguid also subscribed to the much older Canadian ideal of the militia myth. This enduring and ill-defined principle promoted a kind of social Darwinism emphasizing the strength, resiliency, initiative, and pioneer background of Canadian troops. Such qualities made them uniquely suited for the rigours of the Western Front and set Canadians apart from other combatants, particularly the class-conscious British.[16] Canadians, in Duguid's eyes, were "physically strong to endure, mentally alert and independent, spiritually fearless and confident in God's mercy as men are who daily come into contact with the forces of nature." In an early manuscript and in several articles, Duguid expounded upon these themes, stressing the volunteerism and civilian backgrounds of Canadian soldiers and singling out Canadian innovations. In these representations, technology is noticeably downplayed and military success generally explained in terms of national character.[17] The second Battle of Ypres thus became an instance "in which courage and tenacity triumphed over metal and gas," and the horrors of Passchendaele, the third Battle of Ypres, were transformed into a physical and moral test that Canadians met and ultimately overcame.[18]

Duguid's plan extended beyond the official history, and the evidence indicates that Duguid viewed himself and the army's Historical Section as not only the chroniclers of the Great War but also the guardians of its memory. His role, Duguid explained, was "to do everything possible to put the true story of the CEF on paper."[19] Duguid therefore liberally interpreted an already broad mandate and actively set about moulding the memory of the war. In part, he accomplished this through control of the war records and denying access to those researchers whose motives he suspected. One such malcontent was W.B. Kerr, a University of Buffalo history professor and former CEF artilleryman, whose memoir, *Shrieks and Crashes* (1929), was prepared with material provided by the Historical Section. Duguid disapproved of its critical tone and denied Kerr's subsequent requests for information.[20] Only accredited regimental historians were permitted to use the records and war diaries of their units and, even then, they were assisted and directed by Duguid and the Historical Section's staff. Duguid saw regimental histories as more than just specialized battlefield narratives. In his view, they could more readily offer the personal details missing from the top-down narrative of the official history and were a vital and necessary supplement to the official history.[21]

Edmonds, on the other hand, felt that regimental historians were "hacks ... who wanted to earn their fees as quickly as possible, without research or investigation," and warned Duguid that German regimental accounts (and presumably Canadian ones as well) were untrustworthy.[22] The purpose of an official history also differed for Edmonds. He wrote that he wanted his series to appeal to the general reader in addition to the military professional, though he seems to have ignored the former in favour of the latter.[23]

A career British army officer, Edmonds viewed himself not as a historian "but a G.S.O. [general staff officer] writing a military account with the assistance of friends" and felt that he had "the views of [his] comrades to consider."[24] Edmonds later confessed to the military theorist Liddell Hart that he wished to provide officers with enough information to learn the appropriate lessons without revealing too much to the public.[25] Moreover, as another British official historian explained, "Edmonds belongs to the school of thought that an official history should never express a point of view, but should merely state cold facts and leave the reader to form his own conclusions. He also objects to any colour in the work, or any attempt at descriptive writing."[26]

Edmonds also thought that the dominion official historians often exaggerated their own battlefield prowess at the expense of British troops. British soldiers, Edmonds stated, "regarded the Australians and Canadians as the spoiled children of G.H.Q., who were given the most rest, the pick of the fighting pitches, and the most praise."[27] Edmonds was not alone in this view and the wartime efforts of Bean and Max Aitken's (later Lord Beaverbrook) Canadian War Records Office (CWRO) help explain why. Bean's celebratory *Anzac Book* laid the foundations for the Anzac myth, with its depiction of strong, independent, and fearless Australian soldiers and more than a hint of anti-British sentiment, while the CWRO produced an astonishing array of books, pamphlets, films, and other material all dedicated to showcasing the unique qualities of Canadian troops and identifying them as a distinct formation within the British army.[28] The CWRO was successful enough that Lord Horne (GOC First Army) grumbled in 1919 that the Canadian Corps wished to "take all the credit it can for everything, and to consider that the BEF consists of the Canadian Corps and some other troops."[29]

With these competing visions the stage was set for the ensuing controversy. It began in 1924 when Edmonds sent the first drafts of his chapters covering the second Battle of Ypres to Duguid for his comments. The initial drafts of the British history proved to be highly critical of Canadian conduct during the battle, particularly that of then Brig. Gen. Arthur Currie.[30] Edmonds singled out Currie for allegedly ordering his troops to withdraw on three occasions and for leaving his command at a critical point in the fighting to seek out reinforcements. He further charged that Currie and the whole of 1 Canadian Division's staff (including its British commander, Lt. Gen. Sir Edwin Alderson) had lost control of the battle and that only the intervention of a British general from a neighbouring division prevented a catastrophe. Edmonds later told Liddell Hart that Currie's actions had prompted this same British general to exclaim: "If Currie was an English Officer I would have had him put under arrest and he would probably have been shot."[31]

Naturally, Duguid, Currie, and other Canadian officers disagreed with this assessment. Most objected to the narrative's "Anti-Canadian atmosphere or spirit" and felt that the history "does not do credit to the Canadian defence or to the Canadian Command in those trying days."[32] Currie concluded that Edmonds was deliberately targeting him and that Edmonds' mind had been somehow "poisoned" against him. Canadian complaints in 1926 to the secretary of state for dominion affairs, L.S. Emery, and to the chief of the Imperial General Staff, Gen. Sir George Milne, soon made the issue an imperial one. The crisis was eventually resolved in favour of the Canadians, and Edmonds' volume went to press shorn of much of its criticism, thereby avoiding the "calamity in inter-Imperial relations" that Currie predicted would erupt if the original version had been published.[33] Still upset, Edmonds later wrote a scathing report to his superiors in order to set the record straight.[34] Equally unsatisfied, Duguid, it seems, came away from the episode determined to meticulously document Canadian operations in order to pre-empt any future objections by Edmonds.

Two years after the end of their initial clash, Edmonds again complained about Duguid and the lack of assistance he had received from the Canadian Historical Section regarding Canadian operations at the St. Eloi Craters and Mount Sorrel (April and June 1916). Several Canadians, Edmonds wrote, had informed him that Duguid seemed to do nothing but criticize the British drafts, and he requested "a little official pressure through the Dominions Office" to "induce the Canadian Historical Section to produce narratives."[35] After some debate, the task of prodding the Canadians forward fell to the new British high commissioner in Ottawa, Sir William Clark, who duly raised the issue with the minister of national defence. The minister informed Clark that the Canadian Historical Section had indeed sent the requested material to Edmonds several months earlier and had received a letter of thanks from him. Clark surmised that either Edmonds or the secretary of the Historical Section had neglected to inform anyone upon receiving the shipments. Aside from the embarrassment of having "taken rather a toss over the business," Clark felt that no lasting damage had been done except to Edmonds' credibility, as his actions "played into the hands of his enemies in the Historical Section here."[36]

This caught the secretary of the Historical Section unawares and he noted to Edmonds that it was the first he had heard of it. Edmonds acknowledged receipt of the material, but he insisted that he had received only official documents that "the Canadians were bound to give us" and that he should have had much earlier. What he specifically lamented was the absence of prepared narratives that would provide the "Canadian taste," even though he had characterized those compiled for the second Battle of Ypres as inaccurate and untrustworthy. Edmonds closed by noting Duguid's lack of production and that "the onus of compiling the story of the none too brilliant early performances of the Canadians is put on to me[,] and the Canadian Historical Section in previous instances has merely acted as critic."[37] Edmonds' superiors accepted his explanation and agreed to await Duguid's reaction to the British drafts of Mount Sorrel before formulating a response. Duguid and most Canadian commentators deemed Edmonds' drafts to be "a fair and reasonably full account."[38] This positive appraisal seems to have diffused the situation and ended the need for any further government intervention.

Throughout the 1930s, and even the 1940s, Duguid and Edmonds continued to correspond and disagree over just how much credit the CEF should receive. Duguid complained that Edmonds had ignored the contribution of Canadian munitions firms in his first volume on 1916. Duguid's staff felt that the British chapters on the Battle of Vimy Ridge wrongly implied that German errors and not careful Canadian planning and execution had led to the ridge's capture. Similarly, Gen. A.G.L. McNaughton found Edmonds' Passchendaele drafts factually correct yet unsatisfactory, as he felt they failed to emphasize the obstacles that Canadian troops overcame in the course of the campaign.[39] Still bitter, and dealing with what he considered a lack of Canadian cooperation in other areas, Duguid's long-awaited drafts of Second Ypres provoked a similar reaction from Edmonds. The Canadian version, Edmonds wrote, was "incomplete and inaccurate" and unfairly critical of British officers. Edmonds reiterated his negative view of Currie and added that despite this he did not object to covering up the incident. He did, however, consider Duguid's interpretation a violation of a 1926 agreement between the two historians to exclude the affair from both official histories. Duguid, of course, did not recall any such agreement and published an account favourable to Currie over Edmonds' protests.[40]

Even though Duguid attempted to "set Edmonds straight" and secure more recognition for Canadian achievements, it should be remembered that this effort occurred within an imperial or British framework. That is, his criticism of Edmonds did not represent a rejection of Britishness or even a desire to weaken or abandon the imperial link. Given his background, this is hardly surprising. Like many of those in the CEF, Duguid was British-born and his family connection to the British Isles and to Scotland in particular remained strong, and included a brother in the British army.[41] The Canadian army even appears not to have been Duguid's first choice, as his pre-war attempts to qualify for a commission in the imperial army testify. It is also telling that on at least one occasion Duguid referred to Vimy Ridge as "the greatest *British* victory since Waterloo."[42] If, as Linda Colley has argued, it was possible to have multiple loyalties and for someone in Britain to identify himself as "a citizen of Edinburgh, a Lowlander, a Scot, and a Briton," it is again not surprising that Duguid retained something of a British (and likely a Scottish) identity alongside his new-found Canadian one.[43]

Examples of this affection abound. The Canadian official history recounts with pride that the world was taken aback at the unanimity displayed by the Empire. Four years of hardship and sacrifice, Duguid believed, had also "brought a realization of what the British Empire means." For Duguid it meant faith in British values, institutions, and traditions, coupled with a belief in Canada as "the land of Promise, the ideal land of our dreams." This vision of a strong, autonomous Canada within the British imperial family formed the basis for pre-war attitudes that Carl Berger identified as "imperial nationalism," a tradition in which Duguid was firmly rooted.[44] Duguid's ideas were perhaps not as definitive or as precise as Bean's, but they were broadly similar and he certainly shared Bean's 1917 hope that "we may come out of this war as a great empire ... young, beginning, active, thinking."[45]

Imperial symbols and imagery figure in Duguid's other projects as well, including his design for a Canadian national flag. It prominently featured the Union flag along with maple leaves and fleur-de-lys and briefly enjoyed some official sanction.[46] Duguid also assisted in the design and construction of the Memorial Chamber located in the Peace Tower of the Houses of Parliament and proposed the idea for the *First World War Book of Remembrance*. Both are essentially national memorials but intentionally retain an imperial or British component. Along with John McCrae's *In Flanders Fields*, the Memorial Chamber features inscriptions from selected verses of Rudyard Kipling, Laurence Binyon, and John Bunyan's *Pilgrim's Progress*. The Chamber's Altar of Remembrance, itself a British gift, displays the royal coat of arms and was laid in place by Lord Byng, the former commander of the Canadian Corps, in his last act as governor general. A year later, the future Edward VIII performed the altar's dedication.[47] An illustration of St. George slaying the dragon precedes the 1915 list of the fallen in the *Book of Remembrance,* and the original contract dictated that the book be constructed of materials from within the Empire.[48] Nationalist sentiment also did not prevent Duguid from accepting an OBE when his name appeared on the King's honour's list after the Second World War.[49]

Nor was Duguid unique in his imperial sympathies. Canadian veterans warmly greeted their former commander-in-chief Field Marshall Douglas Haig on his 1925 Canadian tour and enthusiastically endorsed his proposal to amalgamate Canadian veterans organizations into a branch of the British Empire Service League. Despite Sir Richard Turner's acrimonious relationship with Alderson and his refusal to shake hands with his former commanding officer, Turner expressed national and imperial pride at the 1923 unveiling of the Canadian memorial at St. Julien. The Canadians never wavered at Second Ypres, he declared, and "in all the annals of the British Empire greater devotion to King and Country has never been shown."[50] Currie also displayed considerable affection for the Empire and, in a speech shortly after the war, he praised British troops and spoke of strengthening the British system to an appreciative London audience. Currie also felt that entombing a Canadian unknown soldier was unnecessary since the Unknown Warrior entombed in London's Westminster Abbey could very well be Canadian, and if not, still represented Canada and all those who fell in defence of the Empire.[51] Even when beset by Edmonds, Currie warmly recalled his association with British officers and reaffirmed his faith and confidence in their "fairmindedness and integrity" and ability "to see that justice is done." At least one other Canadian officer simply found it difficult to believe that Edmonds would deliberately malign Canadian troops.[52]

Official histories imperilled personal, professional, and unit reputations as much as they did national or imperial relations, and determining which was more important, and to whom, is difficult at best.[53] Regimental, battalion, and even divisional pride existed beneath the much-vaunted homogeneity of the Canadian Corps and, like other armed forces, its intellectual and social milieu consisted of a "complex and variable network of relationships running the full spectrum of acquaintanceships, friendships, loyalties, rivalries, and enmities."[54] This desire for personal and unit recognition is an oft-neglected component of the various loyalties and identities held by Canadian soldiers. Thus for some, their outrage over Edmonds' perceived slights against Canadian troops coincided with a measure of personal disappointment at not having been mentioned at all. Sir Richard Turner and Maj. Gen. Garnet Hughes (son of the infamous minister of militia Sir Sam Hughes) took this to extraordinary lengths and petitioned Duguid, the chief of the Canadian general staff, and eventually the prime minister in an attempt to persuade Duguid to revise the Canadian official history in favour of their brigade at Second Ypres and, one assumes, their own conduct. Duguid refused and ultimately prevailed over the two generals, but their protests placed him in an awkward position since he had earlier withheld evidence of their mistakes during the battle from the British official historian because he distrusted Edmonds' willingness to handle it with the proper restraint. Out of consideration for Turner, Duguid admitted that the whole truth had not been told but "General Turner does not realize or appreciate this, and I could hardly tell him."[55] These personal and professional complaints, Duguid concluded, had proven more troublesome than any of Edmonds' criticisms.[56]

As Jeffrey Grey notes, official history is often evaluated without considering the specific context in which it is produced.[57] Duguid, Edmonds, and the British and Canadian Historical Sections worked in relative obscurity, but they were not insulated or immune from the issues and trends of their time. In Duguid's case, the official history, and indeed all of Duguid's efforts, should be considered in terms of the mythic version of the war constructed by Canadians after November 1918. Instead of the horrors of war, this emerging position stressed the justness of overthrowing Prussian militarism and the heroic self-sacrifice of Canadian soldiers, and affirmed the war as Canada's coming of age. Canadians, Jonathan Vance has argued, "conferred upon those four years a legacy, not of despair, aimlessness, and futility, but of promise, certainty, and goodness. It assured Canadians that ... the memory of the war could prove that the twentieth century did indeed belong to Canada."[58] Any criticism of this idealized rendering, be it from Edmonds or anyone else, threatened not only the reputations and honour of Canada's soldiers but the memory of the fallen. Even Duguid's work was not acceptable if he challenged accepted wisdom; indeed, he encountered numerous CEF officers who were reluctant to air the Canadian Corps' dirty laundry in public and urged him to tone down or omit some of his criticisms. One reviewer even noted that at the present it was "not possible or even desirable for the official historian to tell everything."[59]

Edmonds dealt with his own share of ambivalent former officers who were uncertain if the whole truth should be told, meddling government officials, and generally disgruntled parties. Although frequently upset with his dominion counterparts, Edmonds' view of the Australian and Canadian war efforts as supplementary to the British meant that neither Duguid nor Bean were ever his main focus. Instead, he entered into the bitter war of words between wartime military and political figures touched off by the publication of their accusatory and often self-serving postwar memoirs. The degree to which this exchange influenced Edmonds is evident in his admission to Liddell Hart in 1935 that "what ammunition I will use will depend upon what Ll.G [Lloyd George] says in his next volume."[60]

Finally, a certain level of discord, or at least the appearance of it, suited Duguid's and Edmonds' own purposes. Questioned about his lack of progress, Duguid repeatedly answered that checking and correcting Edmonds' work had caused unavoidable delays in the production of the Canadian history. These efforts, Duguid maintained, had compelled Edmonds to rewrite portions not only of the British version of Second Ypres but of numerous other actions. To impress his superiors, Edmonds employed a similar tactic, reporting on his ability to set the dominion historians straight and influence their work. A comparison, however, of the British draft and the published chapters for Canadian operations at St. Eloi (1916) and Hill 70 (1917) reveals only minor changes. Edmonds also had limited success in shifting Duguid's and Bean's opinions when the Canadian and Australian drafts were circulated.[61]

That there were serious disagreements between Edmonds and the dominion official historians over matters of interpretation and emphasis in their respective official histories is without question.[62] Yet in the Canadian case, it is misleading to assume that these disputes heralded the triumph of nationalism over imperialism. The bitterness and resentment displayed by the two historians toward one another is also not indicative of a fundamental shift in Anglo-Canadian relations or perceptions. The militia myth and other stereotypes along with calls for increased Canadian autonomy all existed long before the Great War or Duguid's official history program. British and Canadian commentators also publicly traded many of the same barbs after the Boer War (1899-1902) that Duguid and Edmonds privately exchanged in the 1920s and 1930s.[63] Duguid, however, like many other English Canadians, emerged from the First World War with a heightened sense of a distinct national or Canadian identity. This new Canadianness certainly contributed to his problems with Edmonds, but so did a host of other factors, including methodological differences, personal and professional jealousies, and specific national or internal developments. All of these coalesced to generate the suspicion and resentment that, at times, characterized their differences over Second Ypres and other issues.

For all the sound and fury their differences generated, the clashes between Duguid and Edmonds never seriously threatened the imperial relationship. Vimy Ridge may well have been the turning point in Canada's "road to national maturity" that C.P. Stacey (himself an official historian) thought, but many Canadians, including Duguid, continued to see Britain and the Empire as "their spiritual and sentimental home."[64] Being British, however, did not mean an automatic acceptance of the British view of the war. Duguid certainly wished to see the CEF receive its due from Edmonds, and the British official historian expected the same treatment for British troops from Duguid. That neither appeared fully satisfied in the end is perhaps one example of the many compromises Papineau felt were necessary for the continuation of the imperial relationship.

Notes

1 Talbot Papineau, *The War and Its Influences upon Canada: Address Delivered by the Late Major Talbot Papineau, M.C., to the Canadian Corps School at Pernes in France, 1917* (Montreal, 1920), 4-5. Before his death in 1917, Papineau had been touted as a future political leader and perhaps even prime minister; Sandra Gwyn, *Tapestry of War: A Private View of Canadians in the Great War* (Toronto: HarperCollins, 1992), 94, 98, 399-402, 496.
2 C.E.W. Bean, *The Official History of Australia in the War of 1914-1918*, 6 vols. (Sydney: Angus and Robertson, 1921-42), i, xlviii; vi, 1095; C.E.W. Bean, "The Technique of a Contemporary War Historian," *Historical Studies* 2, 6 (November 1942): 79; Tim Travers, "From Surafend to Gough: Charles Bean, James Edmonds, and the Making of the Australian Official History," *Journal of the Australian War Memorial* 27 (October 1995): 18, 22.
3 Library and Archives Canada (LAC), MG 30 D252, Alan B. Beddoe Papers, vol. 22, Canadian Forces, Colonel Duguid, Historical Section, Duguid to Wilfred Bovey, director of extra-mural relations, McGill University, draft letter, n.d. [late February or early March 1947]; Directorate of History and Heritage, National Defence Headquarters, Biog. D (subsequently cited as Duguid Biographical File [DBF]), file 21, Duguid to Vincent Massey, draft letter, n.d. [mid- to late 1949]. For Duguid and the history's cancellation, see Wes Gustavson, "Fairly Well Known and Need Not Be Discussed: Colonel A.F. Duguid and the Canadian Official History of the First World War," *Canadian Military History* 10, 2 (Spring 2001): 41-54. S.F. Wise offers a broader view of Canadian official histories in his "Canadian Official History: The End of an Era?" in *The Last Word? Essays on Official History in*

the United States and the British Commonwealth, ed. Jeffrey Grey (Westport, CT: Praeger, 2003), 3-25.

4 LAC, RG 24, vol. 2732, HQC 5393, Memorandum on the Historical Section, 5 January 1928, 3; Public Record Office (PRO), CAB 45/155, Edmonds to Gen. Sir George Milne, chief of the Imperial General Staff, 30 April 1926. Andrew Green's recent assessment of Edmonds largely overlooks these clashes; see *Writing the Great War: Sir James Edmonds and the Official Histories 1915-1918* (London: Frank Cass, 2003).

5 Alistair Thomson, "The Vilest Libel of the War? Imperial Politics and the Official Histories of Gallipoli," *Australian Historical Studies* 25 (1993): 628-36.

6 PRO, CAB 45/156, Sir Andrew Macphail to L.S. Amery, secretary of state for Dominion Affairs, 25 April 1926.

7 Tim Travers, "Allies in Conflict: The British and Canadian Official Historians and the Real Story of Second Ypres (1915)," *Journal of Contemporary History* 24 (1989): 319.

8 Quoted in Margaret Macmillan, "Sibling Rivalry: Australia and Canada from the Boer War to the Great War," in *Parties Long Estranged: Canada and Australia in the Twentieth Century,* ed. Margaret Macmillan and Francine McKenzie (Vancouver: UBC Press, 2003), 20.

9 Desmond Morton and Jack Granatstein, *Marching to Armageddon: Canada and the Great War 1914-1918* (Toronto: Lester and Orpen Dennys, 1989), 1; Pierre Berton, *Vimy Ridge* (Markham, ON: Penguin Books, 1987), 290-91. An excellent discussion of the absence of the British connection in Canadian historiography is Phillip Buckner's "Whatever Happened to the British Empire?" *Journal of the Canadian Historical Association* 3 (1994): 3-32.

10 Carl Bridge and Kent Fedorowich, "Mapping the British World," *Journal of Imperial and Commonwealth History* 31, 2 (May 2003): 6. See also Phillip Buckner and Carl Bridge, "Reinventing the British World," *Round Table* 368 (2003): 77-88.

11 LAC, MG 30 E300, Victor Wentworth Odlum Papers, vol. 3, Colonel A.F. Duguid 1926-1933, Duguid to Odlum, Major, 7th battalion CEF at second Ypres; later GOC 11th brigade CEF, 4 October 1938.

12 A.F. Duguid, *Official History of the Canadian Forces in the Great War 1914-1918, General Series,* vol. 1, *Chronicle: August 1914-September 1915* (Ottawa: King's Printer, 1938), v.

13 LAC, MG 30 D252, Alan B. Beddoe Papers, vol. 22, Canadian Forces, Colonel Duguid, Historical Section, Duguid to Wilfred Bovey, draft letter, n.d. [late February or early March 1947].

14 Alistair Thomson, *Anzac Memories: Living with the Legend* (Melbourne: Oxford University Press, 1994), 147; A.F. Duguid, "Canadians in Battle, 1915-1918," *Canadian Historical Association Report* (1935): 50.

15 LAC, RG 24, vol. 6992, chap. 5 (vol. 2), Duguid to Ralph Hodder Williams, draft letter, n.d. [late 1938 or early 1939].

16 Alan R. Young, "The Great War and National Mythology," *Acadiensis* 23, 2 (Spring 1994): 155; Stephen J. Harris, *Canadian Brass: The Making of a Professional Army, 1860-1939* (Toronto: University of Toronto Press, 1988), 86. See also J.L. Granatstein, *Canada's Army: Waging War and Keeping the Peace* (Toronto: University of Toronto Press, 2002), chap. 1; Jonathan F. Vance, *Death So Noble: Memory, Meaning and the First World War* (Vancouver: UBC Press, 1997), chap. 5.

17 LAC, MG 30 E12, A.F. Duguid Papers, vol. 2, file 6, "The Canadian as a Soldier," typed manuscript, 14 July 1920, 6. See also Duguid, "Canadians in Battle," and "The Significance of Vimy," *Canadian Defence Quarterly* 12, 4 (July 1935): 397-402. Bean viewed Australians in a remarkably similar light; see *The Official History of Australia in the War of 1914-1918* (Sydney: Angus and Robertson, 1942), 6, 1078, 1082-86.

18 Duguid, *Official History,* 407; "Canadians in Battle, 1915-1918," 42-43.

19 LAC, RG 24, vol. 1754, DHS 9-1, Duguid to Maj. Gordon Thornton, 2 February 1933.

20 The correspondence between Kerr and the Historical Section is in LAC, RG 24, vol. 1732, DHS 3-2. Kerr was allowed supervised access to the Historical Section's library in 1933 to research an article on Canadian war literature, and his comments on the unfinished official history were likely not appreciated even though he blamed the government and a cavalier Canadian attitude toward history for the delay. See "Historical Literature on Canada's Participation in the Great War," *Canadian Historical Review* 14, 3 (December 1933): 427-28.

21   Tim Cook, "'Literary Memorials': The Great War Regimental Histories, 1919-1939," *Journal of the Canadian Historical Association* 13 (2002): 178, 182-83, 185, 189.
22   Quoted in ibid., 189; LAC, RG 24, vol. 1734, DHS 4-4 (vol. 6), Edmonds to Duguid, 3 February 1928.
23   Brig. Gen. Sir James Edmonds, *Military Operations: France and Belgium 1914,* Vol. 1 (London: Macmillan, 1922), vii.
24   Tim Travers, *The Killing Ground: The British Army, the Western Front and the Emergence of Modern Warfare, 1900-1918* (London: Unwin Hyman, 1987), 203-4; David French, "Sir James Edmonds and the Official History: France and Belgium," in *The First World War and British Military History,* ed. Brian Bond (Oxford: Clarendon Press, 1991), 71, 73.
25   Brian Bond, *Liddell Hart: A Study of his Military Thought* (New Brunswick, NJ: Rutgers University Press, 1977), 82. See also LAC, RG 24, vol. 1503, HQ 683-1-30-5, #1, Edmonds to Duguid, 12 February 1934.
26   Quoted in Travers, "From Surafend to Gough," 15-16. This is not entirely accurate, as there are some descriptive passages in Edmonds' volumes; see for example *Military Operations: France and Belgium 1914, Vol. 2* (London: Macmillan, 1925), 465-66; and *Military Operations: France and Belgium 1916, Vol. 1* (London: Macmillan, 1932), 315.
27   Quoted in E.M. Andrews, *The Anzac Illusion: Anglo-Australian Relations during World War I* (Cambridge: Cambridge University Press, 1993), 170.
28   D.A. Kent, "The *Anzac Book* and the Anzac Legend: C.E.W. Bean as Editor and Image-Maker," *Historical Studies* 21, 84 (1985): 377-79; Dale James Blair, "'Those Miserable Tommies': Anti-British Sentiment in the Australian Imperial Force, 1915-1918," *War and Society* 19, 1 (May 2001): 71-72, 90-91; Tim Cook, "Immortalizing the Canadian Soldier: Lord Beaverbrook and the Canadian War Records Office in the First World War," in *Canada and the Great War: Western Front Association Papers,* ed. Briton C. Busch (Montreal and Kingston: McGill-Queen's University Press, 2003), 54-57.
29   Quoted in Travers, "Allies in Conflict," 319; Duguid blamed British censorship policies for indirectly encouraging favourable press accounts of Canadian troops, *Official History,* 550.
30   Currie went on to command the Canadian corps and was knighted in 1917. The best biography is A.M.J. Hyatt's, *General Sir Arthur Currie: A Military Biography* (Toronto: University of Toronto Press and Canadian War Museum, 1987).
31   Travers, "Allies in Conflict," 301.
32   LAC, RG 24, vol. 2680, HQC 4950 (vol. 2), Maj. Gen. F.O. Loomis to Duguid, n.d.; LAC, RG 24, vol. 1755, DHS 10-10 (vol. 1), G.S. Tuxford to Duguid, 15 April 1926.
33   DBF, file 7, Currie to Duguid, 24 April 1926.
34   Travers reproduces this report in his "Currie and 1st Canadian Division at Second Ypres, April 1915: Controversy, Criticism and Official History," *Canadian Military History* 5, 2 (Autumn 1996): 10-13.
35   PRO, CAB 45/210, Edmonds to E.Y. Daniel, secretary, Historical Section, 25 June 1928.
36   PRO, CAB 45/210, Sir E.J. Harding to Sir William Clark, 15 November 1928, Clark to Harding, 21 December 1928.
37   PRO, CAB 45/210, Daniel to Edmonds, 8 January 1929, Edmonds to Daniel, 9 January 1929.
38   PRO, CAB 45/210, Edmonds to Daniel, 9 January 1929, Sir Maurice Hankey to Sir Harry Batterbee, 10 January 1929; LAC, MG 30 E100, Sir Arthur Currie Papers, vol. 8, Duguid to Currie, 17 September 1929.
39   Duguid, "The British Official History: A Review, and a Summary of the First Six Months of Sir Douglas Haig's Command," *Canadian Defence Quarterly* 9, 4 (July 1932): 514-15; LAC, RG 24, vol. 1897, draft: British Official History, Duguid to Edmonds, draft letter, n.d.; LAC, MG 30 D252, Alan B. Beddoe Papers, vol. 22, Canadian Forces, Col. Duguid, Historical Section, Gen. A.G.L. McNaughton to Duguid, 6 May 1946. In 1932, Edmonds noted with some amusement the attempts of the Canadian government to explain the long delay in the publication of the official history. The secretary of the Historical Section also composed a letter to correct several misstatements made by the Canadian minister of national defence, namely, that "Great Britain has begun work on the Official History, but I would not admit that she is ahead of us in that particular work." See PRO, CAB 45/210, Extracts from Canadian House of Commons Debates, 13 June 1932, and Daniel to Under Secretary of State, Dominions Office, 29 June 1932.

40 Wise, "Canadian Official Military History," 8; LAC, RG 24, vol. 1503, HQ 683-1-30 #3, Edmonds to Duguid, 12 February 1934, 23 September 1936, 12 November 1936, undated letter, Duguid to Edmonds, 22 October 1936; Duguid, *Official History,* 320-22.

41 The CEF did not achieve a Canadian-born majority until 1918. Desmond Morton, *When Your Number's Up: The Canadian Soldier in the First World War* (Toronto: Random House, 1993), 278.

42 G.W.L. Nicholson, "Archer Fortescue Duguid 1887-1976," *The Canadian Historical Association: Historical Papers* (1976): 269; Duguid, "The Significance of Vimy," 400; emphasis added.

43 Linda Colley, "Britishness and Otherness: An Argument," *Journal of British Studies* 31 (1992): 78.

44 Duguid, "The Canadian as a Soldier," 41; Carl Berger, *The Sense of Power: Studies in the Ideas of Canadian Imperialism, 1867-1914* (Toronto: University of Toronto Press, 1970). See also Mark Moss, *Manliness and Militarism: Educating Young Boys in Ontario for War* (Toronto: Oxford University Press, 2001).

45 Dudley McCarthy, *Gallipoli to the Somme: The Story of C.E.W. Bean* (Sydney: John Ferguson, 1983), 376.

46 Duguid, "The Flag of the Canadian Active Service Force," *McGill News* 21, 3 (Spring 1940): 13-14; Alistair B. Fraser, "A Canadian Flag for Canada," *Journal of Canadian Studies* 25, 4 (Winter 1990-91): 73; C.P. Stacey, *A Date with History* (Ottawa: Deneau Publishers, 1983), 67.

47 Ella M. Thorburn and Charlotte M. Whitton, *Canada's Chapel of Remembrance* (Toronto: British Book Service, 1961), 13-19. See also Amelia Beers Garvin [Warnock], *Canada's Peace Tower and Memorial Chamber: A Record and Interpretation by Katherine Hale* (Toronto: Mundy-Goodfellow, 1935), and Jacqueline Hucker, "Lest We Forget: National Memorials to Canada's First World War Dead," *Journal of the Society for the Study of Architecture in Canada* 23, 3 (1998): 88-95.

48 *Books of Remembrance* (Ottawa: Government of Canada, Veterans Affairs, 1984), 5, 7, 14; *Description of the Book of Remembrance in the Parliament Buildings, Ottawa* (Ottawa: King's Printer, 1943), 6; Alan R. Young, "We Throw the Torch: Canadian Memorials of the Great War and the Mythology of Heroic Sacrifice," *Journal of Canadian Studies* 24, 4 (Winter 1990-91): 14-15.

49 Interestingly, Bean refused a number of honours, including a knighthood; see McCarthy, *Gallipoli to the Somme,* 390.

50 John Scott, "Three Cheers for Earl Haig: Canadian Veterans and the Visit of Field Marshall Sir Douglas Haig to Canada in the Summer of 1925," *Canadian Military History* 5, 1 (Spring 1996): 35-40; DBF, file 75, "Notes on a Conversation with General Turner," 2 February 1938; LAC, RG 25, vol. 336, file W 18/26 (45), "Speech at the Unveiling of the St. Julien Memorial," 8 July 1923.

51 DBF, file 2, "Canada and the Empire," n.d.; LAC, MG 30 E100, Sir Arthur Currie Papers, vol. 8, draft reply to an inquiry from the *Halifax Herald,* 7 November 1921. Currie's belief in the inclusive nature of the Unknown Warrior is echoed in the response to the Return of the Unknown Soldier in 2000. In her official address, then governor general Adrienne Clarkson noted that the unknown soldier could easily be "a MacPherson or a Chartrand," or "a Kaminski or a Swiftarrow," and therefore represented all Canadians; see "Eulogy for Canada's Unknown Soldier," *Canadian Literature* 179 (Winter 2003): 15.

52 DBF, file 71, Currie to Duguid, 24 April 1926; LAC, RG 24, vol. 1755, DHS 10-10 (vol. 1), Brig. Gen. F.S. Meighen to Duguid, 29 April 1926.

53 See Patrick Brennan's "The Other Battle: Imperialist Versus Nationalist Sympathies within the Officer Corps of the Canadian Expeditionary Force, 1914-1919," in *Rediscovering the British World,* ed. Phillip Buckner and R. Douglas Francis (Calgary: University of Calgary Press, 2005), 251-65.

54 David Campbell, "Helping Hands and Tender Egos: Cooperation between Canadian Divisions at Passchendaele, November 6, 1917" (paper presented at the eighty-second annual meeting of the Canadian Historical Association, Halifax, May 2003).

55 For this episode, see W. Gustavson, "The Limits of Official History: Remembrance, Recrimination and the Writing of Second Ypres" (paper presented at the eighty-first annual meeting of the Canadian Historical Association, Toronto, May 2002). Duguid quoted in LAC,

RG 24, vol. 2680, HQC 4950 (vol. 2), Duguid to Maj. Gen. E.C. Ashton, chief of the General Staff, 23 April 1934.

56 LAC, RG 24, vol. 1503, HQC 683-1-30-5 #2, Duguid to P. Ashley-Cooper, 30 December 1936; LAC, RG 24, vol. 6992, chap. 5 (vol. 1), Duguid to Ralph Hodder Williams, draft letter, n.d. [late 1938 or early 1939]. A number of other official historians, including Duguid's successor, C.P. Stacey, expressed similar sentiments; see Stacey, *A Date with History*, 233; and Noble Frankland, *History at War: The Campaigns of an Historian* (London: Giles de la Mare Publishers, 1998), chap. 4.

57 Grey, introduction to *The Last Word?* xi.

58 Vance, *Death So Noble*, 266.

59 See for example LAC, RG 24, vol. 1503, HQC 683-1-30-5, #2, McNaughton to Duguid, 19 February 1934, H.D.G. Crerar to Duguid, 12 June 1936, G.S. Tuxford to Duguid, 1 September 1936, Maj. Gen. C.F. Constantine to Duguid, 11 September 1936, R.J. Orde to Duguid, 30 September 1936; W.B. Kerr in *Canadian Historical Review* 20, 1 (March 1939): 63.

60 Green, *Writing the Great War*, 50; French, "Sir James Edmonds and the Official History," 74-76; Grey, introduction, x.

61 Compare Edmonds, *Military Operations: France and Belgium 1916, Vol. 1*, 185-93 and *Military Operations: France and Belgium 1917, Vol. 2* (London: HMSO, 1948), 219-30 with LAC, RG 24, vol. 1896, draft: British Official History, Draft Chapters – St. Eloi and LAC, RG 24, vol. 6998, file 6, Draft Chapter – Hill 70; LAC, RG 24, vol. 1503, HQ 6830-1-30-5 #3, Edmonds to Duguid, 23 September and 12 November 1936.

62 There were a number of difficulties after the Second World War as well; see Stacey, *A Date with History*, 204-13, 217.

63 Carman Miller, *Painting the Map Red: Canada and the South African War, 1899-1902* (Montreal and Kingston: McGill-Queen's University Press, 1993), 438-41.

64 C.P. Stacey, "Nationality: The Experience of Canada," *Canadian Historical Association* papers (1968): 11; David Cannadine, "Imperial Canada: Old History, New Problems," in *Imperial Canada, 1867-1917*, ed. Colin Coates (Edinburgh: University of Edinburgh, 1997), 12. See also Phillip Buckner, "Casting Daylight upon Magic: Deconstructing the Royal Tour of 1901 to Canada," *Journal of Imperial and Commonwealth History* 31, 2 (May 2003): 184-85.

10
Claiming Cavell:
Britishness and Memorialization
Katie Pickles

In Jasper National Park, in the Canadian Rockies, there is a lofty snow-covered peak named Mount Edith Cavell, dedicated by the Canadian people as a monument to the heroic British Red Cross nurse who perished because of the bullets of a German firing squad in Belgium. It is a mountain of striking beauty, from its base to the crown of glittering snow at its peak a little over 3,350 metres high. A glacier, with arms extended in the form of a cross, clings to its slope. Its foot is carpeted with the rosy-hued heather and countless varicoloured flowers of the wold. There is probably no memorial in the world so simply grand as this monument to a humble nurse of the Red Cross.[1]

Throughout the British World the execution of Edith Cavell in Brussels on 12 October 1915 was considered one of the worst atrocities of the First World War. Today, Cavell is forgotten, along with the "British race patriotism" that she personified.[2] Her martyrdom is not a part of the biography of the Canadian nation.[3] As Phillip Buckner has suggested, Canadian historiography has downplayed the significance of the imperial experience in shaping the identity of British Canadians.[4] Yet, at the time of her death, Cavell was considered an important symbol in a British World that "was held together not just by ties of trade, finance, and defence but also by intricate and overlapping networks and associations of all kinds – family, occupational, professional, educational, religious, and sporting, to name a few."[5] The memorials constructed to perpetuate Cavell's memory were expressions of the ties that bound the different parts of the British World together. In the case of Mount Edith Cavell, as Simon Schama had written, "even the landscapes that we suppose to be most free of our culture may turn out, on closer inspection, to be its product."[6] To examine the importance of the British World to Canadians, this chapter rehabilitates discourses of Cavell's execution, focusing on representations of Britishness and womanhood. It then focuses on the Canadian memorialization of Cavell.

Immediately after her death, a British publicist announced that Cavell's name would be shouted and "repeated by generations yet unborn, as long as British tongues have speech and words meaning." "Thrills of horror" and "waves of outrage" purportedly swept through the British World, where "a cry of horror and execration, mingled with agonized pity for her harrowing fate, flashed her name from peak to peak and continent to continent." Cavell was portrayed as a pure, selfless, dutiful British subject, a "heroic daughter of the race that no specious promise of bribe could tempt from the path of honour." Furthermore, "all of the classes, from the highest to the lowest, were desirous of testifying their admiration of one whose devotion to duty and consecrated death will ever be an inspiration to our race." For nurses, the "tragic death of their heroic sister went like a trumpet blast through the ranks of the nursing profession," forming "a lasting memorial to devotion, courage and self sacrifice."[7]

News of the execution of Cavell was widely reported in the Canadian newspapers during the second half of October 1915. An article in the Montreal *Gazette* reported, "General Horror at Execution of Nurse."[8] A front-page cartoon a week later declared, "Who dares say peace while the Beast still lives?"[9] Newspapers were quick to indicate how her death might be avenged, with the front page of the *Toronto Daily Star* exclaiming, "Need for Men Now Urgent, Will Canada Make New Call!"[10] On 22 October the Montreal *Gazette* carried the story "New Recruits to Avenge Murder of Brave Nurse," and featured an editorial three days later stating that "to the British the name of Edith Cavell has become the epitome of womanhood. Today – her name on every lip, and men from the innermost and outermost marches of the world passionately vowing to avenge her death."[11] The immediate use of Cavell's death for recruitment purposes applied throughout the British World. By executing Cavell, the Germans had offended British men's chivalry; to the British prime minister, Lord Asquith, it was "certain that the measures meted out to Nurse Cavell would be gentleness itself compared to the treatment which would befall our womanhood if once the German invasion triumphed over our resistance." Asquith pondered: "I wonder what Nelson would have said if he had been told that an Englishwoman had been shot in cold blood by members of any other nation." He would have made his inquiries by the thunder of the guns of the British fleet, and pressed the question with the Nelson touch that won Trafalgar, as, indeed our own fleet at this moment was only too ready to do. It was estimated that during the two months following her death there were some forty thousand extra recruits in the British army alone, and in her hometown of Norwich, every man of military age was reported to have joined the forces.[12] Cavell's death also appears to have given military conscription, which began on 2 January 1916 and was completed by 26 May 1916, just the boost it needed. In Canada, recruitment posters featuring youthful representations of Cavell also urged men to enlist. One Canadian chaplain noted that the "deciding factor" recruits had given him for joining up was Cavell's execution and declared that "probably no single event during the late war resulted in the enlistment of so many boys as did the execution of Nurse Edith Cavell." He believed that "something about the quiet dignity and incomparable poise of her last moments, captured the admiration and homage of the men and boys of her day."[13]

Immediate portraits of Cavell reinforced her image as an exemplar of British womanhood. She had enjoyed a bucolic childhood in Swardeston, Norwich, where her father was vicar of the local Anglican church.[14] Her youth and early adulthood were typical of British middle-class women of her generation. After leaving boarding school in 1890, Cavell went to work as a governess in Brussels, returning to Britain in 1895 to nurse her sick father. The following year she became a probationer at the London Hospital. By 1899 she had risen to become a staff nurse, and in the following year she went to the St. Pancras Infirmary as a night superintendent, staying here for three years. She was then assistant matron at the Shoreditch Infirmary in Hoxton for three years, and spent some time district nursing in the north of England before returning to Brussels in 1906 to set up a nurses' training school. By 1908 there were thirteen probationers at the school, and by 1912, thirty-two; some were English but most were Belgian. With the German invasion of Belgium on 4 August 1914, Cavell found herself in occupied Belgium. Only seven months later, on 12 October 1915, she was shot by the German forces for "escorting troops to the enemy." Her crime was assisting men of the Allied forces, who had found themselves stranded on the wrong side of the trenches after defeat at the battle of Mons, in passing through Belgium and into neutral Holland. According to Lord Asquith, "She [had] taught the bravest man amongst us the supreme lesson of courage" and was typical of thousands of women throughout the British Empire. She was a "living" example of the best of British womanhood.[15] Canadian imperial women were quick to identify with Cavell. Indeed, it was in Canada that her martyrdom was promoted by the largest women's patriotic organization in the British Empire; at the end of the war, the Imperial Order Daughters of the Empire declared that "among all the horrible deeds perpetuated by the Germans during the Great War, none perhaps excited more loathing and disgust in the minds of British people than the brutal murder of this gloriously loyal Englishwoman. Her execution can only be regarded as a brutal murder, and another illustration of the many which Germans have given in the late war, that in spite of all their vaunted culture they are in fact still a semi-barbarous people and destitute of the very elements of any true culture."[16]

Cavell's conduct during her last days formed a contrast to the use of her untimely death for the prosecution of war. Strong Christian convictions played an important part in her life, greatly influencing how she faced her death. From her cell, she counted down the time to her execution by reading Thomas à Kempis' *The Imitation of Christ,* underlining passages such as "occasions of adversity best discover how great virtue and strength each one hath" and "thou must come through fire and water before thou come to a place refreshing," indicating a quest for courage, forgiveness, and transcendence. Likewise, her last words were in sharp contrast to the subsequent international newspaper coverage. On the eve of her execution she told Rev. H. Stirling Gahan that she had "no fear nor shrinking" in the face of death, having seen death often as a nurse. She expressed thanks to God for the ten weeks that she had spent in solitary confinement (a "time of great mercy"), and even thanked her German captors for their kindness toward her. Then she uttered her famous and controversial words: "But this I would say, standing as I do in view of God and eternity, I realize that patriotism is not enough. I must have no hatred or bitterness for anyone."[17]

The immediate Allied coverage of Cavell's execution portrayed her as a kind and caring innocent nurse set upon by barbaric Germans. On 5 August 1915, Cavell was changing the bandages of a wounded German soldier when "heavy handed barbarians" broke open the door of her hospital with their rifles and rushed into the ward (Cavell's training hospital on Rue de la Culture had been turned into a Red Cross hospital at the beginning of the war). A German "creature" then seized Cavell roughly, tore the bandages out of her hand, gave her a cuff, and dragged a calm and dignified Cavell away to St. Gilles Prison. Once in prison, Cavell was supposedly held on charges cooked up by the Germans, while a "net of accusation" was woven around her. It was alleged that she had given a greatcoat to a French soldier, or (in some accounts) had sheltered two soldiers who afterward escaped into Holland.[18]

As there was no longer a British embassy in Belgium, the British Foreign Office requested the American ambassador in London to ask his counterpart in Brussels to defend Cavell. Following three weeks of silence after her arrest, the Germans announced that Cavell had confessed to concealing French and English soldiers, as well as Belgians of military age, and that she had given them money and provided them with guides to enable them to cross into Holland. Rather than portray Cavell as a weak woman who had quickly broken down and confessed, British accounts justified and celebrated her confession (albeit to a crime they simultaneously declared she did not commit). They referred to Cavell's position as "heroic." Mocking German justice, British accounts asserted that Cavell's trial was rigged, and that her American-led defence team was not fairly updated about the status of her case. The court martial took place on 7 and 8 October 1915 at the Court of

Brussels Senate House. Cavell appeared with thirty-four others; in all, seventy people had been accused of being part of the escape organization. The prosecution asked for the death penalty for Cavell and eight other alleged ringleaders. After the guilty verdict, the American consulate unsuccessfully made a last-minute appeal for clemency, arguing that Cavell had dedicated her life to alleviating the sufferings of others, regardless of their nationality.

Powerful images of Cavell emerged from the trial. First, her martyrdom was equated with that of another historical heroine, Joan of Arc. Second, her identity as a nurse was emphasized, with accounts stating that she appeared in her nurse's uniform, although a photograph at the trial shows otherwise. Her nurse's sense of duty was stressed through statements like: "Even in this supreme hour she had time for a compassionate smile for those who were sharing her peril." Third, emphasis was placed on her ever present British courage; she was portrayed as having composure "too serene for anger."[19] Fourth, and vital to all imaginings of Cavell, was the emphasis on her youth and vulnerability: she was made to appear as much younger than her forty-nine years. Inventing youthfulness contributed to making her death all the more shocking. Although Cavell was a mature and independent new woman with a professional career, she was rendered a young, innocent, sacrificial, and virginal woman, in need of protection by a patriarchy that, until the war, had not had much to do with how she lived her life.

At the trial, Cavell repeated her confession, acknowledging not only that she had helped refugees to escape but also that she had received letters of thanks from those who had reached England in safety.[20] At the time, her apparent frankness was taken by the Allies as proof of her unfaltering patriotism. Later, it came to be thought that she was probably covering up more serious activities and that she had confessed to avoid being accused of spying. Since only those women who were spies were usually executed, it is possible that, by confessing, Cavell hoped to avoid the death penalty. There were also contested accounts of Cavell's execution at the Tir National (national shooting ground). But the common thread in the differing narratives was the assertion that it was essentially wrong to shoot a woman. All of the Allies' attacks on the Germans' "atrocity" would have fallen flat if it had been admitted that Cavell had died exactly as a man might die; that she did not need a man, or a nation, to protect her; or that a man's war had got her into her futile situation and had then failed to rescue her. Seemingly, Cavell chose to rise above hatred and bitterness by making her own tranquil Christian peace. Her reported last words were: "Ask Mr Gahan to tell my loved ones that my soul I believe is safe, and that I am glad to die for my country."

To make the Germans look cowardly, the British accounts gave an execution time of 2 a.m., rather than at the traditional dawn execution time of 7 a.m. One British version stated that the German prosecutor, Eduard Stoeber, announced to 250 parading troops that, owing to the nature of the heinous crimes Cavell had committed, the soldiers need have no worries at the thought of shooting a woman.[21] Another account feminized Cavell, claiming that "her physical strength was not a match for her heroic spirit" and that she fell in a swoon, whereupon the officer in charge of the soldiers stepped forward and shot her as she lay unconscious.[22] This account added to German cowardice by portraying the execution as the shooting of a helpless, unconscious woman, one who was too much of a lady to witness her own death. Another depiction emphasized duty to others before self, suggesting that Cavell fainted as she witnessed the execution of her friend, the architect Philippe Baucq, and *not* at the thought of her own end.

A variation on the theme of an officer shooting Cavell appeared in the *Amsterdam Telegraph,* where it was claimed that each soldier had aimed high so that he might not have the murder of a woman on his conscience. When the volley left Cavell standing unharmed, the officer in charge stepped forward and shot her through the head, close to the ear. The *Amsterdam Telegraph* account posited that, even if the German officers were inhumane, the rank and file could be seen to possess decent impulses. Canada picked up the story. The *Vancouver Daily Province* reported that Cavell was killed "as she lay swooned"[23] and the *Morning Leader* in Regina reported that a "German officer shot her in cold blood as she lay in a swoon."[24] The late 1915 issue of Sir Edward Parrott's *Children's Story* showed an angel appearing over Cavell after a German officer had shot her in the head. Parrott wrote: "In the long, black list of German atrocities there is no more inhuman deed than the murder of Nurse Cavell."[25]

In 1972, Roland Ryder pieced together evidence to reveal that it was most likely that Cavell was shot by the firing squad, according to protocol, within two minutes of entering the Tir National; that she died from two shots to the heart and one to the head; and that she was probably bandaged and tied to a post, alongside Baucq, who yelled out "Vive la Belgique!" emphasizing Cavell's contribution to Belgian resistance. This interpretation had much in common with the 1915 German response to British accounts. The Berlin newspaper the *Vossische Zeitung* stressed that the execution took place entirely in accordance with established regulations and that death occurred immediately after the first volley.[26] Emphasizing equality between women and men, the kaiser's under-secretary for foreign affairs, Arthur Zimmermann, declared that apart from pregnant women, "a man and woman are equal before the law, and only the degree of guilt makes a difference in the sentence for a crime and its consequences."[27] The German authorities also described as hypocrisy British assertions that Germans had no respect for women, pointing out that thousands of Boer women and children had died in Kitchener's concentration camps during the Boer War. To the Germans,

Cavell was a central figure in a conspiracy and she was executed as a deterrent, "to frighten those who might presume on their sex to take part in enterprises punishable by death." Zimmermann insisted that women could be cleverer than the craftiest spy and that those who acted out of patriotism must be prepared to seal their deeds with their blood. Nevertheless, the Germans soon became aware that their action had backfired. After appeals by the king of Spain and the pope, two women and one man sentenced along with Cavell had their death sentences commuted, and the kaiser ordered that no more women were to be executed without his approval.

Authorities across the Empire immediately began discussing appropriate memorials to commemorate Cavell's death. London planned a large monument opposite the National Portrait Gallery, behind Trafalgar Square. Claiming Cavell as a kindred British subject, there was also a proposal in 1915 for a similar $12,000 Canadian monument in her memory. But while the Canadian National Council of Women (NCW) believed that Cavell had "died like a Briton," it was keen to avoid "fostering hatred" and was skeptical of the celebration of Cavell's womanhood in order to prosecute warfare. The NCW suggested that, instead, scholarships and nurses' homes, or even a chair of nursing at a university, would be "more expressive of twentieth century sentiment." As Mrs. W.E. Struthers said at a NCW meeting, "Miss Edith Cavell was a nurse, and speaking from the nursing profession I would say that I think the day and age is past for putting up dead monuments."[28]

In the following years, a wide variety of monuments did appear in Canada, rivalled in number only by those erected in Britain and Australia. But the 3,363-metre-high Mount Edith Cavell trumped all other monuments in its status as the largest Cavell *stone* monument anywhere in the world. Indeed, it was rightfully claimed to be "one of the grandest monuments that commemorates any heroine in history."[29] The directive to name a peak after Cavell came from Prime Minister Robert Borden and the premier of British Columbia, Sir Richard McBride. The peak was selected by A.O. Wheeler, surveyor general in the Selkirk Mountain Settlement and the first president of the Alpine Club of Canada. In 1916 the Geographic Board of Canada approved his choice.[30] Previously, the peak had been "unnamed," although there are suggestions that its indigenous name was White Ghost and that fur brigades using it as a landmark had called it *La Montagne de la Grande Traverse* (The Mountain of the Great Crossing).[31] During the boundary survey, it was referred to for a short time as Mount Geikie, likely after the eminent Scottish geologist and one time director of the British Geological Survey, Sir Archibald Geikie (1835-1924).[32]

Symbolically, Mount Edith Cavell celebrated facing conflict with courage and dignity. The mountain was to become a sacred shrine, transcending the futility of war through an appeal to the sublime of a majestic, triumphant, and emotional landscape. Jay Winter has argued that the First World War witnessed the growth of spiritualism and the return of the sacred,[33] and Mount Edith Cavell emerged out of such a context. For example, there are frequent references to the harnessing of nature to memorialize Cavell. An enthusiastic visitor from Minneapolis found the mountain to be "kissed by the early morning sunrise and caressed by the ever changing sunset, robed always in spotless snow veilings," the whiteness of the snow portraying Cavell's purity. J. Bryan Bushnell continued: "Those who live under the spell of Mount Cavell say that some day people will make pilgrimages to this mountain shrine and that in time it will be as famous as the shrines of the old world."[34] A 1941 article in the *Civil Service Review* described Mount Edith Cavell as a "majestic shrine" and "perhaps the most inspiring of them all ... In the moonlight it is indescribably beautiful suggesting a peace and tranquillity of spirit that recall the last words of Edith Cavell just before her execution, 'there must be no bitterness nor hatred towards anyone.'"[35]

In 1923, keen to contribute to the Canadian memorialization of Cavell, the Toronto-based York Pioneer and Historical Society sought to erect a memorial temple at Mount Edith Cavell. Anxious to secure the "best view of the mountain," the society wrote directly to Prime Minister William Lyon Mackenzie King, seeking his "personal influence with the Department interested to have erected in Jasper Park on a spot facing Mt Edith Cavell a small open-air chapel or sanctuary – to be built of unbarked logs, rustic style – a place for prayer and meditation for the thousands of tourists who will visit this beautiful spot."[36] Involved in constructing Anglo-Canadian heritage, the society viewed Cavell as a suitable figure to memorialize. With similar intentions, J.B. Harkin, the commissioner for National Parks, in Ottawa, had his own plans for a shrine in "Greek temple style" that visitors might go to on a "pilgrimage"[37] that would "perpetuate and emphasize the sanctity and sacredness of the Edith Cavell Monument."[38] The Greek style was proposed to emphasize Cavell's importance by connecting her to historical heroes and heroines. When asked to find a suitable site, the superintendent of Jasper National Park, S. Maynard Rogers, who had served as a colonel during the First World War, recommended a spot "immediately north effacing the Ghost (Angel) Glacier on the floor of the small valley at the foot of the slope facing South."[39] Enthusiasm for a temple subsequently waned and plans did not eventuate.

Significantly, Mount Edith Cavell was situated in Jasper National Park, the flagship of Canada's emerging system of national parks, replete with the ideology of postwar conservation. Just as in general it was felt that Cavell's memory should be constructed as pure and sacred, so too was it was considered necessary to protect the pristine wilderness of the park. In 1924 when considering a tearoom and rest houses or cottages in the vicinity of Mount Edith Cavell, Harkin advised Rogers that sketches for all buildings must be submitted for approval and that "the immediate vicinity of the lake and mountain must be kept absolutely sacred. Any sites to be considered must be away from them."[40] Rogers was in agreement, sharing the desire to "retain the sacrosanct aspect of this locality."[41] Plans for a tearoom, to be open for three months during the summer, were therefore rejected until they were found to be suitably rustic. Over the years, requests for alterations to the tearoom were always carefully vetted in Jasper and Ottawa.[42] In 1931, when the proprietor of the tearoom, Gladys Slark, sought to add accommodation for climbers in the upstairs of the building, Harkin was concerned that such development might be "the narrow edge of the wedge," and feared that there would be "evening amusements," namely "jazz and everything associated with jazz. On grounds of sentiment and on grounds of cold-blooded business I think it is sound policy to keep the Edith Cavell area as nearly as possible a shrine."[43] On the other hand, the sort of accommodation considered appropriate for the national park did include youth hostels, and in the early 1950s the Edith Cavell Youth Hostel was built as one of four log-cabin complexes.[44]

As a monument, Mount Edith Cavell produced off-shoot memorials. In the 1920s the idea arose of transplanting Mount Edith Cavell trees in the United States. A plan to plant three Englemann spruce and three Douglas fir trees in Brooklyn's Prospect Park was abandoned because of "considerable difficulties in getting the trees into the United States."[45] In 1925 however, Fred Leu, a member of the Toledo, Ohio Lions Club, wrote to Rogers that he was sending four trees to Toledo for planting "in the hope that they [would] permanently grow as a memorial to Edith Cavell, and also excellent publicity for this park."[46] In a letter to the president of the Lions Club in Toledo, Rogers suggested that the trees be planted in Court House Square, Ottawa Park: "They may grow and thrive there and serve not only as a memorial to the late nurse Edith Cavell, but as an indication of that splendid fraternal spirit between our two countries."[47]

Unlike Rogers, Harkin did not mention Cavell in his correspondence concerning the trees for Toledo, and he was wary of the implications of using Cavell's name lest it refuel anti-German sentiments and inflame Americans of other than Anglo-Saxon heritage. He warned Rogers, "You will keep in mind, of course, the fact that Toledo contains a good many foreign born citizens so that Anglo-Saxon references will have to be delicately made." Emphasizing Anglo-American-Canadian unity, he sent Rogers a proposal for a speech, based on suggestions from the Immigration Department, that argued that "not only trees but people may be transplanted and do well. Many Canadians have gone to the United States and become successful and on the other hand millions of Americans have come to Canada and found a successful life."[48] The Ohio media coverage focused on the profile of S. Maynard Rogers as a war veteran, and Jasper Park's status as the largest national park in the world, and only brief mention was made of the fact that the "first annual Cavell memorial service was held at the foot of this mountain in August this year."[49]

Rogers was instrumental in encouraging the memorial service for Cavell, held annually after 1935 variously at the foot of the mountain or at the Anglican church in Jasper on the "Sunday nearest the day of her arrest." The chaplain of Jasper Park, Rev. R.E. Bradshaw, conducted the first service, assisted by members of the RCMP stationed at Jasper, the park officials, and the choir of the Anglican church.[50] At a later point, the annual commemorative service moved to the Anglican church of St. Mary and St. George in Jasper, where it is still held every year during the first week of August, commemorating Cavell's "courage and commitment to peace."[51]

In 1927 there were firm plans to build a grandiose inter-denominational church on the shore of Lac Beauvert, near the Jasper Park Lodge, offering views of Mount Edith Cavell. The design was modelled on that of Norwich Cathedral, where "Edith Cavell worshipped as a child and in whose shadow she is buried."[52] The chaplain wrote that "it is hoped to fill the niches on each side with statuettes of the two outstanding heroines nurses – Florence Nightingale and Edith Cavell."[53] The project was supported by "a committee of influential visitors to Jasper Park Lodge" which proposed to "raise funds and build a Memorial to Nurse Edith Cavell."[54] The plans, however, were not wholeheartedly endorsed. In a letter to the *Edmonton Journal,* the Catholic archbishop of Edmonton stated that the Catholic Church would not use the proposed church.[55] In the end, the idea of building a church was abandoned. Another plan, with much more humble intentions, was that of Fred Turnbull of St. Albert, Alberta. In 1936 he wrote to the mayor of Jasper with his idea for a memorial cairn at the foot of Mount Edith Cavell. His suggestion was for people to sign a memorial book "in loving memory of her," and for each to leave a small stone on top of a concrete base. Once the base was covered, it would be bound together with concrete and another layer started, until when a "great height" was reached, a bronze tablet would be affixed to "inform all and sundry of how the monument had been made."[56] The park management was not opposed, but it did not want responsibility for the memorial. The memorial was never erected.

Mount Edith Cavell was not the only memorial to Edith Cavell in Canada. There were at least five schools in Canada named after her. Spread across the country, they were the Edith Cavell School in Moncton, New Brunswick; the Edith Cavell Public School in St. Catharines, Ontario; the Edith Cavell Public School in Windsor, Ontario; Cavell School in Cavell, Saskatchewan; and the Edith Cavell School in Vancouver, British Columbia. It was common in the postwar years to name schools after heroes and heroines who had promoted a strong British Canada within the Empire. For example, schools in the vicinity of the Edith Cavell School in Vancouver were named after Lord Byng and Lord Kitchener. In the same imperial vein, a number of Canadian streets were named after Cavell. In Pointe Claire, in the West of Montreal, there is a Cavell Street, near a Dieppe Avenue and a Duke of Kent Avenue. In Greater Toronto there are two Cavell Avenues, one south of The Queensway in Etobicoke and one to the east in the Danforth neighbourhood. Given Newfoundland's huge losses during the First World War, it is not surprising that there is a Cavell Avenue in St. John's, and in Winnipeg there is a Cavell Drive. In the resource towns of Duncan and Powell River, British Columbia, there is a Cavell Street and a Cavell Place. Port Stanley, Ontario, has a Cavell Street, and in the Sudbury district in Ontario there is a township called Edith next to a township called Cavell.[57]

It was said that for her own retirement Cavell had dreams of setting up a home for retired nurses. In Britain this was the inspiration behind the homes of rest for nurses that were named after Cavell. This idea was also extended to homes for the elderly. Thus there is the Edith Cavell Care Centre in Lethbridge, Alberta, and in Vancouver on the corner of Sophia Street and East Broadway there was the Edith Cavell Hospital, recently rebuilt as Cavell Gardens. After Cavell's death, at the London Hospital where she had trained, a new home for nurses originally intended to be named after Queen Alexandra was instead named after Edith Cavell. When the Toronto Western Hospital had plans for a new nurses' residence, its Women's Board "felt that such a brave person [as Cavell] would be a worthy object for their financial campaign and decided to call their new residence after her." An exhausting fundraising campaign was conducted from 1916 to 1924, but the $59,673 raised was still not enough, and it was only when a member of the Board of Governors matched the sum raised by the Women's Board that the residence was built.[58] The "long-cherished" dream of the Women's Board of Toronto Western Hospital was fulfilled in October 1926 with the opening of the Edith Cavell Memorial Nurses' Residence. At the opening a bronze tablet was unveiled, with an honour roll of the seventy-seven graduates of the hospital who served overseas. Dr. Augusta Stowe Gullen praised Cavell as a devoted nurse who had done her duty, an "inspiration to other members of her profession, as well as to other women of all ranks."[59] Today, redevelopment has claimed the site, but there is still an Edith Cavell Wing dedicated to orthopaedics and rheumatology at the Toronto Western Hospital. Near the ward, just outside of the elevators, there is a picture of Cavell and her two dogs. In Belleville, Ontario, there was an Edith Cavell Regional School of Nursing attached to the Belleville General Hospital. The Edith Cavell Building, originally built as a nurses' residence, is now used for community health care.

The most traditional stone monument for Cavell in Canada is the Edith Cavell Memorial tablet on University Avenue in Toronto. In 1918 the Edith

Cavell Memorial Fund asked the trustees of the Toronto General Hospital "for permission to erect a memorial" at the corner of College and University Avenues.[60] By 11 December 1918, the fund had raised $4,000, a considerable proportion of it from the efforts of schoolchildren. On 12 March 1919, Florence Wyle's sculpture was approved by the trust and the hospital board.[61] The plaque depicts Edith Cavell offering great coats to two soldiers, with the wording: "In memory of Edith Cavell and the Canadian nurses who gave their lives," thus emphasizing that Cavell and the Canadian nurses who had served in the First World War were united in their common Britishness and their willingness to die in the defence of the British World to which they all belonged.

In an interesting twist, in 1922 the Italian Canadian community of Toronto added a small plaque to the memorial. At an unveiling ceremony, which included placing flowers on the cenotaph outside City Hall, Dr. Harley Smith, a former Italian consul, gave a resumé of the Italian campaign in the war and spoke of "the life and sacrifice of Miss Cavell."[62] Chevalier Victor Gianelli, another former Italian consul, praised the "wonderful work of womanhood, at home and as nurses on the field." Edith Cavell, he declared, had won immortality. He continued: "Her name liveth for evermore. We Canadians of Italian birth or descent deem it a high honor as Britons and as Allies of Britain to be privileged on this peace anniversary to do something in tribute to the noble heroes whose names upon the honor roll of history will always inspire us to deeds worthy of the heroism which they displayed that we might live in peace and comfort."[63] How the Italian community became involved remains a mystery. Could it be Cavell's Italian-sounding name? Could it be that before the hospital was built the site was a former "Italian ghetto"?[64] As with the trees that were transplanted to the United States, memorialization for Cavell has a habit of undergoing a process of metamorphosis. As Simon Schama has written, "Once a certain idea of landscape, a myth, a vision, establishes itself in an actual place, it has a peculiar way of muddling categories, of making metaphors more real than their referents; of becoming, in fact, part of the scenery."[65]

In time for the seventy-fifth anniversary of Cavell's death, the Toronto monument was cleaned, and the story of the Italian Canadians and the monument was reinvented. Maria Rosano, a patient-activity volunteer and the daughter of the first president of the Italian Canadian Society, took centre stage and was celebrated for uniting "the First World War, the Italian Canadian Society and the Nursing profession as exemplified in Edith Cavell's life and work." In a multicultural city, it was now the Italian Canadian plaque and not the larger tablet to which it was attached that was receiving the attention.[66]

The anti-German sentiment present in much of the memorialization of Cavell had ongoing repercussions in Canada. During the First World War, some newspapers reported the efforts of German Canadians to distance them-selves from the discourse of barbaric Germans. Gabriel Haas of Walkerton was described as a "young Canadian-German" with "intense hatred for the kaiser," who would be going to war to "avenge Cavell."[67] This issue resur-faced in 1928 when a controversy erupted over the Ontario Board of Censor's banning of the British film *Dawn,* staring Sybil Thorndike as Edith Cavell. The major reason the film was banned was that it would "needlessly embit-ter feelings between the English-speaking population of Ontario and the German-speaking population here as well as Overseas."[68] Significantly, Ontario and Saskatchewan, provinces with considerable German popula-tions, were the two Canadian provinces to ban the film. Internationally, the film met with opposition because it would "fuel hatreds and is histori-cally inaccurate."[69] It was feared that it would interfere with "convalescence from hatred's hell-pains."[70] The Australian prime minister, Stanley Bruce, was concerned that "in view of the efforts of the principal nations to bring about a treaty for the outlawing of war," the film would be a setback.[71] But Canadian Educational Films Limited argued that the film should be shown simply because it was a "great British film" at a time when Americanization in filmmaking was going from strength to strength. British films for British people were much in demand by those who sought to strengthen Canada's links with Britain, especially when the film featured a British heroine. As John M. MacKenzie has pointed out, in the interwar years, film began to replace musicals and pageants as a focus for patriotic entertainment.[72] Ca-nadian imperialists thus opposed the banning of *Dawn,* although they ar-gued that the film provided a lesson in humanity, not patriotism. The Canadian Legion, however, had no reservations about evoking patriotism, making a strong case for screening the film on the grounds that it would perpetuate Cavell's "sacred memory." Yet another perspective took issue with the portrayal of Cavell, especially with the firing squad execution scene at the end of the film. Australia changed the ending, and Quebec cut the shoot-ing of Cavell and a soldier.[73]

Because the memorialization of Cavell was so intimately connected with the notion of Canada as a British nation, Cavell's memory gradually faded as Canada said its "long goodbye" to Britain and the Empire.[74] By the end of the twentieth century, she was largely forgotten. In a post-colonial age, the white, middle-class construction of British womanhood that she had repre-sented was irrelevant. Concurrently, as chivalry came under question, the idea that "the foulest act of all" was to kill a woman was challenged.[75] In-deed, writing in a 1970s climate of equality for women, Phillip Knightley pointed out that Cavell knew her crime was punishable by death, and that the French had already shot a woman for the same offence, and were to shoot eight others.[76] Where Cavell's name does remain, it is often through a process of metamorphosis. The Cavell Parent Child Centre in Toronto used to be located on Cavell Avenue and it simply kept its name when it moved.[77] But the Edith Cavell bust by Sir George Frampton, commissioned by the Toronto City Council for the main corridor of City Hall, can no longer be located, and doubtless many other memorials have disappeared.[78] A 1991 book of Alberta place names says that Mount Edith Cavell was named after a "Norfolk heroine whom some dub a martyr," unintentionally substituting Norfolk for Norwich and being flippant about Cavell's status as a heroine.[79]

In 1990 the Toronto General Hospital had plans for an Edith Cavell Lectureship and a new plaque at the tablet to "indicate The Toronto Hospital's continuing interest in excellence in nursing."[80] But after a meeting of the historical and archives committee, the manager of community relations warned that "the Alumnae people represented on our committee expressed concern[...] at the mention of Edith Cavell as the name for a proposed chair of research nursing. They felt that a Canadian nurse should be honoured in this regard. Two names mentioned were Jean Gunn O.B.E. and Miss Snively, both of whom had many nursing achievements."[81] Times had changed and there was no longer room for Edith Cavell in notions of Canadian nationhood. Canadians were not interested in remembering a British woman who had been a part of a British World that now seemed geographically and historically distant.

Acknowledgments
I am grateful to the editors of the book, to the Government of Canada for a Faculty Research Award to conduct the Canadian research necessary for this chapter, to the University of Canterbury for a research grant in support of the project at large, to Kathryn Rumboldt at the University Health Network Artefact Collection in Toronto, Morag Carnie at the Public Archives of Ontario, and Ethel Irwin, and to archivists and librarians throughout Canada for their assistance.

Notes
1 *Canadian Readers,* book 5 (Toronto: W.J. Gage, 1932), 251.
2 Neville Meaney, "Britishness and Australia: Some Reflections," *Journal of Imperial and Commonwealth History* 31, 2 (2003): 121.
3 Benedict Anderson, *Imagined Communities* (London and New York: Verso, 1983, 1999), 204-6.
4 Phillip Buckner, "Whatever Happened to the British Empire?" *Journal of the Canadian Historical Association* 4 (1994): 3-32. For a development of this argument, see Katie Pickles, *Female Imperialism and National Identity: Imperial Order Daughters of the Empire* (Manchester: Manchester University Press, 2002).
5 Carl Bridge and Kent Fedorowich, "Mapping the British World," *Journal of Imperial and Commonwealth History* 31, 2 (2003): 11. See also Phillip Buckner and Carl Bridge, "Reinventing the British World," *Round Table* 368 (2003): 77-88.
6 Simon Schama, *Landscape and Memory* (New York: Vintage, 1995), 9.
7 Ernest Protheroe, *A Noble Woman: The Life Story of Edith Cavell* (London: Charles H. Kelly, 1916), 63, 25, 84, 115.
8 *Gazette* (Montreal), 22 October 1915, 1.
9 Ibid., 29 October 1915.
10 *Toronto Daily Star,* 23 October 1915.
11 *Gazette* (Montreal), 22 and 25 October 1915.

12 Protheroe, *A Noble Woman,* 117, 95, 86.
13 Library and Archives Canada (LAC), RG 84, A-2-A, vol. 1489, reel T9624, file J-16-82, "The Cavell Memorial. Jasper National Park. Description Written at the Request of the Provisional Committee by the Park Chaplain, Secretary to the Movement."
14 William Thomson Hill, *The Martyrdom of Nurse Edith Cavell: The Life Story of the Victim of Germany's Most Barbarous Crime* (London: Hutchinson, 1915), 6-7.
15 Protheroe, *A Noble Woman,* 95.
16 Imperial Order Daughters of the Empire, *Echoes* 77 (June 1919): 33, 35.
17 Rowland Ryder, *Edith Cavell* (New York: Stein and Day), 188.
18 Hill, *The Martyrdom of Nurse Edith Cavell,* 25, 23.
19 Ibid., 30, 40, 36.
20 Protheroe, *A Noble Woman,* 49.
21 Ryder, *Edith Cavell,* 223.
22 Hill, *The Martyrdom of Nurse Edith Cavell,* 46.
23 *Vancouver Daily Province,* 18 October 1915. Its story had come from the London *Daily Mail's* correspondent in Amsterdam.
24 *Morning Leader* (Regina), 19 October 1915.
25 Edward Parrott, *The Children's Story of the War* (Toronto: Thomas Nelson and Sons, 1915-19), no. 21, 1915, 374.
26 Ryder, *Edith Cavell,* 222-23.
27 Hill, *The Martyrdom of Nurse Edith Cavell,* 53.
28 *Toronto Daily Star,* 26 October 1915.
29 *News London,* 4 October 1924.
30 Alan Rayburn, *The Oxford Dictionary of Canadian Place Names* (Don Mills, ON: Oxford University Press, 1999), 113.
31 *Mount Edith Cavell in the Heart of the Subalpine* (Ottawa: Minister of Supply and Services, 1982), 23.
32 Glenbow Archives (GA), miscellaneous clippings, *Calgary Herald,* 11 November 1990, "Peak Named after Martyr."
33 Jay Winter, *Sites of Memory, Sites of Mourning: The Great War in European Cultural History* (Cambridge: Cambridge University Press, 1995), 54.
34 LAC, RG 84, A-2-A, vol. 1489, reel T9624, file J-56-17, J. Bryan Bushnell, "A Minneapolitan's Pilgrimage to Mount Cavell," *Edmonton Journal,* n.d.
35 LAC, RG 84, A-2-A, vol. 1488, reel T9624, file J-16-82, "Mount Edith Cavell: A Mountain Memorial to a Heroic Woman," *Civil Service Review* 30 (September 1941): 212.
36 LAC, RG 84, A-2-A, vol. 1489, reel T9624, file J-56-17, N.F. Caswell to Mackenzie King, 4 June 1923.
37 Ibid., J.B. Harkin to R.A. Gibson, acting deputy minister of the interior, 26 June 1923.
38 Ibid., J.B. Harkin to S. Maynard Rogers, 26 June 1923.
39 Ibid., S. Maynard Rogers to J.B. Harkin, the commissioner of Canadian national parks, Ottawa, 12 November 1923.
40 LAC, RG 84, A-2-A, vol. 1487, reel T9628, J.B. Harkin to S. Maynard Rogers, 31 October 1924.
41 Ibid., S. Maynard Rogers to J.B. Harkin, 12 November 1924.
42 LAC, RG 84, A-2-A, vol. 1488, reel T9628, file J-16-63. In 1925 Gladys Slark applied for a lease and a permit to build tearooms. In 1930 and 1931 she applied to add sleeping quarters for climbers. In 1946 she sought staff quarters and a ski lodge. In 1948 Annie Guild took over the lease, and in 1955 applied for a building permit for a second floor for overnight accommodation. The tearooms were in operation until 1972.
43 LAC, RG 84, A-2-A, vol. 1488, reel T9628, file J-16-63, J.B. Harkin to H.H. Rowatt, deputy minister of the interior, 27 April 1931.
44 *Edmonton Bulletin,* 20 February 1950, "New Youth Hostel for Jasper's Park."
45 LAC, RG 84, A-2-A, vol. 1488, reel T12990, file J-326-2, Ben Deacon, Canadian National Railways, to S. Maynard Rogers, 19 April 1927.
46 LAC, RG 84, vol. 533, reel T10461, file J-326-1, S. Maynard Rogers to J.B. Harkin, 9 February 1926.
47 Ibid., S. Maynard Rogers to N.E. Hutchens, 9 February 1926.

48 Ibid., J.B. Harkin to S. Maynard Rogers, 8 October 1925.
49 Ibid., clipping from *St. Paul Dispatch,* 15 October 1925.
50 GA, miscellaneous clippings, *Edmonton Journal,* 8 August 1932, "Service to Honor Martyred Nurse: Memory of Edith Cavell to Be Honored in Mountains."
51 GA, miscellaneous clippings, *Edmonton Journal,* 2 August 1987. Winn Sprakes, "British Nurse/War Martyr Remembered in Jasper." A play, "Edith Cavell Returns," was also presented in Jasper in summer 2000.
52 LAC, RG 84, A-2-A, vol. 1489, reel T9629, file J-16-82, *Calgary Albertan,* 11 June 1927, "Nurse E. Cavell Church Is Planned at Jasper Park."
53 LAC, RG 84, A-2-A, vol. 1489, reel T9624, file J-16-82, "The Cavell Memorial. Jasper National Park. Description Written at the Request of the Provisional Committee by the Park Chaplain, Secretary to the Movement."
54 LAC, RG 84, A-2-A, vol. 1489, reel T9624, file J-16-82, H. Edwards, chaplain of Jasper Park, to Charles Stewart, minister of the interior, 7 April 1927: "It will be built by the Construction branch of the C.N.R.[,] the Committee finding the funds, and it will be built under the control of the Manager of Jasper Park Lodge"; "It will be available for use by *all* religious denominations at the discretion of the Manager."
55 LAC, RG 84, A-2-A, vol. 1489, reel, T9629, file J-16-82, *Edmonton Journal,* 15 June 1927. Henry J. O'Leary, Catholic archbishop of Edmonton, wrote, "We have our own church in the town of Jasper. If, later on, the circumstances require a new church in Jasper we will build one."
56 Ibid., Fred Turnbull to the mayor of Jasper, 10 August 1936.
57 Nick and Helma Mika, *Places in Ontario: Their Name Origins and History,* part IA-E (Belleville, ON: Mike Publishing, 1977), 635-36, 384.
58 University Health Network Artefact Collection, Toronto (UHN), *Toronto Western Hospital Auxiliary Ninety Years of Service 1897-1987* (Toronto: Toronto Western Hospital, 1987).
59 Toronto Public Library (TPL) scrapbooks, anonymous clipping, 22 October 1926, "Stands as Memorial to Noble Edith Cavell."
60 Toronto General Hospital Board of Trustees minutes, 11 December 1918, 47. Information supplied by the Alumnae Association of the School of Nursing, Toronto General Hospital.
61 Christine Boyanoski, *Loring and Wyle: Sculptor's Legacy* (Toronto: Art Gallery of Ontario, 1987), 26-27.
62 TPL scrapbooks, anonymous clipping, 13 November 1922, "Italy Pays Homage to Britain's Heroine."
63 Ibid., "Toronto Italians Honor Nurse Cavell."
64 Personal communication with Italian Canadian Society, October 2000.
65 Schama, *Landscape and Memory,* 61.
66 UHN, Cavell file, Speech at Seventy-Fifth Anniversary of Cavell's Death, 1990.
67 *Toronto Daily Star,* 27 October 1915, 3.
68 Public Archives of Ontario (PAO), RG 56-3, Restricted Feature Files, 1918-71, 3.1-3.59, box 3.
69 PAO, RG 56-3, Restricted Feature Files, 1918-71, 3.1-3.59, box 3, anonymous clipping, "German Diplomats at Washington Seek to Prevent Public Showing of War Film Banned by Britain," n.d.
70 PAO, RG 56-3, Restricted Feature Files, 1918-71, 3.1-3.59, box 3, *Herald Tribune* (New York), 10 June 1928.
71 PAO, RG 56-3, Restricted Feature Files, 1918-71, 3.1-3.59, box 3, *Mail and Empire* (Toronto), 14 June 1928.
72 John M. MacKenzie, *Propaganda and Empire* (Manchester: Manchester University Press, 1984), especially chap. 3, "The Cinema, Radio and Empire."
73 PAO, RG 56-3, Restricted Feature Files, 1918-71, 3.1-3.59, box 3, *Telegram* (Toronto), 7 July 1928. The film was shown in New Zealand and Germany. Australia cut the firing squad scene at the ending.
74 Phillip Buckner, "The Long Goodbye: Canadians and the British Connection," in *Rediscovering the British World,* ed. Phillip Buckner and R. Douglas Francis (Calgary: University of Calgary Press, 2005).
75 Jean Bethke Elshtain, *Women and War* (New York: Basic Books, 1987).

76 Phillip Knightley, *The First Casualty: From the Crimea to Vietnam: The War Correspondent as Hero, Propagandist and Myth Maker* (London: Andre Deutsch, 1975), 80.

77 Personal communication with the Cavell Parent Child Centre, October 2000.

78 *Times* (London), 18 November 1915, 7. Photograph in PAO photographic collection with a 24 June 1918 stamp and the description, "Edith Cavell Bust – made by Sir George Frampton (in London). From possession of late Ivor Lewis, January 1959."

79 Aphrodite Karamitsanis, *Place Names of Alberta*, vol. 1 (Calgary: Alberta Community Development and Friends of Geographical Names of Alberta Society, University of Calgary Press, 1991), 77.

80 UHN, Cavell file, memo to Sany Twyon from Peter Honor, manager, community relations, 18 July 1990, and letter to Christine Boyanosky from Peter Honor, 22 April 1986.

81 UHN, Cavell file, memo to Mr. M.L. Louth from Peter Honor, manager, community relations, 30 January 1989.

11
Scrutinizing the "Submerged Tenth": Salvation Army Immigrants and Their Reception in Canada
Myra Rutherdale

"Salvation Army immigrants see the western Eldorado in bright March sunshine – the steamer Kensington arrives with a thousand persons who are to become citizens of this great Canada of ours," trumpeted the *Halifax Herald* in March 1906. A Halifax journalist observed one young man step off the gangway, look toward Halifax, and with sheer delight in his voice exclaim, "The great west." He had finally arrived in what he thought was the land of "vast area, freedom, and opportunity, and the land with a future for every man willing to work." Like the other passengers, this man had travelled to Canada under the auspices of the Salvation Army and was bound for Ontario to work as a farm labourer. Among this new group of 1,180 British immigrants there were thirty or forty families, but most were men travelling alone, although many of them intended to send for their wives and families once they had settled. "The whole aspect of the party was that of physical vigor, self respect, and cheerful confidence," proclaimed the Halifax reporter. "If the status of the remainder of the contingent [of 10,000 immigrants] is as high as this the Salvation Army has done Canada a service in bringing them to the country as settlers ... This first 'ship's load' furnishes a distinct asset for Canada."[1]

In 1903, when Col. David C. Lamb of the Salvation Army in London toured Canada, he laid the foundations for a Salvation Army Emigration Department to coordinate with the one he planned for London. As part of his reconnaissance he arranged to meet James Smart, who later indicated in a letter to W.T.R. Preston, the Canadian commissioner of immigration in London, that he was "rather favourably impressed with the idea that they perhaps would be able to effect a very large saving of both money and trouble to the Department in looking after people on their arrival." He continued, "I believe it is wise for the Department to avail itself of any assistance it can get from this organization, as well as others, but perhaps there is none that can do more for our work than the Salvation Army."[2] Smart realized that the Salvation Army could save his department money and work. It would recruit immigrants from the United Kingdom, assist in their passage to Canada, arrange employment for them, meet them on arrival, and see them safely to their final destination. All the Army expected in return was the usual bonus of 12 shillings for each farmer, farm labourer, or domestic servant brought to Canada, and a sufficient amount to cover the costs for its services. From Smart's point of view, the Army presented him with an irresistible offer. In fact, so well disposed was he to the Salvation Army that he told Preston: "Any young men that call at your office could be referred to the farm which Colonel Lamb is in charge of, to gain for a month or two such information as would be an advantage to them in farm life in Canada."[3] This step would indeed save Preston work.

The Department of the Interior's praise and unanimous approval did not, however, last long. The Salvation Army's relationship with the department quickly began to erode. As the demand in Canada for British immigrants grew, so too did the Salvation Army Emigration Department, but by 1926 the Department of Immigration and Colonization reported that it had been "forced to the unwelcome conclusion that the Army's immigration work is not altruistic as is generally believed and that its present business methods should be completely overhauled."[4] By 1926 a representative of the department wondered why it should be supporting a "parallel organization" at all.[5]

This chapter examines the evolution of the Salvation Army's relationship with the Canadian Department of Immigration from the time the Salvation Army began to sponsor immigration to Canada until 1926, when Canadian immigration officials realized that they had unwittingly encouraged the growth of a parallel organization. This relationship is worth recounting not only because of the role played by the Salvation Army in bringing immigrants to Canada but because it illustrates the willingness of federal bureaucrats during this period to farm out responsibilities to private organizations.[6]

Doug Owram has observed that in terms of the "perception of the proper function of the state and the place of social scientists in defining that role," the period 1918-29 was one of transition in Canada. He concludes that "the professionalization of areas of endeavour that had previously been voluntary and handled by the man of general education or by the theologian marks one key aspect of this transition."[7] These observations are applicable to the relationship between the Salvation Army and the Immigration Branch. In 1903, when the Army began its emigration work, the Immigration Branch could hardly be described as a "professional organization." But by 1926 it had expanded to provide many of the services that had previously been provided by the Army. The Army's emigration work must be seen within the context of the growth of the Canadian state, and the development of an increasingly cautious immigration policy.

An equally important context for understanding the success of the Army's work is that immigration was intricately connected to the promotion of imperialism. Assisted emigration from Britain was not new in the early twentieth century. Commenting on earlier schemes, Adele Perry astutely argues that immigration was nothing if not blatantly political: "Despite the apparent neutrality of terms like 'population,' the effort to draw peoples to British Columbia was an overly racialized process pivoting on entrenched notions of 'legitimate' and 'illegitimate' occupants and 'desirable' and 'undesirable' migrants. While the historiography on migration tends to treat the movement of European peoples as apolitical movements to unoccupied spaces ... immigration was an imperial as well as a social act, part and parcel of the ongoing effort to displace Aboriginal populations and assert a specific brand of white dominance."[8] Imperial imperatives determined the kinds of settlers required in the colonies and ensured that the emigration societies were sending the right kind of people. From middle-class single women to farm labourers and child migrants, emigration was intentional, not happenstance. And, during the Edwardian period, a number of organizations, such as the East End Emigration Fund and the Self-Help Emigration Society, were influenced by social-imperialist ideas and determined to assist worthy immigrants to Canada, although Desmond Glynn concludes that by 1914 they had failed because it was impossible to "translate social-imperialist rhetoric into practice."[9]

As much as colonial considerations were important, so too was gender a critical dimension of immigration policy.[10] The colonial and gendered perspectives on immigration were often conflated with economic needs and labour demands. Aspects of the relationship between labour and immigration are highlighted in Joy Parr's *Labouring Children* and Marilyn Barber's "Sunny Ontario for British Girls 1900-1930." These works concentrate on British immigrants and their transition to permanent settlement in Canada, including their work experiences. Parr and Barber both conclude that the success of these immigrants was due to Canadian demand for farm workers and domestics as well as to the immigrant's "own initiative and determination to succeed."[11] Ross McCormack's "Cloth Caps and Jobs: The Ethnicity of English Immigrants in Canada 1900-1914" presents another aspect of British immigration. McCormack's central argument is that British immigrants used their collective identity to social and economic advantage. Colonization, gender, class, and ethnicity were intrinsic to the Salvation Army's immigration work.

The Salvation Army's interest in emigration can be traced back to the origins of the organization. Its founder, Gen. William Booth, began his evangelical career as a Wesleyan Reformer in 1854, but he found that neither the Wesleyans nor later the Methodist New Connexion could tolerate his revivalist enthusiasm. Working within these two churches, Booth and his wife were continually frustrated that they could not "get at the masses in the chapels."[12] Booth's desire to reach the masses resulted in his separation from denominational churches. In 1865 he created the East London "Christian Mission to the Heathen of Our Own Country." During the 1860s and 1870s the Army spread rapidly throughout Britain, and by the 1880s it could claim members in Canada, South Africa, and Australia, as well as in France, Germany, and Switzerland. Salvation Army doctrine was primarily based on the salvation of souls. "What does it matter if a man dies in the workhouse," queried the Salvation Army's propaganda paper *War Cry* in July 1881, or "if he dies on a doorstep covered with wounds, like Lazarus – what does it matter if his soul is saved."[13] Booth and his Salvationists believed that the source of poverty was sin and that it was their mission to sweep away that sin. Therefore Booth's scheme for salvation, *In Darkest England and the Way Out*, published in 1890, recognized that before the spirit could be restored, the individual's material conditions must be improved. Booth's new scheme was a shift from his old idea that spiritual regeneration was the primary means to salvation. But this is not to say that he was an early social gospel advocate. Booth made it very clear that he did not wish to reform or reconstruct British society. He did not condemn government for maintaining laissez-faire policies or accuse big business of exploiting the working class.

Nonetheless, Booth's strategy had changed. His new objective was to reach the "submerged tenth" in Darkest England, including the unemployed, the homeless, and the criminal, rather than those who were already under the supervision of the Poor Law authorities. His plan was to create "city colonies" where "ship-wrecked" souls would "commence at once a course of regeneration by moral and religious influences." Those who were found to be honest and hard-working would be transferred from the city colonies to Salvation Army farm colonies, where religious and moral regeneration would be reinforced while at the same time they would learn agricultural skills. From the farm colonies these regenerated souls would be placed on farms in the countryside, returned home to their families, or transferred to overseas colonies where they would live on land supervised by the Salvation Army. "Forward them from the city to the country," declared Booth, "and there continuing the process of regeneration, and then pouring them forth on to the virgin soils that await their coming in other lands keeping hold of them with a strong government, and yet making them free men and women and so laying the foundation, perchance of another Empire to swell to vast proportions in later times. Why not?"[14]

The idea of using the Empire as an outlet for the "submerged tenth" was never executed by Booth. The Army's social work continued in London and one farm colony was established in Hadleigh, Essex, but many of the elaborate details of the plan were never realized, primarily because they would have been too expensive to implement and were, for the most part, technically impractical. Booth himself tired of flirting with the ideas of social reform. "I cannot go in for any more 'campaigns' against evils," he remarked to his son Bramwell in 1893. "My hands and heart are full enough. And moreover, these ... reformers of society have no sympathy with the S.A. nor with salvation from worldliness and sin. Our campaign is against sin."[15] Nevertheless, Booth's plan laid the groundwork for the future. The more attainable aspect of Booth's plan was achieved in 1903 when Col. David C. Lamb opened the Emigration office in London. Emigration was the Army's solution to what it regarded as the British problem of overcrowded cities and outcast London. For the sake of Britain and, indeed, for the Empire, the Salvation Army could create the machinery to transport thousands of people to Canada. The imperial connection was explicitly discussed in the Army's propaganda in order to appeal to the jingoistic spirit that had been kindled during the Boer War. "By urging healthy, moral hard-working men and women with their children, to this country is doing just the kind of work to people Canada," claimed the Army's *New Settler,* "with the right sort of population, as well as helping to build up the Empire and to bind it together."[16]

By the turn of the nineteenth century Canada needed immigrants, and Clifford Sifton, minister of the interior from 1896 to 1905, dedicated himself to resettling the Prairies with white farmers. Recalling his first days as minister, Sifton remarked that the major complaint was that it was a "department of delay, a department of circumlocution, a department in which people could not get business done, a department which tired men to death who undertook to get any business transacted with it."[17] Within a few years Sifton improved conditions by strengthening the department in Ottawa with his own hand-picked staff, and he dispatched immigration agents throughout North America, Europe, and Great Britain to promote migration.[18] His greatest success was in increasing the flow of American immigrants to Canada. He was less successful in Britain largely because of an inadequate bureaucracy. Prior to the appointment of his friend and fellow Liberal W.T.R. Preston as an agent to promote and advertise Canada, British and European immigration had been under the jurisdiction of the Canadian high commissioner, Lord Strathcona. Preston set out for London well advised by Sifton that "none of the old officials know anything about [immigration]." At his first meeting with Lord Strathcona, who was then seventy-six years old and not very enthusiastic about immigration, Preston was informed that the high commissioner resented being interfered with, and that there was little possibility of increasing public interest in Canada. In his memoirs, Preston recalled his first impressions of his new work environment:

> When I went into the records of the office on the question of Immigration, very interesting information of the dead and buried type came to light. Recommendations from the time of Sir John A. MacDonald's [sic] regime had been made but a spirit of laissez-faire had taken possession of everyone concerned and nothing of any account had ever been done. The mere fact

that anything might be done seemed to rouse a spirit of resentment. There was an evident hope that I might get sick of the job of trying to stir things up; and go away and let everyone go to sleep again in officialism and peace! It was not an encouraging atmosphere.[19]

The atmosphere did not improve, nor did his relationship with Strathcona. As a result, in 1903 Sifton separated Preston from the high commissioner's office and moved the Canadian immigration offices in London to a new location at Charing Cross.

Smart's enthusiasm for Col. David C. Lamb's visit to Ottawa in November 1903 hardly seems surprising. Canada wanted immigrants from Britain, but the Immigration Branch did not have the machinery to act on this need. The Salvation Army wanted to send people to Canada and it had the system and the organization to carry out its goal. This is not to say that the Salvation Army was the only charitable organization that was willing to assist British immigrants to Canada. The Church Emigration Society, the Self-Help Emigration Society, the Central Emigration Society, the National Association for Promoting State Colonization, and the Church Army had all responded to the same economic crisis that inspired the Salvation Army.[20] However, from the outset the Salvation Army had the distinct advantage of being well established in both Britain and Canada.[21] This was what convinced Smart that the Army's services could be useful to his department.

Upon returning to London after his initial visit to Canada, Col. Lamb immediately began negotiations with Preston. Their first agreement stated that the department would pay the Army a bonus of 7 shillings per immigrant and the sub-agents a bonus of 5 shillings if the immigrant's passage was booked by the Army. Although this was the bonus all agencies received for sending the right class of people (meaning farmers, farm labourers, or domestic servants) to Canada, Lamb was not satisfied. As Preston wrote to Smart: "Colonel Lamb thought this remuneration would hardly be sufficient to meet the expenses which they incur in making a suitable selection among the many thousands coming under their jurisdiction."[22] Determined to increase the remuneration, Lamb convinced Preston that it would be wise for the department to advertise in the Army's publications. Smart approved this plan in February 1904 and the Army agreed to "place for the disposal of the department articles, interviews or otherwise one column in each of their two publications," the *War Cry* and the *Social Gazette*, which had a combined circulation of 450,000 weekly. In addition, the Army was to place thirty-five hundred huge billboards "representing conditions in Canada" in its offices, and distribute literature published by the department for the purpose of promoting Canada.[23] Lamb had won the first round with the department: not only would the Army receive the regular bonus but also the Immigration Branch would subsidize the Army's publications and advertise in its offices. The Army wanted to advertise Canada and promote its emigration scheme and now it had someone to pay for the materials.

Meanwhile, the Army was busy organizing its emigration operations and planning schemes to attract immigrants to Canada. This proved easy. Canada was perceived as the land of opportunity, especially in the first decade of the twentieth century. Readers of the *War Cry* and other Army publications were assured that there was an "unlimited demand" for the "right class" of people in Canada. The Army encouraged prospective emigrants with "ability or adaptability for farm work" to start out as farmhands and eventually move into ownership. Single women were told that "good homes, and good prospects abound" for those willing to emigrate and work as domestic servants.[24] Stories appeared regularly that reinforced the perception that one could achieve economic prosperity in Canada. One woman bound for Canada described how she looked forward to meeting her husband, who had already settled and started work: "All of the fifteen years of our married life we couldn't save £5 – and my husband's teetotal. There was no work for him in the winter and what we saved in the summer wasn't enough to keep us right through the winter. But when I land in Halifax I shall have more than £5 in my pocket and it's all my husband's saving." Another woman, a widow, was settled comfortably in Ontario with her five children, who were all placed in jobs by the Army. "It seems strange; but in my old age I am going to know what it is to be comfortable," she remarked to one Salvation Army officer. "I thought it would be a struggle to the end."[25]

Upon inquiry at a Salvation Army office in Britain, applicants for emigration had to answer questions concerning their past work history, financial status, amount of money required, and anticipated date of loan repayment. They had to state if they were total abstainers, and provide two character references.[26] Those in need of a loan were inspected by Army officers, who subsequently prepared reports on their suitability. Col. Lamb made the final decision on whom the Army would sponsor. Not everyone who hoped to emigrate with the assistance of the Army needed a loan. The majority of emigrants simply booked their passage with the Army either because they trusted it as a booking agency or because they wished to take advantage of its employment services. The London office kept in close contact with the Toronto headquarters, which provided received information on the particular class of immigrants desired in Canada at any given time and the available employment opportunities and kept an updated list of farmers in Ontario who required labourers. Another responsibility of the Toronto branch was to collect from the immigrants the loan repayments, which included a 5 percent interest charge.[27] This well-organized network of communication between London and Toronto was crucial to the Army's initial success.

By 1904 Lamb proudly boasted to Preston that between January and October the Army had sent over "1,000 souls" to Canada. "This is about twice as many as I expected," maintained Lamb. "The work and cost of landing at both ends has been considerable."[28] Since Lamb had apparently underestimated the cost of emigration, he proposed that the Immigration Branch grant a sum of 5 shillings per head on all emigrants over one year old after the first five hundred. He also recommended that the Immigration Branch pay two Army officers £30 per month to travel throughout Britain between November 1904 and April 1905 to promote immigration to Canada. But these proposals were not well received. Smart was willing to continue the same bonus program as in the previous year and the monthly allocation of £20 for office expenses, but he firmly refused the other requests. In fact, the tone of Smart's rejection letter indicated he was losing patience with Col. Lamb. He suggested that Lamb remember that "the Department itself is spending tens of thousands of dollars every year in creating the interest by which the Army, as well as other booking agents[,] are profiting and to a more or less extent this expenditure will be made in the future."[29]

The person responsible for negotiating with the Canadian government was Territorial Commander Thomas B. Coombs. In April 1905 he secured a $1,000 annual grant from the Immigration Branch toward the cost of distributing and looking after immigrants in Winnipeg and points west. Coombs contended that not just Salvation Army immigrants but also those sent out by the Canadian government and other agencies turned to the Army for assistance in western Canada.[30] The Immigration Branch saw Coombs' request as reasonable and legitimate and confirmed that the Salvation Army had "done a great deal in assisting the department."[31] In fact, in April 1905 Bramwell Booth told his father that the Canadian government was very satisfied with Salvation Army immigrants: "A Minister concerned in Ottawa told Tucker [an Army officer], privately of course, that the emigrants we have sent out so far were in every way the very best people they had ever received in Canada under the auspices of any Society or Fund and he intends to say so at the first suitable opportunity in parliament."[32]

In November 1905, however, precisely two years after Lamb's tour of Canada, Commander Coombs found himself in the position of having to defend the Army's emigration work to Frank Oliver, the new minister of the interior. Coombs was alarmed by recent press reports claiming that the Army was receiving an extra allowance per head than was paid to ordinary immigration agencies, and he wrote to Oliver that "while we have no objection that this should be made public we think it is unfair to the Salvation Army not to mention at the same time the whole of the allowance would not pay for the advertisements which Canadian immigration matters receive through Salvation Army publications in England ... and in Canada."[33] Coombs did not mention that these advertisements, written by Army officers and full of praise for the Army's work, were mutually advantageous because they persuaded prospective emigrants to book their passage with the Army.[34] In addition, Coombs claimed that the Army was not in the business of emigration for the purpose of making a profit and that all of the money received by the Army for its emigration work was used to assist the wives and families of men who had moved to Canada earlier. Coombs added that "only about five percent of the number who have come out to this country during the past year under our auspices belong to our organization."[35]

Coombs' concern that people would misunderstand the department's preferential treatment proved warranted. Not long after receiving Coombs' letter, the department received a letter from Alfred Jury, a government immigration agent in Liverpool who predicted that the close relationship between his department and the Salvation Army would end in disaster:

> I understand the Department is giving a special bonus to the Salvation Army. It seems to me that we often bid for the worst class, instead of trying to get the best. The "Army" collects the social and moral wrecks of society, of which we have enough of our own.
>
> The very best people we get for Canada in this part of England are those booked by the local steamship agents, and yet the local agents who are self supporting, are to have less bonus than the "Army" who exist largely by begging. You will find that these chicken(s) will come home to roost.[36]

Jury's letter was inspired by articles in the *Manchester Guardian* and the London *Times* about the opening of a new Salvation Army shelter for men. In his remarks at the shelter's opening, Gen. Booth warned that society should not consider those who use the shelter idle loafers. The London *Times* reported that Booth expected that when the Salvation Army "got all plans in operation it would be possible to find employment either here or across the seas for every man and woman who after being tested for a year was found to be willing and able to work." Booth explained that the emigration office had been overwhelmed by applications: "Only the previous day 450 people applied personally at the emigration depot in Queen Victoria Street and the applications by letter had averaged 700 to 800 daily. These applications were from men and women all over the country pleading to be taken somewhere where they could earn a piece of bread for themselves and their families."[37] Jury was, however, concerned about the quality of Salvation Army immigrants. After reading the *Times* article, he concluded that the Army was sending the "submerged tenth," or the most undesirable type of immigrants to Canada.

The issue of the quality of Salvation Army immigrants had often been raised. Earlier, Sifton had observed that both Preston and Smart "in the fullness of zeal for the work" were "inclined to take too favourable a view of the class of people who are sent out by societies and charitable institutions of one kind or another."[38] Although Sifton insisted on encouraging only agriculturalists and domestics, immigration officials frequently turned a blind eye to non-agricultural immigrants. Sifton's concern was, however, reinforced by Hamilton Trades and Labour Congress. Its secretary declared that "in view of the class of emigrants already sent by [the Salvation Army], being of a class of workers such as clerks, labourers, etc. which will only go to swell the ranks of the workers in the cities of which there is already a superabundance this council protests against the granting of Canadian monies to any emigration scheme."[39] Nonetheless, beginning in January 1907 the system of bonuses was extended by the Immigration Act of 1906 to include adults over eighteen who were domestics, farm labourers, gardeners, stablemen, carters, railway surface men, navvies, or miners and "who have agreed to follow farming or railway construction." But the economic depression of 1907 prompted more complaints against the immigration of those not intending to do farm work or railway construction.

In a letter to W.D. Scott, the Canadian superintendent of immigration, Thomas Howell, Canadian Salvation Army secretary of transportation and immigration, admitted that the immigrants sent to Canada included a small percentage of mechanics and that the Army's policy was to find them work in firms in which stable labour conditions prevailed. The Army, Howell claimed, avoided firms with labour unrest and refused to send immigrants to jobs where they would be acting as strike breakers. "We have the workingman's interest at heart," maintained Howell, "and if the Labour unions would only confer with us instead of publishing all kinds of stories in the press, they would find that the Salvation Army is doing more in the best interests of labour than some of the unions are doing themselves."[40] Howell's claims proved questionable only three weeks later when a number of Salvation Army immigrants were sent to Cape Breton in the midst of a coalminers' strike. The *Halifax Herald* reported on 18 March 1907 that a group of penniless men had been sent by Army officials at Halifax to take positions at the Inverness Coal Company but had stopped at Port Hawkesbury, where they learned that there was no work in Inverness. When they wired the Army officials in Halifax, the Army's response was: "There is good work for you in Inverness if you will go."[41] Not only did the Canadian press condemn the Army's reaction but also questions related to this incident were raised in the British Parliament.

Because of the growing uneasiness surrounding charity-aided immigrants, W.D. Scott ordered an investigation of all the organizations that participated in emigration schemes.[42] This investigation was carried out in London and led to an amendment to the Immigration Act to prohibit entry into Canada by assisted emigrants unless they had been approved by the

Canadian assistant superintendent of immigration in London. Beginning in 1908, all immigrants were to have $25 unless they were going directly to relatives or had prearranged employment.[43] Yet the investigation and the new amendment did not affect relations between the Immigration Branch and the Salvation Army, the largest organization involved in emigration. The amendment essentially relegated the charity organizations to a middle position in terms of emigration and significantly reduced the flow of charity-aided immigrants to Canada from the smaller London societies. The Salvation Army emigration work, however, continued to be sponsored by the federal government and completely escaped condemnation. In fact, although officially the Army's emigrants were to be approved by the assistant superintendent of immigration in London, this rule was not applied.

The Immigration Branch in Ottawa obviously valued the Army's assistance, regardless of the fact that most Salvation Army immigrants ended up in Canadian cities and not in the countryside. The Army continued to receive bonuses from the Immigration Branch, and the Immigration Branch agreed to every scheme that the Army proposed. In addition to continuing its sponsorship of advertisements in the Army's publications, in 1908 the department increased the grant to assist immigrants bound for western Canada from $2,000 to $7,000. Furthermore, the government paid $2,000 toward a Salvation Army emigration lecture tour of Britain and $1,000 annually to assist immigrants on their arrival in Canada. In 1910 the Immigration Branch also gave the Army a grant of $5,000 to open hostels for newly arrived domestics in Montreal, Toronto, Winnipeg, and Vancouver.

One of the reasons for continued government cooperation was the Army's extensive organization. The Army not only arranged employment for those immigrating to Canada but also had officers on board the ships, who looked after passengers on the Atlantic crossing. An article in the Army's *All the World* described how the Army "takes care of families on transport across the Atlantic." One conductress proudly claimed that "all my people were satisfied with the excellent accommodation allotted them."[44] On arrival the passengers were greeted by officers from the Army, and after the new arrivals were settled, the Army sent inspectors to ensure that both the employer and the new employee were satisfied. The Army's administrative organization was thus far more elaborate than that of the other London societies.

Another explanation for ongoing friendly relationship between the Salvation Army and the Immigration Branch is that although Canada was particularly anxious to attract farmers, the government did not condemn the Army for bringing over mechanics and other tradesmen. In 1911, a Halifax shipping agent complained to Scott that the Army was bringing in carpenters, machinists, and other tradesmen who "tell the inspectors, without hesitation, that they will only remain on the land until such time that they can secure a position at their trade."[45] In fact, as Don Avery has pointed out, as the Canadian economy expanded, "the long standing goal of bringing into the country only the settler-labour type of immigrant was displaced by a policy of importing an industrial proletariat.[46] During the postwar period, however, the Canadian economy was unstable, resulting in a depression in 1921 and a recession in 1924. These economic conditions led to a decline in demand for labourers and mechanics. It is true that British immigrants were more welcome in Canada than most, but occasionally even they were criticized. In November 1920 Clifford Sifton wrote to John W. Dafoe of the *Winnipeg Free Press* to challenge the need to attract British immigrants. Sifton disagreed that "as a matter of course we want English speaking immigrants," since British farmers would not immigrate to Canada because they were prospering, nor would agricultural labourers since their wages had recently doubled. Only "the mechanic, the artisan, and the drifter in the Southern towns" would come. Sifton argued that "these are the people that Frank Oliver got in by the thousands and which flooded Canada and would have precipitated a crisis in labour if it had not been for the war. The worst blunder on earth would be to encourage their emigration. They are hopelessly incapable of going on farms and succeeding."[47] During the 1920s Canadian immigration policy became increasingly restrictive. As of January 1921 even British immigrants were required to possess at least $250 on arrival and after 1923 any British subject entering Canada had to "satisfy the immigration Officer in Charge at the port of entry that he has sufficient means to maintain himself until employment is secured.[48]

This shift in immigration policy certainly affected the relationship between the Immigration Branch and the Salvation Army. Even before the war ended, the tone of official correspondence had altered. This change in official attitude toward the Army can be accounted for in part by bureaucratic changes at the Immigration Branch. W.D. Scott remained superintendent of immigration, but F.C. Blair, who had been with the department since 1903, became the departmental secretary in 1919 and assistant deputy minister in 1924. Another significant change was the replacement of W.T.R. Preston by Lt. Col. J. Obed Smith, Sifton's old friend and Manitoba Liberal party organizer, who had previously worked as the Winnipeg Immigration Commissioner. The new mood that prevailed in the Immigration Branch was one of extreme caution.

During the war the Salvation Army emigration work declined, but by 1916 it had already devised a scheme for the postwar period. It proposed that the Immigration Branch grant the Army $100,000 to enable it to send war widows and their families to Canada. Scott did not hesitate to reject the idea: "Notwithstanding all that has been said and sung about immigration after the war, we are not yet in a position to know what conditions we will have to face and the question of immigration of war widows is one that may be safely left in abeyance."[49] Of course, Scott was in no position in 1916 to commit his department to such a scheme, but what was surprising about Scott's response was his sharp repudiation of the Salvation Army's past emigration work: "I am not prepared to admit to the Salvation Army's claim to less than one percent of failures. To my knowledge they have no reliable statistics which can be trusted to bear out such a conclusion. I know personally a good many undesirable Salvation Army immigrants ... The Army is a huge Booking Agency operating in competition with other booking agencies, presumably for a profit and has no adequate follow-up system."[50] This was certainly a dramatic alteration in Scott's earlier view of the Army's work. In the past, when the Army had applied for grants, Scott had usually recommended that Oliver agree to its requests.[51] But in 1916 Scott would not budge. He even recalled the financial crisis of 1907-8 and remarked that those who came to Canada "under such auspices were the first to be out of work and were the hardest to place or intelligently direct" and that those who were aided by the Army were "what is generally referred to as the 'submerged tenth.'"[52]

In October 1918, Lamb prodded James Calder, the new minister of immigration and colonization, to continue to support the Army's work. Lamb had been warned that as of March 1919 all government funding would cease, but he was not willing to give up without a fight. He assured Calder that the officials at the Immigration Branch would testify to the excellence of the Army's work, arguing that "we as social reformers, regard the redistribution of the people of the Empire as part of our reform work."[53] The appeal was successful and the Army's funding was continued, although at a substantially decreased level.[54] Regardless of this setback, Lamb was determined to resume operations. The first group of emigrants, consisting primarily of widows, single women, and a few ex-servicemen, departed from London on 4 November 1919. By this time the government had adopted a regulation that required that unaccompanied women travel with a government conductress. When Lamb learned that women under the auspices of a Salvation Army conductress would be considered "unaccompanied," he fired off a letter to Ottawa. Blair believed that if unaccompanied women were considered accompanied if they had a Salvation Army conductress with them, this would give the Army an unfair advantage over other booking agencies. Lamb thought of the Army's emigration office as much more than that of a booking agency and reminded Blair that the Army "has machinery already at its command to look after young women until they are placed in situations."[55] In the end Lamb's persistence paid off and the Salvation Army was again given full responsibility for its work with domestics, as well as further grants to assist this work.[56]

The next challenge to the Salvation Army came from the Canadian Commissioner of Immigration in London, Lt. Col. J. Obed Smith. Smith was concerned with the quality of Salvation Army emigrants and produced case after case of candidates who would not meet Canadian qualifications yet had been promised assistance by the Army. One such person, William John Hunt, had three years' work experience at a powder mill and four years at a powder foundry, but no experience at farm labour, although the Salvation Army maintained that he had twelve months' experience working with horses and that it would find him work on the land.[57] Another case was that of a young Scottish couple, Albert MacIntosh and his wife, who, according to Smith, had "given up their home in Scotland and burned all their bridges behind them" in anticipation of sailing to Canada. However, Mr. MacIntosh had a "flail joint at the right elbow," and although the Army had promised that he and his wife would be able to emigrate, a government inspector, realizing that there was no way MacIntosh could do farm work, turned them back.[58] Smith's opinion was that the Army was no longer concerned about the quality of emigrants, and he and his staff were growing impatient with the daily problems presented by Salvation Army emigrants: "I regret to have to state that this appears to be the time when the Department should know that without a solitary exception, the whole of our staff in the British isles ... have no confidence, or at any rate not enough confidence, in the Salvation Army methods to warrant anything but the closest supervision of all their operations, and I make this statement advisedly because our own Agents continue to complain to me when they reject a person whom they consider unfit for Canada, so many of these rejected ones shortly after produce a letter from the Salvation Army guaranteeing them work upon the land."[59]

Despite Smith's appeals to Ottawa, Blair was not convinced that the Army was doing such a bad job. Although he agreed that occasionally the Army had demonstrated a lack of good judgment, he felt that Smith's letters were a "tirade against the Salvation Army" and he confessed to the deputy minister that he had "about given up hope that Mr Smith [would] take a reasonable attitude towards the Salvation Army in work which the Army [was] surely qualified to do because of their wide spread organization."[60]

Blair may have sincerely believed that the Army was doing a good job, but it must not be forgotten that the Immigration Act favoured British immigrants above any other group and that Blair himself held anti-foreign views. British immigrants were preferred and if the Army could help further this policy, then Blair felt that the department should be able to tolerate its occasional mistakes. The Canadian government's continued preference for British immigrants was again demonstrated when it agreed to participate in the Empire settlement scheme. The encouragement of state-aided migration throughout the Empire was one of the British government's solutions to declining economic conditions, and the Empire Settlement Act of 1922 stipulated that the British government could enter into immigration agreements with the governments of Canada, Australia, or New Zealand, and with any organization in these countries as long as it was approved by the two governments concerned. The agreement between the Canadian and the British governments stated that the two governments would pay a portion of the transportation fares for immigrants to Canada who were willing to do either farm labour or domestic work.[61] By 1931, 127,654 emigrants had been aided by this scheme, which offered reduced fares, agricultural training, and placement.[62]

This agreement, signed by the British and Canadian governments in May 1922, marked the beginning of the last phase of the relationship between the Immigration Branch and the Salvation Army. Initially, the Empire Settlement Act did not interfere with the Army's emigration work, which continued to be subsidized by the federal government. In 1922, the Army was awarded an annual grant of $25,000 for five years.[63] The government also awarded the Army $227,000 to transport 5,200 boys, $120,000 for 2,000 domestics, and an additional grant of $10,000. But, as Blair observed, the Salvation Army was also "not slow to see the possibilities of making separate agreements with the British government while at the same time participating as far as possible in the benefits of the general agreement between the British government and our government."[64] In May 1923 the Army obtained assistance from the British government for the emigration of children, single women, and families. On its own, this separate agreement was acceptable, but the Army overlapped it with the existing agreement between the British and Canadian governments and was now able to undersell any booking agency and even the federal government. "Their purpose in linking up the two agreements was evidently to get all they could under our official agreement and then something additional from the British government," declared Blair, "so that they were in a position to give better terms than any agency or organization, including the Federal Government of Canada."[65] For example, if a person wanted to travel between Liverpool and Winnipeg, the fare was normally $120, but the Canadian and British government each agreed to pay $45, which reduced the fare to $30. If the emigrant booked his or her passage through the Army, he or she could take advantage of a further reduction based on the arrangement between the Salvation Army and the British government. The Army had a virtual monopoly on all booking arrangements to Canada and, as Blair observed, was in a position to "further their own steamship booking interests," since it was making a profit on each passenger booked.[66] The Army claimed to have misinterpreted the Empire Settlement Act and the federal government accepted this explanation, but when the act came up for renewal at the end of the first year, it expressly forbade the Salvation Army to overlap the agreements.

This was not the end of confusion over grants. In 1922, when the Army was guaranteed a yearly grant, Lamb did not realize that this was subject to an annual review and vote by Parliament. By 1925 Blair had come to believe that the Army no longer deserved the grant. In his opinion, the acting minister approved the grant inadvertently: "I do not understand that the Hon. Mr Stewart intended to commit the department for five years, but was merely discussing a five year program that was proposed by the Salvation Army and had the program been accepted by the department it would have merited support to the extent of $25,000." Blair's suspicion was that Lamb "wrote the above quoted letter and placed it before the Hon. Mr. Stewart for signature before he secured the approval of the five year program."[67] This strongly worded accusation is indicative of Blair's low opinion of Lamb and the Army.

Consequently, when the grant came up for renewal in 1925 and 1926, Blair opposed it. He pointed out that between 1924 and 1925 the Army was able to secure passage assistance for only 279 domestics, yet it received a grant of $25,000, which essentially meant that Canada paid the Army $90 for each domestic it sent to Canada.[68] The Army did continue to book other passengers, including single women who intended to do factory work, but these women did not qualify for free passage under the Empire Settlement scheme. Blair was also critical of the quality of the Salvation Army emigrants. "The operation of the Empire Settlement Agreement brought the Department into direct and personal contact with practically all of your migrants," he wrote to the Salvation Army emigration office in 1926, "and the records confirm the view that a considerable proportion of your migrants have either not been of the agricultural or houseworking classes or were not of a standard of fitness sufficient to warrant passage loans."[69] By 1926 the number of those who were interested in using the Army merely as a booking agency was also greatly reduced.

Considering this reduction, Blair begrudged paying the annual $25,000 grant, especially after he learned that the Army had entered into agreements with the Ontario and New Brunswick governments. Ontario agreed to grant the Salvation Army $10,000 and $40 per person for after-care, while the New Brunswick provincial government agreed to pay the Army $2,000 a year for one hundred immigrants. "Ordinary English almost fails me," remarked Blair, "when I think about the contributions secured by the Salvation Army out of various interests Federal, Provincial and British, to carry out a work that is of very doubtful value to this country."[70] Although Blair's advice to discontinue the grant that had been guaranteed for five years was ignored, it was now only a matter of time before the Army was divested of almost all of its funding for emigration. Even before the $25,000 annual grant ran out in 1927, the Army's methods of operation were again challenged, this time in terms of the Army's treatment of juvenile immigrants.

In September 1924 a delegation of four members chaired by Miss Margaret Bondfield, MP, sailed from Britain to investigate the system of child and juvenile migration and settlement. It had been invited by the Government of Canada, and the members had been appointed by the British secretary of state for the colonies and the president of the Overseas Settlement Committee.[71] The Bondfield delegation visited all of the provinces, inspecting children who migrated to Canada under the auspices of such organizations as Dr. Barnardo's Homes, the Salvation Army, and the Catholic Emigration Association. The delegation's most important recommendation, accepted by both the British and Canadian governments, was that children be prohibited from migrating to Canada until they reached school-leaving age in the United Kingdom. In terms of the relationship between the Immigration Branch and the Salvation Army, however, the most important observation made by the Bondfield delegation concerned juveniles' indebtedness to the Army:

> We found that the organizations referred to in this section even where they receive Government assistance, require a prepayment from the boy, in some cases amounting to as much as 100 dollars, in respect of the expenditure incurred on his migration. We are not sure whether these recoveries are intended to meet a portion of the cost of testing and training, but in any event we feel that this matter should be taken up with the societies concerned and that they should be invited to justify the system under which these recoveries are made. In particular, we would call attention to the practice of one of these organizations of retaining the whole of the boy's wages until his liability has been entirely liquidated.[72]

Bondfield and the other delegates did not make it explicit that the Army collected repayments from the boys, but it did not take the Immigration Branch long to arrive at this conclusion. Their report arrived in Canada in January 1925, and in May Blair reported that he had been "following up a number of references to Salvation Army immigrant lads having to refund ... amounts usually in the neighborhood of $70. The Salvation Army on this side could not explain how the indebtedness was incurred."[73]

The department immediately warned Lamb that it would not tolerate this practice. Lamb did not protest, but when Blair continued to hear rumours that the practice had not ended, he embarked upon a departmental investigation with the assistance of Bruce Walker, superintendent of immigration in London, and George Bogue Smart, supervisor of juvenile immigration in Canada. Walker was asked to approach Lamb in London, but Lamb refused to meet with him and would only state that it was his opinion that the immigration agents were "seeking to obtain information from the boys in an underhand manner."[74] Walker did learn that before emigrating, all boys from the ages of fourteen to seventeen had to sign a form agreeing to make "a voluntary contribution of £8 to help another lad," and they promised to repay £7.10.0 for items such as clothing advanced by the Army to assist on the journey. It must be remembered that the cost of transportation for each boy was divided equally between the Canadian and the British governments, which together contributed £11.10 for passenger fare and £17.18.9 for miscellaneous expenditure. In addition, the Overseas Settlement Committee granted the Army £5 per boy for training at the Hadleigh farm. Altogether the Salvation Army collected £36.18.9 to prepare and send a boy to Canada.[75]

On investigation, George Bogue Smart ascertained that all of the boys brought to Canada by the Army believed that they owed between $70 and $110. This was a sizable fee considering that most boys doing farm labour were paid only between $150 and $200 annually.[76] Not only did the boys feel that they were obliged to repay the Army but the Army sent letters to the boys' employers to ask them to assure that the loan was paid by a certain date.[77] The Salvation Army officials in Canada continued to maintain that the contributions were voluntary, but after questioning several boys, the department concluded that none of them volunteered to give money to the Salvation Army. The boys remembered that before they left London they had signed a document promising to repay the Army, but most of them believed that this repayment was for transportation costs.[78] Blair was now aware that when the department first demanded that the Army stop collecting money from the boys, "instead of changing its theory [it] merely changed its method" to make it appear that the boys were making voluntary contributions instead of forced payments.[79] Based on the evidence that had been gathered, Blair concluded that no further passage grants for boys should be allowed until Lamb promised to abandon this practice.[80] In December 1926 Lamb visited Ottawa to meet with immigration officials and confessed that the "contributions" made by the boys were used to help pay for the overhead expenses of the Salvation Army hostels in Moncton, Smiths Falls, Woodstock, Toronto, Winnipeg, Brandon, and Vancouver.[81] During these meetings, Blair recorded that "Commissioner Lamb feels that he is at a parting of the ways and I concur with this view."[82]

By 1926 the relationship between the Salvation Army and the Immigration Branch had completely deteriorated. Much had changed from the days in 1903 when the Salvation Army was a pioneer in charity-aided emigration work. To men such as James Smart and W.T.R. Preston, the idea that the Army could work with the department in promoting emigration held great appeal. The Army's extensive organization could compensate for the lack of a well-organized bureaucratic system, or, as Smart said at the time, the Army "would be able to effect a very large saving of both money and trouble to the Department."[83] In the pre-war period the Army was responsible for bringing thousands of immigrants to Canada, and the Immigration Branch praised its work. But after the war the demand for labour lessened and so too did Canada's desire for immigrants. In fact, when Commissioner Lamb visited Canada in 1925 to promote the Army's emigration work, he was struck by the government's strict regulations and declared, before a Toronto audience, that "it is harder to get into the Dominion of Canada than into the Kingdom of Heaven."[84] Lamb realized that emigration from Britain was not as welcome as it once had been, and he commented that he had noticed the "existence of what in Australia they call the 'economic bug,' a parasite that affects its victims with the belief that every fresh immigrant is a competitor for an existing job."[85]

Lamb observed that Canadians still complained that the Army was dumping "the submerged tenth." Although the quality of Salvation Army immigrants had always been questioned, in most cases this was a reflection of a downturn in the economy. When the economy was unstable, as in 1907-8 and in the early 1920s, immigrants and immigration policy became targets for criticism, but the "quality of immigrants" argument was often used as a bogey by those who were against immigration. In fact, most of the 200,000 to 250,000 immigrants brought to Canada under the auspices of the Salvation Army between 1903 and 1930 were successful.[86]

Nonetheless, by 1926 the Salvation Army emigration scheme was a vestige from the past. Commissioner Lamb still believed that the "spirit of individual enterprise is our greatest asset," and he still preached that "it is our duty to keep our people in, and for the Empire, and to keep our empire for them."[87] But the golden age of British imperialism had been dealt a fatal blow by the First World War, and social-imperialist ideas held less appeal. Even more central to the deterioration of the relationship between the Immigration Branch and the Salvation Army was the new mood of immigration officials. Bureaucratically, the Immigration Branch had developed a more regulated system than it previously had. There were now government conductresses who worked for the new women's division of the Department of Immigration to escort groups to Canada. The department hired more field staff to inspect and assure the satisfaction of child and juvenile immigrants.[88] There were also more immigration agents to control emigration from Britain. The Salvation Army had become obsolete in the eyes of immigration officials. Why, asked Blair, should the government pay the Army to do the work that his department was "in a position to handle"?[89]

More than anyone else, Blair carried out the campaign against the Salvation Army. It was Blair who called the Army a "parallel organization" and who attempted to end the Army's government grants. Although no biography has yet been written of Blair, some revealing evidence has been uncovered. Not only was he opposed to Russians, Ukrainians, Finns, and Italians, as Donald Avery points out, but, as Peter Neary has argued convincingly,

Blair was also opposed to the immigration of Newfoundlanders to Canada, and it has been proven that he was partly responsible for Canada's rejection of European Jews during the Second World War.[90] Up until 1924 Blair supported the Army's emigration work, but once he was appointed to the powerful position of acting deputy minister, he began to question its motives and operations. There is little doubt that the department had legitimate reason to be concerned by the Army's lack of accountability. When immigration officials questioned the policy of boys' repayment, the Army's only response was that the boys were making "voluntary contributions." Beyond that it remained silent. The Army was not accustomed to having its methods of operation questioned by the government. And F.C. Blair was unaccustomed to being ignored when questions of immigration were concerned.

Much of the Army's emigration work was done in the pre-war period, when Canada welcomed British immigrants by the thousands, primarily to fill agricultural and labour demands, but by 1926 that door had closed for the most part, and the Army's work was perceived as redundant. The Immigration Branch saw itself as a professional organization no longer in need of the services of a turn-of-the-nineteenth-century voluntary organization. However, not everyone agreed with this perception. On the occasion of Commissioner Lamb's visit to Canada, the editor of the *Manitoba Free Press*, J.W. Dafoe, took the opportunity to congratulate the Army on its "happily planned and scrupulously executed" emigration schemes. Looking back to the earlier period of immigration and settlement, Dafoe observed that Canada "once could offer the most attractive settlement on earth. Many, many think it can still. But to show how, and through what means it can become available seems to demand an ability and to require a courage non-existent in the government agencies responsible for it."[91]

Notes
1 *Halifax Herald*, 14 March 1906, 5.
2 Library and Archives Canada (LAC), RG 76, vol. 105, file 17480, part 1, Smart to Preston, 2 November 1903.
3 Ibid. The farm Smart refers to was the 405-hectare Hadleigh Farm Colony in Essex, England, which was purchased in 1891 by the Salvation Army and was used as a training farm.
4 Quoted in R.G. Moyles, *The Blood and Fire in Canada* (Toronto: Peer Martin Associates, 1977), 148.
5 Memorandum of minutes of a meeting between Deputy Minister Egan, Minister Forke, George Bogue Smart, F.C. Blair, and Commissioner Lamb, held in Ottawa on 15 December 1926. The minutes were written by Blair.
6 From 1903 to 1930, the Army transported between 200,000 and 250,000 people to Canada from Britain. Maj. Arnold Brown, *What Hath God Wrought: The History of the Salvation Army in Canada* (Toronto: Salvation Army Printing and Publishing House, 1952), 117, claims 200,000, while Moyles, *The Blood and Fire in Canada*, 262, claims that it was 250,000. The British *Emigrants Information Office Annual Report 1913* gives the breakdown for 1908-13 as follows:

Year	Non-assisted	Assisted by grant	Assisted by loan	Total assisted	Total emigrated
1908	5,396	22	1,879	1,901	7,297
1909	3,673	98	140	238	3,911
1910	7,809	150	904	1,054	8,863
1911	7,913	160	1,026	1,186	9,099
1912	6,717	125	1,279	1,404	8,121
1913	6,937	120	1,324	1,444	8,615
Total	38,445	675	6,552	7,227	45,906

These figures do not coordinate with Maj. Brown's for the year 1908.

7 Doug Owram, *The Government Generation: Canadian Intellectuals and the State, 1900-1945* (Toronto: University of Toronto Press, 1986), 132.

8 Adele Perry, *On the Edge of Empire: Gender, Race and the Making of British Columbia 1849-1871* (Toronto: University of Toronto Press, 2001), 131-32.

9 Desmond Glynn, "'Exploring Outcast London': Assisted Emigration to Canada, 1896-1914," *Histoire Sociale* 10, 29 (May 1982): 235.

10 See Lisa Chilton, "A New Class of Women for the Colonies: *The Imperial Colonist* and the Construction of Empire," *Journal of Imperial and Commonwealth History*, 31, 2 (May 2003): 36-56. The gendered nature of colonial settlement is also discussed in Katie Pickles, "Empire Settlement and Single British Women as New Zealand Domestic Servants during the 1930s," *New Zealand Journal of History* 35 (2001): 22-44, and Michele Langfield, "'A Chance to Bloom': Female Migration and the Salvationists in Australia and Canada," *Australian Feminist Studies* 17 (2002): 287-303.

11 Joy Parr, *Labouring Children: British Immigrant Apprentices to Canada 1869-1924* (London: Croom Helm, 1980), and Marilyn Barber, "Sunny Ontario for British Girls 1900-1930" in *Looking into My Sister's Eyes*, ed. Jean Burnett (Toronto: Multicultural Society of Ontario, 1986), 55-74.

12 Quoted in K.S. Inglis, *Churches and the Working Classes in Victorian England* (London: Routledge and Kegan Paul, 1963), 178. For detailed accounts of the origins of the Salvation Army, see Robert Sandell, *The History of the Salvation Army*, vol. 1, *1865-1878* (London: Thomas Nelson and Sons, 1947), and Fred Coutts, *The Better Fight: The History of the Salvation Army* (London: Thomas Nelson and Sons, 1964).

13 *War Cry*, 7 July 1991, quoted in Inglis, *Churches and the Working Classes*, 176. See also Victor Bailey, "'In Darkest England and the Way Out': The Salvation Army Social Reform and the Labour Movement, 1885-1910," *International Review of Social History* 24 (1984, part 2): 144.

14 Gen. William Booth, *In Darkest England and the Way Out* (1890; reprinted London: International Headquarters of the Salvation Army, 1942), 93.

15 Quoted in Inglis, *Churches and the Working Class*, 211.

16 *The New Settler*, January 1907, Salvation Army, London. For an interesting discussion on imperialism and British identity, see Ross McCormack, "Cloth Caps and Jobs: The Ethnicity of English Immigrants in Canada 1900-1914," in *Ethnicity, Power and Politics*, ed. J. Dahlie and T. Fernando (Toronto: Methuen, 1981), 42-43.

17 Canada, *House of Commons Debates*, 31 May 1906. Quoted in John W. Dafoe, *Clifford Sifton in Relation to His Times* (Freeport, NY: Books for Libraries, 1931), 105-6.

18 D.J. Hall, *Clifford Sifton*, vol. 1, *The Young Napoleon 1861-1900* (Vancouver: UBC Press, 1981), 258.

19 W.T.R. Preston, *My Generation of Politics and Politicians* (Toronto: D.A. Rose, 1927), 218. For more on the relationship between Preston and Strathcona, see Hall, *Clifford Sifton*, vol. 2, *A Lonely Eminence, 1901-1929* (Vancouver: UBC Press, 1985), 66.

20 Glynn, "Exploring Outcast London," 209-38.

21 By 1900 there were approximately 417 Salvation Army corps in Canada. Moyles, *The Blood and Fire in Canada*, 270-81. In Canada the history of the Salvation Army has received attention from historians interested in the nexus between culture, class, and religion. See especially Lynne Marks, "'Hallelujah Lasses': Working Class Women in the Salvation Army in

English Canada," in *Gender Conflicts: New Essays in Women's History,* ed. Franca Iacovetta and Mariana Valverde (Toronto: University of Toronto Press, 1992), and "The Knights of Labor and the Salvation Army: Religion and Working Class Culture in Ontario, 1882-1890," *Labour/Le Travail* 28 (Fall 1991). See also Mariana Valverde, *The Age of Light, Soap and Water: Moral Reform in English Canada 1885-1925* (Toronto: Oxford University Press, 1991), and "The Dialectic of the Familiar and the Unfamiliar: 'The Jungle' in Early Slum Travel Writing," *Sociology* 30, 3 (August 1996): 493-509.

22 LAC, RG 76, vol. 105, file 17480, part 1, Preston to Smart, 27 November 1903.

23 Ibid., Smart to Preston, 5 February 1904.

24 *War Cry* (London), 23 November 1907, and *All the World* 34, 4 (April 1913): 224.

25 *War Cry* (London), 9 March 1907, and *All the World* 34, 4 (April 1913): 224.

26 LAC, RG 76, vol. 105, file 17480, part 1, Salvation Army Loan Form for Those Wishing to Emigrate.

27 Ibid., Allen, who was a Canadian government inspector in London, to Preston, no date but between February 1904 and October 1904, and Smart to Paterson, 21 October 1904. Paterson worked at the Salvation Army headquarters in Toronto.

28 Ibid., Lamb to Preston, 7 October 1904.

29 Ibid., Smart to Preston, 21 October 1904.

30 Ibid., Coombs to Scott, 18 April 1905.

31 Ibid., Scott to W.W. Cory, 26 April 1905.

32 Quoted in Harold Begbie, *The Life of General William Booth: The Founder of the Salvation Army* (New York: Macmillan, 1920), vol. 2, 316-17.

33 LAC, RG 76, vol. 105, file 17480, part 1, Coombs to Oliver, 23 November 1905.

34 *War Cry* (London), 1906, 1907 (especially January to June 1907).

35 LAC, RG 76, vol. 105, file 17480, part 1, Coombs to Oliver, 23 November 1905.

36 Ibid., A. Jury to W.D. Scott, 7 February 1906.

37 *Times* (London), 17 February 1906.

38 Quoted in Hall, *Clifford Sifton,* vol. 2, 69.

39 LAC, RG 76, vol. 105, file 17480, part 1, James Smith, secretary of the Hamilton Trades and Labour Congress, to Sifton, 7 May 1904.

40 Ibid., Maj. T. Howell to Scott, 1 March 1907.

41 *Halifax Herald,* 1 8 March 1907, 1.

42 Glynn, "Exporting Outcast London," 223. Just two days after this event the Public Service Act of Nova Scotia was amended to create a position for a provincial immigration agent and increase funding for immigration from $10,000 to $12,000 annually. Previously, the province had been working in cooperation with the Salvation Army on immigration, but the premier declared that "the Salvation Army had drawn its immigrants principally from European cities and this was not the class of settlers that the province needed most. A number of people thus brought in are now supported by the charity of our own people because we have artisans enough of our own." Of course, this amendment was not prompted by the stranded immigrants in Port Hawkesbury; it had been devised before that incident. But it is indicative of the increasing complaints against charity-aided emigration.

43 Ibid., 225.

44 *All the World* 33, 8 (August 1912).

45 LAC, RG 76, vol. 105, file 17480, part 2, shipping agent in Halifax to Scott, 13 February 1911.

46 Donald Avery, *Dangerous Foreigners* (Toronto: McClelland and Stewart, 1983), 37.

47 Clifford Sifton to J.W. Dafoe, 18 November 1920, quoted in Ramsay Cook, ed., *The Dafoe-Sifton Correspondence 1919-1927* (Altona, MB: Manitoba Records Society, 1966), 41-42.

48 Quoted in Avery, *Dangerous Foreigners,* 94.

49 LAC, RG 76, vol. 105, file 17480, part 2, Scott to Cory, 16 February 1916.

50 Ibid.

51 Ibid. For example, on 11 November 1910, Scott sent a memorandum to Oliver that stated: "I think that the Army continues to do good work and I presume that you will be inclined to look favourably upon their requests."

52 Ibid., Scott to Mitchell, 16 August 1916.

53 Ibid., part 3, Lamb to Calder, 18 October 1918.
54 Ibid., Scott to Calder, 14 May 1919: "I see no justification in continuing either $6000 grant for hostels or $1500 grant for London office." All of the Salvation Army domestic hostels, except for the one in Halifax, were closed in 1919 because government subsidies were discontinued.
55 Ibid., Blair's notes regarding proposal of Commissioner Lamb, 6 March 1920.
56 Ibid., Blair to Smith, 31 March 1921.
57 Ibid., Smith to Calder, 27 April 1921.
58 Ibid., 2 May 1921.
59 Ibid., Smith to Blair, 30 April 1921, and Smith to Calder, 30 April 1921.
60 Ibid., Blair to Cory, 7 June 1921.
61 Empire Settlement Act, 31 May 1922, quoted in Sir John A.R. Marriott, *Empire Settlement* (London: Oxford University Press, 1927), Appendices A and B.
62 Quoted in Avery, *Dangerous Foreigners*, 97.
63 Mr. Charles Stewart to Lamb, 8 June 1922. The letter stated: "Referring to our discussion and your request for assistance of a grant of $25,000 for a period of five years I have taken this matter up with the prime minister and he has consented to agree to your proposal." This agreement signed by Stewart would later plague Lamb.
64 LAC, RG 76, vol. 105, file 17480, part 3, Blair to Egan, 22 September 1924
65 Ibid.
66 Ibid.
67 Ibid., Blair to Egan, 5 February 1925.
68 Ibid., Blair to Stewart, 3 February 1926. In fact, the Army transferred 929 domestics and juveniles who were eligible for the passenger grant in the fiscal year 1924-25. This was a marked reduction from the year before, when the total had been 1,479, but not quite as dramatic as Blair made it sound.
69 LAC, RG 76, vol. 105, file 17480, part 3, Blair to Colonel Tudge, 16 March 1926.
70 Ibid., Blair to Stewart, 3 February 1926.
71 Bondfield Report, *Canada's Child Immigrants Annual Report of the Committee on Immigration and Colonization to the Social Service Council of Canada,* January 1925.
72 Ibid., 82.
73 LAC, RG 76, vol. 105, file 17480, part 3, Blair to Egan, 11 May 1925.
74 Ibid., Walker to Egan, 22 July 1926.
75 Ibid. £36.18.9 was the equivalent of $155.60.
76 Salvation Army Archives, Juvenile History Sheets and Ledgers, 1917-27.
77 LAC, RG 76, vol. 105, file 17480, part 3, Smart to Blair, 19 August 1926.
78 Ibid., Blair to Egan, 6 August 1926.
79 Ibid.
80 Ibid., Blair to Walker, 20 September 1926.
81 Ibid. Meeting between Blair, Smart, Deputy Minister Egan, Minister Forke, and Lamb, 23 December 1926.
82 Ibid., 15 December 1926.
83 LAC, RG 76, vol. 105, file 17480, part 1, Smart to Preston, 2 November 1903.
84 *Manitoba Free Press*, 11 November 1925, 2.
85 Commissioner David C. Lamb, *Our Heritage – The Empire* (London: Salvation Army, London International Headquarters, 1926). Lamb also observed that Canadians generally believed that the Army's emigration work was motivated by a desire to increase its membership. Lamb claimed that in reality only 15 percent of the emigrants belonged to the Army. But compared to 1905, when the number was 5 percent, this was a substantial increase.
86 Salvation Army Archives, Domestic, Children's and Juvenile History Sheets and Ledgers, 1912-27.
87 Lamb, *Our Heritage – The Empire.*
88 Barber, "Sunny Ontario for British Girls 1900-1930," 61, and Parr, *Labouring Children*, 150.
89 LAC, RG 76, vol. 105, file 17480, part 4, Immigration Branch Meeting with Commissioner Lamb, 15 December 1926.

90 Avery, *Dangerous Foreigners,* 94; Peter Neary, "Canadian Immigration Policy and the Newfoundlanders, 1912-1939," *Acadiensis* 11, 2 (Spring 1982): 74; Irving Abella and Harold Troper, *None Is Too Many* (Toronto: Lester and Orpen Dennys, 1983).
91 *Manitoba Free Press,* 3 November 1925, 11.

12
Enigmas in Hebridean Emigration: Crofter Colonists in Western Canada
Marjory Harper

April 1923 was a momentous month in the demographic history of the Outer Hebrides. Within little more than a week, the Canadian Pacific liners *Marloch* and *Metagama* embarked a total of approximately six hundred emigrants from the islands of Barra, South Uist, Benbecula, North Uist, Harris, and Lewis, and took them across the Atlantic to new homes in Alberta and Ontario. The exodus was remarkable not only because it maintained a long-established tradition of mass emigration from the Western Isles but also because it was attended by more positive publicity than was usually associated with that most sensitive and pejorative of issues. By the 1920s the history – and historiography – of generations of emigration had created a Highland population that was deeply antagonistic to the reappearance of any practice that reminded them of forced removal, and proposals to make overseas colonization a key part of postwar reconstruction seemed doomed to failure. Yet that is what was proposed and implemented, with surprisingly little opposition, at least initially. Evidence from the press, oral testimony, government files, and church and estate papers, some of it recently released, allows us to explore puzzling enigmas in Hebridean emigration between the wars, with particular reference to changing perceptions of the British World overseas, the influence of agents in stimulating the movement, and disparities between expectations and experiences.

Opposition to emigration was deeply entrenched in the Highland psyche, especially in the Outer Hebrides, which had witnessed some of the most notorious evictions of the nineteenth century. Tainted by association with a potent mixture of proprietorial compulsion, government ineptitude, and perfidious capitulation by the participants, it seemed highly improbable that emigration would become an integral part of the response to renewed economic crisis in the Western Isles during the 1920s. Among the most unlikely locations for such a response were the southern Hebridean estates owned by Lady Emily Gordon Cathcart of Cluny Castle, Aberdeenshire.

Ever since the brutal evictions perpetrated by Col. John Gordon on these islands in the mid-nineteenth century, anti-emigration sentiment had been prominent in the affected crofting communities of Barra, South Uist, and Benbecula. Antagonism was rekindled in 1883 when Gordon's widow, along with estate factor Ranald Macdonald, orchestrated a further transatlantic exodus to the Canadian Prairies at the same time as the eruption of the Highland land war was bringing the region under an intensifying public spotlight. Prominent among the critics were the islands' Catholic clergymen, who resented Lady Cathcart's uncompromising anti-Catholicism. According to one priest, Donald MacColl, the proprietrix had tried "every means in her power to have the people young and old sent to Manitoba," aided by the sycophantic Macdonald, who "wishes to acquire for himself and Lady Cathcart popularity in making known through the press her kindness and generosity, but not in reality felt."[1]

The ten Long Island families who emigrated in 1883 were located just west of Manitoba, on homesteads in the vicinity of Wapella and Regina, where parsimonious and unsympathetic treatment by the Cluny estate factors earned the Canadian colonization scheme further bad publicity well into the twentieth century. When entrenched bad feeling inhibited Lady Cathcart's attempts to encourage further emigration of "suitable young people" from her island estates in 1911, Ranald Macdonald – aware of the antagonism against his employer – enlisted the help of established settler and loyal land agent of the Cluny estate management, Donald MacDiarmid, to encourage the public promotion of opportunities in the Northwest Territories by persuading some of his neighbours to write laudatory letters for publication in the Scottish press.

MacDiarmid was happy to oblige, but his enthusiasm was not widely shared. Although in 1922 the traditionally landlord-supporting *Aberdeen Journal* referred to Lady Cathcart as a "fairy godmother" to the emigrants whom she had sent from the "wave-tortured islands of the Hebrides to seek their fortunes on the rich prairies of Canada,"[2] continuing public hostility toward emigration throughout the Highlands after the war was both fuelled and reflected by plaintive newspaper editorials, at least in the Liberal press, which equated the exodus of the 1920s with the notorious Highland Clearances. The *Stornoway Gazette* in particular maintained a consistent attack on both the steady loss of the Hebrides' best "bone and sinew" and the government's preference for empire settlement over investment in the development of forestry, fishing, and hydro schemes.[3] The *Oban Times* also held the Board of Agriculture for Scotland culpable for ill-conceived domestic land settlement schemes and warned readers against the Canadian immigration department's "disastrous" propaganda and its disingenuous promise of free prairie land:

When Canada was advertised in the Outer Hebrides as the land of plenty, without doubt, it appealed to many who felt their needs had been unjustly neglected by both Providence and the Government. But less inspired views should have been displayed, showing central Canada with her smile of welcome completely obliterated as she lay, white and dead, for half the year in the cold grip of winter; then, perhaps, another of the brown, parched prairie radiating with the heat of summer; also it should have been depicted that, added to the trials and privations which must be endured, there is never any certainty of recompense.[4]

Yet by the 1920s, press and public hostility was neither universal nor unqualified, and even the crofter-supporting press demonstrated a growing ambivalence toward emigration and empire settlement. The *Highland News* described the sailing of the *Metagama* from Stornoway on 21 April 1923 with more than three hundred Ontario-bound passengers as "in no way marred by the bitter sadness of farewell ... but ... the first glimmer of the dawn of better things," while the *Oban Times* was confident that the equivalent number of emigrants who had left Lochboisdale a week earlier on the *Marloch* for the Canadian Prairies would "do well and be a credit to any community."[5] The *Glasgow Herald* unreservedly welcomed the departure of the *Marloch:* "It is a vastly different exodus this of an enlightened Hebridean community hieing forth of their own volition to a land of assured prospects, compared to the compulsory emigration of the old days, when families were obliged through deprivation of home and livelihood to join the westward flow of the population, not knowing what lay before them. The element of compulsion is not entirely absent from this modern instance of mass emigration, but it is compulsion, not of men's making, but born of the limitations of natural conditions in those barren western isles."[6]

The economic hardships of the 1920s that arose from the harsh Hebridean environment resembled the subsistence crises of the nineteenth century. Not only was agriculture in turmoil, with low livestock prices after wartime protection was removed, but also fuel was in short supply, and fishing was in deep trouble, the loss of the German and Russian markets having devastated the herring industry and curtailed a vital source of supplementary income for crofters, creating conditions reminiscent of those of the famine-stricken 1840s. But the new ingredient after the First World War was the islanders' more positive reaction to emigration as a remedy for their problems, a reaction attributable to the interplay of changing expectations, acceptable opportunities, and the services of professional facilitators.

There is no straightforward explanation of the islanders' revised expectations. Some contemporaries alleged that their apparent enthusiasm for emigration was simply a last despairing resort against the spectres of starvation or tuberculosis, or a statement of frustration at the tardiness of land settlement schemes and disbelief that the state would ever fulfil its promise to provide homes fit for returning war heroes. Between 1886 and 1919 the government had made four legislative attempts to tackle the running sores of Highland overcrowding and unrest, but the failure of the Board of Agriculture for Scotland to make effective use of the legislation to tackle problems of congestion meant that, by the 1920s, Highland land administration was characterized by a "near-absolute incapacity for change."[7] Frustrated tenants, including many war veterans, lost patience with the bureaucracy of the Scottish Office and the recalcitrance of landlords and resorted once more to land raids, simply taking possession of the farms they claimed.

If, as some commentators implied, Hebridean emigrants were provoked partly by the ineffectiveness of land legislation, the changing attitude of proprietors toward their estates encouraged others to regard it as an opportunity rather than a threat. Although landlords remained able to manipulate successive governments until 1919, the gradual erosion of their autocratic authority after 1886, combined with falling profits, high rates, deteriorating land, and the intensified radicalism among their tenants, made them increasingly prone to shedding their responsibilities by encouraging land purchase and peasant proprietorship. As the crofting community perceived that the traditional enforcers of emigration had capitulated, the overseas option came to be viewed as an economic expedient, or even a stepping stone to advancement, rather than a punishment. At the same time that protected tenancies and state pensions released young Hebrideans from the full weight of their former obligation to support elderly dependants, the younger generation was becoming increasingly aware of the insurmountable physical limitations and meagre economic returns of their environment. Ex-servicemen in particular were well placed to compare the subsistence lifestyle of the Hebrides with more comfortable conditions elsewhere, but even those who had never left home had been affected by the official investigations and legislation that had begun to integrate the Hebrides more fully with the rest of Scotland and Britain. Several Lewis emigrants in the 1920s had worked on the short-lived job creation scheme of the island's owner, Lord Leverhulme, building the road between Tolsta and Ness. Perhaps they decided to invest their wages in emigrating in the hope of avoiding a return to the inevitable unemployment that would have been their lot in Lewis. At the same time, Catholics in the southern Hebrides may have been readier to grasp the emigration option in reaction to perceptions of discrimination against their co-religionists in southern Scotland, particularly after the Church of Scotland's Church and Nation Committee was given a remit in 1923 to investigate the "menace to Scottish nationality and civilisation" that had been brought about by Irish immigration.[8]

Attitudes to emigration were revised in response to disappointed expectations in the domestic sphere as well as in response to a growing conviction
that acceptable, even exciting, opportunities were being offered overseas.
On 2 September 1922, *The Scotsman* attributed that conviction to the dissemination of positive information, combined with the erosion of clerical
hostility:

> Although nothing of it has been reported in connection with the Secretary
> for Scotland's visit to the Hebrides, there has been lately a distinct change
> of feeling in the Islands regarding emigration. It is not suggested that this
> movement has made itself an active rival of land settlement schemes, to
> which the lifelong habits of the islanders naturally tend. But unquestion-
> ably emigration is not now regarded with the extreme distaste that was
> almost everywhere found a few years ago. This change is largely to be attrib-
> uted to two causes; one the encouraging reports which are being received
> from crofter families who have gone out from Barra and South Uist, if not
> from other islands, and the other a new readiness on the part of some of the
> priests to consider emigration as a means of improving the condition of the
> people.

The Canadian government was also financing a fact-finding visit by three
crofters and a priest, who were to select suitable areas for settlement, and
The Scotsman concluded:

> Although it would be misleading to represent these incidents as indicating
> a widespread impulse, they are sufficiently significant to warrant the belief
> that the prejudice against the transfer of the home from the Hebrides to the
> prairies is becoming less stiff. If the Scottish Office and the Government
> here were willing to lend financial assistance the necessary money might
> readily be saved in the curtailment of smallholding development which
> can never lead to industrial prosperity, and an emigration policy, adminis-
> tered in conjunction with the Dominion authorities, might at last have a
> fair chance of a thoroughly adequate trial.

Two years later, James Wood, fishery officer in Stornoway, reinforced *The
Scotsman*'s observations when he noted that "the prejudice against emigration is fast breaking down in this region," and emigrants were receiving
both financial and moral support to cross the Atlantic.[9]

While the most acceptable opportunities were undoubtedly those created
by family and friends, the proactive attitude of the British government toward empire settlement in the 1920s simultaneously raised the general profile of overseas opportunities and provided concrete assisted relocation
schemes in collaboration with the self-governing dominions, just as *The*

Scotsman had advocated. Many of those who emigrated from the Hebrides were participants in such collaborative schemes, which came about as a result of the passage of the Empire Settlement Act in May 1922. Even during the war, the British government had begun to consider state-aided emigration as a means of promoting the economic development of the Empire and of preserving its vulnerable political cohesion, while on the other side of the Atlantic the Canadian government in 1919 opened the land settlement schemes already offered to its own veterans to selected British ex-soldiers, who were offered a free passage and assisted settlement to take up farming under the auspices of the Soldier Settlement Board of Canada. That first step toward official transatlantic collaboration was cemented and extended three years later when the Empire Settlement Act made provision for the British government to spend up to £3 million a year for a fifteen-year period on loans and grants for assisted passages, land settlement schemes, training courses, and other approved ventures in partnership with dominion governments or with public and private organizations in Britain or the dominions. Between 1922 and 1935, a total of 405,242 people emigrated from Britain under the auspices of a piece of legislation that not only constituted a marked departure from the British government's traditional reluctance to regulate or assist emigration but also contradicted the emphasis of the 1920s on stringent economy in public expenditure.[10]

Of particular significance for Hebridean emigration was a settlement scheme under the act that involved the extension to Canada of the established Australian practice of nomination. Based on the concept that successful settlers were the most persuasive recruiters of new settlers, individuals in the dominions could nominate friends in Britain for assisted passages, taking on themselves the responsibility for accommodation and after-care of their nominees. In 1923 the system was depersonalized to permit collective nomination of desirable categories of settlers by overseas societies, the selection of individuals being left to the counterparts or agents of those bodies in Britain. Canadian nominees, who were required to take up work on the land, could also, if they were war veterans, qualify for assistance from the Soldier Settlement Board in the acquisition of farms. Final selection was, as always, in the hands of the dominion authorities, but collective nomination clearly increased the scope for assisted migration and settlement, and provided the vehicle for the vast Hebridean exodus of the 1920s.

If the Empire Settlement Act provided the vehicle for crofter emigration, then the fuel was injected by professional emigration agents, whose promotional activities were often a further source of controversy and enigma. Particularly contentious was Andrew MacDonell, who throughout the 1920s orchestrated the collective nomination of Catholic families from the Southern Hebrides and their concentrated settlement in northern Alberta. When in September 1922 *The Scotsman* referred to an increasing warmness toward emigration among Hebridean priests, it probably had in mind the active colonization campaign being waged by MacDonell, who was already a seasoned emigration agent. After ordination as a Benedictine monk at Fort Augustus Abbey, he had spent eight years in charge of the Catholic mission to the surrounding districts of Fort Augustus, Glenmoriston, and Glengarry. In an abrupt change of career, he had then gone to Vancouver Island in 1912 in response to a request from the archbishop of Victoria that he should organize the removal of British orphans to British Columbia. To that end he established a receiving home and training farm at Ladysmith, British Columbia, before returning to Scotland for six months in 1913 as a salaried short-term dominion government immigration delegate.[11]

Following war service in France, for which he was awarded the Military Cross, MacDonell returned to Canada with the intention of resuming his child migration work by organizing the transfer of war orphans from the Highlands to British Columbia. But despite encouragement from the Canadian authorities, he soon dropped those fairly modest plans in favour of a much more ambitious scheme to recruit single men and their families to go from the Highlands to Ontario under the British and Canadian governments' collaborative offer of free passages to ex-servicemen and their dependants.[12] The veterans' scheme was in force from 1919 to 1922, and in the summer of 1921 the Canadian immigration department agreed to MacDonell's request for an expenses-paid recruitment visit to Scotland. Basing himself at Fort Augustus Abbey, he traversed the Highlands from upper Banffshire to the Hebrides, targeting Catholic areas in the hope of creating a Catholic colony in Canada. His meetings were well attended, and he claimed the enthusiastic support of both the Church hierarchy and the Hebridean clergy, while admitting at the same time that there was not a rush of recruits, as interested parties wished to "think it over." Out of a total of 829 applications, including 303 from Barra and 146 from South Uist and Benbecula, MacDonell selected 150 ex-servicemen to go to Ontario in 1922 under the auspices of Canada's Soldier Settlement Board.

On returning to Canada, MacDonell urged the federal authorities to exploit the spirit of restlessness in the Highlands by extending the scheme to civilians. Although the Canadian authorities were reluctant to do this, they were pleased with MacDonell's work, and when in 1922 he proposed to establish a Hebridean colony farther west, they collaborated in his venture to bring at least sixty islanders to northern Alberta, giving him a five-year lease on a disused Indian farm and school at Red Deer, at a peppercorn rent, for use as a receiving and training centre. From there they would move on to wage work or farms of their own. Also involved in the venture were the Catholic Church in the province, which promised to provide the settlers with churches and schools, and the Canadian Pacific Railway's Colonization Department, which was to pass on applications from farmers seeking workers.[13]

In order to benefit from the new collective nomination arrangements under the Empire Settlement Act, MacDonell had to operate through a charitable organization, and to that end he formed the Scottish Immigrant Aid Society, incorporated in Canada but with directors and administrative staff on both sides of the Atlantic. While he was responsible for the nomination and resettlement of the migrants in Canada, recruitment of individuals in Scotland was delegated to the Castlebay priest, Donald MacIntyre, who in the autumn of 1922 had, on MacDonell's invitation, led a four-man delegation to the Prairies to identify the best location for the new settlement, before returning to the islands to promote the venture. In a letter to the bishop of Argyll and the Isles, written on 10 December 1922, John Macneill, priest at Daliburgh in South Uist, wrote that he was expecting MacIntyre that night "on an emigration campaign," and two months later he wrote that "The emigration fever has taken on – about 20 families will leave Uist. I have no accurate information about Barra but from what I hear I should think an equal number, at least, will go from there. If these pioneers thrive there will probably be a general exodus from the Islands next year."[14]

Considerable public excitement and press publicity attended the embarkation of 291 passengers on the *Marloch* at Lochboisdale on 15 April 1923. Travelling with the party, in separate first-class accommodation, were the three island priests and sub-agents, Donald MacIntyre, James Gillies, and John MacMillan, and as evening fell, the passengers sought "encouragement and guidance" from their spiritual leaders. Yet the generally positive tone was reflected in press accounts that contrasted the "bleak island homes, and the bare, drab existence" of the emigrants with the "brave optimism and hope" that underpinned the decision to leave.[15]

After an uneventful passage, the ship docked at Saint John, New Brunswick, to be met by MacDonell, the local mayor, the St. Andrew's Society, and the provincial immigration agent. The welcoming party was apparently impressed with the calibre of the settlers, who were described as "alert, rugged, self-reliant, ... just the right type, physically and mentally, to make good in this country." After disembarkation they split into two groups for the rail journey to the west, taking their leave "with smiling countenances, glad that their long journey was over, and keenly expectant in their outlook towards the country which offer[ed] them greater prosperity than they ha[d] previously known."[16]

Yet MacDonell's colonization scheme was far from straightforward or uncontroversial. In the first place, his enthusiasm for large-group settlement in specially created colonies ignored the lessons of history and ran counter to the general policy of empire settlement in the 1920s. The vulnerability of exclusive group settlements had been demonstrated in 1903 in the Barr Colony at Lloydminster in Saskatchewan, and, more pertinently for MacDonell, by the endemic indebtedness and discontent in the Hebridean colonies established at Killarney and Saltcoats in the 1880s, the second of which had foundered within twenty years of its foundation.[17] MacDonell's venture also contradicted the long-standing opposition to emigration among Catholic clergy. Although Lady Cathcart's enthusiasm for emigration waned in the mid-1920s as her Canadian lands became an economic liability rather than an asset, at the time when MacDonell inaugurated his scheme, emigration was still perceived as a weapon used by the estate management to discriminate against undesirable Catholic tenants and was regarded with suspicion by laity and clergy alike. Whereas MacDonell had put a positive gloss on the mixed response to his 1922 recruitment drive, the Daliburgh priest, John Macneill, believed that the attempt to lure islanders to Ontario had "gone to pieces – Most of those who gave their names have been reconsidering the matter and have come to the conclusion that Canada is too far away."[18] Much stronger criticism of MacDonell's motives and poor organizational skills was expressed a year later by Ardkenneth priest William Gillies:

> Frankly, I am personally not in favour of the methods adopted by the organisers of the scheme. Even at this late date, the prospective settlers have no knowledge of the whereabouts of Fr. MacDonnell, & are quite "at sea" with regard to any practical information. Most of them have sold off their little all, and renounced their holdings. Let us hope they will not be left "in the lurch," tho' developments in this very direction would not in the least surprise me. Given a sound, practical, promising scheme, I am for it at once, but the present Utopian scheme is too uncertain, & the poor people cannot even get into communication with those who are apparently at the head of affairs. Personally, I do not care much for the touch of the hand that presumably guides these matters. And this, *not* from personal feelings, but from sad knowledge of former failures suffered under the same auspices ...
>
> The Uist people undoubtedly must emigrate or starve. They are so simple, & think that whatever the Reverend gentleman says must come true. I sincerely hope the settlers will be successful, & that promises will be fulfilled. At present, however, nobody seems to know where the people are going to; how they are to get there; what is before them; & they cannot even get into communication with the moving spirit!!![19]

Gillies' reservations were subsequently confirmed by the many disparities between the expectations and experiences of those islanders who did cast in their lot with MacDonell. D.J. Murphy, the Canadian government's emigration agent in northern Scotland, claimed that precipitate and irresponsible actions by MacDonell's associates had left the colonists vulnerable to disappointment and even destitution. Not only had they been promised advances of the entire cost of passage, instead of just the 75 percent to which they were entitled under the Empire Settlement Act, but they had lost money by prematurely selling off their meagre stock, and had not been advised of the consequences of a rejected application in a climate of pressing land hunger and competition for holdings.[20]

Indeed, the colonists' disillusionment seems to have been due at least partly to the way in which not only they but also MacDonell himself had been misled by the sub-agents. The four-man delegation that had toured western Canada at MacDonell's invitation in autumn 1922 had agreed that on returning to Scotland they would secure eighteen families for an initial settlement at Red Deer, ensuring that each family had capital of at least $750 to purchase and equip a farm. On that understanding, MacDonell spent the winter negotiating with the Soldier Settlement Board for the acquisition of suitable farms, unaware that his Scottish collaborators were recruiting fifty families, almost half of them penniless. The news of the imminent arrival of a large, impecunious party came to MacDonell at the last minute, forcing him to amend his plan to colonize the Red Deer area and instead seek emergency accommodation and farm work across the Prairie provinces for those who could not afford to take up land and begin farming at once.

In the event, twenty-eight families, comprising 148 people, accompanied MacDonell from Winnipeg to Red Deer for imminent farm settlement, while the remaining 143 migrants were allocated farm work in scattered Prairie locations. Within a few weeks the Red Deer contingent was augmented by the arrival of fifteen of the twenty families that had not accepted such placements, along with six or eight families that had gone to Ontario over a year earlier but had not been settled after completing their farm training. Not surprisingly, disillusionment soon set in among colonists who, having been promised land, houses, and immediate employment, found themselves cooped up in dormitories at the inadequate Red Deer reception centre at their own expense, sitting targets for real estate dealers, as well as for epidemics of infectious, sometimes fatal, diseases. Even those who were in a position to take up farms were unhappy with the properties secured for them by MacDonell, on the grounds that the downpayments were too expensive and the farms too far from the railway.

While MacDonell renegotiated with the Soldier Settlement Board for alternative farms, the conflict entered the political arena when in June 1923, Alfred Speakman, Member for Red Deer, raised in the federal Parliament the "deplorable plight" of the Hebrideans stranded in his constituency, and his sentiments were picked up and reiterated across the Atlantic by a number of Scottish Labour MPs at Westminster.[21] By midsummer, however, all but six of the fifty-six disgruntled families had been settled on acceptable, partially cultivated quarter sections in three main areas: west of Red Deer, north of Edmonton, and east of Camrose. Canadian commentators tended to blame the teething troubles more on the settlers themselves than on MacDonell or his associates, claiming that the impoverished Hebrideans were "a clannish people of peculiar psychology" who were unrealistically optimistic about their prospects of instantaneous success.[22]

Undeterred by early setbacks, MacDonell soon began to plan a further recruitment drive in the Western Isles and a more sophisticated relocation program, which, with extra funding to cover cottage accommodation, farm training, and loans for farm purchase, as well as assisted passages, was meant to overcome the problems encountered by the pioneers. After securing funds and arranging for the construction of one hundred cottages at Red Deer, MacDonell went to Scotland in February 1924 to supervise the recruitment campaign. But once again he had to modify the misleading expectations raised by his associate, Father John MacMillan, who had gone straight to the Hebrides while MacDonell held talks with the Scottish Catholic hierarchy in Glasgow. MacMillan had, according to MacDonell, "been truly eloquent in extolling Canada," but had "said a little too much, for he stated, I was told, that there were farms awaiting every family that would emigrate."[23] This false inducement had to be corrected by MacDonell in his follow-up interviews with applicants, but even without the incentive of immediate independence, the persistence of poor economic conditions at home and the propaganda of MacDonell and his CPR associates convinced many Hebrideans that emigration would be a worthwhile step. As a result, two substantial contingents left Lochboisdale in 1924, the *Marloch* embarking 198 passengers on 28 March and the *Marburn* embarking an even larger party on 31 July. Already on board the *Marloch* when it called at South Uist were 90 Highlanders from the Catholic Highland districts of Lochaber and Mallaig, while the *Marburn* party also included some southern Scots and around 250 impoverished Northern Irish Catholics who had heard about MacDonell's enterprise and had petitioned to be included in it.[24]

The Canadian immigration department's apparent willingness to meet MacDonell's incessant requests for financial and practical support might at first glance suggest official approbation of his activities, and a greater confidence than had been shown in him the previous year. But such approbation was heavily qualified by concern about misleading promises, unsuitable emigrants, unoccupied cottages, and unpaid debts. Harold Roy, a Soldier Settlement Board field officer in Alberta, complained in August 1924 that MacDonell had promised his recruits houses, employment, and, after a year, farms, all without the knowledge or approval of the main land agents, the Soldier Settlement Board. Even worse was the practice of bringing "men of dotage" to Canada in the full knowledge that they and their families, having neither the ability nor the desire to take up farming, would become public charges, often in the cities.[25] Such claims were guaranteed to inflame public and political opinion in a country that had for long suspected British emigrationists of using patriotism as a cloak for the export of misfits. As a result, deportation was exacted swiftly on those who did not meet Canada's requirements.

Complaints were also lodged by disgruntled settlers. Of particular concern to the immigration authorities was a petition sent to the minister of the interior by fourteen disillusioned Hebrideans still at Red Deer, who painted a dismal picture of broken promises, abandonment on unworkable land, and looming destitution.[26] Although some of the petitioners' complaints were subsequently disproved, other settlers became disheartened after the hard winter of 1924 and asked to be sent home. Apparently oblivious to distress, and to the steady deterioration in relations between his Scottish Immigrant Aid Society and the Canadian immigration department, MacDonell maintained as his priority in 1925 the expansion of his empire. In the teeth of Canadian criticism that his controversial ventures were damaging the efforts of the department's Inverness-based agent to recruit settlers under the new 3000 Families Scheme, he pressed ahead with a proposal for empire settlement funding to establish a training farm in Alberta for youths from Catholic public schools in Britain. Predictably, his bid elicited an icy response from the Canadian authorities, who described it as "costly, unnecessary, faddy and impracticable." They were equally dismissive of his proposal to create a female agricultural settlement in the same area, their primary fear being that MacDonell's overcommitment was likely to rebound financially on the immigration department.[27]

Undaunted either by such warnings or by the poor results of his 1925 recruitment campaign, MacDonell launched an even more ambitious venture in 1926, when he attempted to create a colony of Hebridean Catholics at Vermilion in northern Alberta on a 12,140-hectare tract of land purchased on mortgage from the CPR, which he christened Clandonald. It was to be populated partly by earlier settlers brought over from Red Deer and partly by a hundred new immigrant families from Scotland. Once again, however, experiences failed to match expectations, as the newly built cottages proved to be poorly insulated, established settlers resented the absorption of their cattle pasture into the new colony, and the onset of the Depression prevented the enterprise from getting off the ground. The main problem, however, was the Scottish Immigrant Aid Society's ever growing indebtedness. By 1927 only £20 of the £2,000 owed to the British government for the passages of the 1923 pioneers had been repaid. Most of those who had come out under the cottage scheme in 1924 had neither repaid their fares nor paid any rent on their cottages, and in 1939 the Clandonald colonists were still more than $50,000 in debt.

Several enigmas emerge from the story of Andrew MacDonell's long-running campaign to colonize northern Alberta with Hebridean Catholics, including the surprising initial enthusiasm for his venture in a region of entrenched hostility to organized emigration, and the paradoxical accounts of the experiences and prospects of those who went to Canada. But the central enigma is the character of MacDonell himself. Did he orchestrate a "notable piece of work in Canadian land settlement," as one dominion newspaper claimed, or an ill-conceived, egocentric, and mismanaged fiasco?[28] At the zenith of his work, between 1923 and 1928, a total of 1,315 colonists, most of them Highlanders, crossed the Atlantic under his auspices. Undeterred by setbacks, he persistently pursued his goal of creating close-knit, isolated Prairie communities, convinced that group migration would "always be more effective than scattered and haphazard settlement."[29]

In constructing colonies that he intended to be both ethnically and religiously autonomous, MacDonell was following the example of many other emigrationists. His parties were always supervised by at least one priest; the assistant managing director of his enterprise in Canada was the former Barra priest Donald MacIntyre, and one of MacDonell's first priorities at Clandonald was to provide a church in 1926, followed in 1929 by a convent school staffed by Benedictine nuns.[30] In 1955 he was awarded an MBE in recognition of his "great work for the emigrants,"[31] and the Canadian immigration authorities, despite reservations, not only regularly renewed his temporary contract but also agreed to most of his wide-ranging financial demands.

Yet other evidence suggests MacDonell's motives were suspect and his schemes were littered with misjudgments. The decision to expand his horizons from juvenile emigration, in which he had pre-war experience, first to soldier settlement and then to a much more ambitious community colonization venture, was probably the product of a rising desire – made possible by the Empire Settlement Act – to make a name for himself as a successful agent. But perhaps overweening ambition lured him into the tactical error of neglecting the area and people whose needs he understood for wider, but less familiar, recruitment grounds in southern Scotland and Ireland. It is notable that most deportees came not from the Hebrides but from Glasgow and Ireland. Even when his ventures were in obvious difficulties, he continued to pursue ever more ambitious schemes, to the exasperation of his sponsors and the neglect of his pioneers.

MacDonell was overly ambitious for the Church as well as for himself. This was reflected in the denominational exclusiveness of his group settlements, a characteristic that both belied his claim that they were non-sectarian and ran counter to the inclusive tenor of much interwar empire settlement.

Indeed, MacDonell's indiscriminate enthusiasm for Catholic emigration beyond his own colonies further exacerbated his neglect of the Hebridean colonists. By the mid-1920s he was dabbling in juvenile and female emigration projects, although he failed in his attempt to establish farm training schools in the Prairie provinces. These involvements aggravated his penchant for having too many costly irons in the fire and aroused the wrath of the Canadian immigration department, which complained that administrative issues were frequently left to chance – or to the Department – since MacDonell "carries his head office around with him ... and a good deal of business is allowed to run itself or drift because of the utter impossibility of Father MacDonell looking after it personally."[32]

Throughout the 1920s MacDonell had to contend with both the vacillation of the Canadian government and the opposition of anti-emigration elements on both sides of the Atlantic. Resenting the way in which the assertive imperialism of the Empire Settlement Act threatened to eclipse long-standing Canadian settlement strategies, the dominion authorities sometimes procrastinated when processing applications from would-be emigrants – a tactic that frustrated MacDonell – on the grounds that good recruits were being diverted to Australia. Empire settlement was widely regarded as a euphemism for the dumping of the unemployed and unemployable dregs of Britain's population, an image reinforced by evidence of deficiencies among MacDonell's recruits, but when he offered to make an example of selected defaulters, the immigration department demurred, anxious "not to give rise to the idea of persecution as that would be fatal to the work."[33]

Official disquiet about the calibre of assisted migrants was matched by a simmering public antagonism in Canada at large. One caustic correspondent warned the immigration department in 1923 that before assisting Hebrideans to come to Canada, the department should note that the descendants of their countrymen who had come to Cape Breton a century earlier were "absolutely unreliable citizens," who were crowding the asylums and were content to remain in poverty.[34] MacDonell alleged that some of his Clandonald colonists were victimized because they had required financial assistance to emigrate, while group settlement in general was regarded with suspicion on the grounds that "a group of Britishers would immediately set about forming a union and having a strike."[35] Perhaps MacDonell entertained similar fears himself, for he was haunted by the fear that "inimical interests" were hatching Communist plots to subvert the colonists by encouraging them not to pay their debts or to demand immediate access to ready-made farms.[36] When this multifaceted disquiet found its way across the Atlantic, it fuelled the arguments of anti-emigrationists, both at Westminster and in the Hebrides. While the Labour Party used it as a stick with which to beat imperialists over the Empire Settlement Act's viability, the *Stornoway Gazette* on more than one occasion castigated MacDonell for his negative response to the "Highland Problem," which, it claimed, had simply depopulated the Hebrides and encouraged the government to neglect its economic responsibilities to the region.[37]

MacDonell's enigmatic relationship with his sponsors, politicians, and the press was paralleled by ambiguities in his relationship with Southern Hebrideans on both sides of the Atlantic. While unusually large numbers had overcome their antipathy to emigration and rallied to the agent's call, MacDonell rapidly jeopardized their welfare and squandered their trust through his own carelessness and overcommitment. In both 1923 and 1924 he should have kept a tighter rein on his overzealous associates in Scotland to prevent them making rash promises and bringing out vast numbers of people on false pretences. First impressions were crucial to the success of the work, especially in 1923, when better-off islanders who had been unable to release themselves from their tenancy agreements were keeping a watchful eye on the fate of their countrymen who had sailed on the *Marloch*. Furthermore, the Canadian Immigration Department was particularly concerned when bad publicity arising from MacDonell's enterprises began to damage its own recruitment campaign in Catholic areas of the Highlands. In 1924 MacDonell admitted that careless selection was partly to blame for the failure of several Irish recruits in particular, and, some years later, in confronting the continuing indebtedness of his colonists, he conceded that he should have encouraged a greater sense of responsibility in the Clandonald settlers by drawing up formal rental contracts instead of loose agreements of sale.[38]

Were Andrew MacDonell's problems the fruit of wilfulness, ignorance, or simply misfortune? To some extent he was a victim of circumstance, contending not just with over-expectant colonists and political opposition on both sides of the Atlantic but also with an increasingly chilly economic climate. Having launched his enterprise in the optimistic era of the early 1920s, his recruits were still finding their feet when the onset of worldwide depression in the 1930s put an end to any hope of debt repayments and plunged some families into utter destitution. His cottage scheme was thwarted by the increasing inability of established Canadian farmers to offer a living wage or to employ men all year round, and even the critical immigration department admitted in 1938 that the Clandonald venture had been bedevilled by economic circumstances over which the colonists had little control. But economic hardship does not fully explain the intense resentment that MacDonell engendered in the Southern Hebrides, a lingering resentment that continued to fuel speculation and controversy about his motives long after he had stopped sending colonists to Canada. A question mark remains over the extent to which he collaborated – deliberately or unwittingly – with the detested Lady Cathcart, whose shareholding interests in the Canadian Pacific Railway and the Hudson's Bay Company added an extra dimension to her long-standing enthusiasm for sending crofters to the Dominion.[39] Although specific evidence for such collaboration is lacking, it is not difficult to understand why, in the face of the collapse of the much-vaunted colonization schemes, disillusioned colonists and their relatives in the Hebrides tarred the agent and the proprietrix with the same vilifying brush. Perhaps their bitterness was even more acute because their perceived betrayal was at the hands of a clergyman and his priestly associates, and, even worse, a clergyman who was suspected of collaborating with a landowner whose aggressive emigration policy had long been directed particularly against Catholics. MacDonell's links with Lady Cathcart, real or imagined, may also help explain why the Scottish Catholic hierarchy, having allegedly supported his venture at first, soon became determined to frustrate it, and distanced itself completely from MacDonell as the volume of public criticism grew.

Some enigmas therefore remain unanswered, the subject of speculation rather than verifiable evidence. In the last analysis, however, perhaps MacDonell's venture failed not just because of mistiming, political and public antagonism on both sides of the Atlantic, or his own ambitions, but because the Canadian fever of the 1920s was a departure from the established and expected pattern of crofter antagonism to emigration. As disillusioned colonists wrote – or returned – home, that antagonism re-emerged with full and enduring force, bringing into sharp relief the many enigmas of an apparently aberrant enthusiasm for overseas relocation that had gripped the Outer Hebrides for a short time after the First World War.

Notes
1 Scottish Catholic Archives, Edinburgh (SCA), DA66/77/3. D. MacColl, priest, Ardkenneth, South Uist, to bishop of Argyll and the Isles, 28 October 1883, 27 September 1883.
2 *Aberdeen Journal*, 30 September 1922.
3 *Stornoway Gazette*, 7 February 1924.
4 *Oban Times*, 5 April 1924.
5 *Highland News*, 28 April 1923; *Oban Times*, 21 April 1923.
6 *Glasgow Herald*, 16 April 1923.
7 Ewen A. Cameron, *Land for the People? The British Government and the Scottish Highlands, c. 1880-1925* (Edinburgh: Tuckwell, 1996), 204.
8 *Report on the Schemes of the Church of Scotland, Church and Nation Committee* (1924), 639.
9 National Archives of Scotland (NAS), AF62/1964/1, Emigration of Fishermen: Proposed Settlement of Scottish Crofter Fishermen in British Columbia, letter dated 25 November 1924.
10 For discussion of the political and economic implications of the act in particular, and interwar emigration policy in general, see Stephen Constantine, ed., *Emigrants and Empire: British Settlement in the Dominions between the Wars* (Manchester: Manchester University Press, 1990).
11 Library and Archives Canada (LAC), RG 76, C-10446, file 968592, part 1, R.A. MacDonell to Department of the Interior, 19 November 1913; F.C. Blair, secretary, Department of Immigration and Colonization, Ottawa, to Thomas Gelley, commissioner of immigration, Winnipeg, 27 March 1923. For a detailed discussion of MacDonell's colonization schemes,

see Marjory Harper, "Crofter Colonists in Canada: An Experiment in Empire Settlement in the 1920s," *Northern Scotland* 14 (1994): 69-108.

12 LAC, RG 76, C-10446, file 968592, part 1, G. Bogue Smart, chief inspector of British immigrant children, to R.A. MacDonell, 6 November 1919.

13 R.A. MacDonell, "British Immigration Schemes in Alberta," *Alberta Historical Review* (Spring 1968): 5-13. The paper was published posthumously, MacDonell having died in 1960.

14 SCA, DA66/28/15, 10 December 1922; DA66/28/16, 19 February 1923.

15 *Press and Journal,* 16 April 1923.

16 *Gazette* (Montreal), 30 April 1923. See also *Stornoway Gazette,* 3, 17 May 1923.

17 Wayne Norton, *Help Us to a Better Land: Crofter Colonies in the Prairie West* (Regina: Canadian Plains Research Center, University of Regina, 1994).

18 SCA, DA66/28/6, Macneill to Bishop Donald Martin, 2 March 1922.

19 Ibid., DA66/78, William Gillies to Bishop Donald Martin, 19 February 1923. Original punctuation (including ellipses) retained.

20 LAC, RG 76, C-10446, file 968592, part 1, Murphy to J.O. Smith, 17 April 1923.

21 *Stornoway Gazette,* 14, 28 June 1923.

22 LAC, RG 76, C-10446, file 968592, part 1, W.J. Black, deputy minister, Department of Immigration and Colonization, undated report, quoted in *Saturday Night,* 21 July 1923.

23 SCA, DA9/26, R.A. MacDonell, "British Immigration Schemes."

24 Ibid.

25 LAC, RG 76, C-10446, file 968592, part 3, Harold Roy to F.C. Blair, 20 August 1924; J. McCabe, Satuffer, Alberta, to W. Cory, deputy minister of immigration and colonization, 28 October 1924; J.K. McCormack, Edmonton Trades and Labour Council, to Edmonton City commissioners, 15 November 1924. ,

26 Ibid., petition sent to the Hon. Charles Stewart, 23 January 1925, with covering letter from Archibald McLellan, Red Deer.

27 Ibid., F.C. Blair to W.J. Egan, deputy immigration minister, 1 April 1925; Blair to W.R. Little, 2 April 1925.

28 Ibid., part 1, *Saturday Night,* 21 July 1923.

29 Ibid., MacDonell to Robert Forke, minister of immigration, 4 January 1928.

30 Diana Sim, "Clandonald: A Rural Catholic Colony" (undergraduate paper, University of Calgary, 1987), 27.

31 *Inverness Courier,* 2 December 1960.

32 LAC, RG 76, C-10446, file 968592, part 4, F.C. Blair to M.V. Burnham, supervisor, Women's Branch, Department of Immigration and Colonization, 26 May 1926.

33 Ibid., MacDonell to Egan, 16 July 1925.

34 Ibid., part 1, R. Law, Toronto, to Department of Immigration and Colonization, 22 February 1923.

35 Ibid., part 5, MacDonell to Forke, 4 January 1928.

36 Ibid., part 4, MacDonell to Blair, n.d. (late autumn 1925); part 5, MacDonell to W.R. Little, 7 August 1927; part 6, MacDonell to Blair, 17 July 1939.

37 *Stornoway Gazette,* 7 February 1924, 10 July 1925.

38 Sim, "Clandonald," Appendix, notes from MacDonell's undated typescript, "Report for St Benedict Abbey, Fort Augustus" (Glenbow Alberta Institute).

39 See Saskatchewan Archives Board, collection R-E2494, accession numbers R87-48 and R86-610, for correspondence regarding the Hudson's Bay Company in the Cluny Castle Archives.

13

Nation-Building in Saskatchewan: Teachers from the British Isles in Saskatchewan Rural Schools in the 1920s
Marilyn Barber

> It comes as a shock to many English teachers, who fresh from the "Old Country" with very British and well-meant sentiments, are apt to overlook or be blind to the great differences between a truly British Englishman and a truly British Canadian.[1]

The teacher who sent this report home to England in 1927 had been employed for more than three years in the rural elementary schools of the western Canadian province of Saskatchewan. She was one of more than five hundred British Anglican teachers encouraged by Church of England missionary societies to migrate to western Canada in the decade after the Great War. Recruited to transmit British values and culture through their work and their example, the teachers discovered that they themselves had to learn and adapt in order to be accepted. The correspondent who communicated her insight that great differences existed between the Canadian and the English concepts of Britishness had developed this understanding only through personal experience living and teaching in isolated rural schools. Ironically, she recalled her happiest time as the two years spent in a mixed district of Ukrainians and French where she received nothing but kindness and appreciation from the settlers, extending even to her efforts to provide religious instruction. By contrast, her most painful experience of the "age-long quarrel of national and religious differences" occurred in a district divided between Canadian Methodists and adherents of the Church of England.[2] Her account indicates the need to explore more fully the contested meanings of Britishness in western Canada in the 1920s. Women and men had an equal task as teachers in Saskatchewan's one-room rural schools. Nonetheless, cultural assumptions of femininity and masculinity affected their reception in the local community, their relations with the male educational hierarchy, and the interpretation of the values they were to transmit. Focusing on the experiences of teachers from the British Isles within the context of Saskatchewan educational policies helps to reveal the continuation of common ties of British heritage but also the evolution of a distinctive Canadian view of Britishness arising from settlement conditions and the mingling of peoples.

The death of imperialism as a result of the First World War has been a central tenet in the Canadian narrative of political nation-building.[3] Generations of Canadian schoolchildren have learned the signposts from colony in the nineteenth century to full national sovereignty after the First World War. More recently, however, British cultural studies have stimulated widespread interest in understanding the cultural meaning of Britishness as expressed through empire and nation. Building on this interest, the British World Conferences held in Cape Town in 2002 and Calgary in 2003 have promoted analysis of the sense of British identity in the former dominions. Focusing on cultural evolution over time, instead of on specific political events, leads to a reassessment of the impact of the First World War. Rather than the war constituting an abrupt division, the interwar decades form a transitional period during which Canadians struggled to forge an identity based on Canada's distinctive duality as both a British and a North American nation. Benedict Anderson, in his seminal book investigating nations as "imagined communities," claims that "from the start the nation was conceived in language, not in blood, and that one could be 'invited into' the imagined community."[4] Migrants from the British Isles to Canada had an ambiguous status as members of the nation in the 1920s. Unlike continental European immigrants, they did not have to be "naturalized" (a wonderful word, as Benedict Anderson notes) to acquire the privileges of citizenship.[5] In the Canadian census, the British Isles (England, Ireland, Scotland, Wales, and the lesser isles) were grouped with Canada in the section for British born, which was distinguished from the section for foreign born.[6] Hence migrants from the British Isles could occupy positions of influence that were usually closed to foreign migrants. Nonetheless, migrants from the British Isles had to adapt before they could identify with Canada as home or be fully accepted by Canadians as members of the national as opposed to the imperial community.[7] Teachers from the British Isles accepted responsibility for the education of Canadian citizens at the same time as they dealt with issues of their own identity.

Saskatchewan schools in the 1920s faced the challenge of preparing for Canadian citizenship the children of settlers of diverse national and ethnic origins. Prairie settlement had been so rapid in the period before the First World War that schooling had not been able to keep pace with the ever increasing need. The war that interrupted the influx of immigrants allowed provincial educational officials more opportunity to assess progress and problems. The intense patriotism associated with fighting the war also aroused public fear that the schools were failing in their mission to assimilate non-

English-speaking immigrants into the province. Concern focused especially on the large number of Ukrainians and other immigrants from central and eastern Europe, in part because they often formed large bloc settlements where, according to a survey for the government, "they live largely unto themselves, using their own mother tongue, their own manners and customs, often to the utter disregard of Canadian standards and ideals."[8] The resulting campaign to legislate conformity through the schools singled out language as the practical and symbolic key to identity. In Saskatchewan in 1918, politicians responded to the strong demand for "English only" in the provincial elementary schools by abolishing the hour each day in the school curriculum allowed for languages other than English. While the political schools controversy centred on language legislation, educators continually stressed the pre-eminent influence of the teacher as "the one great factor" in improving schools.[9] They believed that the background, qualifications, and initiative of the teachers would be critically important in determining how Saskatchewan schools met the challenge of building a strong postwar nation to ensure that the sacrifice of sixty thousand Canadian soldiers' lives had not been in vain.[10]

In postwar Saskatchewan, the one-room rural school carried the greatest responsibility for education in citizenship. With the sole exception of Prince Edward Island, Saskatchewan had the highest percentage of rural population of any Canadian province. At the time of the 1921 census, 71 percent of Saskatchewan residents lived in rural areas; by contrast the majority of the population of Ontario and Quebec resided in urban centres.[11] The children of non-English-speaking parents were also concentrated in rural schools. Less than half (46 percent) of the rural population was of British origin, whereas those of British origin composed 70 percent of the smaller urban population.[12] The number of teachers employed in Saskatchewan had dramatically risen from 1,017 in 1906 to more than 6,000 by the end of the First World War. Because of the constantly escalating demand, the provincial Department of Education in the immediate postwar years still struggled to provide sufficient qualified applicants, especially for the more isolated rural schools. The need for teachers opened the way for Church of England missionary societies to recruit British teachers in order to maintain British Christian values in Saskatchewan. At the same time, previous migrants from England, Scotland, Ireland, and Wales entered the teaching profession by training at Saskatchewan normal schools. One of these migrants, Robert England, with his wife, Amy, became the model for a group of scholarship teachers specially selected and prepared to teach Canadian citizenship in what educational authorities considered the more difficult rural schools among "new Canadians."[13] Shared membership in the British Empire helped immigrants from the British Isles take a position of potential community leadership beside Canadian-born teachers, many of whom were migrants from eastern

Canada. A comparison of the work of Robert and Amy England with the Church of England teachers contributes to unpacking the assumptions hidden within the discourse of British values and Canadian citizenship.

With a rather misleading name, Robert England migrated to Saskatchewan from Ulster, Ireland, shortly before the First World War.[14] Born in 1894, the thirteenth of fourteen children of a devout Portadown Methodist family, England, at the age of eighteen, rejected becoming a probationer on the Methodist circuit and instead followed one of his brothers to Canada. After working on Saskatchewan farms and taking extramural courses from Queen's University in Ontario, England joined the Canadian Expeditionary Force (CEF). Commissioned as a lieutenant, he went over the top with the Canadian forces at Vimy Ridge, was twice severely wounded, and was awarded the Military Cross. After marrying an English Nursing Sister in 1919, he returned to Canada. Unable to farm because of his war wounds, he studied at Queen's University, reading books dealing with Canadian schools issues. These included the 1918 publication *The Education of the New Canadian,* by J.T.M. Anderson, a Saskatchewan teacher and school inspector who from 1918 to 1922 filled a special position in the provincial Department of Education as director of education among new Canadians.[15] Anderson, who in England's words "preached vigorous Canadian citizenship," induced England and his wife, Amy, to take Slawa school in a Ukrainian district thirteen kilometres from the nearest village of Hafford, Saskatchewan, in May 1920.[16] The initiatives of Robert and Amy England at Slawa led to the War Memorial Scholarship Project, which encouraged fifty-one scholarship teachers to go forth as "apostles of the highest type of Canadian citizenship" into Saskatchewan's isolated immigrant blocs.[17] England not only provided leadership for the project but also analyzed it in a book, *The Central European Immigrant in Canada,* which received national and even international attention when published in 1929.[18] In addition, the work of Robert and Amy England at Slawa became the subject of a silent film, *Nation-Building in Saskatchewan: The Ukrainians.*[19]

The War Memorial Scholarship Project sought to "keep faith with those who sleep in Flanders fields" by sending the best-qualified teachers as nation-builders into the most difficult districts, districts that seldom could attract or keep a qualified teacher.[20] George Weir, principal of the Saskatoon Normal School and Grand Master of the Masonic Grand Lodge of Saskatchewan, which funded the project, noted that "the real values of the Scholarship Project depend very largely, not so much on what these teachers actually teach, as on what they *are,* – on their character, influence and personality."[21] Neither Weir nor Anderson (who enthusiastically promoted the project), although both Canadian-born, commented on any perceived impediment to accepting Robert England, a recent Irish immigrant, as a model of Canadian citizenship. A 1922 article in the *Grain Growers' Guide* noted that England "[was] a young Irishman by birth but ha[d] chosen Canada for his home."[22] England himself indignantly refuted a later claim that he could not share in the distinctive attitude of native Canadians because he had not been born in Canada.[23] In his memoirs, he rebuked such "parochial thinking" by reiterating that he had chosen his country, and his task had been to live for Canada. He underlined the depth of his commitment to Canada by asserting that his activities "reaffirmed [his] *consent* to Canadian citizenship, made its *conservation* significant, and by *co-operation* [he] came to share in its rewards, responsibilities and opportunities."[24]

England's identification with his chosen country cannot be disputed, but his active consent to Canadian citizenship does not in itself fully address the transition from his Irish youth to his Canadian adult years. Unlike the central European immigrants whom he hoped to educate for Canadian citizenship, England obviously considered that he himself immigrated to Canada with an excellent knowledge of the cultural values essential for good Canadian citizenship. Although there definitely were national variations in curriculum, his Irish education had acquainted him with the same British literature, history, and ethical concepts that his Canadian pupils were expected to learn. In addition, the Methodism so important to his Irish family was a dominant Christian denomination claiming a nation-building role among immigrants in western Canada. Thus a shared British heritage helped eliminate seams in the journey from Ireland to a Canadian teaching position. An Ulster Irish perspective on Britishness that included an emotional and intellectual distance from the hegemonic conflation of English with British may also have assisted Robert England in identifying with Canadians' similar resistance to English hegemony. Beyond these cultural connections, however, the impact of the First World War on England's life must be taken into account. The war years separate England's Irish youth from his Canadian adulthood. His commitment to Canadian citizenship was forged in the crucible of war as he bonded with his fellow Canadian soldiers fighting in France. One of England's two brothers who preceded him to Canada also enlisted in the CEF and was killed fighting in France; the other emigrant brother returned to Ireland. In spite of having many immediate family ties in Ireland and none in Canada, in spite of marrying an English bride, at the end of the war Robert England returned to the country that he had made his own through his war service.

The men who directed Saskatchewan educational policy praised Robert and Amy England as ideal apostles of Canadian citizenship because, as a married couple, they represented the family values at the heart of British civilization. By the 1920s far more women than men were attracted to elementary school teaching across Canada. In Saskatchewan, female teachers outnumbered male teachers by a ratio of more than five to one. Education officials regretted the scarcity of men, particularly married men, whom they regarded as the best candidates for teaching positions among non-English-speaking settlers. A 1918 Survey of Education prepared for the Saskatchewan government strongly recommended "that specially prepared Canadian teachers – preferably married men with practical wives – be subsidized by the Government" to teach in central European communities.[25] Therefore the War Memorial Scholarship project deliberately recruited an unusually high proportion of men. Of the fifty-one teachers, including England, selected for the project, over half were men, and at least fourteen of the men were married. Most of the scholarship teachers were Canadian-born but, interestingly, the eight scholarship teachers identified as born in the British Isles were all men, five of whom were married. The lack of appropriate living conditions for single female teachers was often cited as one reason why men were considered more suitable for schools in central European communities. Accommodation could be improved for both male and female teachers by providing better small houses for teachers, called teacherages, on the school grounds, but the security of a young female teacher in an isolated district remained an issue. By contrast, a married man with a practical wife not only meant two workers for the price of one but also brought Canadian family life to the community. As explained by one of the scholarship teachers, "The married teacher can establish a home and give the people an opportunity of seeing Canadian customs and manners."[26]

Historians interested in the gender dimensions of colonialism and nation-building have emphasized the importance of everyday life and of the domestic realm of the home and indeed of the school to the formation of the imagined community that is the nation.[27] Slawa school by its very name conveyed the impression that Ukrainian immigrants were making on the landscape and material culture of western Canada.[28] The community at Slawa, however, was reportedly disillusioned with previous short-term teachers of Ukrainian background and was prepared to cooperate with a well-qualified, native-English-speaking teacher like Robert England who would remain in the school for more than a few months. The Ukrainian parents desired that their children be educated, to take advantage of Canadian opportunities. They strongly rejected the proposal made by one of the few English-speaking ratepayers in the district that the school be closed in the winter months to save taxes.[29] At Slawa, Robert and Amy England moved into a new teacherage, which Amy made into a "cozy home" intended not only for their own comfort but as a model for the surrounding community.[30] In addition, Amy England assisted her husband with his social work. Her background in England had equipped her with excellent skills for her new occupation. Reared in a comfortable bourgeois environment in rural Hampshire, Amy Hale spent some years as a school nurse in the east end of London before joining Queen Alexandra's Imperial Military Nursing Service – Territorial Force.[31] She thus knew the social proprieties of English middle-class domestic life but also the problems of those lacking resources to maintain middle-class standards.

At Slawa, Amy England took charge of hygiene, health, and first aid for both school and home. Cleanliness was a value that scholarship teachers closely associated with the moral order of British civilization, in contrast to their observations of dirt and disorder within many Ukrainian homes built with mud floors and walls.[32] They realized that far from being an isolated private sphere, the domestic realm directly affected the public social order. England and the other scholarship teachers believed that inappropriate gender relations in Ukrainian families threatened the development of a strong Canadian nation. Therefore, in the questionnaires that he devised for a school and community survey by the scholarship teachers, Robert England specifically asked for comments on women's work and women's status in the family.[33] The interest reflected the concern that central European women were not able to carry out their essential domestic role of raising healthy children and creating a proper home environment because they were too fully occupied working outside the house in the fields and because they did not receive sufficient respect from their husbands. In the view of one scholarship teacher near Insinger, if the women stayed in the home, "the home would probably become a real place in which to live, instead of merely a shelter from inclement weather. Well kept and comfortable attractive homes, neatly dressed clean children, well cooked, well served meals would undoubtedly have a good moral effect upon the men. They would rise to the occasion and endeavor to help the wife keep up the standard of living."[34] England himself considered the women in his community underprivileged because a "woman [was] thought of as a chattel, rather than a wife, in the marriage relation."[35]

The teacher could attempt to instill more approved concepts of domesticity and gender relations through school activities, sometimes in subtle ways. For instance, England worked out a system of responsible government in his school to establish confidence in elected representatives and respect for authority. By his system, the girls chose captains to be in charge of "inside duty," that is, inside the school, whereas the boys elected captains for "outside duty."[36] The school arrangements thus mirrored the desired division of work within the family. While England could instruct the boys in British precepts of manliness and the girls in British precepts of feminine duty and responsibility, no instruction educated as well as personal example. Through their own home and their relations with each other, Robert and Amy England presented a model of Canadian family values to the surrounding community. In circumstances in which British values were set against the customs of immigrants from outside the British Empire, the issue of whether Robert from Ireland and Amy from England represented a distinctive Canadian outlook became less important than the shared British heritage uniting

Canada with the British Isles. England conveyed this sense of Britishness defined against the other when he wrote: "The school, especially the rural school, is the buffer between our culture and the cultures of the new Canadian."[37]

Like Robert England, the British Anglican teachers recruited by the Church of England missionary societies were forced to reflect on the meaning of Britishness in Canada. Unlike Robert England, they had little or no opportunity to adapt to Canadian ways before they began teaching. Those who were trained went directly to Saskatchewan schools with their British teaching qualifications. Those without training started teaching after only a short course at Regina or Saskatoon normal school. The continuing close ties within the Church of England between western Canadian dioceses and the British Isles brought the British teachers to Canada. Lacking sufficient Anglican workers, western dioceses relied on the traditional support of British missionary societies more than on the Toronto-based Canadian church to fill the need. Not only was the educational work of teachers a vital component of missionary activity, but in western Canada, Anglican teachers could compensate for the shortage of Anglican clergy. Indeed, through the provincial schools they could reach communities where Anglican clergy were not welcome.

One ardent imperialist clergyman, Rev. George Exton Lloyd, initiated the teacher schemes.[38] He first persuaded the Ladies Association of the evangelical Colonial and Continental Church Society (CCCS) to begin sending female teachers to Saskatchewan shortly before the First World War. Toward the end of the war, Lloyd expanded the teacher recruitment efforts by founding a new missionary society, the Fellowship of the Maple Leaf (FML), that was specifically devoted to the supply of British teachers for western Canada and sponsored both women and men. An English emigrant who came to Canada as a young man, Lloyd dedicated most of his life to the motto he gave the FML: "Keep Canada British and Christian." Although in the 1920s there was debate within mission circles concerning the relation of Christianity to British culture, that debate did not seem to include mission work among white settlers in Canada.[39] Lloyd personally had no doubt that British progress and the advance of Christianity were inextricably intertwined. As he later wrote, "I am a firm believer in God's call to the British race ... Not because we are White or Black but because, as far as I can see, we are the most Christian nation."[40] In particular, Lloyd believed that the Church of England with its strong imperial connections represented the essence of Britishness in Canada. He urged Anglicans in the British Isles to support FML work in Canada because "the more we can do to make that great nation of the future *Christian,* according to our own Anglican form, the more we are helping to keep them British as well."[41] Lloyd did not cherish any false hopes that all western Canadian settlers could be converted to Anglicanism. Instead, he wanted to maintain as high a proportion as possible of British Anglicans, especially in leadership positions. British Anglican teachers in the schools could exert a vital influence in ensuring that Canada fulfilled its rightful destiny as a British Christian nation.

The recruitment of the Church of England missionary societies significantly increased the number of British Anglican teachers in Saskatchewan, even though the societies failed to supply as many as they wished. From 1918 to 1930 they sent more than five hundred teachers to western Canada, the great majority going to Lloyd's home province of Saskatchewan. Although the societies stressed that candidates must be of good character and background, the chief criterion for selection was religion. The Ladies Association of the CCCS sought evangelical churchwomen, ages twenty to thirty, who could witness for God in the Empire, and, as teachers in the prairie and bush schools of Saskatchewan, would be "above all, desirous of winning their scholars for Christ."[42] The FML, casting a wider net, accepted women and men over the age of eighteen provided they were "baptized confirmed communicants" of the Church of England.[43] Advertising in the daily press, the FML received a wide range of applications but destroyed "those from Roman Catholics, Presbyterians, and others that were evidently no good."[44] While a few of the candidates selected were of Welsh, Scottish, or Irish background, the great majority were English, reflecting the main national strength of the Church of England. Hence, in referring to national identity, "British" was often used as identical to "English" by the Church of England societies. All of the CCCS candidates and over 80 percent of the FML candidates were women. Accepting the numerical dominance of women among both elementary school teachers and missionary workers, Lloyd stressed the need for British women on the western Canadian frontier. The emigration of young female teachers would provide the future good-quality British wives and mothers so essential for establishing British family life and sustaining the race. As Lloyd noted, "'English men, of all nationalities in the West, marry more than any others, out of their own nationality.' This is not a desirable thing."[45]

While the scholarship teachers were directly selected by Saskatchewan educational officials, the British Anglican teachers, after selection by the church societies, had to obtain approval from the provincial Department of Education before they could be employed in Saskatchewan schools. In the immediate postwar years, the Saskatchewan government warmly welcomed the British teachers, asking the assistance of the Church of England societies in filling the teacher shortage.[46] J.T.M. Anderson, himself an Anglican, enthusiastically supported the importation of Anglican teachers from the British Isles, in contrast to his opposition to the employment of naturalized Canadians. As he wrote to Premier Martin, "I thoroughly agree with you that young men and women of our various races must be given equal chances with our own sons and daughters, but I feel that we are justified in limiting our selection to those *born here* and fully trained in our schools."[47] By 1922, however, the supply of teachers in the province began to meet the demand. As teaching positions became more difficult to obtain and average salaries for Saskatchewan teachers steadily declined, Canadian teachers vigorously objected to organized efforts to import British competition. In the later 1920s the Department of Education retained a limited number of places in Saskatchewan normal schools for candidates selected by the Church of England societies only because "it has been pointed out that it might be exceedingly unwise in the long run to close the doors to such a desirable class of immigrants."[48] The main desirability of the teachers was not their educational qualifications but their British identity. Controversy was mounting in the late 1920s as continental European immigration once again began to exceed British immigration to Canada, so the federal Department of Immigration and Colonization wanted to show encouragement to suitable British immigrants.[49] Preferred immigration status in contrast to central European immigrants did not mean that British teachers always received local acceptance even in English-speaking communities, where they might appear as outsiders lacking a Canadian outlook.

Unlike the scholarship teachers who had been given a mission to educate for Canadian citizenship, the British Anglican teachers had been recruited as "living links of Empire" to transfer the best British cultural values to the imperial frontier in western Canada. Yet to carry on their work they had to receive local acceptance. When they left the British environment of the Anglican teachers' hostels in Regina and Saskatoon, they scattered to schools across the province. By default if not by choice, many taught at least initially in outlying rural schools, often in communities of mixed ethnicity and religion. Experienced British teachers realized the importance of community acceptance. One CCCS teacher informed the Ladies Association: "The first thing is to have the confidence of the people and then they are willing to let you do pretty much as you like in the school."[50] Another pointed out: "The teacher must be able to adopt the Canadian viewpoint if her influence was to tell."[51] For newly arrived Anglican teachers, usually identified as English rather than British, fitting into the community or adopting a Canadian viewpoint was often not easy. Having been told that they were bringing culture and education to Canada, British teachers might be met by resentment from Canadians who felt that they were being treated as inferior colonials. One FML teacher left her first school after only six weeks because, as she explained, "one family did not like me being English and I was very English."[52] Canadian-born settlers often resented what seemed to be presumptions of unwarranted superiority on the part of the English. An English accent, an indicator of class at home, became a sign of ethnic difference in Canada and was sufficient to arouse suspicions of claims to English cultural superiority.[53] A teacher who had been advised "not to push the

English side of things" because the English were not popular on the Prairies recalled how she unwittingly gave cause for criticism by insisting that her pupils use the English pronunciation of words like "vase." She was unappreciative, however, when the inspector who informed her of the correct Canadian pronunciation also spent twenty minutes telling her of all the foolish things other English teachers had done.[54] In addition, British teachers were ridiculed because they did not possess the skills naturally acquired by Canadians growing up in the west.[55]

Like Robert and Amy England, the British Anglican teachers taught the health, hygiene, and appropriate behaviour that they, too, considered British values. Leadership through personal example, however, was more challenging for them. Young single women, as many were, did not have the same community authority as a married man nor the same ability as a married couple to serve as a model of family life. Most also lacked the personal negotiating skills, resources, and contacts that Robert England had acquired. At the same time as they tried to maintain suitable standards in domestic and public life, they themselves had to adapt to a new environment with a harsh climate, a foreign landscape quite unlike the cultivated domesticity of rural England, and a more informal lifestyle. Instead of importing middle-class British domesticity, a number of British teachers reflected instead on the character-building attributes of fitting into boarding houses or ill-maintained teacherages. Often they had to cope with a lack of privacy, lower standards of cleanliness, and families whose manners might differ considerably from their own. If they were to be accepted, especially in English-speaking communities, they could not seem to have pretensions of British superiority.

Even as "great differences between a truly British Englishman and a truly British Canadian" created problems for recent English immigrants in their mission to build a British nation, so Christianity was a divisive as much as unifying force in western Canada. In the 1920s, almost all Saskatchewan settlers, regardless of ethnicity, shared a Christian heritage.[56] Nonetheless, Saskatchewan politicians and educators did not challenge the belief of the Church of England societies that Britishness and Christianity had a symbiotic relationship. Long-standing denominational rivalries within Christianity, however, could lead to bitter conflict. In English Canada, the dominant Protestantism particularly remained suspicious of Catholic loyalty. Therefore, Saskatchewan political policy upheld the principle of the separation of church and state. Non-denominational provincial schools were established to build a united nation and especially to overcome the major divide between Protestantism and Catholicism. Teaching at Slawa among Ukrainian settlers who were mainly Greek Catholic or Greek Orthodox adherents, Robert England based his citizenship training on the new social theories of the progressive education movement rather than on the morality of religious education. He viewed religion as an impediment rather than an aid to achieving his objectives. England was certainly not alone among Methodists in the 1920s in taking a more secular route to building an earthly kingdom. Nonetheless, he turned down a request from Rev. C. Endicott, superintendent of Methodist missions in Saskatchewan, to operate a Methodist social centre at Hafford because he thought even the sponsorship of the Methodist Church might be misunderstood.[57] As an expression of both his own beliefs and his ideals for the Canadian nation, England quoted the verse:

> This is the land where hate should die,
> Though dear to me, my faith and shrine,
> I serve my country best, when I
> Respect the creeds that are not mine.[58]

When he appealed for an end to religious strife, England had in mind not only long-standing denominational rivalries within Christianity in Canada but also what he referred to as the dark stories of religious hatred that he found imported from Europe by the immigrants at Slawa. Therefore, instead of religious faith, he stressed the British ideals of freedom, tolerance, and respect for others regardless of race or creed, which he believed should guide the building of the Canadian nation.[59]

Rev. Lloyd had a very different viewpoint from Robert England regarding the relation of religion and education. Although he accepted that the government schools could not be made Anglican, he stressed the importance of Christianity for educating British subjects. "We can help to make these schools British in tone and ideal. We can have a Christian atmosphere in the daily work. We can give plain Scripture instruction to the children on the week day as far as the law allows, and open and close the schools with daily prayer."[60] Teachers sent to Canada by the Church of England societies did not all share a missionary vocation; some applied primarily because they needed employment or wanted to travel. Nonetheless, those whose letters were selected for publication in Anglican periodicals particularly emphasized their efforts to teach religion. Some could only inculcate Christian principles through other school subjects and personal example. One teacher in a Roman and Greek Catholic settlement reported: "I dare not do very much, but as you say, indirectly I can help a great deal. We use the Lord's Prayer, of course, and we have learnt three simple hymns, but it is in everyday life and intercourse that one can try and instil Christian principles, and they are certainly needed."[61] Other teachers in districts of mixed religion succeeded in starting Sunday schools, often on Friday afternoon, which were welcomed by people who felt deprived of spiritual sustenance. A teacher in a mixed English and Ukrainian district later recalled, "I took Sunday School with them and they were very pleased to have it and the parents were too, although the trustees said to me, 'You'll get those old Ukrainian priests after you.'"[62]

Religion could fill a social as well as a spiritual need in rural districts cut off from the commercial entertainments of the 1920s. When an Anglican teacher and her Seventh-day Adventist suitor together began a Sunday school, adults as well as children flocked to the gathering.[63] Thus, on one hand, the scattered settlement and mixed population in many rural districts encouraged religious cooperation. One male FML teacher who had had some theological training in England before emigration noted that in Canada he became quite ecumenical and remained so ever since.[64] On the other hand, not only Catholic leaders but also other Protestants strongly resisted any British Anglican efforts that seemed designed to exert control by the Church of England over other denominations. Hence, the English Anglican teacher who started an Anglican Sunday school in a district where the children already attended a Methodist Sunday school encountered the "age-long quarrel of national and religious differences." In this community, the equation of Methodist with Canadian settlers and Anglican with English immigrants exacerbated the conflict. Although recruited as living links of empire, British Anglican teachers could not claim a special status for the Church of England as defender of Britishness in Canada.

While religion had a tenuous place in Saskatchewan schools because of its potential divisiveness, Saskatchewan educational officials enthusiastically embraced a British youth organization that they viewed as ideal for training all students in good Canadian citizenship. They found the Scout and Guide movement so appealing not solely because of the British ideals conveyed but also because of the potential inclusiveness of the organization. Divorced from explicit religious teaching, Boy Scouts and Girl Guides provided a program for building the qualities of moral and social character considered essential for successful participation in Canadian family, community, and national life. In the opinion of J.T.M. Anderson as director of education for new Canadians, "no activity is calculated to assist in the 'getting together' of our various races to a greater degree than the Boy Scout and Girl Guide movement. No race or creed but may join and the training towards good citizenship cannot be overestimated."[65] Scouting, which Lord Baden-Powell founded in England in 1908, grew rapidly in Saskatchewan at the end of the First World War. By 1920 the number of Scouts in Saskatchewan almost equalled the number in Ontario, a much more populous province, and greatly exceeded the membership in any other Canadian province. In Canada, as in Britain, the associations of Scouting with military men and war aroused suspicions of militarism.[66] In 1920s Saskatchewan, however, the leadership of Department of Education officials validated the acceptability of peace scouting in postwar provincial schools. A.H. Ball, deputy minister of education, was provincial commissioner, and R.F. Blacklock, departmental registrar, was provincial president.[67] Robert England shared their enthusiasm for the educational benefits of Scouting. At Slawa he organized the first Ukrainian Boy Scouts and Wolf Cubs with the aid of the Saskatoon Rotary Club, which supplied the uniforms. Dress is important as an indicator of identity and at first his Ukrainian community did not approve of the strange clothing. They were disturbed by the military overtones of the uniform but also by the short pants, which were accepted masculine attire for English boys but not for western Canadian farm lads or Ukrainian peasants. As England explained, "The uniform lent colour to the suspicion that the teacher was trying to make soldiers and there was objection to the 'bare knees.'"[68]

Although certain English accoutrements of Scouting did not transfer easily to the western Canadian Prairies, England, with his persuasive powers, overcame obstacles to make Scouting a central force for youth training and community development. Nonetheless, perhaps it was fortunate that he did not provide uniforms for the girls, who simply wore white dresses and straw hats. England approved so highly of Scouting because he believed the movement simultaneously promoted racial cooperation and taught what he defined as Anglo-Saxon ideals. Unlike the uniform, these cultural ideals at the heart of the movement conveyed citizenship values that were both British and Canadian. England wanted to develop in his community "that characteristic British sense of fair play – the Anglo-Saxon spirit of sportsmanship."[69] Through the youth organization attached to the school, he hoped to instill in his students citizenship qualities that he believed were lacking in many of the homes. In his words, "Anglo-Saxon ideals of sportsmanship and service are not, in many cases, understood ... There is no better way to inculcate some of the humaneness of the Anglo-Saxon than to adopt the Scout programme, with its emphasis on self-discipline, obedience to parents, kindness to animals and old people, courtesy, thrift and industry."[70]

The Scouting movement crossed ethnic boundaries but it did not challenge prescribed gender divisions. Although teachers in one-room schools, whether male or female, organized both Scouts and Guides, the men in the Saskatchewan educational hierarchy concentrated their leadership and thinking on the Scouts. Men most appropriately undertook the training of boys, and, like Baden-Powell himself, they undoubtedly valued Scouting for its ability to capture the interest of boys who were considered less amenable to direction than girls. In Saskatchewan, where the organization of Girl Guides lagged well behind Boy Scouts, several of the Anglican women teachers from England led in developing and sustaining the movement for girls. Ella Bashford, superintendent of the Saskatoon CCCS teachers' hostel, organized several companies before 1921, when the provincial council was formed. Her influence encouraged teachers at the hostel to participate in the Guide movement, but some teachers were particularly valuable because they arrived in Canada as experienced Guiders. For example, Mary Cameron, a FML teacher, not only organized the children at her school but also trained other Guide officers and took responsibility for the Lone Department, the branch for Guides who were too isolated to belong to a local company.[71] Because Guiding was an imperial and international movement, the British teachers could readily transfer their organizational knowledge from the British Isles, where Guiding was better established, to western Canada, where experienced leaders were in very short supply. In addition, although Saskatchewan educators found the Scout and Guide movement attractive because of its ability to transcend religious divisions, Anglican leaders often found the movement attractive as an organization for youth training that could be sponsored by the Church.[72] The British Anglican teachers could draw on their religious as well as their educational background in promoting Guides in Saskatchewan. This flexibility of the Guide and Scout movement helped to ensure its popularity.

Through their example and their work, teachers from the British Isles contributed to building the Canadian nation. In 1930 the Saskatchewan Royal Commission on Immigration and Settlement reported: "We have found two schools of thought. One is that we should establish Saskatchewan as a province of British blood; and the other is that that is too late, and we should establish a Province of Canada with British conditions and ideals."[73] The commission's report encapsulated some of the contested meanings of Britishness in the province of Saskatchewan that affected the teachers' mission. Lloyd, the Church of England societies, and also Anderson particularly supported teachers from the British Isles because of their British blood. Not only would they reinforce the British-born population of Saskatchewan but they would also carry cultural ideals from the British Isles to the new society being created in western Canada. When the teachers were working among new Canadians, the shared British heritage that united Canada with the British Isles became more important than issues of national difference among the British-born. Viewed from other perspectives of Canadian nation-building, however, being born in the British Isles did not guarantee acceptance. Those in Saskatchewan who wanted a Canadian province with British ideals often had a distinctive Canadian outlook on Britishness. Unlike Robert England, who had become identified with Canada through his war service, teachers arriving from the British Isles after the war had to adapt to Canada as their home while they were teaching. Like other immigrants, they had to be "invited into" the Canadian community. Because almost all the Anglican teachers were from England, they were subject to Canadians' anger at being treated as mere colonials by English immigrants, something which, as an Irishman, Robert England did not encounter. Although sharing a supposedly common language with English Canadians, teachers from England found that their accent set them apart. While Robert and Amy England became models for British domesticity at Slawa, many of the young female teachers from the British Isles, lacking similar authority, had to accept the unfamiliar Canadian manners of their community in order to proceed with their work.

Through the school and school-based organizations such as Scouts and Guides, Robert England and the British Anglican teachers attempted to convey the ethical and social values that both they and Saskatchewan educational officials defined as British ideals. The space to be accorded Christianity, however, was much more controversial. Because religion was potentially such a divisive force in Saskatchewan, Robert England, reflecting the views of many Saskatchewan educators, did not attempt to link British ideals with Christianity. He stressed instead the British ideals of freedom, tolerance, and respect for others regardless of race or creed, which he believed should guide the building of the Canadian nation. By contrast, many of the British Anglican teachers responded to the religious mission that Church of England leaders in both Britain and Saskatchewan expected them to undertake. Finding a desire for spiritual nourishment in many rural communities, they attempted to maintain the Christian foundation of British ideals in Canada. They could not, however, promote a special status for the Church of England as defender of Britishness.

Notes

1 Anglican Church General Synod Archives, Toronto (ACGSA), Fellowship of the Maple Leaf Papers (FML), *Magazine* (December/January 1927-28): 13.
2 Ibid.
3 R.G. Moyles and Doug Owram, *Imperial Dreams and Colonial Realities: British Views of Canada 1880-1914* (Toronto: University of Toronto Press, 1988), conclude that the war brought both the climax and the extinction of the imperial era. Similarly Carl Berger, *A Sense of Power: Studies in the Ideas of Canadian Imperialism, 1867-1914* (Toronto: University of Toronto Press, 1970), 264, argues: "Many factors limited and curtailed the appeal of imperialism: the First World War killed it."
4 Benedict Anderson, *Imagined Communities: Reflections on the Origin and Spread of Nationalism*, rev. ed. (London: Verso, 1991), 145.
5 Ibid. As explained in *The Canadian Encyclopedia*, vol. 1, 2nd ed. (Edmonton: Hurtig Publishers, 1988), 427, "Before 1947, Canada's Naturalization Acts conferred British subject status on immigrants being naturalised in Canada and on native-born alike. The Canadian Citizenship Act, the first nationality statute in Canada to define its people as Canadians, came into force on 1 January 1947."
6 Anderson analyzes the census as an institution of power in shaping the nation. *Imagined Communities*, chap. 10.
7 Carl Bridge and Kent Fedorowich, "Mapping the British World," *Journal of Imperial and Commonwealth History* 31, 2 (May 2003): 2, point out that mapping the British World includes the encounters millions of British migrants had with earlier generations of people who were curiously very much like themselves but also quite different. They note that these encounters are little addressed in the literature on colonialism, which focuses on relations between colonizer and the colonial "other."
8 H.W. Foght, *A Survey of Education in the Province of Saskatchewan* (Regina: King's Printer, 1918), 73.

9 Ibid., 152.
10 This chapter concentrates on the role of teachers from the British Isles within Saskatchewan educational policy. The perspective of continental European immigrants on educational efforts to build a nation in western Canada is beginning to be examined by those with the necessary language skills, but most attention has been given to the period before and during the First World War. See Stella M. Hryniuk and Neil G. McDonald, "The Schooling Experience of Ukrainians in Manitoba, 1896-1916," in *Schools in the West: Essays in Canadian Educational History* (Calgary: Detselig, 1986), and Orest T. Martynowych, *Ukrainians in Canada: The Formative Period, 1891-1924* (Edmonton: Canadian Institute of Ukrainian Studies Press, University of Alberta, 1991).
11 *Census of Canada*, 1921, vol. 1, 345.
12 Calculated from *Census of Canada*, 1931, vol. 1, 718-19. The statistics are for 1921.
13 At the end of the war, Canadian educators were among those who began to use the term "new Canadian" instead of "foreign immigrant" as an indication of the increased emphasis placed on assimilation to a Canadian identity.
14 The biographical information on Robert England comes from a combination of sources, especially his memoirs, Robert England, *Living, Learning, Remembering: Memoirs of Robert England* (Vancouver: Centre for Continuing Education, University of British Columbia, 1980); his personal papers, Library and Archives Canada (LAC), MG 30 C181; and the author's interview with Robert England, Victoria, British Columbia, 29 May 1983. See also Susan E. Wurtele, "'Apostles of Canadian Citizenship': Robert England, the CNR and Prairie Settlement," in *Reflections from the Prairies: Geographical Essays*, ed. H. John Selwood and John C. Lehr (Winnipeg: Department of Geography, University of Winnipeg, 1992), 18-23.
15 Born in Ontario in 1878, Anderson went from education to politics in Saskatchewan. In 1924 he became leader of the Saskatchewan Conservative party and in 1925 was elected MLA for Saskatoon City. He was premier of Saskatchewan from 1929 to 1934, leading a cooperative government of Conservatives, Progressives, and independents.
16 England, *Living, Learning, Remembering*, 175.
17 George Weir, introduction to Robert England, *The Central European Immigrant in Canada* (Toronto: Macmillan, 1929), x.
18 Susan E. Wurtele, "Assimilation through Domestic Transformation: Saskatchewan's Masonic Scholarship Project, 1922-23," *Canadian Geographer* 38, 2 (1994): 132, notes that reviews of England's book appeared in every major newspaper in Canada, and the book received international coverage in the *Times Literary Supplement* and the *London Morning Post*.
19 A copy of the film is in the film archives at Library and Archives Canada.
20 England, preface to *The Central European Immigrant*, viii.
21 LAC, MG 30 C181, vol. 5, file 23, Scholarship Report, n.d.
22 Amy J. Roe, "Teachers and Schools," *Grain Growers' Guide* 15 (13 September 1922): 22.
23 England, *Living, Learning, Remembering*, 133.
24 Ibid. Emphasis in original.
25 Foght, *A Survey of Education*, 153.
26 LAC, RG 30, Canadian National Railway Papers, vol. 5937, Final Report, G.J. Tomlinson, April 1923.
27 Recent Canadian examples are Jean Barman, *Sojourning Sisters: The Lives and Letters of Jessie and Annie McQueen* (Toronto: University of Toronto Press, 2003), an account of two sisters from Nova Scotia who by teaching in British Columbia in the late nineteenth century helped to domesticate the province; and Myra Rutherdale, *Women and the White Man's God: Gender and Race in the Canadian Mission Field* (Vancouver: UBC Press, 2003), especially chap. 4, "'Oh, to Be in England': Making a Home Away from Home."
28 James Darlington, "The Ukrainian Impress on the Canadian West," in *Canada's Ukrainians: Negotiating an Identity*, ed. Lubomyr Luciuk and Stella Hryniuk (Toronto: University of Toronto Press, 1991), 53-80. See also the numerous articles of John C. Lehr, including "Ukrainian Houses in Alberta," *Alberta Historical Review* 21 (1973): 9-15; "The Landscape of Ukrainian Settlement in the Canadian West," *Great Plains Quarterly* 2 (1982): 94-105; "The Cultural Importance of Vernacular Architecture," in *Continuity and Change: The Cultural*

Life of Alberta's First Ukrainians, ed. Manoly Lupul (Edmonton: Canadian Institute of Ukrainian Studies, University of Alberta, 1988): 87-99; "The Ukrainian Sacred Landscape: A Metaphor of Survival and Acculturation," *Material Cultural Bulletin* 29 (1989): 3-11; "Preservation of the Ethnic Landscape in Western Canada," *Prairie Forum* 15 (1990): 263-76.

29 Interview with Robert England, Victoria, British Columbia, 29 May 1983.

30 "Teachers and Schools," *Grain Growers' Guide* 15 (13 September 1922), 22.

31 England, *Living, Learning, Remembering,* 15.

32 Some teachers also observed that young people returning from working for English Canadians tended to build homes that more closely resembled a standard Canadian house and could be kept clean. Money obtained through the work as well as the exposure to Canadian-style architecture would help explain the change.

33 England, *The Central European Immigrant,* Appendix B, 217-30, contains the complete questionnaires used for survey by scholarship teachers. The first group of teachers in 1922 submitted three reports. The second group in 1923 answered only the first questionnaire.

34 LAC, RG 30, vol. 5937, George J. Tomlinson, Rural Municipality of Insinger, Second Report.

35 LAC, RG 30, vol. 5938, Robert England, First Quarterly Report, 31 July 1922.

36 "Teachers and Schools," *Grain Growers' Guide* 15 (13 September 1922), 22.

37 England, *The Central European Immigrant,* 8.

38 Born in London, England, in 1861, Lloyd came to Ontario in 1881, completed his theological training at Wycliffe College, Toronto, and served in Ontario and New Brunswick. He worked for the CCCS and came to Saskatchewan in 1903 as chaplain of the All-British Colony that settled around Lloydminster, named after Lloyd. Lloyd was bishop of Saskatchewan from 1922 to 1931.

39 Andrew Porter, "Empires in the Mind," in *The Cambridge Illustrated History of the British Empire,* ed. P.J. Marshall (Cambridge: Cambridge University Press, 1996), 204-5; Jeffrey Cox, "Audience and Exclusion at the Margins of Imperial History," *Women's History Review* 3, 4 (1994): 508.

40 ACGSA, George Exton Lloyd Papers, I A2, H.B. Hall correspondence 1938-39 re Chapter 3 "On Migration."

41 ACGSA, FML, *Magazine* (March/April 1917): 5.

42 *Greater Britain Messenger,* 223 (July 1918): 68; 276 (January/February 1926): 2. An advertisement, "Teachers Wanted for Canada," appeared in *Greater Britain Messenger* until the issue of May/June 1930.

43 ACGSA, FML, *The Future of Western Canada,* n.d., 1.

44 Ibid., minutes, 22 August 1919.

45 ACGSA, FML, *Magazine* (July 1917): 13. Lloyd was quoting the president of the University of Saskatchewan about the marriage statistics of English men, but the comment about desirability was entirely his own. See also Marilyn Barber, "The Fellowship of the Maple Leaf Teachers," in *The Anglican Church and the World of Western Canada 1820-1970,* ed. Barry Ferguson (Regina: Canadian Plains Research Center, University of Regina, 1991), 159.

46 ACGSA, FML, minutes, 25 April 1919. Premier Martin asked for the help of the FML because an average of 750 extra teachers were needed each year. In 1920 the province expected to fall short of its requirements by more than 500 teachers.

47 Saskatchewan Archives Board, Saskatoon (SAB), W.M. Martin Papers I 56(2), Anderson to Martin, 3 October 1921.

48 SAB, Department of Education Records, file 101 (2) FML deputy minister to M.J. Coldwell, 24 September 1927.

49 Ibid. The latter also stated that "as the situation was somewhat complicated with the operations of the Immigration and Colonization Department of the Dominion Government, it was not deemed advisable to close our schools completely to such students."

50 *Greater Britain Messenger* 204 (November 1916): 159.

51 *Greater Britain Messenger* 209 (December 1921): 111.

52 Interview with Doris (England) Perry, Saskatoon, 11 November 1983.

53 Dirk Heorder, "'To Be or Not to Be – British': The Many Worlds of British-Origin Immigrants in Canada" (paper presented at the second British World Conference, Calgary, July 2003), refers to English immigrants as an audible if not a visible minority who attempted to rid themselves of their mother-country accent and vocabulary in order to acculturate.

54 Interview with Adeline (Cheeseborough) Fraser, Victoria, British Columbia, 30 May 1983.

55 The adaptation of the Church of England teachers was previously examined in Marilyn Barber, "'A Religious and Patriotic Way of Earning One's Daily Bread': Church of England Teachers in Western Canada, 1909-1939," *British Journal of Canadian Studies* 16, 1 (2003): 126-36.

56 Approximately 0.5 percent of the population was Jewish and small numbers claimed other religions or no religion, according to census statistics.

57 England, *Living, Learning, Remembering*, 18

58 England, *The Central European Immigrant*, 204.

59 Interview with Robert England, Victoria, British Columbia, 29 May 1983.

60 ACGSA, FML, *The Future of Western Canada*, 13.

61 ACGSA, FML, *Magazine* (September/October 1928): 8-9

62 Interview with Grace (Warwick) Christie, Saskatoon, Saskatchewan, 24 May 1979.

63 Ontario Institute for Studies in Education, Toronto, Ontario, Women's History Archives, Winnifred Galbraith typescript memoir, 38.

64 Interview with Donald Banks, Dunmow, Essex, England, 20 May 1992.

65 Saskatchewan Department of Education, annual report for 1920, 37.

66 See Patricia Dirks' chapter in this book (Chapter 7).

67 Boy Scouts of Canada Records, Ottawa, the Canadian General Council of the Boy Scouts Association, annual report for 1920. According to the Scout census returns, in 1920 there were 6,091 Scouts in Saskatchewan, compared with 6,258 in Ontario, 2,645 in Alberta, 1,970 in Manitoba, and 803 in British Columbia.

68 England, *The Central European Immigrant*, 148.

69 Robert England, "Hafford School Sports," *The Grain Growers' Guide*, vol. 15, 16 August 1922.

70 LAC, Robert England Papers, MG 30 C181, vol. 5, file 23, "The Boy Scout and Canadianization." See also England, *The Central European Immigrant*, 148-50.

71 The Canadian Girl Guide Association, Canadian Council, Saskatchewan Report, A. Hooke, provincial commissioner, 1925; ACGSA, FML, *Magazine* (November/December 1926): 18.

72 In Chapter 7 of this book, Patricia Dirks notes that clergymen, especially Anglicans, played an important role in the dissemination of Scouting. For example, the first three Boy Scout troops in Calgary were all sponsored by the Church of England.

73 SAB, Saskatoon, R249, *Royal Commission on Immigration and Settlement* (Saskatchewan, 1920), vol. 35, 20.

14

Brushes, Budgets, and Butter: Canadian Culture and Identity at the British Empire Exhibition, 1924-25

Christopher Tait

> The fundamental purpose of the British Empire Exhibition is serious. It is to stimulate trade, to strengthen the bonds that bind the Mother Country to her Sister States and Daughter Nations, to bring all into closer touch the one with the other, to enable all who owe allegiance to the British flag to meet on common ground, and to learn to know each other. It is a Family Party, to which every part of the Empire is invited, and at which every part of the Empire is represented.[1]

Thus went the official rhetoric of the program at the British Empire Exhibition, held at Wembley, England, in 1924 and 1925. It was an assessment of the Empire in the wake of the Great War, and by all accounts the Empire presented itself impressively for the metropolitan audience. On a site of eighty-seven hectares in the London suburbs, virtually every corner of the globe was represented in a small city of pavilions and amusements. Visitors to the exhibition, mostly British, could marvel at the still unrivalled extent of their Empire and the variety of peoples and products that were on display.

But was it merely a Potemkin village for a declining power? The war had taken its toll on not only the population and resources of the Empire but also its spirit. The Australians still remembered Gallipoli all too well – they observed Anzac Day just two days after the opening of the exhibition in April 1924.[2] Two years earlier, during the Chanak crisis, Australia, South Africa, and Canada had all refused to support the British in their Turkish campaigns. In 1923 Canada signed its first treaty independent of Britain.[3] Now these dominions, each slowly moving toward independent nationhood, were being called home to present themselves with the rest of the Empire. All answered the call, but what was outwardly a show of solidarity under the Union Jack offered an occasion for subtle demonstrations of national identity and cultural differentiation as well. The challenge for Canadians was the reconciliation of these two sentiments.

The 1924 Wembley Exhibition *was* still an opportunity for Canadians to display their continuing loyalty and commitment to the Empire. In fact, most people credited the original proposal for such an event to the Canadian Lord Strathcona in 1913.[4] Even if many Canadians no longer shared the "Ready, aye, ready" imperial spirit, they were not looking to cut their ties to Britain. But the exhibition was also a chance for Canada to express some sense of self, some aspects of national distinction. The Liberal government of Prime Minister William Lyon Mackenzie King was, as ever, not attempting any bold actions in the direction of Canadian sovereignty, but the government pavilion was intended to have a Canadian character, to show the products of a unified and prosperous dominion. And while cultural nationalism was not a government priority in the organization of the Canadian pavilions at Wembley, the cultural products on display at the exhibition, especially the paintings by the Group of Seven, were recognized by both Canadians and foreign audiences as expressions of identity.

These were only hesitant steps in proclaiming to the world what Canada was. Behind the scenes, the preparations for the exhibition showed that many groups in Canada were still not sure what kind of Canada they wanted to present to the mother country, to the Empire, and to the world. The Dominion government was not financially supported by the provinces in its attempt to present a united Canada. The Group of Seven paintings were but a part of the Canadian art display at Wembley, and their inclusion had been the subject of considerable controversy in Canadian art circles. The literature presented was a strong showing of Canadian talent, but it was not all articulately "Canadian" in spirit, and it included many older works, rather than showing just what modern Canada could produce. Still, "hints of independence from Britannia" were there.[5]

On 24 April 1924, the Montreal *Gazette* took pride in the symbolic placement of Canada at the head of the procession in an exhibition cartoon in *Punch* magazine. The front page of the newspaper crowed that Canada's pavilion had been finished on time, ahead of most of the exhibition, and was quite a crowd pleaser, as visitors "walked in its long corridors and gazed with awe at the impressive physique and picturesque uniforms of the Royal Canadian Mounted Police and with a curiosity and admiration at the exhibits. Then they viewed the rival pavilions and by the time they had finished their inspection were ready to concede Canada best with India in second place, followed by South Africa and Burma. The Australian building was not ranked so highly, a disappointment under which the Australian officials bore up bravely."[6] A less charitable visitor remarked that the Australian section had "more or less of the appearance of a fruit stall."[7] By contrast, the Canadian pavilion, its exhibits, and the Mounties stood as symbols of national accomplishment and identity. Canada remained loyally within the fold, but it also took pride of place as the senior dominion.

The pride in the larger project of Empire was evident as well. The Montreal *Gazette* cheerfully reported the opening of the ceremonies, which had "an assemblage of more than 150,000 persons of white, black, yellow, brown and intermediate hues, standing with bared heads in a stadium far larger than any erected by the Greeks and the Romans in the days of their Imperial glory, [to see and hear] King George V, as he formally opens to the whole world this exhibition of the lives and labors of the hundreds of millions of people under his sceptre."[8] The newspaper also fawned over the Prince of Wales, noting his practical contributions to peace and diplomacy, as well as his generally excellent character, and adding that "the present heir to the British throne may be numbered amongst the very elect. Were he not a prospective monarch by birth, nobody would be the least bit surprised to see him elected president of any republic by universal acclamation."[9] Prominently displayed among the Canadian exhibits was a photograph of the Alberta ranch purchased by the heir to the throne in 1919.[10]

The seeming paradox between support for a separate Canadian identity and continued connection to Britain was best exemplified by the speech of Sir Campbell Stuart, the Canadian-born managing editor of the *Times* of London, at the St. George's Day Banquet in Montreal. The very day that King George V opened the exhibition, Stuart called for Canadians to remain true to their own country and national interests: "[I have] never forgotten the land I came from, and for that reason my happiest days are like today when I am back at home. We have two types of Canadians in England – one is the type that has become so English that he is more English than the English, and the other is the type who realizes that his duty to his country should not cease because he is not residing within its borders. For, after all, gentlemen, it is a poor man that has no country." Later in his speech, he made an even stronger declaration of his belief that all Canadians should work for "that great national resolve – to keep Canada Canadian ... [and] must develop more and more a national consciousness." That national consciousness was to be found in Canada's British and French origins, as well as a sense of belonging to the Canadian landscape. Moreover, his vision of Canada was a centralist, unified nation: "We must be true to the Fathers of Confederation who builded [sic] that we might enjoy a united country, and not a Canadian league of provinces."[11] Implicit in this call to arms was resistance to American influence and control, as well as a condemnation of loose federalism and parochial provincialism, all of which could be viewed as veiled criticism of the Mackenzie King Liberals and their policies.

Indeed, Mackenzie King was not particularly excited about the British Empire Exhibition and its symbolism. He wrote in his diary after meeting with exhibition organizers that it was "a cut and dried affair ... It is an imperialist scheme, but of the 'safe' variety, the antithesis of war – the outlay is large, but we cannot afford to be represented by a vacant lot."[12] Whatever his personal feelings, he knew Canada would have to be at Wembley, for which he conveniently blamed Arthur Meighen's prior commitment to the venture while prime minister. Although Mackenzie King would outwardly endorse the event, even his public remarks suggested his emphasis lay elsewhere. In a telegram to the *Times* of London, he called the exhibition "the physical expression of a union such as the world has never seen before, with local freedom existing to so large an extent that it is substantially true that here is a League of Nations, functioning with hardly any friction, and suggesting the possibility of the larger League which is the vision of lovers of peace and good-will among all the nations of the world."[13]

Mere cooperation, and reluctant cooperation at that, was obviously not enough for some Canadians. Unlike Sir Campbell Stuart, Conservatives at the time were not so subtle in their attacks on Mackenzie King. *Le Devoir* reported on 25 April 1924 that Conservatives had labelled him an "enemy of the Empire," and assaulted his weak resolve on protectionism and his apparent support of Canadian nationalism.[14] In the view of *Le Devoir*, this was nothing to apologize for: "Never has a more propitious occasion presented itself to extract the country from the mess into which the war and the false peace treaties have thrown it. If he knows to take advantage of it, Mr. King has every chance to react energetically against the adventurous policy pursued from 1899 to 1919 and to prepare the resistance to entanglements of the future." Extraction from imperial commitments was long overdue, and external circumstances were right for a move in the direction of Canadian sovereignty. The new Labour government in Britain, perceived (incorrectly, it would turn out) as anti-imperial, and the movements for independence in other parts of the Empire, from Ireland to India, offered the prime minister an opportunity to adopt "a nationalist policy – in the broadest sense of the term – eminently proper for consolidating the accord between Quebec and the Western provinces, better still, to restore all across Canada the sense of unity and national preservation."[15] At this point, the militantly French Canadian voice of *Le Devoir* seemed to be the strongest supporter of Canadian unity and nationalism.

But that did not mean that *Le Devoir* did not give meaningful coverage of the exhibition. The front page of that paper on opening day carried more or less the same message as the others: Canada was looking to the Empire for prosperity. Perhaps this was because the Dominion government had chosen to emphasize the commercial rather than the imperial aspects of participation, making the event less distasteful for Henri Bourassa and French Canadian nationalists.

Did British tourists of the mini-Empire care about expressions of national feeling in the pavilions? Some might, but the organizers realized that for many visitors, this was meant to be a pleasant excursion as well. Those who found little to keep their attention in the commercial and industrial pavilions were reassured by the official guidebook that

> there is no undue insistence at Wembley upon the educational side ... Those who wish merely to see a few of the more spectacular exhibits and then to amuse themselves, will find that their every want has been anticipated. The Amusements Park covers nearly fifty acres [twenty hectares], and while it has not overlooked any form of amusement that has been devised for folk bent on pleasure in times past, it has discovered new ones. Those who seek their recreation in Gardens will find a floral display that has no rival in or out of London. Numerous cafes and restaurants provide for the material needs of visitors, and the musical arrangements are on a lavish scale. The Stadium, which provides accommodation for 110,000 people, is the scene of pageants and contests of every kind.[16]

Never mind that this carnival atmosphere contradicted the serious purpose of the exhibition. From most accounts, it was what the majority of visitors really wanted. As Kenneth Walthew writes, "However deplorable and contrary to the original intentions, ... Wembley, which had started life as a cure to the [British] nation's ills, had become merely the antidote, a Roman circus where the populace could release its frustrations and seek a refuge from reality."[17] About 27 million people visited the exhibition in the two years that it was open, and it is safe to assume that many were there for the diversions as much as for a show of support for the Empire.[18] It was in this spirit that two of the more popular attractions outside the amusement park were the Queen's Doll Houses, complete with properly stocked wine cellars, and the sculpture of the Prince of Wales and his horse made entirely out of Canadian butter.[19] The latter might be viewed as the perfect marriage of art and commerce, or else as a testament to the sometimes bizarre marketing ploys that were used at the exhibition.

Butter art aside, as far as the Canadian government was concerned, the main priority for the country at the British Empire Exhibition was neither starry-eyed idealism (of the imperial or national variety) nor a ride on the Giant Switchback roller coaster. Canadian participation was based on the assumption of economic gains for the nation – new markets for trade and immigrants to augment the workforce. According to J.S. McKinnon, the director of the Canadian industrial exhibits at Wembley, three things made a nation great: "Busy workshops, Fertile fields, [and] Easy conveyance of man and goods from place to place." The Canadian exhibits would show the Empire that "Canada to-day is fully and well equipped with regard to these three very material activities."[20] It was not merely a question of trading volume but also of direction. McKinnon would later remark that "Canada takes part of the balance resulting from her trading with the United Kingdom and spends it in the United States, I am sorry to say. Why cannot we get together and trade within the Empire, and keep money within the family?"[21]

The Montreal *Gazette* also presented the exhibition as an important business venture, and the tone of an editorial describing the Canadian pavilion and its exhibits made this clear: "In the Canadian building ... [the visitor] can see exactly what manner of country this great Dominion is and what its natural resources are; he sees the farms, the orchards, the forests, the factories and the railways of Canada, the processes and products of manufacture ... The Department of Trade and Commerce has, in this connection, prepared a pamphlet showing at a glance what this country can produce and sell, what is now being produced and sold, and the routes over which the trade of Canada is carried. All of which is good business."[22] No mention of the presentation of Canadian culture was made in any of the articles or editorials concerning the opening of the exhibition.

The Toronto *Globe* viewed the exhibition in much the same way. In May 1924 the paper reported the international acclaim not for art but for fruit. Canadian apples were very popular with attendees, which was a good prospect for Canadian fruit growers and sellers.[23] Another story that day suggested that Australia was showing increased interest in trade with Canada.[24] In another indication that Canada was all business at Wembley, the editors even suggested that perhaps what the United States needed was a Wembley of its own to boost its sagging economy.[25] Obviously, the imperial symbolism was not a defining feature of the event as far as the *Globe* was concerned.

Nevertheless, beneath the surface there were indications that Canadians wanted to do more than hawk apples from a fruitstand outside a theme park. Despite the sense of businesslike conduct and frugality that surrounded the Canadian presence at Wembley, Members of Parliament did not want Canada to appear overly stingy in its presentation to the world. The Conservative S.F. Tolmie recalled in a 1923 speech to the House of Commons that "when I was in England I attended the big Royal Show, and I found that the Canadian exhibit there was not nearly equal to that of South Africa. South African products and the capabilities of that country were all well represented and their corner was crowded, while Canada's exhibit attracted very little attention ... If any important effect is to be produced we must make a showing at least as good as that put up by other countries."[26] A few months later, Charles Stewart, the minister of immigration and colonization, expressed a similar sentiment: "We found that the other overseas dominions were making heavy expenditures in connection with it [the Wembley exhibition]. If we go into it, it appears to me we ought do so in a way commensurate with our standing as a dominion."[27] And a few weeks later, when a request for further sums of money for the Canadian exhibits was put forward, the fact that Australia was outspending Canada seemed sufficient to justify the increased allocation.[28] Competitiveness about attracting business and immigrants to Canada over the other parts of the Empire was prevalent.

The final result was an enormous set of buildings and displays covering nearly two and a half hectares. There were 268 exhibits and numerous elaborate dioramas on display, highlighting Canadian businesses and goods of all kinds, with a particular emphasis on agricultural products.[29] Included, not surprisingly, were such staples as wheat, minerals, fish, timber, and furs, although in 1924 some visitors were disappointed by the meagre display of only four pelts, hardly what they expected "from the country English folk always associate with fur-bearing animals."[30] Here one might think that the Canadian pavilion was attempting to break free of a stereotype, but the next year the display was much more elaborate, with dozens of furs representing numerous species.[31] Other English misconceptions about Canada were challenged, however, by the industrial displays, which "proved a great surprise to visitors who seemed to have thought of Canada as almost destitute of factories."[32]

The Canadian section actually comprised three pavilions: the main Canadian building was flanked by two smaller structures, one for the Canadian National Railway and one for the Canadian Pacific, suggesting both the economic and symbolic importance of these enterprises for the country. All three conformed to the concrete neo-classical design that was found in all of the major British and dominion buildings, with the notable exception of South Africa's more vernacular style of architecture.[33] In outward appearance then, Canada was not looking to stand out from the imperial crowd. It became instead a symbol of unity with the Empire. This may not have been entirely conscious: the Canadian government had given the building contract to a British firm, chosen primarily because it had constructed Canada's pavilions at earlier shows.[34] In this case, familiarity was more important than self-expression.

As with all government projects, there were cost overruns. As of June 1924, the total costs for Canadian participation in the exhibition were $649,859.09, and a further $300,000 was requested for the next fiscal year.[35] But on a visit to Britain in August, James Robb, who replaced Charles Stewart as minister of immigration and colonization, was "much annoyed" to discover that A.W. Tolmie, the senior Canadian official at Wembley, had "underestimated requirements to the extent of about $200,000."[36] All told, by 1926 the Dominion had spent over $1.3 million.[37] That was a large outlay for a project for which, as the government admitted, there was no way of measuring the overall return on investment.[38]

The government wanted the Canadian pavilion to be a national project, with all provinces contributing to one unifying display of Canadiana. The idea had been floated by some of the exhibition's organizers and promoters to have each province, state, or region of the various dominions represented individually, but the Canadian government resisted the idea and decided on the national representation. James Robb explained it thus: "Our building represents Canada as a whole, but every exhibit is distinctly labelled showing the province and the locality in that province from which it comes ... I remember that our Canadian exhibit at San Francisco was recognized to be the best on the grounds, because we had the one outstanding idea – Canadian."[39] In this scheme, each province was asked to contribute funds proportional to its population. So, theoretically, all would enjoy the benefits of pooled resources but still have some recognition for their local ventures.

Typically, however, the provinces, especially Ontario and Quebec, resisted giving overall control to the Dominion government, arguing that "unless they got their own provincial exhibit they would not exhibit and would not contribute." While the exhibit did come together as a national pavilion in the end, the provinces refused to pay their proportion of the total expenses. Opposition Leader Arthur Meighen sighed, "He [the minister] will never get anything from the other provinces unless Ontario and Quebec come forward ... We may count that we are paying the whole shot."[40] Other than the provinces paying for their own representatives to attend, it appears that Meighen's assessment was correct.

Such federal-provincial squabbles extended down to the level of individual exhibits. Although Canadian apples of all types were widely appreciated at Wembley, various provincial representatives had proposed to show and sell their apples separately. Although doing so "would obviate any possibility of interprovincial jealousy," it would also create problems of space, organization, and quality control that Dominion officials wanted desperately to avoid, and the Department of Agriculture demurred.[41] The Canadian pavilion, though perhaps successful in portraying Canada as a unified country to the outside world, offered numerous examples of provincial interests at odds with the federal government's vision of national unity.

A related problem for the government's vision of the Canadian pavilion was the near-absence of the French language on-site. One Quebec MP repeated the complaint of a French visitor to the pavilion who had been unable to read the inscriptions for the various exhibits, and pointed out that there was, to his knowledge, only one French Canadian representative in the pavilion.[42] A group representing French Canadian businessmen denounced the "ostracism of the French language and bilingual employees," and called for "immediate measures to remedy this deplorable situation."[43] Prime Minister Mackenzie King promised that these problems would be addressed as quickly as possible, and that the government had no intention of excluding French Canadians or their language from the exhibition.[44] But the presentation of Canada at the Empire Exhibition was still primarily as a British dominion, without significant recognition of the French presence.

In the summer of 1924, with the exhibition underway, only four French Canadian businesses were displayed in the Canadian pavilion.[45] This problem of French Canadian representation extended to some of the artistic displays as well. Only a handful of French Canadian artists were listed in the 1925 booklet cataloguing the Canadian art exhibition.[46]

The major exception to this pattern of under-representation was in the literature. Here, with nearly 180 works, the French section was not small, and it included some defiantly nationalist works, from three books by Lionel Groulx to a play that warned of the dangers of Anglomania in French Canada. Translated works in the English section, such as Pierre Jean Baptiste Duchassois' tale of the Grey Nuns in northern Canada, and French contributions to the *Makers of Canada* series, provided exposure for some francophone literature to the mainly British audience.[47] So it would be incorrect to suggest that French Canada was entirely excluded from the imperial gathering. Indeed, it was there in full literary flourish, even thumbing its nose at both English Canada and the British Empire. The English Canadian literary contribution, by comparison, was tame and conventional (of which more later).

The real artistic sensation, however, was caused by paint, not ink, despite some unpromising circumstances. To begin with, the exhibition organizers had decided that all of the art at Wembley, whether from Britain or elsewhere, would be housed in the Palace of Arts (where only one-fifth of the total space was allotted to the dominions) in the metropolitan section of the grounds, rather than in the individual pavilions.[48] The exception was Native art, which was treated as an artefact or decoration in most of the dominion and colonial pavilions.[49] Aside from the convenience of having all of the pictures in one main gallery, there was an aesthetic imperialism at work. The director of the UK exhibits, Sir Lawrence Weaver, declared that "now first can be seen in one place how the Daughter Nations have developed their art from the English school which is represented so splendidly in the Retrospective Galleries." In other words, art from the Empire was all derivative. Needless to say, nationalist sensibilities, from Quebec to Queensland, were offended.[50]

The next hurdle was the selection of the more than two hundred canvases for the Canadian section of the Palace of Arts. Here, the problems were homegrown. This was not only a question of artistic taste – conservatives versus modernists – but also, as Ann Davis has pointed out, a clash of institutions: the Royal Canadian Academy versus the National Gallery of Canada.[51] As the self-appointed guardians of the artistic community in Canada since 1880, the slightly older academy had for years sought to gain control over the gallery, along with its acquisitions policy and budget.[52] But government officials, gallery directors, and even some critics had strongly resisted the idea that the state-funded gallery should be "even in appearance, allied to any other body." So by the time the preparations for the Wembley show began, the two institutions had been squabbling for almost forty years, although not nearly to the degree that they would over the Empire Exhibition. The root of the renewed fighting lay in the connection between the gallery – whose curator since 1910, Eric Brown, had brought new "dynamism and enthusiasm" to its activities – and the nascent Group of Seven. Brown and the chairman of the gallery's board of trustees, Sir Edmund Walker, supported the idea that the National Gallery should encourage young and struggling Canadian artists, especially those who, like the Group of Seven, were "painting their own country and realizing its own splendours and its character."[53] At least this arm of the government, then, was giving active support to nationalist feelings in the 1910s and 1920s.

But in the meantime, other styles of painting had matured and were recognized by the Royal Canadian Academy. Now many Canadian painters were in a position to show their work in foreign exhibitions, where recognition was crucial "in the making of reputations at home or abroad."[54] It seemed especially important for the Group of Seven, since in the early 1920s not many Canadian critics or collectors valued their work. A.Y. Jackson scoffed that "they wanted Canadian art to be a mild form of European art of thirty-five years ago," so a foreign audience was the real proving ground.[55] The two institutions wrestled for control of the selection process for foreign shows, an area where in the past there had been no consistent policy.[56] Thus the Wembley battle was seen to be significant not only as a demonstration of Canadian artists' talent to the world but also as a determination of who would organize international showings in the future.

As a government organ, the National Gallery was approved by both the Wembley organizers and the Dominion government to select the eight-member jury for the Canadian section. But with the threat of a Royal Canadian Academy boycott looming, the gallery wisely decided to compromise, and, in the end, the jury, which included both the academy's president and Arthur Lismer from the Group of Seven, was more or less balanced between the academy and the gallery, the conservatives and the modernists.[57] Most of the academy's artists were satisfied, and the final selection seemed to be balanced as well.

As it turned out, the Group of Seven stole the show in the eyes of many critics, both Canadian and foreign. One London critic, "without previous acquaintance with Canadian pictures," drew a very clear distinction between the older styles and the more exciting modern works in the Canadian galleries:

One's first impression of the Canadian paintings at Wembley depends to a great extent on which room one enters first. Should you enter by the door nearest the turnstiles, you are likely to feel an apathy of disappointment ...

In the first room, you will find principally paintings similar to those which find their way in such great numbers into our own Royal Academy. [They] have the least possible relation to painting as an art. In the second room [containing the work of the Group and Tom Thomson] ... one has the feeling that Canadian art, whatever the level of its achievement measured against the world's productions, is very much alive. Moreover, it seems as if the new leaven was working from inside rather than being, as is so evident in English art, an influence borrowed elsewhere.[58]

The *Art News,* from New York, shared these sentiments exactly: "There are two galleries, one of which is filled with rather tame performances, but in the second larger gallery one finds a collection of works by new men who are practically unknown ... Here are people with something vital to say, who say it well and with emphasis, and at the same time with a typical Canadian outlook."[59] It should be emphasized that the Group of Seven and Thomson had only twenty canvasses in the Palace of Arts in 1924, out of the 270 selected by the Canadian jury.[60] Even so, these were the Canadian works most frequently mentioned by critics, with works such as Thomson's *The Jack Pine,* Macdonald's *Beaver Dam,* and Lismer's *September Gale* receiving particular attention.[61]

From the art community present at Wembley, the Group of Seven had gained the critical recognition that had eluded them thus far in North America.[62] More international success would follow. Paintings from Wembley were toured through galleries in the United Kingdom and Europe in 1924 and 1925. The exhibition reopened in 1925 and included an all-new display of Canadian art, with the Group again featured prominently.[63] Critical response continued to be favourable, and even those who were more attached to the British Empire than to Canadian nationalism could take heart in the fact that King George V himself, "who showed a connoisseur's appreciation of the paintings on view, remarked upon the vigour and vitality of the Canadian school."[64] The imperial metropolis, it would seem, was more than happy to see the dominions gaining in self-confidence and self-expression, at least in terms of culture.

In the selection of books to represent English Canada there would be less outspoken nationalism, so it is not surprising that here there was also less public controversy than in the selection of art. The government designated the three-year-old Canadian Authors Association (CAA) as the official organizers of the literary display. A committee from the Toronto Public Library, working with the CAA, selected the hundreds of books, English and French, that would represent the fruits of Canadian literary talent.[65] And, like the art collection, the Dominion government encouraged the committee in its efforts with financial support for the purchase and binding of books. The

French section requested assistance from the government of Quebec to fund its contribution to the exhibits. The Dominion archivist, Arthur Doughty, even offered to the committee a selection of historical manuscripts for the displays, but these had to be refused, with regrets, because of the lack of space allotted in the Palace of Arts.[66]

The final list of Canadian books at Wembley was quite impressive. The chief librarian in Toronto, George Locke, introduced the catalogue of English books as "fairly representative of what is current in Canadian literature ... It is by no means exhaustive nor yet exclusive nor 'academic.'"[67] "Current" in this case seems to have referred to books that were in print at the time, even if they had first been published decades earlier, such as some of the works of the Confederation Poets and Lucy Maud Montgomery. Some books had first appeared in the mid-nineteenth century – Susanna Moodie's *Roughing It in the Bush* and Anna Jameson's *Winter Studies and Summer Rambles*, for example. It would perhaps have been more accurate to describe the collection as a survey of the development of Canadian literature from colonial times. Nevertheless, many contemporary writers were represented, from well-established figures like Ralph Connor to more recent arrivals on the literary scene, like Frederick Philip Grove.[68]

The collections also covered a multitude of genres in Canadian writing, including fiction, poetry, drama, biography, history, religion, science, and even children's literature. The curious visitor to the Canadian library at the Empire Exhibition – who was allowed to take the books from the shelves and peruse their contents – could get a variety of information about Canadian life, thought, and art from the selection, which ranged from *Anne of Green Gables* to Prime Minister Mackenzie King's own *Industry and Humanity*.[69] The inclusion of the latter, along with two of Dominion archivist Doughty's works, might cast some doubt as to whether the collection was assembled purely on the basis of popularity and literary merit, but these were exceptional cases.

While the literary committee may have done a commendable job of picking a sample of Canadian work, the presentation at the Empire Exhibition was apparently less commendable. One irritated correspondent wrote to the *Canadian Bookman* of the "unsatisfactory arrangement" of the books on display. She pointed out that "the book-cases in which the books have been placed contain only three, and in some cases, two shelves, thus the majority of the books are only a few inches from the ground and their titles cannot be read with any degree of comfort. The average sightseer knows that glass is usually used to prevent exhibits being handled, so he does not attempt to slide back the glass fronts of the shelves and examine the contents of the books." A lack of seating and helpful background information for visitors unfamiliar with Canadian literature contributed to the initially unaccommodating atmosphere of the Canadian section. Moreover, the organization of the books on the shelves was apparently quite haphazard: "*The Drama of the Forest* [stood] next to *The History of Medicine,* which ha[d] as its other neighbor, *A People's Life of Christ.*"[70] No official response appeared to confirm whether these organizational problems had been resolved or not.

Indeed, for all of the *Canadian Bookman* and CAA's attempts to promote Canadian writers and writing, their sense of marketing was not impeccable. They seem to have done very little by way of publicizing their participation in the British Empire Exhibition in order to stimulate the domestic appetite for homegrown authors. This had, after all, been viewed as one of the main reasons for artists to participate in the paintings section of Wembley. In his 1924 presidential address to the CAA, Robert J.C. Stead made brief mention of the exhibition and its importance: "Our work as an Association, and Canadian literature generally, have been signally honored by the Canadian Government in its decision to display a Canadian literary section at the British Empire Exhibition, and in intrusting the detail of the work to the officers of the Association. So far as I am aware, this is the first occasion upon which a Canadian Government has officially recognized Canadian literature as a product worthy of display before the nations of the world."[71] After all, the CAA was only three years old at the time, and such an important project must have been extremely valuable in legitimating it for Canadians.

But if momentum was gathered through this work, it was not fully exploited, and especially not in the pages of the *Canadian Bookman.* Curiously, most of the coverage of the Empire Exhibition in the magazine dealt not with the country's literature but with the art. Bess Housser, the magazine's art commentator, wrote a number of articles in which she praised the work of the Canadian painters on display, and reprinted many laudatory reviews from British papers.[72]

There was nothing unusual about art being the topic of discussion in the *Bookman,* but it does seem strange that no comparable discussion of British reaction to the books would be printed, given that the pages of *Canadian Bookman* and *Canadian Forum* were filled with hand-wringing and soul-searching articles on the state of Canadian literature and culture in general at this time. A sample of headlines from the *Canadian Bookman* in the period 1924-25 makes this plain: "Manifesto for a National Literature," "Attributes of a National Literature," "One Way to Write 'Canadian,'" "Let the Arts Tell the World about Canada," and "Finding a Market for the Canadian Writer."[73] It may be that the Canadian literary community, which constantly proclaimed its frustration with the lack of support for Canadian work at home, was simply latching onto the unpredicted resounding success of the Group of Seven and their colleagues in attracting world attention to unique Canadian artistic expression.

The British Empire Exhibition in 1924-25 was perhaps not a defining moment for Canadian identity, but it was a landmark event for one element of Canadian culture. The Group of Seven finally got their due in terms of international critical recognition, and although there would be many other occasions for their work to garner legitimacy and respect over the years, the Wembley show in particular would stand out as a milestone for the Group's development.[74] But the Canadian government, reluctant to define an ideological battleground for imperialists and nationalists, or tradition and modernism, especially in those economically difficult years, upheld the notion that Canada's presence at the Empire Exhibition was all about commercial growth. Along the way, representations of Canadian culture – painting and literature in particular – were given government assistance and encouragement, and made their mark, to varying degrees, on the world stage.

What Canadian participation at Wembley reveals is the complex and insecure conception of Canadian national identity that existed in the aftermath of the First World War. Midway between Vimy Ridge and the Statute of Westminster, Canadians could not agree on what made Canada unique, or even whether uniqueness was a desirable quality. But the exhibition was a chance to take stock of the country, from economic resources and ethnic makeup to the progress made by the arts in the past century. This cataloguing of Canadiana coincided with growing feelings of nationalism, however unsure. So perhaps, after Wembley, it was easier for some to identify what made Canada distinctive: whether it was the vast untapped economic potential, the varied population, the political system, or a sense of connection to the landscape. As Canadian scholar Thomas O'Hagan argued in the wake of the British Empire Exhibition: "We have no patriotism in Canada ... I do not believe that the safety of this Commonwealth of Nations depends on waking up at midnight to sing 'God Save the King!' We can best serve the Commonwealth by being above all loyal to our own land – a component part of the Commonwealth ... We must create a great Canadian life, and then from this spiritual endowment will come forth in due time the true Canadian genius of art and literature."[75] By the 1920s the hand-wringing over Canadian culture and identity was evidently well underway, but Canada's participation in the pageantry at Wembley reminded all that the search for identity could still take place within the context of the British World.

Notes

1 *The British Empire Exhibition, 1924: Official Guide* (London: Fleetway Press, 1924), 13.
2 *Globe* (Toronto), 24 April 1924, 2.
3 Tom August, "Art and Empire: Wembley, 1924," *History Today* (October 1993), 38.

4   See for example S.R. Parsons, "The British Empire Exhibition: A Study in Geography Resources, and Citizenship of the British Empire," *Empire Club Speeches 1924* (Toronto: Empire Club of Canada, 1924), 287, and John S. McKinnon, "A Canadian's View of the Empire as Seen from London," *Empire Club Speeches 1926,* 102.
5   August, "Art and Empire," 38.
6   *Gazette* (Montreal), 24 April 1924, 1.
7   Parsons, "The British Empire Exhibition," 294.
8   *Gazette* (Montreal), 24 April 1924, 1.
9   Ibid., 23 April 1924.
10 McKinnon, "A Canadian's View," 105.
11 "Would have young Canada active in country's affairs," *Gazette* (Montreal), 24 April 1924, 7.
12 Library and Archives Canada (LAC), MG 26 J13, William Lyon Mackenzie King Papers, Diary, 13 October 1922, 108.
13 Mackenzie King to the *Times,* 26 February 1924, LAC, MG 26 J1, William Lyon Mackenzie King Papers, reel C2262, vol. 97, 82306.
14 "M. King 'ennemi de l'Empire,'" *Le Devoir* (Montreal), 25 April 1924, 1. Author's translation.
15 Ibid.
16 *Official Guide,* 15.
17 Kenneth Walthew, "The British Empire Exhibition of 1924," *History Today* (August 1981), 39.
18 A Canadian pavilion official reported that the official attendance in 1924 was 17,395,031. LAC, RG 17, Agriculture, vol. 3207, file 150-21(1), Ernest Rhoades to H.S. Arkell, 17 December 1924. The deputy minister of immigration and colonization reported that 1925 attendance "almost reached the 10,000,000 mark." Canada, "Report of the Department of Immigration and Colonization," *Annual Departmental Reports,* 1925-26, vol. 2 (Ottawa: F.A. Acland, 1927), 42.
19 *Official Guide,* 58; Denis Judd, *Empire: The British Imperial Experience from 1765 to the Present* (London: HarperCollins, 1996), 274.
20 "Canada's Part in the Exhibition," *English Review* 38 (April 1924): 579.
21 McKinnon, "A Canadian's View," 109. Behind such comments, made after the close of the exhibition, was growing support for imperial preferences, which free-trading Britain would adopt only gradually and piecemeal before 1931.
22 *Gazette* (Montreal), 24 April 1924, 12.
23 *Globe* (Toronto), 1 May 1924, 2.
24 "Australia turning to Canada's market," *Globe* (Toronto), 1 May 1924.
25 "To emulate Wembley," *Globe* (Toronto), 2 May 1924.
26 Canada, Parliament, House of Commons, *Official Report of Debates* [hereafter *Debates*], 14th Parliament, 2nd Session, Vol. 156 (23 March 1923), p. 1454.
27 Ibid., Vol. 158 (14 June 1923), p. 3950.
28 Ibid., Vol. 159 (29 June 1923), p. 4704.
29 Ibid., Vol. 163 (23 June 1924), p. 3533.
30 Canada, "Report of the Department of Immigration and Colonization," *Annual Departmental Reports,* 1924-25, vol. 3 (Ottawa: F.A. Acland, 1926), 47.
31 LAC, RG 17, Agriculture, vol. 3207, 150-21(1), F.D. Burkholder to C.M. MacRae, 30 March 1925.
32 Canada, "Immigration and Colonization," 46.
33 August, "Art and Empire," 42.
34 *Debates,* Vol. 163 (23 June 1924), p. 3533.
35 Ibid., p. 3548.
36 LAC, MG 26 J1, reel C2269, vol. 107, 90764, J.A. Robb to Mackenzie King, 2 August 1924.
37 The public accounts for fiscal years 1924-25 and 1925-26 reported expenses of $599,796.85 and $70,611.08 respectively. See "Public Accounts" in the *Annual Departmental Reports* for those years.
38 *Debates,* Vol. 156 (23 March 1923), p. 1454.

39 Ibid., Vol. 163 (23 June 1924), p. 3534.
40 Ibid.
41 LAC, RG 17, Agriculture, vol. 3207, file 150-21, "Memorandum on proposed selling of apples at Wembley."
42 *Debates*, Vol. 162 (6 June 1924), p. 2861.
43 LAC, MG 26 J1, reel 2278, vol. 117, 99996, Paul LeClair to Mackenzie King, 25 September 1924. My translation.
44 *Debates*, Vol. 162 (6 June 1924), p. 2861.
45 Ibid., Vol. 163 (12 June 1924), p. 3106.
46 See *Canadian Section of Fine Arts: Catalogue* (London: British Empire Exhibition, 1925).
47 See *Catalogue of Canadian Books* [English Section] (London, British Empire Exhibition, 1924).
48 *Official Guide*, 55.
49 August, "Art and Empire," 41.
50 Ibid., 38-39.
51 Ann Davis, "The Wembley Controversy in Canadian Art," *Canadian Historical Review* 54, 1 (March 1973), 48.
52 Ibid., 53.
53 Ibid., 60-63.
54 Ibid., 66.
55 Charles C. Hill, *The Group of Seven: Art for a Nation* (Toronto: McClelland and Stewart, 1995), 117.
56 Davis, "The Wembley Controversy in Canadian Art," 67.
57 August, "Art and Empire," 40.
58 Rupert Lee, "Canadian Pictures at Wembley," *Canadian Forum* 4 (August 1924): 338.
59 *Press Comments on the Canadian Section of Fine Arts, British Empire Exhibition, 1924-1925* (n.p., n.d.), 16.
60 Hill, *The Group of Seven*, 143.
61 See for example "Palace of Fine Arts, Dominion Tendencies," *Times* (London), 6 May 1924; Anthony Bertram, "The Palace of Arts, Wembley," *Saturday Review* (London), 7 June 1924; "Canadian Art: Brought from Wembley Exhibition to Glasgow," *Bulletin* (Glasgow), 29 December 1924. All cited from *Press Comments on the Canadian Section of Fine Arts*.
62 Hill, *The Group of Seven*, 142.
63 Ibid., 150.
64 "Royal visit to Wembley," *Times* (London), 15 May 1925.
65 "Section of the Canadian Authors Association" *Canadian Bookman* 6, 4 (April 1924): 97.
66 Ibid.
67 Preface to *Catalogue of Canadian Books* [English Section] (London: British Empire Exhibition, 1924).
68 For perspective on this period in Canadian literature, see Mary Vipond, "Best Sellers in English Canada, 1899-1918: An Overview," *Journal of Canadian Fiction* 24 (1979): 96-119, and "Best Sellers in English Canada, 1919-1928," *Journal of Canadian Fiction* 25-26 (1980): 73-105.
69 For the complete list, see the *Catalogue of Canadian Books* [English Section].
70 "A Wembly [sic] Protest," *Canadian Bookman* 6, 6 (June 1924): 142.
71 "Third Annual Convention, C.A.A.," *Canadian Bookman* 6, 7 (July 1924): 164.
72 See for example Bess Housser, "What the Critics Are Saying at Wembley," *Canadian Bookman* 6, 7 (July 1924): 159.
73 Lionel Stevenson, "Manifesto for a National Literature," *Canadian Bookman* 6, 2 (February 1924): 35-36, 46; "Attributes of a National Literature," *Canadian Bookman* 6, 3 (March 1924): 61-63; Georges Bugnet, "One Way to Write 'Canadian,'" *Canadian Bookman* 6, 10 (October 1924): 209-10; Russell MacDonald Ray, "Let the Arts Tell the World About Canada," *Canadian Bookman* 7, 5 (May 1925): 79-80; John Macklem, "Finding a Market for the Canadian Writer," *Canadian Bookman* 7, 8 (August 1925): 127-28.
74 Hill, *The Group of Seven*, 173.
75 "A Pregnant Bit of Criticism: An Interview with Dr. O'Hagan," *Canadian Bookman* 7, 12 (December 1925): 198.

15
Instructor to Empire:
Canada and the Rhodes Scholarship,
1902-39
David E. Torrance

In the will that created his scholarships, Cecil Rhodes expressed the hope that each of his scholars would "esteem the performance of public duties as his highest aim."[1] Nowhere were his expectations more fully gratified than in Canada. Moreover, though Rhodes might have expected South Africa or the United States to play the leading role in his scholarships, it was Canada that exerted the most influence on the Rhodes Scholarships in the first two decades of their existence. It did so in the person of Sir George Parkin, who was selected by the Rhodes Trust to construct and organize the entire scholarship system – its rules, regulations, and procedures – so that the provisions of Rhodes' will would be implemented as fully and faithfully as possible. In delineating criteria for future Rhodes Scholars, Parkin placed priority on character and public service rather than on Empire loyalty. Although identified as one of the more imperially minded figures in Canada, he also reflected wider currents of thought in the Dominion. It was this wider cultural context as well as Parkin's broad-minded approach to imperialism that ensured that the scholarships would enjoy a favourable reception in Canada. It can be further claimed that the Rhodes Scholarships, in turn, made a constructive contribution to Canadian public life in the early twentieth century.

Although Cecil Rhodes is customarily characterized as a British imperialist, his conception of imperialism was so expansive that it transcended Britain and even the Empire. He envisioned the creation of an English-speaking political union between Britain and the United States, and he would as readily have based its capital in Washington as London. It was not part of Rhodes' imperialism to strengthen the imperial connection in any specific way. Indeed, as the prime minister of the Cape Colony, he had urged removing the "imperial factor" from South Africa. Rather, he sought to create an Anglo-American elite that would share the same cultural outlook and promote English-speaking values. What precisely these were Rhodes did not specify, but he was confident that French Canadians and Afrikaners could share them too.

To be sure, Rhodes hoped that the Oxford experience would engender kind sympathies toward Britain, but he never prescribed imperial commitment as a condition for his scholarships. Instead, he stipulated academic achievement, fondness for sports, and "qualities of manhood[,] truth[,] courage[,] devotion to duty[,] sympathy for and protection of the weak[,] kindliness[,] unselfishness[,] and fellowship."[2] Interestingly enough, such qualities suffused Canadian university life in the early twentieth century, and Rhodes' priorities accorded well with those of Parkin and his intellectual contemporaries in Canada.

It might also be noted that the vagueness of Rhodes' will left considerable creative space for those, like Parkin, who were entrusted with putting Rhodes' wishes into practice. To interpret the will was to define it, and, to a significant extent, what Rhodes' will "meant" amounted in practice to what Parkin and the trustees *thought* it meant.

The announcement of Rhodes' death in the Toronto press on 27 March 1902 failed to evoke a stream of unqualified eulogies, but the revelation of his will about a week later tapped a spring of enthusiastic support. One of the notables whom the Toronto *Globe* interviewed when details of Rhodes' will became known was Sir George Parkin, who had not yet become the trust's organizing secretary. He admitted that Rhodes had made mistakes, such as his conspiracy with Dr. Jameson to topple the South African republic in 1895. The Jameson Raid was a fiasco, ending with Jameson's capture by Republican forces and Rhodes' resignation as prime minister of the Cape Colony. Parkin believed that since then, however, Rhodes had redeemed himself, especially through his will: "For some years past, I have very strongly had the feeling that a little lack of scrupulousness had ruined one of the greatest careers that our age had known, and that the Jameson Raid was the gravest mistake to which any public man of modern times had lent himself. It is a great relief to find that Mr. Rhodes has taken such a noble way of rehabilitating himself in the opinion of the nation to which he belonged. If he made a mistake he has redeemed himself in a very noble way."[3]

Whatever criticisms Canadians had toward Rhodes as a person, few criticized his will. Who could condemn such magnanimity? True, French Canadians might be uncomfortable with the avowed objective of promoting the English-speaking races, but they could take succour in clause 24, which stoutly affirmed that "no student should be disqualified for election to a scholarship on account of his race or his religious opinions." And those Canadians who were worried about the extension of British power over the dominions could find reassurance in the will's express desire to inculcate among the scholars an attachment to Britain "without drawing them or their sympathies from the land of their adoption or their birth."[4]

Virtually the only voice of dissent came from Professor James Loudon, president of the University of Toronto. He told the *Globe* "that Mr. Cecil

Rhodes' foreign scholarships would have but little effect on Canadian students. Oxford and Cambridge had no attraction for Canadians, as there was practically no research, in which the English were particularly deficient." Adding patronizing insult to injury, "President Loudon hoped that the effect of the scholarships would be to awaken Oxford and Cambridge to the fact that they were behind the times, and that research is what is now being sought."[5] Loudon was attacking not Rhodes but Oxford, and he brought the Rhodes Scholarships into the debate that was raging throughout the Canadian intellectual community between the research scientists and the philosophical idealists. Loudon was the foremost spokesperson in Canada for the camp that believed that universities should be creating knowledge through rationalistic scientific enquiry and research. Inspired by German educational ideas, he preached the "gospel of pure research" and argued that the university's mission should be the production of new knowledge. His views were not incompatible with those social theorists who urged that society be refashioned along the lines of rational functionalism, conducive to industrial progress.

The opposing line of thought was embodied by philosophical idealists such as John Watson, professor of philosophy at Queen's University from 1872 to 1920, and George M. Grant, principal of Queen's from 1877 to 1902, who propounded what might be termed humanistic idealism. As A.B. McKillop has explained: "The philosophical idealism of the late nineteenth and early twentieth centuries was an elaborate and elegant edifice intended to provide a sense of intellectual and moral unity in an age of increasing pluralism and fragmentation. But it was also more than this: it was also a sustained and heroic attempt to prove that the individual could still be a meaningful moral agent, in control of his own destiny, at a time when impersonal and unseen social forces seemed to be propelling society in directions seemingly beyond individual control."[6] Although descended from the biblical theology of Christianity, philosophical idealism of this kind had become more rationalist and humanistic. To be sure, its essence was Christianity, and, indeed, its proponents described it as *essential* Christianity. Nonetheless, Christianity as taught in Ontario universities concerned itself less with God's transcendence and more with God's immanence in the world.[7] This immanence gave meaning, content, and urgency to moral action.

The moral philosophy of Watson and Grant was predicated on an organic conception of society, which conceived of individuals not as isolated atoms but as integrated parts of a greater whole. Such ideas were in wide currency in Britain, where what became known as the "new liberalism" became increasingly influential in Edwardian politics. The thought of L.T. Hobhouse, the foremost apostle of these new liberal ideas, bears close resemblance to that of the Canadian idealists. The main object of this idealist philosophy, whether in Britain or Canada, was to reconcile on an ethical level the moral claims of the individual with those of society. To John Watson the central question was what freedom could mean in such an "interdependent social university." His answer was similar to that of Hobhouse: self-realization, the development of character and personality. And like Hobhouse, he believed that self-realization and true freedom required devotion to and effort for the common good.[8] Watson's ideas were shared not only by liberal-minded Canadians but also by imperially minded ones like Parkin.

Thus, the notion of duty that this idealism informed permeated Canadian universities. It is no surprise that Adam Shortt, a student of Watson and Grant at Queen's and himself a Queen's professor, left Queen's in 1908 to assume the role of civil service commissioner. Nor is it a surprise that his student Oscar Douglas Skelton would follow his mentor's steps and lay the foundation of Canada's modern civil service. Undergraduates, too, imbibed the doctrine of duty. During this period missionary agencies attracted students for service not only abroad but also in newly explored western Canada. Others joined organizations like Frontier College to teach English to immigrants. It is interesting that this missionary zeal embraced athletics. In McKillop's words, "Late Victorian and Edwardian university sports in Ontario were conducted with a mixture of missionary zeal and martial ardour. In a complementary inversion of the way in which the 'Christian soldiers' of the period were 'marching to war' in their attempts to convert other races and to Canadianize the European immigrants within Canada, rugby and hockey players did manly battle with muscular Christians in the name of moral virtue." Indeed, "manliness became a necessary attribute of university life." Athletics were believed to build up courage, self-control, and fair play.[9] Thus, the ground in Canada was fertile for the enthusiastic reception of the Rhodes Scholarships, which valorized both service and manly sports.

The sublimation of religious idealism into a social mission had as a by-product the infusion of culture with a spiritual purpose. The Edwardian period saw in Canada the dramatic rise of English literature as an academic and critical discipline. For certain academics, it had become a "surrogate religion." To quote McKillop again, "Where once the unity of Christendom had been the vessel responsible for the voyage of moral continuity from age to age, this duty was now seen to lie in a tradition of English literature."[10] The endowment of culture with such spiritual qualities would have imperial ramifications. It certainly added moral urgency to the idea behind the Rhodes Scholarships of uniting and reinvigorating the English-speaking world.

Indeed, the imperialist implications of this line of thought are obvious, for the idealization of culture could easily entail the idealization of Britishness itself and the sanctification of the Empire that embodied it. This is precisely the conclusion James Cappon, a professor of English at Queen's from 1888 to 1910, reached: "The Empire represents an ideal of high importance for the future of civilisation, the attempt to assemble in a higher unity than even that of nationality the forces which maintain and advance the white man's ideals of civilization, his sense of justice, his humanity. It is an attempt to transcend the evils of nationality ... without impairing the vigour which the national consciousness gives to a people."[11] Many other academics, like G.M. Wrong of the University of Toronto, would have agreed.[12] And, while some idealistic social reformers found themselves leaning toward imperialism, imperialists such as Parkin and Grant embraced the social gospel at home. As Carl Berger put it, "The social gospel was a necessary ingredient of imperialism; or, put another way, it was an expression on a different but interconnected level of the sense of mission. The ends of both were identical and the realization of the civilizing mission abroad was dependent upon the existence of a sound society in the imperial state."[13]

It says something about the centrifugal force of empire that it drew Sir George Parkin (1846-1922) to its centre from its remote rural periphery. To be sure, Parkin, whose father was an English immigrant and whose mother was of loyalist descent, was imbued with British sympathies from birth. Nonetheless, his personal experience was of a small town in New Brunswick. He received all his education in the village of Salisbury until he entered a normal school in Saint John to train for teaching. He then went to the University of New Brunswick, after which he served in various teaching posts in the province, including that of headmaster of the university's collegiate school in Fredericton, but he did not step into the world beyond Canada until 1873. Securing a leave of absence from his post in Fredericton, he set out for Oxford to study Latin, Greek, and history as a non-collegiate student. Although only there for a year, he made a considerable impression on Oxford, as it did on him. He joined the Oxford Union, a private debating society, where he delivered a formidable speech on the need for imperial unity, after which he was elected secretary, a rare honour for a first-year university student. While at Oxford, he came into contact with individuals who would in the future occupy commanding heights of power in Britain and the Empire. Of particular importance in Parkin's intellectual and personal development was Alfred Milner, who became interested in Parkin's notion of extending representation in imperial bodies to the more important colonies. When Parkin returned to Canada, he maintained his connections with his imperial friends in Britain. In 1888, on a research trip to Britain, he was introduced to the most important members of the Imperial Federation League and was later asked to conduct a lecture tour of Australia and New Zealand on its behalf. He jumped at the opportunity, resigning his post in Fredericton to undertake the mission. In Berger's words, "He threw himself into the work as though the whole imperial question depended upon his efforts alone."[14]

Parkin's imperialism certainly included geopolitical elements, but it went well beyond mere considerations of power. For Parkin, imperialism was deeply spiritual and constituted a divine mission. Although Parkin did not overlook the need for domestic reform, his emphasis was on Canada's mission abroad, which constituted, in a sense, an overseas version of the social gospel. To quote Berger again: "The sense of mission, then, grew out of this conception of the immanence of God in the world: history has not accidentally placed millions of the 'weaker races' under the protection of the Empire, nor was the evolution toward a stronger union a fortuitous and fitful process. The main justification for imperial power was work directed toward the Christianization and civilisation of these races. Such work would not only fulfil God's own purposes, but would also burn away the selfishness and pride bred by power." To Parkin, this work needed to be performed not only by Britain but also by the more "advanced" portions of the Empire (i.e., the dominions), which had to recognize that their imperial duties involved leadership as much as loyalty. Indeed, in his mind, the criterion of real nationhood was a willingness to shoulder these responsibilities. For Canada, such a willingness must lead it into a more active role in the Empire rather than to independence.[15]

Needless to say, not every Canadian was capable of shouldering such enormous responsibilities, and Parkin sought to entrust the future of Canada and the Empire to an elite qualified for the purpose. The question was how to discern who was fit to rule and how best to train such men. As a product of his time, Parkin assumed that society's leaders would be men – usually, though not always, white men. Like most British imperialists, Parkin gave pride of place to the Anglo-Saxon "race." He did not, however, think in purely racial terms. The danger of linking Parkin's Anglo-Saxonism too closely with race was demonstrated during the First World War, which he viewed as a great Anglo-Saxon struggle against German militarism. If the term "Anglo-Saxon" referred to race, the distinction between German and British would, of course, break down. Also meaningless would be Parkin's comment about America's gradual shift toward the Allies: "Thinking America is almost entirely with us, almost passionately so; but there is a vast mixed multitude from many nations scattered through the Empire which can scarcely be expected to take a large view on questions of liberty and international law. But the Anglo-Saxon is still on top in the United States and so are his ideas, and these will prevail in the present struggle."[16] As Berger put it so incisively: "Equally clear is that the entire notion of [a] civilising mission would have collapsed in futility had it been assumed that race character was intractable and unchangeable. For then they would have been summoning the Anglo-Saxon race to perform Sisyphean labour, which, however much it might exalt the character of those who performed it, would none the less be hopeless and self-defeating in the end."[17]

The point is that Parkin did not believe that the elite would arise spontaneously through race or wealth. It must be shaped by godly men. This brings us back to the crucial importance of education to Parkin; for him, education meant inculcating character or, as he often termed it, manliness. The end aimed for was well described by Bliss Carmen, one of Parkin's former students: "Good breeding is scrupulous in requiring the sacrifice of our comfort for that of others."[18] At the imperial level, an education had not only to convey to students an understanding of the Empire of which they were a part but also to infuse in them the desire to serve it unselfishly. In 1895 Parkin got a chance to put his ideas into practice when he accepted the position of principal of Upper Canada College. In Toronto he was able to associate with many of the key leaders in Canadian imperial circles.[19] With his reputation as an educator and his connections in Canada and Britain, it was not surprising that in July 1902 the Rhodes Trust appointed Parkin organizing secretary for the scholarships.[20] He would occupy this position until 1920.

Canada profited more from Parkin than from Rhodes, whose will accorded only two scholarships to Canada – one for Quebec and one for Ontario. Before Parkin even undertook his initial tour of the Rhodes constituencies around the world, he strongly suggested that the trust rectify this paltry provision by creating six additional scholarships for Canada's remaining six provinces. The trust acceded to this request in 1903 with little hesitation.[21] Thus, when Parkin toured North America, he assumed with good reason that Canada would have eight scholarships and Newfoundland one. (The latter was remembered in the will.) The first conference of Parkin's Canadian tour was held in Sackville, New Brunswick. In opening the proceedings Parkin declared that the Rhodes trustees' "main object was to establish some impartial system of selection absolutely free from political[,] sectarian[,] or local bias."[22] To that end, he presented two alternative schemes for selection. The first involved the nomination of candidates by universities, each of which would have a quota based on student numbers. Then, a provincial Committee of Selection would make a disinterested choice. The second option was rotation, whereby the scholarship would be assigned to each university on a rotating basis. After touring the rest of Canada (the Maritimes, Montreal, Toronto, Winnipeg, Regina, and Victoria), Parkin pragmatically decided to adopt the plan best suited to each province. For those that had several institutions liable to compete, he opted for rotation. These included New Brunswick (University of New Brunswick: 3/7 (3 nominations in a 7-year interval); Mount Allison: 3/7; and Saint Joseph's: 1/7); Nova Scotia (Dalhousie: 6/12; Acadia: 3/12; Saint Francis Xavier: 2/12; and King's College: 1/12); Quebec (McGill: 3/7; Laval: 3/7; and Bishop's: 1/7); and Ontario (Toronto: 4/10; Queen's: 3/10; Trinity: 1/10; McMaster: 1/10; and Ottawa: 1/10). In Manitoba, Prince Edward Island, British Columbia, and the Northwest Territories, committees of selection were appointed.[23]

Parkin managed to frame the regulations for scholars without great contention. There was no quibble, as there had been in the United States, about the need of scholars to secure exemption from the standard examinations required by Oxford as a prerequisite for admission (known as responsions) either by passing an equivalent qualifying examination or by the status of the university attended. As with other commonwealth schools for higher education, eight Canadian universities enjoyed special recognition from Oxford, which exempted students from such schools from responsions. These eight were McGill, Laval, University of Toronto, Queen's, King's, Dalhousie, University of New Brunswick, and Mount Allison University. There was also wide agreement that scholars should have completed at least two years of work at a Canadian university. In addition, scholars had to be unmarried and between nineteen and twenty-five years of age. They could apply from either their province of domicile or from that in which they attended university.[44]

The position of Quebec in the scholarship scheme did raise some controversy. Doug McCalla, in a recent study of the Rhodes Scholarships in Canada, perceptively observed that "French Canadian participation in the scholarships was ... a vital element in liberal imperialists' dreams for Canada." Indeed, McCalla gives evidence of Parkin's own commitment to French Canadian representation in the scholarship system. What should be emphasized, however, is that Parkin faced opposition from less sympathetic members of the trust and from the French-speaking universities themselves. These latter received almost half of Quebec's scholarships. (Over a seven-year rotation, McGill and Laval received, alternately, three scholarships, and Bishop's secured one every seventh year.) Laval, however, did not play the part assigned to it. Even at the outset, its rector, O.E. Matthieu, expressed doubts about the scheme, and Laval's first nomination did not exactly fit the founder's criteria, one of which stipulated that the candidate have a fondness for manly sports. Although an excellent linguist, Joseph Belleau was not, by his own admission, a sportsman, because he had a physical handicap with his feet that prevented his participation in "violent sports." "Besides," he added, "I like them not." Although Parkin made representations on his behalf to the trust, Belleau spurned his nomination. Despite persistent pressure from Principal William Peterson of McGill to have Laval's scholarship for 1905 transferred to McGill, Parkin insisted that this could be done only if Laval agreed. As he wrote to Bourchier F. Hawksley, Rhodes' late solicitor and now a trustee, "the matter was a delicate one to handle as it is a very distinct object for us not to touch French Canadian sensibilities." Scrupulous about Laval's legal rights, Hawksley agreed with Parkin, but another trustee, Lord Grey, then governor general of Canada, believed that, because of Laval's misguided nomination, Quebec should forfeit the scholarship for 1905. He blamed the situation on the Roman Catholic hierarchy, which, he surmised, did not want gifted Frenchmen to come under the influence of Oxford.[25] Parkin, however, strenuously resisted Peterson's persistent attempts to appropriate to McGill the 1905 Quebec Rhodes Scholarship. Initially, he gained his point, but when it became clear that Laval would offer no suitable alternative, the trust acceded to Peterson's request.

Ironically, McGill selected Talbot Papineau, whose name could be expected to resonate throughout the French Canadian community, though his accent would not because his first language was English. A descendant of Joseph Papineau, the great French Canadian leader of the 1837 Rebellion in Lower Canada, Talbot Papineau, according to Grey, possessed some "mental instability which characterises the Papineau race." Fortunately, Grey continued, Papineau took after his American mother and was himself more American than French Canadian. Indeed, he could barely speak French when he arrived at Oxford. The Oxford experience would prove a positive one for Papineau, though he wrote in a letter, "I need to work, work, work!"[26]

In 1907, when the rotation came again to Laval, there were two strong contenders for the position: Gustav Lanctot and Marius Barbeau. After much deliberation, Laval chose Barbeau, who later became a distinguished anthropologist. In 1909 Laval deferred to its Montreal branch, which selected Lanctot (who later became a well-respected historian). Unfortunately, the trust ruled him out, for he was now well over the age limit. As usual, Peterson immediately started clamouring for the position, but this time the trust refused to accede to his demand, although some trustees favoured letting Quebec's position lapse for the year, and Lord Milner, a trustee, wanted to parachute in a candidate who had been "badly treated" in Prince Edward Island. Eventually, the Montreal academics made a new selection: Laurent Beaudry. On hearing this, Peterson grumbled to Parkin that "the Beaudry family have a good deal of English mixture in them," and that, rather than having a real competition, Laval had just handed the scholarship to anyone who would take it. In later life, Beaudry would become a senior member of the Department of External Affairs.[27]

In May 1912 the resentment toward Oxford that had simmered beneath the surface from the beginning erupted into the open. Rev. A.E. Gosselin, who had replaced Mathieu, declared that Laval was boycotting the scholarships because Oxford had not extended to Laval the same privileges regarding course credits that it had to English-speaking universities in Canada. Although Parkin was genuinely sympathetic, he informed Gosselin that the Rhodes Trust did not have the authority to challenge regulations that Oxford University had established. As usual, McGill's president agitated for the scholarship and suggested the abolition of the entire system of rotation so that the province could have open competition. Eventually – and months past the deadline – Laval sent in its nominee: Alexandre Gérin-Lajoie, who was accepted by Worcester.[28] In 1914 the problem arose again.

Laval procrastinated in choosing a candidate, which prompted Parkin to ponder the prospect of altering the system of rotation. Two weeks later, he remarked that "it is all very provoking, but it is a very peculiar situation we are dealing with." When over three months later still no choice had been made, Parkin vented to Peterson his frustration with Laval:

> I have been strongly tempted to make an imperative demand for an imme-
> diate answer. On the other hand I do not like to give up on the French
> Canadians as one of our elements at Oxford. The men hitherto sent over
> have been distinctly interesting ... and I am sure that Oxford captured them.
> I am also sure that there are lots of young fellows waiting for the chance, if
> their authorities did not stand in their way. I fear that you will be a great
> deal disgusted at my long suffering in this matter. I do not care a fig about
> the Laval people and I would be glad to transfer the whole thing into an
> open competition for the Province. But I do care a great deal for the young
> Frenchman and in his behalf I think one is bound to go to the extreme
> limits of patience.[29]

Eventually, Laval chose as its candidate Joseph Rochette, who would read law at Pembroke College and later become minister of labour, mines, and maritime fisheries in Quebec.

In 1916 the selection went smoothly, but Parkin's mind was still turning toward the abolition of the system of rotation. In 1919 the trust did abolish the system of rotation in Canada, a change that entailed the creation of an appointed Committee of Selection in each province. In Quebec E.W. Beatty, president of the Canadian Pacific Railway, agreed to serve as chair. As Peterson anticipated, the French universities made a poor showing in open competition. Indeed, few French Canadians succeeded in winning scholarships for several years after the change. Whereas before open competition seven French Canadians and eleven English Canadians were appointed, between 1920 and 1925 only one French Canadian won a scholarship, while four English speakers did. To rectify the situation (and to satisfy the wishes of the Quebec Rhodes community), the trust granted Quebec the scholarship forfeited by Prince Edward Island, on the expectation that it would be filled by French Canadians. To reserve such scholarships explicitly for French Canadians would have violated the terms of Rhodes' will, but it was hoped that a sufficient number of qualified French Canadian applicants would justify the annual selection of one French Canadian. To forestall criticism from Ontario, the trust created a new scholarship for that province. Thus, the trust went to great trouble and expense to undertake what was essentially an affirmative action policy to embrace the French Canadian community in Canada.[30]

In addition, as McCalla has clearly shown, the trust took active measures to include francophone representatives on Quebec's Committee of

Selection. Barbeau was asked to serve on the first Committee of Selection. In the late 1930s the first francophone secretary (Ariste Brossard) was appointed to the Committee of Selection, and since 1953 only francophones have been appointed to the position. As McCalla concluded, "By the 1930s, the second scholarship had begun to create a larger group of French-speaking scholars resident in Quebec and to give the trust access to voices within French Canadian society."[31] And yet, as one Rhodes Scholar put it eloquently, Canada itself contained "two solitudes."[32] Although the Rhodes Scholarships attempted to break through these solitudes (and on occasion did so), it is doubtful that they succeeded on a wide scale.

Aside from the Quebec issue, certain miscellaneous matters arose before the war that revealed Parkin's priorities as well as his probity. For example, he had to contain certain irregular pressures brought to bear by members of the Rhodes community itself. He could not, for instance, accede to the suggestion of Lord Grey to add a new scholarship so that an exceptionally brilliant young scholar of whom he had heard many good things could procure a scholarship. Similarly, Parkin had to explain to James MacKerras Macdonnell, the Ontario scholar for 1905, that the trust could not show favour to his brother. At the same time Parkin would not bend in the direction of the underprivileged. As he explained to Elven Benbough, registrar of McMaster University in 1915:

> In some of the communities with which we have to deal I think I have discovered a tendency to award the Scholarship to a poor and struggling student because he is such. This is certainly a mistake. The object Rhodes had in view was not to do an act of charity, but to find strong men to have an influence in the future in their own countries. I would like to see the sons of well-to-do people treated on exactly the same terms with those of poorer men, in contending for the honour of winning the Scholarship.
>
> I think perhaps that Scholars who have had something of what are looked upon as social advantages fit more easily into Oxford life than those who have had few. On the other hand I know of no place in the world where real merit, whether provided with money or not, meets with readier recognition than in the Colleges of Oxford.[33]

Some questions did arise about the criterion of "fondness for outdoor sports," and Parkin usually recommended a generous interpretation of the athletic requirement. Remembering an Upper Canada College football player with only one arm, he tended to stress the spirit rather than the letter of the provision. Thus he viewed favourably the case of an intellectually gifted but physically disabled student at Dalhousie. Although the Dalhousie senate disqualified the student's candidature in 1911, the student presented himself again two years later when Dalhousie's turn came. This time, Parkin referred the case to the trust:

> A student, said to be of rather unusual ability, and with a course of law in view, has always as the result of infantile paralysis, had to use crutches. He is keenly interested in the athletics of the University – plays quoits skilfully – and sometimes keeps goal in hockey ...
>
> I confess that I am somewhat perplexed in my own judgement about the matter. I do not like to say that a man of marked intellectual power should be excluded entirely. On the other hand I wonder whether the appearance at Oxford of a Rhodes Scholar on crutches would cause undue surprise, or whether such an appointment would be setting an undesirable precedent.

He ended his letter on a positive note. "I saw the young fellow, and he struck me as a man of weight and character." Unfortunately, the trust did not share Parkin's sympathies and sent back a terse cable: "Undesirable elect Dalhousie cripple."[34]

Parkin was also keenly aware that, however good it might be to cultivate among the scholars a sense of imperial enthusiasm, it was neither desirable, nor part of Rhodes' intention, to have his scholars denationalized by the Oxford experience. In 1911 Edward Peacock lamented to Parkin that this had happened to one Alberta scholar:

> This chap returned last summer, after two years at Oxford, to visit his parents. They found that his head had been completely turned by his success, with the result that he attempted to ape all the peculiarities which he conceived to be those of the Oxford man – as to dress, accent, and mannerisms to such an extent as to make himself quite ridiculous in a small Canadian town. His attitude towards everything with which he has been formerly connected was so completely changed that his parents were terribly wounded and disappointed, and the feeling in the community has been very strong over the matter.

This scholar's "Britishness" was, however, not mere affectation, for he fought and died for the Empire in the First World War.[35]

It is not surprising that a large portion of Canadian Rhodes Scholars served in the First World War. Of the 118 Canadian Rhodes Scholars before 1918, 78 served in the armed services. Of these, 9 were killed, including 5 Maritimers. The last Canadian Rhodes Scholar killed was Talbot Mercer Papineau. In 1914 he had proclaimed to the Associated Canadian Clubs that "there would be as many French Canadians as English Canadians to take up arms in defence of the Empire in this crisis." On 28 February 1915 he distinguished himself at St. Eloi, winning the Military Medal "for con-spicuous gallantry," and in March 1916 he took issue with the French Cana-dian nationalist Henri Bourassa (his cousin) for stating that the war was of marginal importance to Canada or to Quebec. "At this moment as I write," Papineau retorted from the front, "French and English Canadians are fight-ing and dying side by side. Is their sacrifice to go for nothing, or will it not cement a foundation for a true Canadian nation?"[36]

Between the wars Rhodes Scholars occupied distinguished positions of trust and influence in finance, high politics, university academics, and gov-ernment service. We find them across the political spectrum, but, more likely, on the left. Of course, some remained in England, like John Lowe (Ontario and Christ Church 1922), who entered the Anglican clergy and became dean of Christ Church in 1939, a Rhodes trustee in 1940, and vice-chancellor of Oxford in 1948. Most, however, returned home to Canada. Doug Owram has argued that the interwar period witnessed the emergence of a new government elite in Canada, the members of which tended to be male, anglophone, and of the same postwar generation. Although most came from the upper or middle classes, the primary basis for this elite was educa-tion. School connections, university friendships, and scholarly or profes-sional associations linked this elite together and gave them the sense of an exalted group identity. Foremost among the educational institutions that furnished members for Canada's upper echelon was Oxford, whose gradu-ates tended to form the apex of this elite. Lured by an "imperial mystique," which lingered after the war, and by the financial aid available from various scholarships, Canadian students came out of Oxford with supreme confi-dence, a shared experience (within an exclusive group), and powerful con-tacts, national and international. It was this group that provided Canada with its leading public servants. Needless to say, Rhodes Scholars occupied a key position in this elite configuration.[37]

Norman Robertson was emblematic of the Rhodes Scholar who would dedicate his life to the performance of public service. Born in Vancouver in 1904, he was brought up in a family that valued the intellect. Though not a sportsman at university, he showed such intellectual promise that he won a Rhodes Scholarship. Contemptuous of conservatism, he was a socialist when he entered Balliol in 1923, and he retained his passionate commitment to labour. As he confided to Alfred Rive, a friend in Vancouver, "I feel that however badly the workers may be led, whatever tactical blunders they or their leaders may commit, still in the long run the Lord is on their side. This is the only question in the world about which I ever cared." During the British General Strike, he supported the labourers by working in the Lon-don office of the *Daily Worker*. Yet he was also becoming aware of a pro-found and general skepticism that was dampening his romantic radicalism: "I don't know how I'll end up but I have a vague fear that sometime my radicalism will vanish. Already I know I can't be a revolutionary. It is a physical impossibility for me to believe absolutely in any side on any issue. And yet one must take sides."

Robertson was not unhappy to return to North America. In 1928 he joined the Department of External Affairs, which included several Rhodes Scholars, including Laurent Beaudry (counsellor) and John Read (legal advisor). In charge of the department was O.D. Skelton, whose son, Douglas Alexander, had accepted a Rhodes Scholarship the previous year (1927). In this position, Robertson's politics drew him gradually to the centre. In fact, at the Ottawa Conference of 1932, at which he was a delegate, he showed considerable sympathy with Britain's position: "It is altogether an absurd and rather tragic situation. I've never been much of an imperialist but do believe that what's left of the Empire is worth keeping." In 1941 he moved up the ladder, becoming undersecretary to replace the ailing Skelton. Although relatively junior, circumstances favoured his appointment, as did the recommendation to Mackenzie King, the prime minister, from Arnold Heeney, a Rhodes colleague at Oxford and now secretary to the cabinet. Robertson's Rhodes connections also assisted him when he, along with Malcolm MacDonald, his counterpart in the British Foreign Office, needed to act as a buffer between Mackenzie King and Britain's prime minister, Winston Churchill, during the Second World War. (MacDonald was well connected with many Rhodes trustees who were prominent in British politics; he would himself become a trustee in 1948.) The presence of so many Rhodes Scholars and British-educated men in the Canadian Department of External Affairs caused many outsiders to criticize it "for its Oxbridge manner, its old boy networks, its tea and sherry atmosphere."

Robertson had other postings after he left the Department of External Affairs: he was high commissioner to London twice (1946-49, 1952-57), clerk of the privy council and secretary to the cabinet (1949-52), ambassador to the United States (1957-58), and a second stint as undersecretary for external affairs (1958-63). In the words of his biographer, "Norman Robertson was one of the men who made modern Canada. With a handful of other mandarins, he created for the Canadian public service the ethos of duty, high competence and intelligence that animated it in its heyday, and with Hume Wrong and Lester Pearson, he made the Department of External Affairs into the pre-eminent ministry of that service and into one of the ablest foreign offices anywhere. He was, John Holmes said, 'the greatest mandarin of them all,' a servant who served his country and Canadians as well."[38]

Canadian Rhodes Scholars also distinguished themselves outside government. In education, there was the imperial historian A.L. Burt (Ontario and Corpus Christi 1910) and the Canadian historian Chester Martin (New Brunswick and Balliol 1904). After teaching history at McGill, Terrence MacDermot (Quebec and New College 1918) became principal of Upper

Canada College in 1935. From 1929 to 1935 he also served as assistant secretary for the Rhodes Scholarships in Canada. James Corry (Saskatchewan and Lincoln 1924) became a legal expert, joining the Department of Political Science at Queen's University in 1936.[39] Norman Rogers (Nova Scotia and University 1918) also taught at Queen's, but in 1935 he was elected to Parliament and became minister of labour. In 1939 he was made minister of defence, where he served only a year before dying in an airplane accident.

The Rhodes Scholar who cut the highest political profile was Daniel Roland Michener (Alberta and Hertford 1919). From Oxford he went on to study for the English bar, becoming a barrister in 1923. In the next year he returned to Canada, where he enjoyed both a distinguished legal career and one equally distinguished in politics. Elected to the House of Commons in 1953, he was Speaker of the House in 1957 and 1958. From 1964 to 1967 he served as high commissioner to India, after which he became governor general of Canada. From 1936 to 1964 he also served the trust as general secretary for the Rhodes Scholarships in Canada. While a Progressive Conservative, Michener was a quite moderate one. His predecessor as general secretary was James MacKerras Macdonnell (Ontario and Balliol 1905), who interrupted his budding legal career to serve in the Great War, in which he won the Croix de Guerre. During the war he married Christine Marjorie Randolph, a daughter of Sir George Parkin. Like Michener, Macdonnell enjoyed a distinguished legal career and was a Progressive Conservative MP in the House of Commons.[40]

Those more radical in outlook included F.R. Scott, Eugene Forsey, Graham Spry, and David Lewis. Although left-leaning and a socialist, Francis Reginald Scott was not atypical of Canadian Rhodes Scholars between the wars. He was born in Quebec City in 1899 and, though educated at the elite Bishop's College, was raised in a family sympathetic to the cause of labour. When his father, an Anglican canon, publicly expressed his support for the Winnipeg strike, he was ordered to leave the city. While at Oxford, F.R. Scott was active in the Christian Social Movement, and he was inspired by R.H. Tawney's *The Acquisitive Society*, which drew him to Fabian socialism. In his "afterlife," he was a law professor, poet, and political activist. In 1929 he felt an urgent call to work for social democracy and so teamed up with Frank H. Underhill, a University of Toronto history professor who, albeit not a Rhodes Scholar, was Oxford educated. In 1931 the two men organized a Fabian research group, which became known as the League for Social Reconstruction. Out of the league there emerged in 1932 the Co-operative Commonwealth Federation (CCF). Its party program, the Regina Manifesto, was substantially drafted by Scott.[41]

Perhaps the best-known case of a left-leaning Canadian student receiving a Rhodes Scholarship was that of David Lewis. The son of Jewish immigrants, David was twelve years old when his family came to Canada from

Russia, in 1921. He quickly mastered English and achieved such success at school that he gained admission to McGill, where he received his undergraduate education. In 1932 he secured a Rhodes Scholarship. His socialism ran deep. While a student at McGill, he was active in student socialist organizations. When in 1932 the principal's assistant recommended that he apply for a Rhodes Scholarship, he dismissed the idea as ridiculous, but when Frank Scott, now a McGill professor, suggested the same thing, Lewis gave the matter some consideration, though he nonetheless dismissed it. As he recounted, "To him [Scott] I pointed out that ... the committee would know that I was a Jewish immigrant only ten years in the country and would also know of my noisy socialist role on and off the campus. I simply could not see a committee of businessmen and professionals picking a candidate like myself." While Scott admitted the force of his points, he nonetheless placed more faith in the committee's fair mindedness than Lewis did and urged him to apply. Eventually, Lewis was persuaded to do so.

The first hurdle for the fifty-odd candidates chosen for the initial round of competition was to write a three hour essay on a topic the candidates could select from a prescribed list. Lewis wrote his on the proposition "Modern culture is ugly." The selection committee was sufficiently impressed to grant him an interview. The chair was Sir E.W. Beatty, president of the Canadian Pacific Railway and chancellor of McGill. As Lewis described the interview, "At one point, Sir Edward Beatty turned to me and, with a quizzical sparkle in his eyes, asked, 'Lewis, if you became the first socialist prime minister of Canada, what would you do?' I could not suppress a defiant glint in my eyes as I answered with emphasis, 'Nationalise the CPR, sir.'" Valuing intellectual integrity more than political correctness, the committee awarded Lewis a scholarship.[42]

At Oxford Lewis was just as forthright as he had been in his interviews. Academically, after reading jurisprudence for a year, he decided that he would like to switch to PPE (philosophy, politics, and economics), which meant that he would have only a year to prepare for the examinations. Although C.K. Allen, the warden, feared that his exam results would suffer, he conceded to Lewis "after a couple of weeks of obstinate discussion." As for extracurricular activities, Lewis was active in the Labour Club and the Oxford Union. He was elected president of the latter, despite his strong left-wing views.

During his years in England, Lewis was aggressively outspoken in his socialist views. As he admitted in his memoirs:

> On reflection, I can see how my single-minded political commitment made other people in the Union uncomfortable from time to time. Quite often, they were forced to listen to an intense "colonial" who did not hide his contempt for the genteel dilettantism of supercilious members of the "upper

class," or his scornful impatience with those who preferred to sit on the sidelines. I must admit that I thundered against the evils of what was in the thirties a sick and dying system as lustily and as angrily as few others. It may be that there were occasions when a softer less accusatory tone might have accomplished more, but that was not my mood in those years, nor, indeed, was it the mood of many other social activists.

On his election to the presidency of the Union, the *Isis,* a student journal, remarked: "The almost ferocious energy with which Lewis defends his convictions is, however, the root of his most dangerous fault. Tolerance comes hard. He cannot help attacking hypocrisy, snobbery and muddled thinking with a scathing, merciless sarcasm. His forthright earnestness has antagonized many of the more timid and soft-spoken Oxonians. At the same time it has won their respect."[43] It also won the respect of the Oxford secretary, C.K. Allen, who, in one of his annual reports for 1933-34, wrote: "Apart from public success, he [Lewis] has charmed everybody, by the honesty of his character, the keenness of his mind, and the natural delicacy of his instincts and manners; and though he has changed none of his views, he has quickly got the 'feel' of Oxford and has behaved with discretion. His career should be very interesting. I should hate to be a millionaire if he were in power, but I should be sure of being sent to the guillotine with the most charming and sympathetic of farewells."[44]

Shortly after his return to Canada from Oxford, Lewis abandoned his legal career to devote himself to the political cause of labour, becoming in 1936 national secretary of the CCF. He was not only a constant campaigner for the cause of labour; he was also one of the movement's key theorists. Although he fought several elections, he failed to secure a seat in Parliament and returned (intermittently) to the practice of law in the 1950s. Nonetheless, he continued his political work for labour and was one of the founders of the New Democratic Party, which came into being in 1961. Though profoundly committed to socialism, he worked consistently to keep the labour movement in Canada free from Communist ties.

In the interwar years, authorities in the Rhodes Trust became aware of the sense of nationalism developing in Canada. In 1925 the general secretary, Philip Kerr, toured North America. On his visit he reported gloomily, "I am afraid that things in Canada are not at present as satisfactory as they are in the United States ... I even found in places a certain feeling that it was a mistake for returned Scholars to avow themselves as Rhodes Scholars, and that the best would be that they should merge themselves in the population and forget their unhappy past!" In 1932 Sir Francis Wylie, the recently retired Oxford secretary, reported that there was little enthusiasm for the formation of Rhodes associations in Canada: "It was suggested, or hinted, on at least two occasions, that a good many Rhodes Scholars would be out of sympathy with the kind of Imperialism for which, it was assumed by the speaker, Mr Rhodes stood."[45]

Despite the fears of Kerr and Wylie, it could be argued that Canadian scholars fulfilled the expectations that Rhodes had held up. True, they were not empire-builders, but they were public spirited in the ways that the will exhorted. While American Rhodes alumni tended to become lawyers or academics in "afterlife," Canadian scholars tended to devote themselves to public service. Norman Robertson, D.R. Michener, F.R. Scott, David Lewis, and many other Canadian Rhodes Scholars did indeed "esteem the performance of public duties as [their] highest aim." Rhodes bequeathed the funds, but it was a Canadian (George Parkin) who defined the will for all Rhodes constituencies around the world, and it was Canadian scholars whose lives gave it meaning in Canada. They were guided not by Rhodes' example but by their own sense of duty. It might indeed be claimed that they made the Rhodes Scholarships something better than Rhodes had even envisioned.

Notes

1 Rhodes' will, 1 July 1899, clause 23; this can be found at Rhodes House, Oxford, shelfmark 610.1 5.6.
2 Ibid.
3 "Cecil Rhodes' Will: Views of a Number of Canadian Educationalists," *Globe* (Toronto), 8 April 1902, 4. Rhodes' death was announced in the *Globe* on 27 March 1902; two days later, the broad details of his will became known, and on 5 April 1902 the text of his will was published. See the *Globe* (Toronto), 27 March 1902, 1; 29 March 1902, 1; 5 April 1902, 1.
4 Rhodes' will, 1 July 1899, clauses 16 and 24.
5 *Globe* (Toronto), 8 April 1902, 4.
6 A.B. McKillop, *Matters of Mind: The University in Ontario, 1791-1951* (Toronto: University of Toronto Press, 1994), 152-54, 190.
7 Ibid., 216-17.
8 In both Canadian idealism and British new liberalism we see traces of German idealism as mediated by Oxford philosophers like T.H. Green. This common intellectual ancestry could explain the similarities in the thought of Watson and Hobhouse.
9 McKillop, *Matters of Mind*, 197-99, 230-31, 243-44, 246. About Adam Shortt and O.D. Skelton, McKillop observed, "In their own ways both Shortt and Skelton were simply fulfilling the logic of nineteenth-century idealism, and in so doing they helped shape a liberal-democratic ethic by taking the sense of mission and stewardship they had learned and acted out at the university into the public realm." See McKillop, *Matters of Mind*, 202.
10 Ibid., 204, 219-24.
11 James Cappon, quoted in S.E.D. Shortt, *The Search for an Ideal: Six Canadian Intellectuals and Their Convictions in an Age of Transition, 1890-1930* (Toronto: University of Toronto Press, 1976), 74.
12 McKillop, *Matters of Mind*, 225-26.
13 Carl Berger, *The Sense of Power: Studies in the Ideas of Canadian Imperialism, 1867-1914* (Toronto: University of Toronto Press, 1970), 186.
14 Ibid., 35.
15 Ibid., 226, 231-32.
16 Library and Archives Canada (LAC), A-794 (Rhodes Trust File [RTF]), 1378, Parkin to Kettlewell, 15 July 1915.
17 Berger, *Sense of Power*, 229.
18 Bliss, quoted in ibid., 211-13.

19 Berger, *Sense of Power*, 38-41.
20 Rosebery Papers (Scottish Record Office, Edinburgh), 10131, Rosebery to Alfred Beit, 3 July 1902; Papers of the Fourth Earl Grey (University of Durham), 191/1, memorandum, 11 July 1902; notes on Rhodes Trust meeting, 29 July 1902; see also Milner Papers (New Bobleian Library, Oxford University), dep. 467, fol. 336, Hawksley to Parkin, 29 July 1902; fol. 348, Parkin to Hawksley, 2 August 1902.
21 The only complaint came from Sir Lewis Michell, a business associate of Rhodes in South Africa and at the time a Rhodes trustee. He believed that Rhodes' omission of the remaining six provinces was not an oversight; rather, he surmised, Rhodes felt that Canada was wealthy enough to supply its own educational needs. Nonetheless, Sir Lewis fell in with the majority, assuming that South Africa would receive reciprocal treatment later, especially considering that it had prior claims. See Rhodes Trust Archives (Rhodes House, Oxford University), file 1256, Michell to Hawksley, 30 March 1903.
22 *Daily Sun* (Saint John), 20 December 1902.
23 Rhodes Trust Archives, Report by Parkin on North American Tour, March 1903; see also Appendix A of the report.
24 Rhodes Trust Archives, file 1256, Scheme for Selection of Rhodes Scholars, in Parkin to Boyd, 27 July 1905; George Parkin, *The Rhodes Scholarships* (London: Constable, 1913), 117-18.
25 Doug McCalla, "The Rhodes Scholarships in Canada and Newfoundland," in *The History of the Rhodes Trust, 1902-1999*, ed. Anthony Kenny (Oxford: Oxford University Press, 2001), 205; LAC, A-621 (RTF 1269), Joseph Belleau to Parkin, 2 December 1904; Parkin to Belleau, 17 December 1904; Peterson to Parkin, 30 March 1905; Parkin to Hawksley, 24 January 1905; Grey to Parkin, 20 March 1905.
26 LAC, A-621 (RTF 1269), Grey to Parkin, 13 March 1906 and enclosure; Papineau to Mr. Fleet (at McGill University), 4 February 1906; see also McCalla, "Rhodes Scholarships," 206.
27 McCalla, "Rhodes Scholarships," 206; LAC, A-621 (RTF 1269), D. Mavor to Wylie, 3 May 1909; G. Dauth, vice rector, to Parkin, 17 June 1909; secretary for Rhodes Trust to Wylie, 9 July 1909; G. Dauth to Parkin, 13 September 1909; Parkin to Hawksley, 17 September 1909; Hawksley to Parkin, 22 September 1909 (received).
28 LAC, A-621 (RTF 1269), A.E. Gosselin to Parkin, 25 May 1912; Parkin to Gosselin, 20 June 1912; memorandum by Parkin, 27 June 1912; memorandum by D. Mavor (for Rhodes Trust), 4 December 1912.
29 LAC, A-621 (RTF 1269), memorandum by Parkin, n.d.; Parkin to Wylie, 5 March 1914; Parkin to Peterson, 8 June 1914.
30 French Canadians were not guaranteed a position. When in 1929 none of the candidates who applied from Montreal or Laval seemed suitable, the committee wondered whether to leave one scholarship vacant. The chair, however, argued that, although it was practice to split the scholarships between McGill and Bishop's on one hand and Montreal and Laval on the other, there was no hard and fast rule that the second scholarship should not be filled by English Canadians if no qualified candidates appeared from Laval or Montreal. In the event, McGill students filled both positions. Philip Kerr, the trust's secretary from 1925 to 1939, expressed his full approval and observed that if the decision caused disappointment among the French universities, they would have to improve the calibre of their candidates. See LAC, A-621 (RTF 1269), J.M. Macdonnell (for Quebec Committee of Selection) to Kerr, 12 January 1929; Kerr to Macdonnell, 14 January 1929; see also LAC, A-621 (RTF 1269), Rhodes Trust to E.W. Beatty, 29 August 1919; Rhodes Trust Archives, Report to the Rhodes Trust by the Oxford Secretary (Sir Francis Wylie) on his Visit to the US and Canada, 28 October 1925; McCalla, "Rhodes Scholarships," 216.
31 McCalla, "Rhodes Scholarships," 216; LAC, A-621 (RTF 1269), Rhodes Trust to Barbeau, 29 August 1919.
32 See Hugh MacLennan, *Two Solitudes* (Toronto: Macmillan, 1945).
33 LAC, A-727 (RTF 2357), Grey to Parkin, 21 March 1908; Parkin to Grey, 7 April 1908; A-729 (RTF 2157), J.M. Macdonnell to Parkin, 27 May 1909; Parkin to Macdonnell, 9 June 1909; A-621 (RTF 1202), Parker to Benbough, 21 September 1915.

34 LAC, A-730 (RTF 1250), Parkin to Murray, 9 March 1911; memorandum by Parkin, 22 November 1912; Augury (for Rhodes Trust) to Parkin, 14 December 1912 (cable); see also McCalla, "Rhodes Scholarships," 206.
35 LAC, A-727 (RTF 2357), E.A. Peacock to Parkin, 18 April 1911; see also *Register of Rhodes Scholars, 1903-1945* (Oxford: Oxford University Press, 1950).
36 Desmond Morton and Jack Granatstein, *Marching to Armageddon: Canadians and the Great War* (Toronto: Lester and Orpen Dennys, 1989), 6, 29, 168; Rhodes Trust Archives, file 2252, extract from report 139: Record of War Service of Rhodes Scholars from Dominions beyond the Seas and the US.
37 Doug Owram, *The Government Generation: Canadian Intellectuals and the State, 1900-1945* (Toronto: University of Toronto Press, 1986), 135-47. Owram noted that "the very possession of a Rhodes Scholarship tended to facilitate acceptance by others in this able and ambitious group" (145-46).
38 Jack Granatstein, *A Man of Influence: Norman A. Robertson and Canadian Statecraft, 1929-68* (Toronto: Deneau, 1981), 7, 15, 17, 18, 42, 55, 103, 112n., 243, 385.
39 See J.A. Corry, *My Life and Work, A Happy Partnership. Memoirs of J.A. Corry* (Montreal and Kingston: McGill-Queen's University Press, 1981), passim.
40 When president of the Canadian Clubs of Toronto, he worked with the more left-leaning Graham Spry. As Owram, *Government Generation*, 169, notes, "For his part Macdonnell, though a Conservative in a group that was increasingly radical in outlook, seems to have received about universal respect within the intellectual community."
41 Sandra Djwa, introduction to *On F.R. Scott*, ed. Sandra Djwa and R.St.J. Macdonald (Montreal and Kingston: McGill-Queen's University Press, 1983), ix-xxi.
42 David Lewis, *The Good Fight: Political Memoirs, 1909-1958* (Toronto: Macmillan, 1981), 32-36.
43 Ibid., 52, 55-57.
44 Rhodes Trust Archives, Annual Report by Oxford Secretary, 1933-34.
45 Rhodes Trust Archives, Report to the Rhodes Trust by the Secretary [Philip Kerr] on his Visit to the US and Canada, 28 October 1925; Report to Rhodes Trust by the Late Oxford Secretary [Sir Francis Wylie] on his Visit to Canada, July 1932.

16
The Canadian Radio Broadcasting Commission in the 1930s: How Canada's First Public Broadcaster Negotiated "Britishness"

Mary Vipond

After the First World War the bonds that held together the British Empire, including those between the mother country and the settler colonies, began to weaken. This was certainly the case in Canada, where English Canadians increasingly shared with their francophone counterparts an impulse toward independent nationhood and closer continental ties. This is not to say, however, that the imperial connection vanished in Canada in the interwar period. Continuing official relationships, immigration, trade, and personal intercourse served to maintain the British tie. Moreover, English Canadians continued to respond to culturally evocative ideas of a British World that embodied superior "institutions, ethos, literary culture, and forms of civility."[1] Because of its continued popularity, the concept of Britishness remained useful to certain elites and institutions. The imagery by which the meaning of the British World was communicated also changed after the war. Not only were the settler dominions like Canada searching for new (and multiple) identities, but also the imperial identity was itself evolving from a spirit of militarism and conquest evoked by images of chivalric knights and heroic soldiers to what some have called the "peace Empire," an empire representing cooperation, mutually advantageous trade, and international leadership by Anglo-Saxons.[2] For Canadians, the interwar period was one of balance and tension, point and counterpoint, tradition and new ventures, as they attempted to sort out their country's future, and its future relationship with Great Britain and the rest of the Empire and Commonwealth.

As Simon J. Potter observed in his contribution to *The British World: Diaspora, Culture and Identity,* the significance of networks of communication, both personal and commercial, has remained underexamined as a factor in building imperial bonds in the period just before the First World War.[3] His study highlights the importance of press relations and the dissemination of news both between the centre and the periphery and among the settler colonies. It ends, however, with the war – in other words, with the end of the age of traditional high imperialism. Potter's article also stresses structural and functional ties rather than those of emotion, whether naturally occurring or deliberately created by agencies of imperial propaganda.

This chapter addresses a subsequent period, the 1930s, when imperial sentiment within the British World became increasingly subtle, and when radio began to establish its predominance as a medium uniquely capable of transmitting live entertainment and news right to the family hearth-side. Radio's utility as a nation- (and Empire-) binding medium was quickly recognized, and that is the focus of this chapter. More specifically, it will examine the relationship between Canada's first public broadcaster, the Canadian Radio Broadcasting Commission (CRBC), and the British Broadcasting Corporation (BBC). Some of the problems in that relationship were clearly institutional in their origin, but others reflect the reality that English Canadians were not only members of the British World but increasingly part of a North American cultural and media environment. For Canadians, and for institutions like the CRBC that were charged with developing a common sense of what it meant to be Canadian, the tensions along the imperial, national, and continental axes were complex and intertwined.[4]

The CRBC was born in 1932 into an environment of continental private-ownership broadcasting. For ten years, Canadian and American corporations and entrepreneurs had been constructing radio stations financed as loss leaders or by third-party advertising. In the American case, two national networks tied the strongest of these stations together. In both cases, programming was aimed at an audience that was assumed to be diverse and mainly interested in diversion. The challenge for the CRBC was to establish itself as a credible alternative to this North American norm. Otherwise it had little reason to exist.

The formation of the CRBC was strongly supported by Anglo-Canadian cultural elites, many with British links and fearful of American cultural domination. Some of them, notably Graham Spry of the Canadian Radio League, were also alarmed by the commercialization of radio. One route the three commissioners who ran the CRBC might have taken in attempting to stake out an alternative broadcasting identity, then, would have been to stress the British connection and to forge links with the non-commercial BBC. This chapter will examine how the CRBC negotiated the British question, with its various implications for issues of cultural authority. Did the CRBC deliberately promote Britishness, and if so, how and why? It will focus on two aspects of the CRBC's programming practices: its use of BBC programs, and its own Empire-oriented broadcasts as illustrated by the program the CRBC produced for Empire Day in 1935.

Contrary to what many assume, the BBC was not a strong institutional model for the CRBC. Not only were the legislative base and formal structure very different, but the environment in which the commission operated was not monopolistic but rather competitive with still-existing private stations.

Of the three commissioners, only one had visited Britain in the BBC era, and that was W.A. Steel, who was the technical man. Hector Charlesworth, the chairman of the commission and the person who, at least in theory, guided the broad outlines of programming policy, was not particularly anglophilic. He was, on the contrary, a Canadian-born self-educated journalist and art and drama critic as fond of American as of British high (or middlebrow) culture.[5] The commissioners were aware as well that the BBC had a bad image in North America as too serious, boring, stiff-necked, and centralized. Through the two or three years of political and newspaper debate immediately prior to the creation of the commission, much of the criticism of the idea of establishing a public broadcaster focused on the perception that in Britain radio was dictated by the government, and the British system was frequently negatively contrasted with the "free" North American model in which the listeners were the "masters of the air."[6] There was no pressure on the commissioners to adopt the BBC model from the much more anglophile prime minister, R.B. Bennett. Not only was Bennett generally a free enterprise man, but he seems to have taken heed of the views of Howard Ferguson, the Canadian high commissioner to London, who advised him: "Perhaps I should say to you that there is a tremendous lot of criticism here of the B.B.C. not only of the style of programme that is being furnished to the public, but of what is alleged to be the very autocratic attitude of the management with regard to everything that has to do with broadcasting. I think you know [Director General] Sir John Reith and you will have carried your own impressions of his temperament."[7]

Nevertheless, the idea of using a substantial amount of BBC programming surfaced as soon as the commissioners got down to planning their first full fall schedule.[8] The advantages were obvious: the material would be of good quality, inexpensive to acquire, and distinctive. A balanced schedule could be developed that would have a mix of serious British programming and lighter more North American fare, or possibly even a mélange of both serious and light material from both sources. Such a programming package would kill two birds with one stone: the CRBC could make itself credible by demonstrating its difference while at the same time not alienating listeners who over the course of the previous ten years had come to assume that radio existed primarily for their entertainment. Insofar as the CRBC's highest priority throughout its existence had to be the establishment of its cultural authority, BBC programming could serve a useful function in the balancing act.[9] In the end, however, regular British programming was heard on the CRBC for only one brief experimental period, from September 1935 to February 1936. While there was also a number of special programs from Britain, and much was made of the King's annual Christmas messages and other royal and imperial special events, a number of difficulties precluded more structured links.

Before those problems are outlined, a few words need to be said about the BBC's position on supplying programs overseas. The BBC's Empire Service, which formally commenced on 19 December 1932, had been discussed for several years before that, but quarrels over who should pay (the Colonial Office? The colonies or dominions themselves?) delayed action. The plans came together only in late 1930 when the BBC reluctantly accepted full financial responsibility, and a new short-wave transmitting station was set up at Daventry. While within BBC management the initial motivation for such a service seems to have been the maintenance of a consolidated British Empire, by the mid-1930s this was coupled with a strong concern to compete with the growing use of short-wave radio for propaganda purposes, particularly by Germany and Italy.[10] By 1933 the BBC offered five services to different parts of the world via directional transmitters. These could be heard, however, only by listeners with short-wave receivers. Arrangements with colonial or dominion broadcasters to retransmit the programs on their own stations and networks were more difficult to achieve, as the Canadian case attests. In fact, there was a considerable split in opinion within the BBC as to whether its programs (and its aerials at Daventry) should be oriented toward the "lonely listener in the bush" or toward relaying or recording programs for rebroadcast by dominion or colonial broadcasters.[11] Generally, up to 1935 the former sentiment prevailed, which helps explain some of the frustration felt by the officials at the CRBC.

Among the obstacles in the way of BBC and CRBC exchanges was the time difference. The CRBC broadcasted only in the evening hours. So while a short-wave station was erected in the summer of 1935 just outside Ottawa primarily to receive and relay BBC programs, they could not be neatly fitted into the schedule. Transmission V, the one aimed at Canada and the West Indies, aired at 11 p.m. GMT each weeknight. This is the service that the CRBC did broadcast for five months, at 6 p.m. on its Eastern network. But it was not a prime time, and could not be extended westward without a costly expansion of network hours. Moreover, the programs provided by the BBC to this service were mostly light music, with the occasional light talk such as one described as "an illustrated excursion by motor-car along the waterfront from London Bridge to the Docks, with a farewell in passing to that famous old inn, 'The Turk's Head.'"[12] CRBC officials felt the programs could be improved in a number of ways but did not find the BBC particularly helpful on that score. From the BBC point of view, the resources of the Empire Service were stretched thin; there was not much money for creating original programs for overseas, particularly as that would involve bringing artists into the studios in the middle of the night. Moreover, a news service, which might have appealed to the Canadian broadcasters, was delayed until late 1934 pending an agreement between the BBC and Reuters.

The most appropriate type of program service also engendered a lengthy debate at the British end: Did the potential imperial audience want sentiment and nostalgia, or did it want highbrow high quality? This paralleled another simmering debate within the BBC about its imperial programming in general. While Reith consistently supported quite a traditional patriotic programming format (he believed, according to one scholar, that patriotic music by composers such as Sir Edward Elgar was "a vital adjunct of national life"), and such programs attracted huge domestic audiences, many of his subordinates were embarrassed by this kind of "unimaginative flag-waving," much of which was not even very good radio.[13] The CRBC managers tended to prefer more highbrow programs from London, especially if the voices were "typically British."[14] They were perfectly capable of providing light music from the "homeland" from their own studios, and the reception would be much more reliable than short-wave transmission from Daventry. On the other hand, the Canadians did not want stuffiness from the BBC. Commissioner Steel especially thought the programs offered on the Empire Service were "terrible," and he wrote confidentially to Canadian expatriate Gladstone Murray, the BBC's director of publicity, that too many of the broadcasts contained "the very thing which is unpopular in Canada, namely, long drawn-out talks without any point to them."[15] He also had come to the conclusion, however, that it did not matter what he thought; he was convinced that Reith had "made up his mind that Canada will take what he is willing to give them [sic] or nothing at all."[16] It must be noted, however, that what the CRBC officials thought was the most appropriate or best BBC programming was not necessarily that which Canadian audiences preferred. The data on audience response is limited given the lack of listener surveys in Canada at the time, but it may well be that, as in Britain, it was precisely the combination of light entertainment with pageantry, especially of the monarchical sort, that was most popular among English Canadians.[17]

An alternative to direct short-wave reception was to record the programs at the Canadian end and play them at more convenient times of the day. The CRBC invested a considerable amount of money and even more time and frustration in a primitive machine called the Blattnerphone to pick up and record the BBC short-wave broadcasts. The Blattnerphone was based on a discovery by Danish physicist Valdemar Poulsen at the end of the nineteenth century, further developed by Dr. Curt Stille in Germany in the 1920s. Simply put, its technique involved making magnetic impressions on steel wire or tape. One of Stille's machines was apparently imported to Britain by a movie producer named Blattner, and the name Blattnerphone was adopted in Britain. The British Marconi Company purchased the UK rights to Stille's patents and worked with the BBC to make a recorder that used three-millimetre-wide steel tape for use by the Empire Service from 1932 on. Although there were problems getting a pure sound, the great advantage of the machines was that thirty-three minutes of material could be recorded on one reel (containing no less than three kilometres of wire); moreover, the tapes could be erased and reused.[18] At the suggestion of early CRBC employee Austin Weir, while on a trip to England in 1933 Commissioner Steel met with the Stille people, and signed an agreement with Marconi to supply and service a Blattnerphone to be set up in the commission's Ottawa studio in the Château Laurier Hotel. The order was submitted in March 1933, less than two months after the CRBC had begun to function, and the machine arrived and was installed by October.[19] Two more recorders were ordered before the end of 1933. The machines were not purchased from Marconi but were rented at the not inconsiderable sum of $2,200 per year each.

Despite high hopes, the Blattnerphones quickly turned into "a great disappointment."[20] There were a number of technical problems: there was a hum on all recordings, the tapes had a bad habit of seizing after running only ten minutes, and the local Marconi technician was unable to help much. The CRBC initially refused to pay Marconi its rental fees until the difficulties were cleared up, but it gradually became evident that the commission had bought into an experimental technology that had been put on the market too soon. The bottom line was that the experiment was a failure – but the amount of effort and money expended does indicate a serious interest on the Canadian end in using BBC programming.[21]

There were other problems as well. BBC programs ran at odd lengths – for instance, thirty-five minutes – which was inappropriate for the already rigidly scheduled North American broadcasting market, and the British refused to allow the programs to be cut off midstream.[22] More serious were copyright problems. To record any program using a registered artist, the CRBC would have had to clear copyright in Britain.[23] As Charlesworth baldly summed it up to a government colleague: "The BBC prohibits us from recording its best programmes by blattnerphone and rebroadcasting."[24] Moreover, it was the custom in North American broadcasting that all evening programming was live. Both broadcasters and audiences believed that recorded programs were somehow inferior, sometimes in quality but also because they did not take advantage of one of radio's greatest assets, its spontaneity. Indeed, the CRBC regulated Canadian private stations to limit the amount of recorded material they used during prime time. For the CRBC to schedule much Blattnerphone-recorded programming in the evening hours, then, might have raised hackles.[25] Yet another frustration for the Canadians was that they wanted to exchange programs with the BBC, as was done with the American networks. This, it was anticipated, would publicize Canada in England to good effect. But the BBC had little interest in taking Canadian programs for its domestic service, so this plan also fell through.[26] Steel's bitterness at the whole situation, especially at being patronized, and his comfort with the obvious North American alternative, are revealed in another letter to Gladstone Murray: "I might also point out to you that the Canadian Radio Commission can obtain all the first class exchange features we require from the two American systems, with both of whom we are on very excellent terms. I am sorry that the matter has developed in this way but I can assure you that this Commission does not intend to be dictated to by the British Broadcasting Company [sic]."[27]

Many years later Bob Bowman, a CBC man who also worked with the Empire Service in Britain before and during the Second World War, reminisced that when he tried to encourage Charlesworth to use more BBC programs, the latter replied that "the B.B.C. would not cooperate." When Bowman then went to London and asked the same question, the response was that "they wanted some of their programs to be rebroadcast by the Canadian Radio Commission, but ... they couldn't get any cooperation."[28] The way Bowman recounted the story, the blame lay with the CRBC. But whichever side was at fault, it is clear that there was mutual misunderstanding and frustration – and few opportunities to listen to the BBC in Canada.[29]

While the BBC and the CRBC did not establish an exchange arrangement for regular programming, the Canadian public broadcaster did pick up a large number of special programs from Britain via the BBC. These were aired on the national network, usually with great fanfare. An analysis of the list of seventy-two special programs mentioned in the CRBC annual reports between April 1933 and March 1936 reveals that the largest single group (thirty-one) may be classed as imperial in orientation – for example, the wedding of the Duke of Kent or a Royal Empire Society speech by the British high commissioner to Canada. Among these imperially oriented special programs, the most important concerned the monarchy; most celebrated of all were the annual Christmas messages of King George V. In fact, the very first program the commission coordinated, even before all its members had been sworn in, was the first Empire-wide Christmas message in December 1932. Three years later the annual report described the 1935 message as "the chief event broadcast in Canada" that year.[30] These broadcasts involved not only the King's brief speech but pickups of greetings from various parts of the Empire. For the 1932 broadcast, for example, greetings from Halifax, Montreal, Toronto, Winnipeg, and Vancouver (all by radio officials) were exchanged via short-wave with London, Dublin, Wellington, Sydney and Melbourne, Cape Town, Gibraltar, and a ship in mid-Atlantic.[31] In 1934 good wishes were sent by, among others, a fisherman in Tasmania, a toll-keeper on the bridge at Sydney Australia, and Capt. Malcolm MacLean from a fisherman's cottage in the Maritimes. The Canadian segment also featured part of a hockey game between the Toronto Maple Leafs and the Montreal Maroons, narrated by Foster Hewitt, and a children's skating party in Winnipeg.[32] In 1935 the CRBC went all out with a program Austin Weir described as "the apogee of network broadcasting for the CRBC." On this occasion, a "moving panorama," primarily of music, forged choral and orchestral chains across the country, culminating in roving reporter interviews and the exchange of felicitations between the CRBC and NBC in New York.[33] Paddy Scannell and David Cardiff rightly point to the King's Christmas messages, with their emphasis on him as the head of the royal family and also of the family of nations in the Empire, as an "invented tradition," one that "set a crowning seal on the role of broadcasting in binding ... together" both the British nation and its overseas dominions and colonies.[34] Even the titles of the Christmas programs evoke this familial message: "All the World Over" in 1932, "Absent Friends" in 1933, "Empire Exchange" the following year, and "The Great Family" in 1935. The ability of the CRBC as a national network to fully participate in such programming fostered not only the imperial linkage but also a sense of national accomplishment.

In addition to the Christmas broadcast, the BBC's other significant regular flagship program with an imperial orientation was the Empire Day broadcast. Starting in the late 1920s, the BBC devoted a considerable amount of time each 24 May to programming about the Empire. In the 1930s, with the initiation of the Empire Service, an exchange program was developed with the broadcasters of the settler colonies. The first such program was coordinated from Australia in 1934.[35] In 1935, the CRBC supplied the special program to the BBC Empire Service for airing throughout the Empire. While the CRBC did not initiate this program but put it on at the request of the BBC, it nevertheless created and produced it, and the choices made by Chairman Hector Charlesworth and his program directors reveal some of their assumptions about Canada's role in the Empire and about the CRBC's role in Canada. The arrangement was that the CRBC would organize and finance the program, it would be sent to the BBC on the transatlantic "beam," and then be retransmitted from the BBC's Empire station around the world. The survival of both the script and the background correspondence fortunately enable a close analysis of the 1935 Empire Day program.

Late in 1934, once alerted to the task of creating the broadcast, Chairman Hector Charlesworth got together with his program planners to discuss various possibilities: What kind of program would it be? Would the prime minister and governor general speak? Would it be aired from one location or several? How much should the CRBC spend on it?[36] Fairly quickly they focused on the idea of highlighting the fact that the Empire Day movement had been originally conceived in the late 1890s by Mrs. Clementina Fessenden of Hamilton, Ontario, and had been promoted in turn by the Canadian Club of Hamilton. One may speculate that Charlesworth, who had been born in Hamilton, might have suggested this idea.[37] Information about the role of Mrs. Fessenden and the Canadian Club was quickly acquired, and the contract to write a fifteen-minute script for a dramatized story about Mrs. Fessenden's "glorious" idea was given to Mrs. Evelyn Biddle, a writer who had previously been used by the commission and who lived near Hamilton.[38] In addition to this short drama, the program featured orchestral music and greetings from Prime Minister Bennett. The music is not fully described in the surviving script, but it apparently included what a planning document called "national music" from Canada and the other dominions, as well as at least one rendition of "Rule Britannia," "Pomp and Circumstance," and, of course, "God Save the King."[39] By the mid-1930s these imperial anthems, which were particularly well suited to use in radio broadcasts, possessed iconographic status.[40]

The script's opening and closing announcements were in both English and French. The latter gives the tone. It stated: "This broadcast, which has circled the globe, has brought together in bonds of unity the sons and daughters of the British family of nations. Canada is proud of her heritage, and of the part she has played in the building of the Empire, and today expresses, as she links hands across the seas with her brother and sister nations, her allegiance to the Motherland ... on this, our Empire Day, as we unite in singing ... God Save Our King."[41] It was arranged that the production would initiate from the studios of the privately owned Hamilton station, CKOC, the commission not having its own facilities in that city.[42] It was also arranged that the program be Blattnerphoned for later rebroadcast.

In his instructional letter to Mrs. Biddle, CRBC official G.A. Taggart suggested that she begin the script with the meeting of the Wentworth Historical Society at which Mrs. Fessenden first broached the Empire Day idea, and that Mrs. Fessenden's granddaughter Kathleen be somehow included. Scene B, he suggested, should show the celebration of the first Empire Day. Scene C was to portray "the patriotic results" derived from Empire Day. The commission wished to end with two brief interviews with children "as to their opinion of Empire Day and what the word 'Empire' means to them."[43] He reminded Mrs. Biddle that she had been chosen because of her ability to "write dialogue of a human and homely, yet impressive quality," and added: "You understand, of course, that the basis of the broadcast will be to stimulate patriotism throughout the Empire but at the same time it is our wish to have a dramatic story that will appeal to the audience." In a similar letter to the prime minister's private secretary, Charlesworth pointed out that because Mrs. Fessenden's original idea had involved school-based celebrations, the broadcast played up Empire Day as "a young people's celebration."[44] He went on: "In the Prime Minister's remarks, it might be well to aim at the young people and of [sic] the conception of 'Empire,' which means the spread of civilized ideals and free institutions around the world in contrast with the old Imperialism, which signified domination and tribute. The vast audience in every clime, which he will be addressing, should be borne in mind and the marvel of modern communication, which enables a single voice to reach listeners around the world, might be touched upon."

Almost immediately, however, a difficulty ensued. It had been understood from the beginning that the BBC would check the CRBC's plans and scripts. When Charlesworth offered to supplement that material with pictures of Mrs. Fessenden – "There is no question that she originated the idea" – the reply from the BBC was less than enthusiastic.[45] The difficulty, from the BBC's point of view, was that while Mrs. Fessenden possibly founded the Empire Day movement in Canada, there might be those in the other dominions and in Britain itself who would take exception to the claim that she originated it for the whole Empire. "I think you will agree with me," the Empire Programme Director J.B. Clark told Charlesworth, "that it would be unfortunate if an Empire Day programme gave rise to controversy."[46] He therefore politely declined the offer of the photographs and added, "We shall wait your observations with interest." Charlesworth was cooperative. As he explained to Clark: "If we ignored [Mrs. Fessenden] in an Empire Day broadcast we would be in hot water with all the Loyalist organizations in Canada. However, I had already given instructions that this portion of the broadcast not be parochial and recognition must be given to the fact that the movement was spread through the plan being taken up in Great Britain."[47] More candidly, he wrote to Prime Minister Bennett's private secretary: "The BBC asked us not to stress the idea that Empire Day originated in Canada (although this is a fact) on the ground that it might cause feeling in other Dominions, but we are giving the main portion of the broadcast from Hamilton because it was the birthplace of the idea."[48]

Charlesworth was partially right. Mrs. Fessenden had indeed conceived the idea on her own in the late 1890s, but English imperialist activist the Earl of Meath had had a similar idea in 1896, and the spread of what came to be called the Empire Day Movement to Britain and other parts of the Empire was due to his work.[49] Lord Meath's beliefs, all the scholars seem to agree, were very much of the old-school (more specifically public-school) brand of imperialism focusing on training youth to build up an "imperial race" – "worthy of responsibility, alive to duty, filled with sympathy towards mankind and not afraid of self-sacrifice in the promotion of lofty ideals."[50] In essence, writes J.A. Mangan, Lord Meath's concept of Empire Day "comprised a belief in the qualities of self-denial, discipline, subscription to duty, [and] fealty to the state."[51] This was the kind of imperialism Charlesworth, as cited above, explicitly rejected; it was not appropriate either to the 1930s or to Canada. Meath's Empire Day Movement, which began as a voluntary enterprise in Britain in 1904 and was officially endorsed there in 1916, apparently reached its peak of popularity in the 1920s and 1930s, an acceptance which at least one authority, John M. MacKenzie, suggests may be attributed to the Empire Day radio broadcasts.[52]

In the end, the script prepared by Mrs. Biddle differed considerably from that first suggested by the CRBC. While it begins with the narrator's voice saying, "We present now a dramatized story of the founding of Empire Day in Canada," followed by a swelling few seconds of Elgar's "Pomp and Circumstance," the script immediately moves on to two sketches, the first about the arrival of the United Empire Loyalists at Saint John, New Brunswick, and the second on the westward movement of Canadian pioneers. The first presents the classic Loyalist myth: the Loyalists had abandoned everything they owned in the United States to "willingly face a life of hardship in the virgin wilderness – rather than forfeit their British heritage."[53] The first voices heard are those of British military men welcoming the arrival of the fleet from the "States" with a bugle call and a gun salute. Repeatedly, the narration stresses the themes of toil and privation and the *"privilege* to sacrifice for England."[54] The Loyalists themselves speak in five or six anonymous voices about the task before them and their children and grandchildren: to "build another England."[55] Terms such as "British soil" and "fellow-Britishers" are frequently used. Interestingly, the Loyalists' endeavour is compared to that of their predecessors, the French Canadians, whose "example of loyalty and devotion to the British Empire undoubtedly was an inspiration and an encouragement."[56] The episode, whose dialogue can only be described as stiff and traditional, climaxes with a prayer – "We thank Thee for our safe arrival in this dear, British land, over which waves our beloved Flag" – and the "Doxology," followed by "Rule Britannia."[57] Comprising only four pages of the script, the Loyalist sketch is significant because it sets the tone for the program. Its presentation, in words and music, of militarism, religion, patriotism, and British family values strongly evokes the old imperialism of the pre-war period.

A rather abrupt transition then takes us to 1896, and a brief dialogue between two farmers, one of whom is selling his farm and heading to western Canada. Again, the theme is the sacrifice of the comfortable life for the hardship of pioneering, because "that's the spirit that's made the British Empire."[58]

At the middle of the sixth page of the fourteen-page script we get to the Wentworth Historical Society's fateful meeting of 6 June 1896. Amid pieties about the "great responsibility we, as sons and daughters of the Empire, must bear," Mrs. Fessenden reveals her project.[59] She explains that it was inspired by an event that had occurred at the previous meeting, when her little granddaughter Kathleen had been presented with an honorary badge in recognition of the work of the late Mr. Fessenden. Kathleen's emotions had been stirred by the presentation – "an expression ... of pride ... and youthful understanding seemed to light her whole face."[60] And so Mrs. Fessenden had conceived a project that would stir the loyalty of all children, to ignite a "pride of race" and a surge of "national energy."[61] More concretely, she suggested that the schools be persuaded to set aside one day for a Flag Day – or perhaps it might be called Loyalty Day, "Our Country's Day," or Britannia Day. And so the members immediately decided to approach the newspapers, "influential people," the minister of education of Ontario, and the provincial teachers convention to promote their plan. Meanwhile, we are told, in Britain Lord Meath was working along the same lines, and soon Empire Day became established throughout the British World. "The question of who was responsible for its institution is secondary," the narrator tells us, for it was the product of "the united co-operation that has made the British Empire what it is."[62]

The script concludes, as had been the original intention, with children. A scene is painted of a "typical Canadian home" at breakfast time on Empire Day in 1935. A letter has just arrived from the children's Uncle John in Australia. Replete with pompous patriotism and sentimentality, it is read aloud at the table:

> I cannot help but mention a feeling of pride that envelopes [sic] me, meeting and mingling with British Citizens of all races, creeds and colour ... united in bonds of understanding and singleness of purpose ... I'm brought to the realization that there must be some mighty power behind such a commonwealth of nations ... a power of brotherhood and purpose, governed by high ideals and a sincere desire to elevate mankind ... It means much to the peace and prosperity of the earth ... The responsibility of each of us, I feel, is great, but the satisfaction derived from a realization of the part each one plays is sufficient compensation.[63]

The script continues with dialogue as the children question their parents about the meaning of all this, and many pious platitudes are expressed. The emphasis is on the Empire as one big family with Great Britain as the mother; "We are *all* children of the Empire," the mother declares.[64] British public school values are invoked by the father, who declares that the "spirit of Britain the world over" is "to play the game ... not to pick on the little fellow ... to do unto others as you would have others do unto you."[65] The drama ends as the mother quotes from her brother's letter again, as quiet background music begins to play: "'I trust and pray that this spirit of honour and united understanding will never waver or fall before selfish motives.' Oh, John, you said it so perfectly."[66]

All in all, this script is strong neither in conception nor dialogue. Two strong ambivalences are evident: between the desire to highlight the Canadian story and the need to include the rest of the Empire, and between the more traditional images and language of imperialism and the more modern "peace Empire" notions already common by the mid-1930s. While some of the 1935 family's dialogue does reference newer ideas of imperialism such as peace and prosperity, the use of the phrases "high ideals" and "spirit of honour" gives the script a traditional aura, as of course does the Loyalist segment. Moreover, as John M. MacKenzie has wryly remarked about imperial programming in general, "The militarist devils of the historic, heroic Empire had all the best tunes."[67] The emphasis on Britain as the "mother" and the dominions the "children" in the Empire family also harks back to imagery increasingly inappropriate in the post-Statue of Westminster era. By stressing high-minded spiritual values so much, the Empire Day drama loses its rootedness in real interwar Canadian or Commonwealth life and becomes a vehicle for sentimental pap. The congratulatory telegram Reith sent to Charlesworth after the broadcast praised only the prime minister's speech; it made no mention of the drama.[68]

The CRBC's attempt to pacify the BBC by including mention of Lord Meath's contribution to the spread of Empire Day predictably aroused the wrath of some elements in Canada. Fiercely proud of Mrs. Fessenden's, and therefore Canada's, claim to origination, Mrs. Helen Coy of the New Brunswick branch of the Imperial Order of Daughters of the Empire wrote to Charlesworth to complain that "some gentleman" had been heard on CFNB Fredericton giving Lord Meath the credit for the Empire Day idea.[69] Charlesworth's reply was again frank. He explained that he was well aware of Mrs. Fessenden's work but that the BBC had feared controversy if the Canadian claim was "asserted too emphatically." "Under the circumstances," he went on, "I was obliged to accept the suggestions[,] and the introduction of the name of Lord Meath was recognized as a judicious one by old Imperialists in Canada."[70] The tale concludes on a rather sour note. When CKOC Hamilton presented the CRBC with a bill of $120 for the use of its facilities, Ernest Bushnell replied huffily that it was much too high, given the "honour" the station had been accorded in being asked to stage the program.[71] One may note as well that the CRBC only very reluctantly aired the Empire Day program from South Africa in 1936 and was not otherwise involved in it.[72]

Not only does this story reveal a tension between the Canadians' desire to assert Mrs. Fessenden's primacy and the need to play the story the way the BBC wanted it, but this in turn reflects the implicit and explicit debate still occurring in Canada in the 1930s about exactly what the nation's relationship to the Empire and Commonwealth should be. The battle for Mrs. Fessenden's claim was, after all, a battle about who was the best imperialist. The CRBC's programming decision was intended to satisfy the Empire patriotism of a group of old-fashioned Canadian imperialist nationalists, some of whom were personal friends of the chairman. As Carl Berger and others have amply demonstrated, in the late nineteenth and early twentieth century, one prominent form of Canadian nationalism was imperial federationism, the notion that Canada's destiny lay in becoming a dominant member of the Empire.[73] But the idea died during the First World War as it became evident that it was impractical to imagine Canada truly contributing to imperial decision making. While the Canadian and British governments continued to cooperate after the war, it was on a more ad hoc basis than the federation idea had promoted; despite common underlying ideals, the differences in the interests and positions of the two countries became increasingly evident. The 1935 broadcast rings a false note, then, for it attempts to revive a Canadian mood and a type of imperialist imagery that was indeed alive in Mrs. Fessenden's day but that was by 1935 drawing some of its last breaths. The CRBC asserted its authoritative voice in this case, but its attempts to give a Canadian flavour to an Empire Day broadcast only produced a program replete with a traditional high-minded imperialism very much out of date in English Canada by the mid-1930s.

Nevertheless, the broadcast was significant. Chairman Charlesworth clearly believed that the CRBC had a larger duty to the Canadian people than simply to present Canadian material, it was also important for the commission to bring major imperial events to Canadians, and vice versa. Those who worked at the CRBC considered themselves to be part of an important Canadian institution, with responsibilities that were symbolic, moral, and national. And part of the commission's mandate as a national broadcaster, with access to the living rooms and parlours of a large number of Canadians, was respectful attention to moments of importance to the Empire and the British World. The lesson of the 1935 Empire Day broadcast, however, is that the commissioners lacked a contemporary sense of the appropriate tone in which to broadcast such moments either to Canadians or to the rest of the Empire and Commonwealth.

In this example, we see the CRBC playing a mixed game in the 1930s in promoting BBC links and British programming on its network. While there was none of the hostility to the British model that existed in some other North American radio circles, there was no automatic respect or imitation either. What did remain was respect for the institutions of imperial life, including the monarchy. There was also clearly a sense that the Empire connection should be conveyed in tones that resonated simultaneously with majesty and sentiment, with glorious music and depictions of everyday life. Programs of this type enhanced the authority of the commission in the competitive North American radio environment and helped justify the cost of its network. But even conservatives like Charlesworth were strongly oriented toward North America and accepted that radio was an entertainment medium catering to the Americanized tastes of Canadian listeners. Britishness was useful for special events programming. For both practical and cultural reasons, however, it was not for everyday fare.

Notes

1 John Darwin, "A Third British Empire? The Dominion Idea in Imperial Politics," in *The Oxford History of the British Empire*, vol. 4, *The Twentieth Century*, ed. Judith M. Brown and Wm. Roger Louis (New York: Oxford University Press, 1999), 86. See also Carl Bridge and Kent Fedorowich, "Mapping the British World," in *The British World: Diaspora, Culture and Identity*, ed. Carl Bridge and Kent Fedorowich (London: Frank Cass, 2003), 6-9.

2 See John M. MacKenzie, "'In Touch with the Infinite': The BBC and the Empire, 1923-53," in *Imperialism and Popular Culture*, ed. John M. MacKenzie (Manchester: Manchester University Press, 1986), 183, 186. One must not exaggerate the abruptness of this transformation. As Jonathan Vance has clearly illustrated, Canadian memorials to the war dead continued to use heroic, Christian, and chivalric motifs in the 1920s and 1930s. See Jonathan Vance, *Death So Noble: Memory, Meaning, and the First World War* (Vancouver: UBC Press, 1997).

3 Simon J. Potter, "Communication and Integration: The British and Dominion Press and the British World, c. 1876-1914," in *The British World*, 190-202.

4 John D. Jackson, "Contradictions: Cultural Production, the State and the Electronic Media," *Fréquence/Frequency* 3/4 (1995): 27-35.

5 See Dennis Salter, "Hector Willoughby Charlesworth and the Nationalization of Cultural Authority, 1890-1945," in *Establishing Our Boundaries: English-Canadian Theatre Criticism*, ed. Anton Wagner (Toronto: University of Toronto Press, 1999), 137-76, and Charlesworth's own books, including *Candid Chronicles* (Toronto: Macmillan, 1925), *More Candid Chronicles* (Toronto: Macmillan, 1928), and *I'm Telling You* (Toronto: Macmillan, 1937).

6 Mary Vipond, "Desperately Seeking the Audience for Early Canadian Broadcasting," in *Nation, Culture, Identity: Essays in Honour of Ramsay Cook*, ed. Michael Behiels and Marcel Martel (Don Mills, ON: Oxford University Press, 2000), 86-96.

7 Library and Archives Canada (LAC), MG 26 K, R.B. Bennett Papers, mfm M-1292, Ferguson to Bennett, 2 March 1934, 363535-36.

8 LAC, RG 41, CBC Records, vol. 615, mfm T-3040, CRBC minutes, 1 June 1933.

9 It should be noted that the CRBC also included a number of NBC and CBS programs in its schedule, mostly more serious fare, like the NBC Philharmonic Orchestra.

10 Gerard Mansell, *Let the Truth Be Told: 50 Years of BBC External Broadcasting* (London: Weidenfeld and Nicolson, 1982), 9. See also Asa Briggs, *The History of Broadcasting in the United Kingdom*, vol. 2, *The Golden Age of Wireless* (London: Oxford University Press, 1965), part 3, chap. 5.

11 Mansell, *Let the Truth Be Told*, 11.

12 LAC, MG 30 E250, Ernest Bushnell Papers, vol. 2, file: CBC – Bushnell-Murray Correspondence 1935, "Empire Programmes – Transmission V."

13 John M. MacKenzie writes: "Reith was ... 'in love with symbolism, pomp, dressing-up and orders.' He was a devotee of hierarchical values, a self-dramatist and a conformist. The Empire programmes appealed to all these sides of Reith's nature, and provided for him a sense of participating in great national ritual"; MacKenzie, "In Touch with the Infinite," 172-73, 180. See also Siân Nicholas, "'Brushing Up Your Empire': Dominion and Colonial Propaganda on the BBC's Home Services, 1939-45," in *The British World*, 209, and Paddy Scannell and David Cardiff, *A Social History of British Broadcasting*, vol. 1, *1922-1939: Serving the Nation* (Oxford: Basil Blackwood, 1991), 288-89.

14 LAC, MG 30 E250, Ernest Bushnell Papers, vol. 2, file: CBC – Bushnell-Murray Correspondence 1935, J.C.S. MacGregor memo to J.B. Clark [late September 1935].

15 LAC, W.A. Steel Papers, MG 30 A42, vol. 26, file 144, Steel to W.E.G. Murray, 1 March 1934.

16 Ibid.

17 John M. MacKenzie, "Propaganda and the BBC Empire Service, 1932-42," in *Propaganda, Persuasion and Polemic*, ed. Jeremy Hawthorn (London: Edward Arnold, 1987), 43.

18 On the British use of the Blattnerphone, see Briggs, *Golden Age*, 99-100, 382.

19 LAC, RG 41, CBC Records, vol. 76, file 3-4-3, part 1, Steel to R.M. Brophy, 14 March 1933.

20 Ibid., vol. 37, file 2-2-6-8, part 1, Charles Shearer to Steel, 18 June 1934; ibid., Steel to R.M. Brophy, 16 July 1934.

21 The commissioners were also interested in similar pickups from French radio, but technical difficulties intervened there as well. See LAC, MG 30 A42, W.A. Steel Papers, vol. 29, file 165, Léopold Houlé to Colonel Chauveau, 30 August 1935.

22 LAC, MG 30 E250, Ernest Bushnell Papers, vol. 2, file: CBC – Bushnell-Murray Correspondence 1935, Bushnell to W.E.G. Murray, 25 August 1944. See also ibid., Murray to J.B. Clark, 30 September 1935.

23 Ibid., J.B. Clark to Bushnell, 12 February 1935, and BBC Written Archives Centre (WAC), E1/522/1, Empire Broadcasting in Canada, Malcolm Frost to Steel, 15 March 1934.

24 LAC, RG 12, Department of Transport Records, vol. 404, file 5558-1, Charlesworth to C.P. Edwards, 9 May 1936.

25 LAC RG 41, CBC Records, vol. 615, mfm T-3040, CRBC minutes, 1 June 1933; see also ibid., vol. 390, file 20-9, part 7, E.C. Buchanan to Malcolm Frost, 9 July 1935. This was also the main reason why the CRBC did not take transcriptions (programs on records) from the BBC, although they were apparently of high quality and very popular in the other dominions. See Mansell, *Let the Truth Be Told*, 27. Other factors included the cost of the transcriptions and the competing appeal of similar recordings offered by the American networks. See WAC, E5/9, Empire Transcriptions: Canada.

26 LAC, MG 26K, R.B. Bennett Papers, mfm M-1293, T. Maher to Bennett, 9 February 1934, 365478.

27 LAC, MG 30 A42, W.A. Steel Papers, vol. 26, file 144, Steel to Murray, 24 January 1934.

28 LAC, MG 30 D304, T.J. Allard Papers, vol. 6, file 6-4, "Reminiscences of the CBC by Bob Bowman" [1963], 2. There is extensive discussion of the difficulties in the relationship in the BBC's files on the CRBC. See particularly WAC E1/522/2, Empire Broadcasting in Canada, "Resumé of Correspondence and Reports Covering the Period December 1932-April 1935"; ibid., E1/492, Canada: Canadian Broadcasting Commission 1934-1936, "Report: Empire Broadcasting in Canada," [labelled "Mr. Frost's Final Report"], c. March 1934; ibid., E1/528, Felix Greene: Reports 1935-1936. Greene was the BBC's North American Representative, based in New York.

29 At least one private station affiliated to the CRBC, CHNS Halifax, did broadcast BBC programs. These were picked up off short-wave for direct broadcast in daytime hours, a use not open to the commission. One final comment may be added. It may only be an artefact of the record-management policies of the CBC Historical Section that long ago winnowed the CRBC papers, but it is notable how little correspondence survives on the Canadian end between BBC and CRBC managers, and how rarely the BBC came up in official minutes or other records. The relationship was sporadic, and lukewarm at best. While more extensive files exist on the British end, they often reveal the frustration of BBC officials when their correspondence and queries were left unanswered. See for example WAC, E1/508, Canada: Canadian Radio Broadcasting Commission A-Z, for J.B. Clark's frequent pleas in early 1936 for some comment from the CRBC about what kinds of programs it would like to receive from the Empire Service.

30 CRBC *Annual Report*, 1935-36 (Ottawa: King's Printer, 1936), 13. Similar hyperbole was used on the British end. See MacKenzie, "In Touch with the Infinite," 181-82, and MacKenzie, "Propaganda and the BBC Empire Service," 43.

31 See E.A. Weir, *The Struggle for National Broadcasting in Canada* (Toronto: McClelland and Stewart, 1965) 41-46, for his first-hand account of the "fiasco" that prevented the broadcasts from beginning in 1931 and for the arrangements for the 1932 broadcast.

32 D.R.P. Coats, "Canada's Fifty Years of Broadcasting and Stories Stations Tell: Featuring the Pioneer Station XWA, Later Given the Call Letters CFCF, 1919-1969" (manuscript, Canadian Marconi Library, Montreal, n.d.), 281-83.

33 Weir, *Struggle for National Broadcasting*, 197-98.

34 Scannell and Cardiff, *Social History of British Broadcasting*, 280-83.

35 The 1933 program, which seems to have been entirely a British production (and entitled "News from Home"), was aired in Canada, interestingly enough, not by the CRBC but on a chain of private stations. This was likely because the CRBC had barely got its network set up at the time. "Radio," *Globe and Mail* (Toronto), 24 May 1933, 16. On the evolution of

the Empire Day programming, as well as the reluctance of some BBC programmers for this kind of patriotic endeavour, see WAC R/34/213/1, E.J. King Bull memo, "Programme for Empire Day, 1930," 22 February 1930; ibid., Lindsay Wellington memo, "Empire Day Programme," 10 February 1931; ibid., E.A.F. Harding to Assistant Director (Programmes), "Empire Day Programme, 1933."

36 LAC, MG 30 D67, E.A. Weir Papers, vol. 17, file 6, C.G. Graves to Charlesworth, 28 September 1934 and 29 October 1934.
37 For more on Mrs. Fessenden, Empire Day, and the imperial sentiments of late-nineteenth-century Ontario, see R.M. Stamp, "Empire Day in the Schools of Ontario: The Training of Young Imperialists," *Journal of Canadian Studies* 8 (1973): 32-42, and Cecilia Morgan, "History, Nation, and Empire: Gender and Southern Ontario Historical Societies, 1890-1920s," *Canadian Historical Review* 82 (2001): 491-528. See also Michihisa Hosokawa, "Making Imperial Canadians: Empire Day in Canada," paper presented to the second British World Conference, Calgary, July 2003. The commissioners were well aware that Reginald Fessenden, the first experimenter to successfully transmit sound by wireless, was Mrs. Fessenden's son.
38 LAC, MG 30 D67, E.A. Weir Papers, vol. 17, file 6, CRBC, "Empire Day Dramatization," 8.
39 Ibid., CRBC, "Empire Day Broadcast Skeleton."
40 MacKenzie, "Propaganda and the BBC Empire Service," 43, and MacKenzie, "In Touch with the Infinite," 179.
41 LAC, MG 30 D67, E.A. Weir Papers, vol. 17, file 6, CRBC, "Empire Day Announcements," 3.
42 Ibid., Charlesworth to C.R. McCullough, 5 February 1935; G.A. Taggart to Mrs. Biddle, 28 February 1935.
43 Ibid., Taggart to Mrs. Biddle, 4 March 1935.
44 Ibid., Charlesworth to R.K. Finlayson, 20 May 1935.
45 Ibid., Charlesworth to Maj. Murray, 11 February 1935.
46 Ibid., J.B. Clark to Charlesworth, 6 March 1935.
47 Ibid., Charlesworth to Clark, 14 March 1935.
48 Ibid., Charlesworth to Finlayson, 20 May 1935.
49 The sources differ somewhat on this question. J.O. Springhall, who has written most extensively on the British youth movements of the period, does state that "the idea ... came from Canada in the 1890s," but John M. MacKenzie is quite explicit that Meath wrote a letter to the *London Times* in 1896 calling for patriotic school assemblies with flag salutes on the Queen's birthday followed by a half-holiday, although unfortunately he does not provide the precise date of the letter. See J.O. Springhall, "Lord Meath, Youth, and Empire," *Journal of Contemporary History* 5 (1970): 105, and John M. MacKenzie, *Propaganda and Empire: The Manipulation of British Public Opinion, 1880-1960* (Manchester: Manchester University Press, 1984), 231-32. See also J.A. Mangan, "'The Grit of Our Forefathers': Invented Traditions, Propaganda and Imperialism," in *Imperialism and Popular Culture*, 130-31.
50 Lord Meath, "Duty and Discipline in the Training of Children" (1910), quoted in Mangan, "The Grit of Our Forefathers," 130.
51 Ibid., 132.
52 MacKenzie, "'In Touch with the Infinite,'" 168.
53 LAC, MG 30 D67, E.A. Weir Papers, vol. 17, file 6, CRBC, "Empire Day Dramatization," 1.
54 Ibid., 4. Emphasis in original.
55 Ibid., 2.
56 Ibid., 4.
57 Ibid., 3.
58 Ibid., 6.
59 Ibid., 7.
60 Ibid., 8.
61 Ibid.
62 Ibid., 10.
63 Ibid., 11-12.
64 Ibid., 13. Emphasis in original. Another contemporaneous locus of emphasis on the Empire as one big family was the propaganda of the Empire Marketing Board. See Stephen

Constantine, "'Bringing the Empire Alive': The Empire Marketing Board and Imperial Propaganda, 1926-33," in *Imperialism and Popular Culture*, 217.
65 LAC, MG 30 D67, E.A. Weir Papers, vol. 17, file 6, CRBC, "Empire Day Dramatization," 13.
66 Ibid., 14.
67 MacKenzie, "In Touch with the Infinite," 186.
68 LAC, MG 30 D67, E.A. Weir Papers, vol. 17, file 6, Reith to Canadian Radio [Broadcasting]
    Commission, 24 May 1935.
69 Ibid., Helen Coy to Charlesworth, 16 July 1936. Mrs. Coy seems to have been a bit slow off
    the mark; this letter was sent more than a year after the broadcast.
70 Ibid., Charlesworth to Coy, 29 July 1936.
71 Ibid., Bushnell to L.E. Edwards, 18 June 1935.
72 Ibid., Bushnell memo to Colonel Steel, 20 May 1936. The CRBC's successor, the CBC, coor-
    dinated the 1939 Empire Day broadcast, which featured George VI speaking from Winnipeg
    in the midst of the month-long Royal Tour of Canada and the United States. See Mary
    Vipond, "The Mass Media in Canadian History: The Empire Day Broadcast of 1939," *Jour-
    nal of the Canadian Historical Association*, n.s., 14 (2003): 1-21.
73 Carl Berger, *The Sense of Power: Studies in the Ideas of Canadian Imperialism, 1867-1914*
    (Toronto: University of Toronto Press, 1970). The alternative interpretation, as developed
    by Douglas Cole, is that the Canadian imperial federationists were not Canadian but rather
    Britannic nationalists. See Douglas Cole, "The Problem of 'Nationalism' and 'Imperialism'
    in British Settlement Colonies," *Journal of British Studies* 10 (1971): 160-82.

17
Canadian Labour Politics and the British Model, 1920-50
James Naylor

Among the more oft-quoted remarks of J.S. Woodsworth, the parliamentary leader of the Co-operative Commonwealth Federation (CCF), is his call to build a specifically Canadian socialism. To the founding convention of the CCF in Regina in 1933, he declared his refusal "to follow slavishly the British model or the American model or the Russian model. We in Canada will solve our own problems along our own lines."[1] While voiced as a declaration of Canadian nationalism, the remark was primarily aimed at Woodsworth's political opponents on the left, both inside and outside the CCF. Certainly the Russian-oriented Communists figured centrally here, as did those CCFers who considered themselves heirs of the Bolshevik revolution in one way or another. This chapter, though, will consider the British model, which, despite Woodsworth's disavowal, figured prominently in the world view of the CCF.

Historians of Canadian labour are familiar with the deep roots Canadian labour activism had in Britain. Vast numbers of trade union and socialist activists – often of quite different perspectives – belonged to unions and socialist parties in the old country, and it is commonplace for biographers to try to gauge the ways in which their British roots shaped their Canadian socialism.[2] Equally noticeable was the air of privilege these activists brought with them. They were hardly outsiders. For example, Bill Pritchard arrived in Vancouver on 19 May 1911. On the 21st he attended a Socialist Party of Canada meeting. On the 23rd he applied for membership and, by the end of the year, he was writing for the party's paper and organizing unemployed workers.[3] Like so many before and after him, Pritchard's movement within the Empire did not mean crossing cultural borders.

The Canadian socialist movement, then, was deeply shaped by this British connection, although in complex ways that transcended this initial colonization of activists from a more developed industrial setting. Immigration, and the experience of so many within labour and socialist organizations in

Britain, gave workers in Canada a language and a set of familiar examples of organizations and strategies that persisted long past the settlement era. In the troubled period between the two world wars, Canadian socialists oriented themselves within the Canadian left regarding British developments and debates. The Canadian socialist press encouraged and assumed a familiarity with analogous movements in Britain.

Historians' focus on political leaders and party programs tends to obscure the heterogeneity of the Canadian left and particularly the CCF. The CCF truly was a federated organization with very different streams flowing into it. As well, the CCF was organized on a provincial basis, and affiliates to the Federation varied considerably in composition and influence across the country. It was, though, increasingly an electoralist party, attracting those who were eligible to vote – British subjects – and those familiar with the British parliamentary system. It was, therefore, within Canadian liberal democracy, a privileged political formation with potential access to governmental power. At the same time, it encouraged familiarity with, but also criticism of, the British model.

It is useful to draw examples from Winnipeg, perhaps the most cosmopolitan of Canadian cities in this era, and one noted for its broad, multinational political labour movement. Veteran socialist Jacob Penner noted that before the Great War, the non-English speaking sections were numerically the largest branches of the Socialist party.[4] Radicalism was associated with the city's sprawling multi-ethnic north end. This was clearly evidenced in some of the heirs of this tradition, but the most enduring strain, the CCF tradition, reflected a clear and pervasive Britishness. The *Weekly News*, published by the Manitoba Independent Labour Party (ILP), which was affiliated to the CCF, was fairly typical of papers from this current. Reports from Britain were regular features, as were articles regularly republished from British sources, particularly *Forward* and the *New Leader*, giving readers considerable understanding of debates within the British Labour Party (BLP). The bulk of the paper consisted of reports of Winnipeg municipal politics, where the ILP was quite strong; occasional reports from Ottawa; and regular ones from Britain. In the late 1920s, page one carried a weekly article by J.S. Woodsworth and another by the BLP's parliamentary leader, Ramsay MacDonald (the latter reprinted from *Forward*). As well, other British labour and socialist figures, such as British ILP leaders Fenner Brockway and H.N. Brailsford, had their criticisms of Labour Party policy published in the Canadian press. Indeed, the *Weekly News* editorialized that such criticism was symptomatic of a healthy labour movement dedicated to ushering in a new social order.[5] Interestingly, this contrasted with a paucity of reporting from the United States. Continental integration of the trade union movement had relatively little impact on political debate.

British political figures regularly travelled to Canada, as they had before the First World War. The most celebrated was perhaps Ramsay MacDonald's 1928 tour, replete with large banquets of labour figures, although Arthur Henderson, J.H. Thomas, and former Communist J.T.W. Newbold all arrived in 1926.[6] In 1927 the head of the British Railway workers' union who was also a leader of the British ILP toured Canada with Aaron Mosher of the Canadian Brotherhood of Railway Employees, speaking on the importance of political action.[7] A Miss Luty, of the British ILP, spoke to ILP women and to the Labour Church as part of her tour of the Empire, "earning the where-withal as she travel[ed]."[8] Indeed, Britishness provided a connection beyond social class as when Scottish ILP MP Jennie Lee addressed the Women's Canadian Club at the Royal Alexandra Hotel. The *Weekly News* savoured the irony: "How many of them realized ... she was telling them that the old order of things was perishing?"[9] At the same time, Canadians trekked to Britain. R.B. Russell, of Winnipeg General Strike fame and a leader of the One Big Union (the radical competitor to both the ILP and the Communists), spent much of the summer of 1926 in Britain, his first trip back in seventeen years. Interestingly, he felt the labour movement there trailed that of western Canada. As we shall see in a moment, the British movement was more of a reference point than a model for many Canadians.[10]

This connection to the British labour movement manifested itself in predictable ways. Well-attended meetings were held in 1926 in support of the British General Strike, and the election and collapse of the second Labour government dominated attention from 1929 to 1931.[11] On other occasions, local leaders, like Winnipeg MLA William Ivens, analyzed the British situation at local forums. But all of this was nested in a broader cultural sense of identity. Sometimes there was direct emulation, as with the Manitoba ILP's decision to create a Dramatic Society modelled on the British ILP Arts Guild, directed by Miles Malleson, which would produce plays obtained from the British movement.[12] Other times the depth of working-class history was reflected. The William Morris centenary was marked by both meetings and knowledgeable editorials in the labour press. And such labour newspapers reminisced of the days of the Clarion movement, remembering the British paper's regulars: Nunquam, the Bounder, Gaggle, and the Clarion scout movement.[13] More broadly, a cultural Britishness suffused the movement, as the Winnipeg Women's Labour Federation sang the Jacobite hymn "Will Ye No Come Back Again," and CCF rallies opened with bagpipes and highland dancing.[14] Since socialists argued that small-l liberalism was dead in the Liberal Party, their examples were primarily British: Gladstone, Cobden, and Bright.[15] There was little fear that readers would misunderstand. When labour MLA and future Winnipeg mayor John Queen travelled to Britain to the Commonwealth Labour conference in 1925 and 1928, he encountered a familiar idiom among the "British Labour Parties," as he no doubt expected.[16]

Toronto labour leader J. MacArthur Conner certainly proudly publicized the fact that he had grown up in the house next door to the family of Scottish labour icon Keir Hardie.[17] Annie Hood Turner of Clarkson, Ontario, bragged of growing up next to the English socialist poet and homosexual activist Edward Carpenter.[18]

What did this all mean for Canadian labour politics? As has often been noted, their deeply British-Canadian character made it difficult for labour parties, and especially the CCF, to gain a purchase among non-British workers and within Quebec.[19] This was widely observed. When a letter to the *Hamilton Spectator* commented that there were "too many Britishers" in the CCF, the CCF did not deny the charge but attempted to explain it in terms of the precocious development of capitalism in that country.[20] The Communist Party was much more successful than the CCF among Eastern Europeans, and Quebec was difficult for the left to address at all, both culturally and because of its increasing support of a centralized Canadian state. But what this British orientation did not mean was that Canadian workers attempted, at least not before the Second World War, to emulate the BLP. Although often done, it is quite incorrect to equate the CCF as it emerged in the 1930s with the BLP, for a couple of reasons. First, the failure in 1931 of the British Labour government led by Ramsay MacDonald to meet the challenges of the Depression, and its subsequent collapse, undermined the BLP as a model for Canadian socialists. But British-Canadian labour activists had long considered the BLP inadequately socialist. As Norman Penner commented more than twenty-five years ago, "Most of the British socialists who came to Canada during this period [before the First World War] were in fact staunch opponents of laborism and fabianism."[21] What seems apparent is that Canadian socialists identified not with the BLP but with the ILP and, during its brief existence, the Socialist League. These were individual-membership organizations (unlike the BLP with its affiliated union membership) that acted as the left-wing conscience of the Labour Party, whose connections with the institutions of the unions and the British state dampened its potential radicalism. To the extent that a party organizationally analogous to the BLP had existed in Canada, with direct trade union affiliation, such a party was the Canadian Labour Party of the 1920s.[22]

The British ILP had predated the BLP, pressed for its formation, and continued on within it, as a kind of party within a party. Its goal was to push the BLP, with its broad trade union affiliation, toward socialism, which it succeeded in doing – more or less – in 1918. For neither the BLP nor the ILP was this socialism concrete. This was particularly the case with the BLP, which remained, in essence, a labourist rather than a socialist party. It was particularly unable to deal with the challenges of the Great Depression, and the second Labour government collapsed in 1931. Ramsay MacDonald went on to lead an essentially Conservative National government in what most labourites and socialists considered a betrayal. Through the 1920s the ILP had acted as the internal left wing of the BLP, although this was a broad category, as the ILP explored guild socialism, the living wage campaign, and became increasingly overtly critical of the BLP's lack of direction. Following the Labour Party's dramatic electoral drubbing in 1931, the ILP disaffiliated. The ILP's place within the BLP was, in essence, taken by the Socialist League.

Neither the ILP nor the Socialist League was particularly large in the 1930s, but they both contained an extraordinary number of key left-wing thinkers in the English-speaking world. These included Fenner Brockway, G.D.H. Cole, Stafford Cripps, Harold Laski, and H.N. Brailsford, among many others. There were several strands of thinking here, but they collectively tended to move to the left under the pressure of the Depression. Indeed, the ILP's decision to leave the BLP was prompted by a sense of impending capitalist crisis. The ILP and the Socialist League shared a belief that capitalism had entered a period of potentially terminal crisis and its immediate manifestation was the rise of fascism, which they considered as much a domestic as an international threat. There were increasingly urgent demands that the Labour Party break with gradualism and from the trade union bureaucracy, and revolution seemed to move onto the political agenda. It was not entirely clear what this meant. It certainly meant a rejection of mere palliatives that would only shore up capitalism, and it included a criticism of electoralism. But it did not mean that either the ILP or the Socialist League had anything that might be considered a revolutionary strategy, though they created some furor on different occasions as they discussed the extraordinary steps an elected socialist labour government would have to take to prevent capitalists from undermining the transition to socialism.[23]

For our purposes, what is important is the extent to which Canadian socialists followed and understood these debates, and the extent to which they identified with the left-wing critique of the BLP. That they did so to a large extent is not surprising given that, in terms of composition, Canadian socialist parties, including the CCF, were analogous to the ILP and not the BLP. The ILP had been the prime individual-membership affiliate to the BLP; most of its members were affiliated via the unions. Those who self-identified as socialists, then, tended to be in the ILP in Britain and the socialist parties or the CCF in Canada. Equally interesting is the extent to which the British ILP appealed to heterogeneous currents on the Canadian left. The combination of the vagueness of its socialism and the radicalism of its language appealed broadly – from the Manitoba ILP, which was basically a municipal reform party, to the socialist parties in Ontario and British Columbia, which represented the left wing of the CCF, to the middle-class League for Social Reconstruction, to some elements of the Trotskyist movement. As the British Columbia Socialist Party commented, the British ILP "is divided between apologists for the Second International, a large section which is in favor of some sort of affiliation with the Third International, and a small group agitating for the formation of the Fourth International and mixed with these an influential percentage of reactionaries who are satisfied with the 'Laborites' in the government."[24] Its appeal, then, to a broad section of the Canadian left is hardly surprising. Most of all, it reflects a broad identification with the British left and an attempt to use it to find a way out of the abyss of Depression politics, as well an inability to decide between revolutionary and reformist political projects. This was not lost on contemporary observers. Even the Communist Party of Canada, which had in the early 1930s dismissed any potential within the CCF, publicly acknowledged the existence of a large leftward-moving current within the CCF modelled on the British ILP.[25] Privately, the Communist Party of Canada noted that in the 1935 elections the CCF program had "moved somewhat to the Left" and "is almost the program of the Wise group in the British Labour Party."[26] The reference is to E.F. Wise, leader of the Socialist League.

Again, Manitoba provides a good example. "The real trouble with the MacDonald Government," opined the Manitoba ILP's *Weekly News* in February 1931, "is that it has failed to do anything really radical. It has had, we admit, cruel and terrible problems to face and solve ... Nevertheless, the crisis called for radical measure."[27] The criticism, and its vagueness, typified the response to the collapse of the MacDonald government. The Manitoba ILP had already praised the ILP's anti-war stance in 1914, and defended Brailsford, and other ILPers' criticism of the BLP.[28] This criticism harkened back to the ethical socialist paradigm that the Canadian and British socialists shared. As one correspondent to the Manitoba CCF paper commented, the BLP had been built on a "poor foundation, and the foundation crumbled."[29] The provincial CCF's Educational Council was more explicit. In presenting its plans for educational programs in every constituency in Manitoba, the council cited the secretary of the Scottish Labour Party: "The greatest tragedy of the Labor movement of Great Britain in 1931, was not the lack of leadership, but lack of education."[30] In Britain and Canada, socialists' goal was as it always had been (to cite New Brunswick CCF Watson Baird, who in turn quoted William Morris): educational; it was to "make socialists."[31] Sometimes, the sentimental affinity to the British ILP caused rather transparent ideological contortions. In 1931, as the Manitoba ILP regularly confronted the Communist Party of Canada at its most sectarian, the *Weekly News* attacked the Soviet Union but also regularly reprinted articles in the defence of the Soviet Union from the British ILP's press.[32] The paper was able to resolve this by 1934, arguing that flirting with the Communists had undermined the British ILP.[33] As an interesting aside, the One Big Union, although critical of both the Manitoba ILP and the CCF, debated these issues on the same terrain. The *One Big Union Bulletin* criticized the British ILP as a means of addressing its Canadian supporters. At one point, the One Big Union suggested that the ILP was as remote from socialism as was the British Labour Party, though it would later acknowledge that some British ILPers recognized that the BLP operated as a defender of British capitalism.[34]

The Manitoba ILP's and CCF's affinity with the British ILP was ironic because, in their day-to-day activity, these organizations appeared very remote from the concerns of the British movement. In city councils and in the provincial legislature, signs of radicalism or anti-capitalism were scarce. For sections of the CCF that were more explicitly critical of both the leadership of the national CCF and gradualism in general, the identification with the ILP or the Socialist League was even more explicit. This is particularly true of the Socialist Party of Canada (SPC) in Ontario (a small regroupment in the early 1930s that was instrumental in the creation of the Ontario CCF) and of the SPC in British Columbia (which dominated the CCF in that province).[35] The latter, incidentally, had changed its name from the Independent Labour Party over the objection of some, according to party leader Wallis Lefeaux, who retained a "sentimental attachment" to the British party by that name.[36]

These two parties developed independently, and as they sent out feelers to each other, they described themselves in British terms. As Ontarian Bert Robinson, writing to E.E. Winch of the BC party, suggested: "We have always considered that the British I.L.P. outlook is generally correct."[37] The Ontario group was interested in the British ILP's call for an "International Conference of Revolutionary Socialist Parties of the World," although it was unable to afford to send delegates, and it explicitly followed the British ILP's lead on issues like building a united front of socialist and labour organizations.[38] Indeed, it felt that its greatest audience in Ontario would be former "British ILP men."[39] Notably, the Ontario group attempted to retain its affiliation with the Ontario CCF since it considered it, "in comparison with the British Labour Party," to be "much more advanced."[40] Former British ILP MP Jennie Lee addressed the founding convention of the Ontario SPC in 1932. The minutes of the convention referred to her as representing the "extreme left" of the British movement. Socialist Party chairman Thomas Cruden commented that "the Socialist Party now being formed felt exactly the same way about these things as our British comrade."[41] Not surprisingly, the visit of ILP leader Fenner Brockway to Toronto in 1934 prompted considerable excitement and, in some quarters at least, a desire to affiliate directly to the British movement, although for the most part the Ontario SPC hoped to be part of a new international party that included the British ILP.[42] The infatuation with the British ILP was apparent to the Trotskyists in Toronto who, trying to describe the Ontario Socialist Party, declared, "Its character is probably well summed up when it is said that it admires the British I.L.P."[43] Interestingly, the Ontario SPC's negotiations with the CCF leadership addressed the question of whether an ILP-type formation within either the British Labour Party or the CCF continued to be warranted.[44]

The story of the BC Socialist Party is similar. Its newspaper often highlighted statements from ILP or Socialist League figures on pressing issues of the day, as a claim to authority. For example, as the issue of participating with the Communists in constructing a popular front of labour and liberal organizations raged in the CCF, a sidebar in the *British Columbia Clarion* entitled "Divide and Rule" carried this quote from Harold Laski: "The effective issue that is raised is simply that of the United Front. I take the view that it is morally obligatory upon the Labor Party to enter the discussion with the Communist Party to see whether an adequate common base can be found."[45] The *Manitoba Commonwealth* chose to print excerpts from Laski's *Communism* to buttress its opposition to the popular front.[46] That the BC group had a more nuanced attitude to Communism can be seen in its more careful reading of Laski, who noted the contradictory character of the Soviet Union, and in its discussions on Spain, which included references to the ILP's Fenner Brockway.[47]

Interestingly, in Ontario, the Socialist Party's relationship with the CCF quickly floundered as the national leadership of the CCF expelled the SPC-dominated Labour Conference that had, in fact, founded the Ontario CCF, and which some, including Elizabeth Morton, explicitly identified as a "Socialist League" within the CCF.[48] (Arthur Mould considered this split analogous to the BLP-ILP split in Britain.)[49] Woodsworth turned to Graham Spry to rebuild the movement in Ontario in its place. Spry quickly became vice-president of the Ontario CCF and editor of its newspaper, the *New Commonwealth*. Ironically, Spry was closely associated with the British Socialist League, particularly with its leading light, Stafford Cripps. Spry's wife, Irene, introduced him to George Cadbury, another Socialist League member, who had been a fellow student at Cambridge.[50] The new leadership was not to the liking of all who stayed in the CCF and, almost immediately, some dissidents, including Ontario CCFer Fred Fish, called for the formation of "a Socialist League for Canada" within the CCF.[51] Fish was pushing at an open door, or at least a door that was half open. The Ontario CCF leadership clearly identified with the Socialist League. This was apparent in its newspaper's report of British politics: it cheered on the Socialist League within the BLP, and twice hosted Stafford Cripps on his visits to Ontario.[52] (The support seemed to be mutual; the CCF printers in Toronto were named the Stafford Printers, in honour of Cripps, who had made a significant donation toward its purchase.)[53] There was no reticence in criticizing the BLP, such as when its 1936 conference was declared, by the Ontario CCF editorial, a "distressing and discouraging failure," with "dangerous implications" that could lead the BLP to supporting an imperialist war. "The fact of the matter," opined Spry's newspaper, "is that the undemocratic card vote has given the reactionary trade unions a stranglehold on the party."[54] This willingness to attack the BLP was shared by others, including the BC Socialist Party-dominated CCF, whose paper editorially attacked the BLP's narrow electoralism: "If the CCF will remember one thing at this stage in its history it has in its power to become a movement unique in world politics. The British Labor Party and kindred movements have surrendered to the 'votes first' principle."[55] Returning from England in 1936, Sam Lawrence, the deeply respected leader of the Hamilton labour movement, expressed "some alarm about the tendencies in the Labor party and felt that the right wing in both the Party and the Trades Union Congress was holding back the Labor movement from giving the country and Europe, a real lead."[56]

What is notable about Spry's cohort within the CCF, who were mostly associated with the League for Social Reconstruction (LSR), was their strong connection to the group of intellectuals who led the Socialist League in Britain.[57] On one hand this is hardly surprising. The LSR has been repeatedly described as Fabian in inspiration. While this popularly denotes gradualism, depression-era Fabianism is somewhat more complicated. In Britain, the Socialist League was fed by two streams: those ILPers who, led by Wise, remained in the BLP; and the SSIP (the "Zip" – the Society for Socialist Inquiry and Propaganda), closely allied to the New Fabian Research Group. Like the LSR itself, the SSIP was a particularly donnish group. Ben Pimlott notes the group's Cambridge and Oxford ties "to the exclusion of the few working-class leaders who had previously been associated with either side."[58]

LSRers seemed to make the trek to Britain en masse, and particularly to Oxford, where several – Eugene Forsey, King Gordon, and David Lewis among them – held Rhodes Scholarships. Others had been to Cambridge and the London School of Economics.[59] It was a powerful attraction, one strong enough to counterbalance other roots, such as David Lewis' deep connection to the North American Jewish left, although some elements of this left had their own British ties, for example, to the Poale Zion, which was itself affiliated to the British Labour Party.[60] According to the Lewis family's biographer, David Lewis quickly adopted Cripps as his mentor and was later offered a position in Cripps' law office.[61] Although he "tended to sympathize with the critics" of the BLP, Lewis drew a conclusion more in keeping with his future role as the central functionary in the CCF: there was no place in the BLP or CCF for a permanently organized opposition, particularly one that would alienate "moderate sections of the party."[62] Judging from his central role as leader of the Ontario CCF, Lewis' classmate at Oxford, Ted Jolliffe, presumably agreed.[63] Certainly for many in the CCF, the isolation and shrinkage of the ILP demonstrated the fate of "splinter groups."[64]

While Lewis' view would prevail, many of his cohort were, for the time being, determined to focus on keeping the CCF on the revolutionary path, in the rather vague manner of the ILP and Socialist League. Still, Lewis, too, used British politics as his ideological and organizational compass. Although the LSR was well aware of American co-thinkers, there was no parallel to the network of intense relations between Canadians and Britons.

Consequently, then, *Canadian Forum*, closely associated with the LSR, was a major conduit of these ideas into Canada. In the early 1920s the journal had been particularly interested in guild socialism, as articulated by G.D.H. Cole and promoted by the ILP.[65] The election of the second Labour government was met with some enthusiasm,[66] but the journal soon focused on the ILP and Socialist League critique. David Lewis obtained an article by Cripps explaining the weaknesses of the Labour Party.[67] Subsequently, historian Frank H. Underhill urged the formation of a group of intellectuals within the CCF, somewhat along the lines of the Socialist League, although he did not mention the league by name.[68] Central members of the LSR published extended reviews of major British works, including critical reviews of works sympathetic to Communism; among these were E.A. Havelock on John Strachey's *Theory and Practice of Socialism* and King Gordon on R. Palme Dutt's *World Politics, 1918-1936*.[69] In 1938 *Canadian Forum* debated the trajectory of the British Labour Party. G.M.A. Grube's (the Toronto classics professor had been a member of the British Labour Party through the 1920s[70]) contribution, in which he managed to defend the Labour Party as the appropriate vehicle for British working-class political action and support Cripps' and Laski's activities in and outside the party, reflected the LSR's ambivalence to the British model but its inability to break with it.[71]

Even those who can be more easily considered to be in the revolutionary tradition – Trotskyists – toyed with such issues. The British ILP was also, of course, the ILP of George Orwell's *Homage to Catalonia,* and a haven for those who considered themselves revolutionary socialists and anti-Stalinists. The main group, associated with former Communist Party of Canada leaders Maurice Spector and Jack MacDonald, was quite critical of the British ILP, although it discussed the ILP evolution in its executive committee.[72] Another group, the League for a Revolutionary Workers' Party, which had gained a considerable foothold in Canada, was largely of a similar opinion, referring to the "well-intentioned muddle-heads" of the British ILP. Standing outside the international left opposition, the league assessed but eventually rejected the ILP's call for a new international organization. Nevertheless, it channelled the funds it raised for anti-fascist fighters in Spain through the British ILP.[73]

Both the British ILP and the Socialist League had stormy histories, particularly through the popular front period as political coalitions that included the Communist Party led to a series of deep ruptures on the British left, as elsewhere. Again, those within the CCF who supported a working alliance with the Communists, at least on immediate issues, pointed to the British example. Both the ILP and the Socialist League supported the united front (as opposed, in most cases, to the popular front), proposing from the start an alliance of purely working-class organizations (but excluding liberals, whom the Communist parties everywhere were increasingly interested in wooing).[74] CCFers of similar views were well aware of the distinction and the British experience, and cited them in their arguments.[75] Similarly, even at the end of the decade, the ILP was held up as an example of an alternate politics. Those, such as the Saskatoon CCF executive, who opposed the approach of the Second World War as another imperialist slaughter, urged the CCF to emulate the anti-war position of the ILP.[76] Others relied strongly on their British co-thinkers to explain such complex events, as was the case with Ontario CCF vice-president Ted Jolliffe, whose analysis of the Soviet war against Finland relied explicitly on Laski.[77] Similarly, David Lewis told up-and-coming labour leader Charlie Millard to read Laski to understand the war. "It has the whole stuff," he added.[78]

This orientation toward the British ILP and the Socialist League did not consist simply of references made by a cosmopolitan elite. Although the intensity varied across the country, socialist organizations, including the CCF, conducted sustained education. This was key to their idea of "making socialists," and, judging by their reading materials, the socialists they hoped to make were British in character. This was a literate movement, and working-class autodidactism was alive and well. The BC CCF, dominated by the SPC, is the best example of this, since it was the most arduous in this campaign. Until destroyed in a fire in 1935, a lending library of five hundred books, of which two hundred were usually in circulation, was maintained by the BC CCF.[79] In the early 1930s the BC SPC remained a relatively small party with a membership "founded on a clear understanding of Marxian principles." In January 1933 it had about sixteen hundred members in forty-eight branches around the province. The party's literature agent reported, for instance, having sold sixty copies of Everyman's edition of *Capital* in connection with one of the party's education classes. More interesting for our purposes was the source of the literature sold through the party's literature agent. She reported "about 220 copies of the Socialist classics, 470 from the I.L.P. of England, 250 from the Socialist Party of Great Britain and 150 miscellaneous pamphlets from different publishers."[80] The Alberta reading library run by the CCF newspaper there, *The People's Weekly*, was even more extensive, including titles by all the major leaders of the ILP and the Socialist League.[81] Across Canada, CCF study groups relied heavily on British sources. Everywhere, members discussed Fred Henderson's *The Case for Socialism*, and the Manitoba ILP even produced its own edition. G.D.H. Cole's works were widely circulated, particularly his *Principles of Socialism, How*

Capitalism Works, and *The Intelligent Man's Guide through World Chaos.* The *Saskatchewan CCF Research Review* recommended predominantly British works. In 1933 and 1934 its recommentations included Cole's *Intelligent Man's Review of Europe Today,* Harold Laski's *Democracy in Crisis,* British pro-Communist John Strachey's *The Coming Struggle for Power,* and Fenner Brockway's exposé of the armaments industry, *The Bloody Traffic.*[82] As well, it republished Brailsford's critique of the BLP in its own columns.[83] In the *Research Review's* columns, Alberta professor W.H. Alexander acknowledged "his own great indebtedness to various pronouncements of Cole, Tawney, and Brailsford, who are putting the whole world under obligation to them for their vigorous and lucid writings."[84]

As the decade wore on, literature from individuals associated with the left-wing critics of the BLP leadership became increasingly invaluable to socialists in Canada. In Ontario the CCF's newspaper, *New Commonwealth,* serialized G.D.H. Cole's *How Capitalism Works* and in 1936 a front-page editorial encouraged every Canadian to read Stafford Cripps' new book, *The Struggle for Peace.*[85] The approach of war only heightened interest as Harold Laski's explanations of the defeat of France or analysis of postwar prospects were printed in CCF papers.[86] *Canadian Forum* focused particularly on the themes of war and social change raised by Francis Williams in *War by Revolution* and Laski in his Penguin volume *Where Do We Go from Here?*[87] The *New Commonwealth* in 1943 suggested H.N. Brailsford's study of India in the wartime Empire and John Strachey's book *Banks for the People* as potential Christmas gifts.[88] The list of left-wing literature seems endless, extending beyond the CCF. The Canadian League Against War and Fascism published its own edition of John Strachey's pamphlet *Fascism Means War,* the Winnipeg Women's Labour Federation was studying G.D.H. Cole on Marx, and the United Church urged its members to keep in touch by reading a short list of authors that included R. Palme Dutt, John Strachey, and Stafford Cripps.[89] This was the intellectual world that dominated the CCF and greatly influenced the Canadian left as a whole. The lineage was quite conscious. As late as 1942, one of the CCF weekly study topics organized by the BC CCF Education Committee was to compare the CCF with the British and New Zealand Labour Parties. It was suggested that branches set aside a minimum of thirty minutes for discussion of this topic.[90]

Predictably, then, the fate of this current in Britain would have a deep impact on Canadian socialism. The onset of the war in Europe of course brought dramatic changes. In Britain, the war drew the Labour Party into a coalition government, and it drew intellectuals into the wartime state. During, and particularly after, the war the British state proved reformable in ways that Depression-era socialists had doubted. Labour leaders transformed the state. Under labour ministers, energy and transportation and the Bank of England were nationalized. Left-winger Aneurin Bevan led the creation of the National Health Service. After playing a key international role with India and the Soviet Union during the war, Cripps became identified with economic austerity in the tough postwar years. This was not the ILP or Socialist League program, but it was new and significant, and it did require the insight and expertise of experts. Canadian socialists' pole of attraction moved into the mainstream of Labour politics.

In Canada the war enforced a new reality that threatened, as in the First World War, to trump working-class politics, at least at the outset. None of this means that Canadian socialists rallied easily to Britain's side. The story of the CCF's reticence on this score is well known.[91] It had taken seriously Cripps' warnings to the Ontario CCF convention of the possibility of a British homegrown "country-gentleman" fascism.[92] And certainly its criticism of British imperialism was a staple of CCF politics throughout the 1930s and central to its debate over the character of the war in 1939. There was no way, CCFers believed, they would allow Canada to become a pawn of British imperialism.[93] Nonetheless, CCFers' identification with their British comrades made their organization susceptible to an analogous process of identification with the British state. In November 1940 the *New Commonwealth* reprinted a cable from the leadership of the BLP on its front page: "The battle line is in London," it read, "but we urge our Canadian comrades to realize that our cause is world-wide and that the future of human progress depends upon a democratic victory over the Nazi and Fascist menace."[94] CCF attitude to the war was complex, yet clearly its reference points abroad had shifted. Unlike the British Labour Party, the CCFers had never faced the responsibilities and pressures of governmental power. In Britain during the war, the Labour Party developed a national-patriotic identity whereby class and nation became redefined, because Labour was seen as embodying the defence and aspirations of the British, and the Labour Party played a key role in modernizing the British state through economic planning and nationalizations.[95]

The growing prestige of the BLP was an important resource for the CCF, which it gleefully used (for instance, in radio broadcasts[96]), but one that provided a shifting basis for an oppositional politics in Canada. The Labour Party displaced the socialist groupings as the model for the CCF, and although the CCF was placed much further from power than the Labour Party, it followed events there vicariously. Charles Lister, a long-time socialist and former editor of the *One Big Union Bulletin,* was in Britain during the war and provided a weekly "London Letter" for the *British Columbia Federationist,* the paper of the BC CCF. Debates over the Beveridge report, which harkened the new welfare state in Britain, waged through the CCF. Overall the CCF supported such measures, although it invariably painted them as palliatives falling far short of socialism.[97] Nonetheless, as M.J. Coldwell pointed out, the enthusiasm for a postwar world without the insecurities of capitalism had pervaded Britain and encouraged wartime morale, and *Canadian Forum* waxed enthusiastic about the possibilities of planning.[98] By and large, criticism of Britain focused on the imperial role the Labour Party inherited. During the war, the issues of India and Greece loomed large. The CCF debated "not only for weeks but months," criticizing the British government for its repression in India.[99] And British attempts "to foist reactionary governments on peoples who have been bravely battling for freedom" in Greece and elsewhere raised hackles in the CCF, as it did in the BLP.[100] The CCF leadership tried to squelch such criticism, arguing that the fate of the CCF was directly tied to that of the Labour Party, although it too often became embroiled in debates over the trajectory of its British co-thinkers, which included personal comments based on individual knowledge of Labour Party leaders.[101] Dorothy Steeves, however, wondered what the CCF had to lose if it came clean and declared its support for left-wing oppositionists in the BLP.[102] As David Lewis told Winnipeg MP David Orlikow, "Most of us are not prepared to add to the attacks on the British Government unless we are convinced that such attacks on our part will do some good to offset the undoubted harm which would flow from reducing the prestige of that Government in the eyes of the world."[103] Despite shying away from official statements – except on the issue of British policy in Palestine – the CCF press fully reported debates within the BLP, particularly those on foreign policy.[104]

Some within the CCF cringed at its tendency to be publicly identified with the BLP. The Stanley Park Club in Vancouver, a long-time centre of oppositional politics in the CCF, urged that the CCF separate itself from this image, pointing out in 1946 that "the tendency to a reformist policy is forcing the British Labour Government to adopt in some instances, anti-labour and imperialist policies."[105] On the other hand, oppositionists in the CCF continued to look to the BLP for examples. The left-wing current within the Ontario CCF known as the "ginger group" identified with the Bevinite group within the Labour Party and used the occasion of left-BLP leader Michael Foot's visit to Toronto in 1950 to explain its principles.[106] The relationship had shifted but persisted.

The ties were complex, however. While Canadian socialists looked to Britain for models and for organizational inspiration, they did so within a context that was reinforced during the war. While they were highly critical of the British class structure and British imperialism, they were themselves British. It was this sentiment that David Lewis spoke to at the end of the war: "We now have socialist governments in Australia, N.Z., and Britain. If Canada were in the same position the major nations of the British Commonwealth would be united not only by history and constitutional ties, but also by the bonds of a common social philosophy, and common economic and political ends."[107] The Ontario *CCF News* commented that the "only truly socialist governments in the entire world existed within the British Commonwealth, New Zealand, Australia and Great Britain."[108] The British connection had become a progressive one, but one based on a shared heritage.

Certainly, in a war defined, in classless terms, as democracy versus fascism, the lexicon of "British justice" made a resounding return. The roots of such language are deep, although they were largely avoided, or even lampooned, by socialists. The report of a BC demonstration attacked by police in 1932 was typical: "Canada, in theory, the land of the free, the brave and good, land of British justice ... So I thought."[109] Chad Reimer's close reading of hegemonic power and the use of language in the Winnipeg General Strike – a situation in which "British justice" was both assailed and appealed to – is useful here.[110] This popular concept has a long and complex history, as documented by historian Greg Marquis, who insists on its deep roots as well as the ways it served to legitimize the social and legal order.[111] During the Second World War, such meanings would once again be contested, although with different outcomes and important consequences for socialists who had looked to Britain for leadership.

Prevented – internally by division and externally by the threat of revision – from continuing to debate international questions, the CCF turned its attention to the homefront during the war. It focused on the preservation of civil liberties, workers' rights, and the articulation of a postwar program of social security. In the latter instance, the model of the BLP proved particularly important, as already suggested by the Beveridge report, and by Leonard Marsh's *Report on Social Security for Canada*.[112] However, it was the assaults on civil liberties that heralded a political response that revealed a deep connection to both liberalism and British roots. Even before the war, those to the left of the CCF had lampooned such language. One Trotskyist paper reported that "J.S. Woodsworth, speaking before the Montreal C.C.F., criticized the recent anti-labor bills and the Padlock Law of Duplessis as 'a violation of British Justice.' We thought that British justice had died a natural death ... this is a capitalist society in which there is only one kind of justice – capitalist justice."[113]

Many in the CCF did indeed have very little faith in capitalist democracy,[114] but there was little in their wartime rhetoric to reflect this. Although the language of course varied, appeals to pre-war civil liberties like British justice were widespread. To some extent the reference to Britain was both convenient and opportune. As had been the case with the sweeping definition of sedition in the infamous section 98 of the Criminal Code, the weakness of the Canadian record on civil rights in comparison with the British was widely drawn. For instance, as the CCF editorialized at the time, "Section 98 is the embodiment of all that is opposed to British liberty or any other kind of liberty. No similar law is to be found on the statute books in any other democratic country."[115] Given the wartime aim of defending Britain, such references became even more specific after 1939. Regular comparisons were made between British legislation and what was seen as the far more restrictive wartime regulations in Canada. For instance, while Canada interned Communists, the British government allowed the Communist-inspired People's Convention to go ahead: "Proof," according to *Canadian Forum*, "that the British tradition of free speech and free assembly is still a living reality, even in bomb-racked London."[116] In the same issue of *New Commonwealth* that reported the arrest of Canadian Congress of Industrial Organizations secretary (and prominent CCFer) Charlie Millard under the Defence of Canada Regulations for "making statements prejudicial to recruiting," the Co-operative Commonwealth Youth Movement announced an essay contest on comparing civil liberties in Britain and Canada during wartime.[117] A month later the paper began running a series of articles on this very issue.[118] Privately, the CCF recognized that civil liberties were under attack everywhere, but still suggested that the British comparison was important. The Ontario CCF Committee on Civil Liberties reported to the provincial executive that "protest should be made against this all the time. At a time when we are supposed to be fighting for British democracy, we might at least attempt to practice it – if only to the extent that it is still practiced in Great Britain itself."[119] This language should be seen as particularly important, given that the CCF was largely remade during the war as waves of recruits to the movement were drawn into it by wartime struggles over wartime labour issues, the promise of social security after the war, and the desire to defend democratic liberties.

The references to British practices were more than opportunism. The report of an early CCFer at the time of the emergence of the movement reflects the much deeper cultural heritage of British justice, much in line with the argument of Greg Marquis. The 1934 report read:

British traditions and institutions are still cherished and revered by the vast majority of Canadians as abundantly evidenced by their vote at the polls time after time in the history of our political and constitutional development to the present day which finds us a self-governing dominion, or state, within the British Commonwealth of Nations. It is noteworthy that the Canadian unit of the *British Family* appears now to be seriously undertaking the establishment of a Co-operative Commonwealth as its own interpretation of a social democracy – the kind of democracy, in fact, which British peoples have ever been striving for since the day in 1215 when King John signed the Magna Carta.[120]

This view of British justice, however, had been challenged during the 1930s as fascism seemed to be the fate of capitalist democracies, and not least in

Britain, where the Tory hierarchy seemed weakly committed to democracy. Interestingly, this analysis was based on a branch of this tradition, combined with Marxism, within the ILP and the Socialist League. By 1940 this tradition was very much exhausted, and a reinvigorated labourism in Britain was closely identified with the British state and claimed a particular patriotic aim, that of bringing peace and prosperity to all Britons.

In Canada it was in part Britishness that accounted for the trajectory of the CCF. In the 1930s it seemed to count for little, although the unselfconscious culture, for instance, of the Winnipeg ILP-CCF reflects how deeply it ran. In wartime, however, it became a valuable political and social resource. The fact that it was there to be used brings us back to our original observation. "Britishness" had meaning in interwar Canada, even on the left, where such identities were often overtly dismissed in favour of a broader internationalism. In wartime it provided a powerful language – for CCFers, at least. But it was also exclusionary. Being British meant having a particular heritage and set of rights. This was the kind of particularism that an oppositional politics had hoped to challenge. That it had failed meant that socialism after the war was potentially more focused on creating either egalitarian British subjects or Canadian citizens. But it would be less likely to create an internationalist working-class subject. This was a fate that would prove disabling for alternate politics in a world divided by the Cold War and by ongoing colonial struggles. Although the CCF by the 1950s would be less interested in Britain than it was in the 1930s, its politics had been deeply shaped by its Britishness and the privileges Britishness brought.

Notes
1 Quoted in Kenneth McNaught, *A Prophet in Politics: A Biography of J.S. Woodsworth* (Toronto: University of Toronto Press, 1959), 262.
2 There are countless examples. Peter Campbell examines four prominent Marxist socialists with exactly these roots in his *Canadian Marxists and the Search for a Third Way* (Montreal and Kingston: McGill-Queen's University Press, 1999). Among others see Thomas H. McLeod and Ian McLeod, *Tommy Douglas: The Road to Jerusalem* (Edmonton: Hurtig Publishers, 1987); Irene Howard, *The Struggle for Social Justice in British Columbia: Helena Gutteridge, The Unknown Reformer* (Vancouver: UBC Press, 1992); Gene H. Homel, "James Simpson and the Origins of Canadian Social Democracy" (PhD thesis, University of Toronto, 1978).
3 Campbell, *Canadian Marxists*, 79-80.
4 Jacob Penner, "Recollections of the Early Socialist Movement in Winnipeg," *Marxist Quarterly* 2 (Summer 1962). See also Tom Mitchell and James Naylor, "The Prairies: In the Eye of the Storm," *The Workers' Revolt in Canada, 1917-1925,* ed. Craig Heron (Toronto: University of Toronto Press, 1980), 179-80.
5 *Weekly News* (Winnipeg), 13 September 1929.
6 *Weekly News* (Winnipeg), 17 August 1928, 15 October 1926.
7 *Weekly News* (Winnipeg), 22 April 1927.
8 *Weekly News* (Winnipeg), 15 May 1925.
9 *Weekly News* (Winnipeg), 15 April 1932.
10 *Weekly News* (Winnipeg), 11 February 1927.
11 *Weekly News* (Winnipeg), 14 May 1926.

12 *Weekly News* (Winnipeg), 29 April 1927.
13 *Manitoba Commonwealth,* 14 September 1934.
14 *Manitoba Commonwealth,* 16 November 1934, 22 January 1937. Burns night was also regularly marked. John Queen presided in 1934; *Manitoba Commonwealth,* 19 January 1934.
15 *Weekly News* (Winnipeg), 7 December 1928.
16 See Ray Clinton Barker, "The Commonwealth Labour Conferences, the British Labour Party Model, and Their Influence on Canadian Social Democratic Politics" (MA thesis, Carleton University, 1996). They continued to refer to themselves as the "British Labour Parties" into the 1940s, *CCF News* (Toronto), 19 October 1944.
17 *New Commonwealth* (Toronto), 25 May 1935.
18 University of Toronto, J.S. Woodsworth Memorial Collection (WMC), box 8, Socialist Party of Canada, Turner to Bert Robinson, 19 June 1932.
19 On Quebec see Andrée Lévesque, *Virage à Gauche Interdit: les communistes, les socialistes et leurs ennemis au Québec 1929-1939* (Montreal: Boréal Express, 1984). On the Communists, see especially Walter Rodney, *Soldiers of the International: A History of the Communist Party of Canada, 1919-1929* (Toronto: University of Toronto Press, 1968); Ian Angus, *Canadian Bolsheviks: The Early Years of the Communist Party of Canada* (Montreal: Vanguard, 1981); Norman Penner, *Canadian Communism: The Stalin Years and Beyond* (Toronto: Methuen, 1988).
20 *New Commonwealth* (Toronto), 26 January 1935.
21 Norman Penner, *The Canadian Left: A Critical Analysis* (Toronto: Prentice-Hall, 1977), 45.
22 See the Ontario Socialists analysis of this in University of British Columbia, Special Collections, Angus MacInnis Memorial Collection (AMMC), box 54A, file 54A-5, Correspondence 1934, unsigned letter from Ontario, 24 July 1934.
23 There are many sources for all of this, but most useful are Geoffrey Foote, *The Labour Party's Political Thought: A History* (London: Croom Helm, 1985), and Ben Pimlott, *Labour and the Left in the 1930s* (London: Allen and Unwin, 1977).
24 *British Columbia Clarion,* July 1935.
25 G. Pierce [S. Smith], *Socialism and the C.C.F.* (Montreal: Contemporary Publishing, 1934), 21.
26 Library and Archives Canada (LAC), MG 10 K3, Communist International Fonds, file 169, "Meeting of Sect. Com. Marty Report of Comrade Porter on Canadian Elections," 9 November 1935, 9.
27 *Weekly News* (Winnipeg), 20 February 1931.
28 *Weekly News* (Winnipeg), 15 May 1925, 13 September 1929.
29 J. Bellamy, Rivers, Manitoba, to *Manitoba Commonwealth,* 15 January 1937.
30 *Manitoba Commonwealth,* 12 November 1937.
31 LAC, MG 28 IV, 1, CCF Records, vol. 89, file: Watson Baird, 1933-1946, Baird to David Lewis, 10 October 1943. On this tradition, see particularly Stanley Pierson, *Marxism and the Origins of British Socialism: The Struggle for a New Consciousness* (Ithaca, NY: Cornell University Press, 1973).
32 *Weekly News* (Winnipeg), 20 February 1931.
33 *Weekly News* (Winnipeg), 20 April 1934.
34 *One Big Union Bulletin,* 22 May 1930, 19 June 1930.
35 See James Naylor, "Politics and Class: The Character of 1930s Socialism in Canada" (paper presented at the Seventy-Second Annual Meeting of the Canadian Historical Association, Ottawa, 1993), and "Pacifism or Anti-Imperialism?: The CCF Response to the Outbreak of World War II," *Journal of the Canadian Historical Association,* n.s., 8 (1997): 213-37.
36 *The Challenge* (Vancouver), July 1932. Nevertheless, this current in British Columbia was both knowledgeable of the British ILP, and tended to be somewhat more critical, as reflected in its criticism of the ILP's living wage campaign, *The Challenge,* April 1932.
37 University of Toronto, Thomas Fisher Rare Book Library, WMC, box 8, Robinson to Winch, 19 April 1933.
38 WMC, box 8, A.H. Downs Jr. to E.E. Winch, 7 December 1933; A.H. Downs Jr. to Fenner Brockway, 14 February 1934; Bert Robinson to Arthur Mould, 11 July 1933.
39 WMC, box 8, Fred Hodgson to Bert Robinson, 17 August 1933.
40 WMC, box 8, Bert Robinson to Fred Hodgson, 11 August 1933.

41 WMC, box 9, "Minutes of Conference Called to Consider the Formation of a Socialist Party, Winchester Hall," 7 February 1932.

42 This was the case with the York Township branch of the SPC; WMC, box 9, minutes, SPC (Ontario Section), PEC, 27 January 1934. In 1931 an editorial in the Ontario Labour Party's paper foresaw the internationalization of the ILP and mused that the annual conference might some day be held in the Rocky Mountains. *Labour Advocate*, 25 April 1931.

43 Archives of Ontario (AO), Macdonald-Spector Papers (now located at Library and Archives Canada and renamed the Trotskyist Collection), box 1, Toronto Branch report, 1934.

44 WMC, box 10, J.S. Woodsworth to Bert Robinson, 3 February 1932.

45 *British Columbia Clarion*, April 1936.

46 *Manitoba Commonwealth*, 13 September 1935.

47 *British Columbia Federationist*, 13 January 1938, 22 October 1936.

48 LAC, MG 28, IV, 1, CCF Records, vol. 41, file: Ontario General Correspondence 1932-1934, circular letter, 17 November 1933.

49 LAC, MG 28, IV, 1, CCF Records, vol. 41, file: Ontario General Correspondence 1932-1934, Arthur Mould to Woodsworth, 10 October 1933.

50 Rose Potvin, *Passion and Conviction: The Letters of Graham Spry* (Regina: Canadian Plains Research Center, University of Regina, 1992), 12, 91.

51 *New Commonwealth* (Toronto), 4 August 1934. Fish actually returned to live in England; *New Commonwealth* (Toronto), 9 October 1937. There is an interesting report of his 1936 visit to Transport House in the Canadian popular front magazine, *New Frontier*, December 1936.

52 *New Commonwealth* (Toronto), 24 November 1934, 16 March 1935, 31 October 1936.

53 Potvin, *Passion and Conviction*, 92.

54 *New Commonwealth* (Toronto), 24 October 1936, 31 October 1936.

55 *British Columbia Federationist*, 14 January 1937.

56 *New Commonwealth* (Toronto), 25 June 1936.

57 Spry's report to the LSR "on a trip to Britain to visit the Socialist League and Labor Party offices" (very much in that order), gives a fascinating picture of the connections of Spry and others. He also arranged that a Socialist League leader (perhaps Cadbury) would be at the next LSR convention. LAC, MG 30 D204, Frank H. Underhill, vol. 8, file: Graham Spry, 1928-1936.

58 Pimlott, *Labour and the Left*, 46.

59 For individual biographies see Michiel Horn, *The League for Social Reconstruction: Intellectual Origins of the Democratic Left in Canada, 1930-1942* (Toronto: University of Toronto Press, 1980).

60 LAC, MG 28, IV, 1, vol. 90, file: M.J. Coldwell, 1933-1938, L. Cheifetz, secretary, United Jewish Socialist Labor Party, Paole Zion, to CCF, n.d. [March 1936].

61 Cameron Smith, *Unfinished Journey: The Lewis Family* (Toronto: Summerhill Press, 1989), 184. David Lewis, *The Good Fight: Political Memoirs, 1909-1958* (Toronto: Macmillan, 1981), 75.

62 Lewis, *The Good Fight*, 63.

63 Smith, *Unfinished Journey*, 173.

64 For example, *Manitoba Commonwealth*, 20 April 1934, 25 May 1938.

65 See *Canadian Forum*, by J.T. Gunn: "The Building Guild Movement," February 1921; "The Progress of the Guild Idea in Britain," December 1921; "Expansion of the Guild Movement," August 1922.

66 *Canadian Forum*, October 1929.

67 LAC, MG 30 D204, Frank H. Underhill Papers, vol. 3, file: C.C.F., 1928-1956 (1), David Lewis to Underhill, 5 December 1939; *Canadian Forum*, January 1934.

68 *Canadian Forum*, September 1934.

69 *Canadian Forum*, January 1937, October 1936.

70 *New Commonwealth* (Toronto), July 1942.

71 See especially *Canadian Forum*, February 1938.

72 AO, MacDonald-Spector Papers, box 1, file: "Workers Party of Canada," E.C. Meeting, 21 May 1935. For an important reappraisal of this current see Ian McKay, "Revolution Deferred: Maurice Spector's Political Odyssey, 1928-1941" (paper presented at the eighty-second annual meeting of the Canadian Historical Association, Halifax, May 2003).

73 *Workers' Voice* (Toronto), January 1937, 2 October 1937.
74 Pimlott, *Labour and the Left*, 89-108.
75 For example, letter to the editor, *British Columbia Federationist*, 27 May 1937.
76 Saskatchewan Archives Board – Saskatoon, Carlyle King Papers, A225, 1, file 42, CCF War Policy, Carlyle King, chairman, Saskatoon CCF to M.J. Coldwell, 6 September 1939; 2, file 2, Canadian Fellowship of Reconciliation – Correspondence with Members 1938 to 1947, Carlyle King to Eunice Sibley, 16 September 1939.
77 LAC, MG 28, IV, 1, CCF Records, vol. 362, file: Comments and Statements by the CCF, 1938-1951, "Letter to a Social Democrat," 15 October 1940.
78 LAC, MG 28, IV, 1, CCF Records, vol. 102, file: CHI, Millard, Lewis to Millard, 30 December 1940.
79 UBC, AMMC, vol. 45A, file 45-5, Socialist Party of Canada, 1934-1935, annual convention, 20 and 21 January 1934, secretary-treasurer's report; and provincial executive minutes, 14 April 1935.
80 UBC, AMMC, vol. 45A, file 45-3, Socialist Party of Canada, minutes, 1931-33, annual convention, 31 and 33 January 1933.
81 *People's Weekly* (Edmonton), 12 September 1936.
82 "We Recommend," *CCF Research Review*, October 1933, and "We Recommend," March 1934.
83 *CCF Research Review*, December 1934.
84 *CCF Research Review*, August 1935.
85 *New Commonwealth* (Toronto), 28 July 1934, 31 October 1936.
86 *British Columbia Federationist*, 25 July 1940, 11 June 1942.
87 *Canadian Forum*, January 1941.
88 *New Commonwealth* (Toronto), 9 December 1943.
89 University of Toronto, WMC, vol. 104, file: Lobe, Alice F., "A few good things to read..."; *Manitoba Commonwealth*, 14 December 1934; McMaster University Archives, Canadian Youth Congress Papers, box 11, file 4, "National Young People's Union of the United Church of Canada."
90 *British Columbia Federationist*, 8 January 1942. Not all idolized these sources however, judging by a very critical review of Cole's *Fabian Socialism*, in which he and Laski were assailed as too radical to provide guidance to the CCF. *New Commonwealth*, 30 March 1944. I have found no similar views before this date.
91 James Naylor, "Pacifism or Anti-Imperialism? The CCF Response to the Outbreak of World War II," *Journal of the Canadian Historical Association* 6 (1997).
92 LAC, MG 28, IV, 1, CCF Records, vol. 48, File Ontario Conventions, 1935-1945, minutes, annual convention of the CCF (Ontario Section), 20 April 1935.
93 For example, *British Columbia Federationist*, 3 February 1938, and "War Nears as Imperialisms Clash: Britain to Fight for Her Empire," 20 March 1939.
94 *New Commonwealth* (Toronto), 30 November 1940.
95 See particularly Donald Sassoon, *One Hundred Years of Socialism: The West European Left in the Twentieth Century* (London: Fontana, 1996) for a discussion on the role of left-wing parties in modernizing the state in this period.
96 LAC, MG 28, IV, 1, CCF Records, vol. 100, file: David Lewis, miscellaneous, 1936-1954, Radio Broadcast, CBR, 18 October 1941.
97 LAC, MG 28, IV, 1, CCF Records, vol. 43, file: Ontario General Correspondence 1942 (December-October), Robert F. Hardy to David Lewis, 8 December 1942, and Lewis to Hardy, 12 December 1942; vol. 79, file 79-5, British Columbia: Conventions, "Proceedings of the Tenth Annual Provincial Convention C.C.F. (B.C. Section), 16 April 1943. See also "Beveridge Plan Freezes the Status Quo of Ownership," in *British Columbia Federationist*, 17 December 1941, as well as Angus MacInnis' defence of the report in UBC, AMMC, box 54A, file 54A-15, correspondence 1942, MacInnis to David Lewis, 31 December 1942.
98 *Manitoba Commonwealth*, 6 June 1941, *Canadian Forum*, March 1943, and particularly the special section on "Planning Post-War Canada," May 1945.
99 For instance, in Ontario: LAC, MG 28, IV, 1, CCF Records, vol. 43, file: Ontario General Correspondence 1942 (December-October), David Smith to David Lewis, 5 December 1942, and Lewis to Smith, 11 December 1942; vol. 48, Ontario Conventions, 1935-1945, "Final

Agenda, Ontario CCF Annual Convention, 1944," resolution 117. The CCF national office statement is UBC, AMMC, box 54A, file 54A-15, Correspondence 1942.

100 The quote is from Harold Thayer: LAC, MG 28, IV, 1, CCF Records, vol. 77, file 77-2, British Columbia: Correspondence, Thayer to David Lewis, 15 December 1944. Such sentiments came from several quarters. See also vol. 60, file: Manitoba: General Correspondence 1938-1953, David Orlikow to Lewis, 26 November 1945.

101 For example, LAC, MG 28, IV, 1, CCF Records, vol. 101, file: Angus MacInnis, Lewis to MacInnis, 1 October 1940.

102 LAC, MG 28, IV, 1, CCF Records, vol. 104, file: Mrs. D.G. Steeves, Steeves to David Lewis, 17 November 1946.

103 LAC, MG 28, IV, 1, CCF Records, vol. 60, file: Manitoba: General Correspondence 1938-1953, Lewis to Orlikow, 5 February 1947 and 6 March 1947. There is considerable debate about British foreign policy in 1945 and 1946. See particularly LAC, MG 28, IV, 1, CCF Records, vol. 98, file: Dr. Carlyle King, David Lewis to King, 10 January 1946; file: Stanley Knowles, 1940-1945, Lewis to Knowles, 12 December 1945.

104 *CCF News* (Toronto), 22 August 1946, 12 September 1946, 12 December 1946.

105 Provincial Archive of Manitoba, MG 14, B64, Magnus Eliason, file 194.

106 McMaster University Archives, CCF (Ontario Section) Papers, vol. 2, file: Ginger Group.

107 Quoted in LAC, MG 28, IV, 1, vol. 93, A.F. Colwell to Lewis, 16 August 1945.

108 *CCF News* (Toronto), 8 November 1945.

109 *Challenge,* April 1932.

110 Chad Reimer, "War, Nationhood and Working-Class Entitlement: The Counterhegemonic Challenge of the 1919 Winnipeg General Strike," *Prairie Forum* 18, 2 (Fall 1993).

111 Greg Marquis, "Doing Justice to British Justice: Law, Ideology and Canadian Historiography," in *Canadian Perspectives on Law and Society: Issues in Legal History,* ed. W. Wesley Pue and Barry Wright (Ottawa: Carleton University Press, 1988).

112 See particularly *Canadian Forum,* April 1943.

113 *Workers' Voice* (Toronto), 1 May 1938.

114 See Naylor, "Politics and Class."

115 *New Commonwealth* (Toronto), 28 July 1934.

116 *Canadian Forum,* March 1941.

117 *New Commonwealth* (Toronto), 14 December 1939.

118 *New Commonwealth* (Toronto), 18 January 1940.

119 University of Toronto, WMC, box 1, "Report of the Ontario C.C.F. Committee on Civil Liberties to the Provincial Executive," [December 1939].

120 *New Commonwealth* (Toronto), 21 July 1934 (emphasis added).

18

Historical Perspectives on Britain: The Ideas of Canadian Historians Frank H. Underhill and Arthur R.M. Lower

R. Douglas Francis

Frank H. Underhill and Arthur R.M. Lower were two noted Canadian historians who wrote extensively on Canadian-British relations in the interwar and post-Second World War eras from both a historical and a polemical approach. Both were ardent Canadian nationalists, deeply committed to helping Canada become a strong and independent nation state. Both came to see Canada's association with Britain through the British Empire as the greatest detriment to Canada's evolution from colony to nation. To them, British imperialism was the antithesis of Canadian nationalism. To offset this imperial dominance, both historians emphasized the influence of the North American environment on Canada's history. They believed that Canada's destiny lay in closer association with the United States and a distancing of the country from Britain. Still, to label these two historians as being purely anti-British is too simplistic. For there was an aspect of Britain that both historians greatly admired: its liberal-democratic tradition and values. They believed that Canada had benefited from its association with liberal Britain in its democratic tradition, its strong sense of individualism, and its parliamentary form of government. As both men matured, they came to dwell on this aspect of Canada's association with Britain, particularly after the Second World War when the imperial connection no longer seemed to pose much of a threat to Canada's existence as an autonomous nation.

In essence, both Underhill and Lower saw two Britains: the imperial Britain, the Britain of power, dominance, exploitation, and colonial possessions; and the liberal Britain, the Britain of the British Isles that valued freedom, democracy, individualism, and justice. Canada, they both believed, should keep some kind of association with Britain so as to acknowledge and strengthen its own liberal tradition while at the same time avoiding the pitfalls that came in an association with imperial Britain. Both historians looked at Britain through the eyes of avid Canadian nationalists. Imperial Britain was a monolith that Canadians needed to resist as they strived to create an independent nation; liberal Britain became the prototype for the ideal Canadian society when independence was achieved. The difficulty both men faced was in attempting to reconcile these two opposing perspectives of Britain. This chapter explores the roots of Underhill's and Lower's perspectives on Britain and analyzes those ideas in the context of their antithetical views of imperial and liberal Britain.

Both Underhill and Lower were born in 1889 in small Ontario towns about eighty kilometres apart: Underhill in Stouffville, Lower in Barrie.[1] Both towns were made up predominantly of British settlers. Both men came from British stock. Underhill's British ancestral heritage was in a more distant past, being two generations removed. Lower's was more immediate, since both his parents were born in London, England, and they were the first generation to settle in Canada. Lower's father never lost his attachment to the "homeland." In his autobiography, *My First Seventy-Five Years,* Lower recalled: "My father remained an English exile to the day of his death and as he got older his thoughts and words turned more and more towards 'home.'"[2] Arthur R.M. Lower attributed his own "hostility to ... things English" in part to a reaction to his father's Britishness, a father with whom he admits having had a negative relationship; certainly, his reaction to his father's anglophilia made him a passionate Canadian.[3]

Underhill and Lower had similar recollections of experiences in their community that should have reinforced their identification with, and admiration for, the British Empire. As boys, they recalled the celebrations for Queen Victoria's Diamond Jubilee in 1897, and the excitement over Canadian soldiers going off to fight for the Empire in the Boer War, from 1899 to 1902. Underhill remembered the enthusiasm he felt in collecting the special stamps that were issued on the occasion of the jubilee, "containing a map of the world that was splashed with red wherever there were British possessions, with a proud declaration at the bottom of the stamp: 'We hold a greater empire than has been.'" He went on to note: "A small boy in a little Ontario village was well prepared by 1899 to sing *Soldiers of the Queen,* that most vulgarly boastful of all imperialist war-anthems."[4] Arthur R.M. Lower recalled: "The Boer War rapidly became our own Canadian war ... The geography of South Africa became more familiar than our own, and I could reel off astonishing lists of British generals. The Boers, of course, were bad people. Why? Don't ask embarrassing questions! We young Canadians took it for granted that honesty, decency, mercy, justice, the love of freedom, were the peculiar prerogatives of the British world."[5] Both recalled that for them the world was unfolding as it should at the turn of the nineteenth century, with Britannia ruling the waves and the world.

Underhill and Lower both attended the University of Toronto: Underhill in combined honours in classics and English and history; Lower initially in the Faculty of Education and then in English and history "with Moderns option." Both received a good dose of British history. From here their career paths differed. Underhill went to Balliol College, Oxford, where he did first the *Literae Humaniores* or "Greats" program, and then modern history. Lower taught high school for two years and worked for the Board of Historical Publications, an adjunct of the Public Archives of Canada, until the late 1920s when he did a PhD in history at Harvard University.

While at Oxford, Underhill came to have a love-hate attitude toward the English. He greatly admired their polished ways, their sophisticated culture, and their social graces. At the same time, he felt that the polished manners and social graces were often substitutes for serious thought and moral ethics. The university, he was convinced, was more concerned with producing a social class with polished manners than an educated elite with a social conscience. He also found the reserved manners and cold nature of the upper-class English students hard to take. "Those who declare that the Englishman is self-centered, and hard to get acquainted with and uninterested in strangers can count me among their supporters,"[6] Underhill informed his Toronto history professor, George Wrong. This initial encounter with the British elite would colour Underhill's perception of the British for the remainder of his life. He would alternate between periods when he idealized the British as he reflected on their intellectual greatness, liberal values, and cultured ways, and periods when he condemned the British ruling class because its haughty ways and self-righteous attitudes reminded him too much of the snobbish upper-class students who had been his Oxford colleagues. The experience also made him a strong Canadian nationalist. "I had made up my mind during my stay at Oxford," he recalled years later, "that I was a Canadian, I wasn't an Englishman. I had that strong national feeling that was deeper than reason."[7]

Both Underhill and Lower joined the First World War out of a sense of duty to Britain. Underhill joined in 1915 while a professor at the University of Saskatchewan, a position he had received in 1914 upon completion of his studies at Oxford. In an article written for *The Sheaf*, the student newspaper at the University of Saskatchewan, Underhill wrote: "Sending soldiers to Europe is not an act of generosity but of duty, that we are in the war on the same basis as England, that being part of the Empire means that we have obligations to fulfill just as much as she has."[8] He joined the Canadian army, but was then transferred on request to the British army, where he served as a subaltern officer in an English infantry battalion. Wounded at the Battle of the Somme, he nevertheless served out his time until the armistice. His experience in the British army reinforced the dislike for the upper-class English elite that he had felt at Oxford. He wrote in later life: "I discovered that this Edwardian-Georgian generation of Englishmen made the best regimental officers in the world and the worst staff officers. The stupidity of G.H.Q. and the terrible sacrifice of so many of the best men among my contemporaries sickened me for good of a society, national or international, run by the British governing classes."[9]

Lower joined in 1916, during his second year of high school teaching. He too joined out of a sense of duty, a duty to the Anglo-Saxon race, as he recalled in his autobiography: "It was a matter of *the race;* far more the race, I think, than the Crown or historic tradition ... The English-Canadian sense of identity existed very strongly before the First World War, but it was almost entirely within the family, as it were."[10] Lower joined the British navy; it was his first direct encounter with England and the English. He was appalled by the class differences. "It was this steep distinction between rich and poor that I found hardest to take in England," he recalled.[11] On a personal level, he found it difficult to get to know the English because of their reserved manners. "England is not an open country; people do not stop you on the street and ask you home to dinner ... Some of the English I liked, some I did not; some were congenial, others not. Few were easily intimate."[12] Beyond that, Lower's only other recollection of the British was their total indifference to colonial affairs. In hindsight, he recalled: "My three years in the British navy have been marked by no unpleasantness arising out of my 'colonial' origin; I had just been accepted as another of the breed. But it had also shown me how completely indifferent was the centre of the imperial faith, England, to my native land, which was only one of a score of countries 'out there.' I came back from the war much more of a Canadian than I went to it."[13]

It was this British indifference to its colonies that became the subject of one of Lower's first major publications. In "The Evolution of the Sentimental Idea of Empire: A Canadian View," Lower argued that the idea of the British Empire as "similar to a family, held together merely by ties of affection" evolved not by the efforts of the British, who up until the turn of the nineteenth century had no real interest in the Empire beyond the economic advantages, but by the efforts of the colonies, especially Canada. He believed that British indifference had caused the Thirteen Colonies to go their own way, and the same might have happened in the British North American colonies if it had not been for the desire of British settlers in the colonies to maintain the tie: "The settler carried out with him memories of the motherland, the glamour of her civilization, and pride in her strength. Naturally, his pleasurable recollections did not lose anything with the lapse of years. He passed many of them on to his children, who added to their imaginative fancies of the distant and omnipotent *alma mater,* their hopes and ambitions for their native land."[14] The resulting amalgam of nationalism in the colonies and imperial pride was the British Commonwealth of Nations, Lower contended, "a world-wide British unity, growing ever larger and more powerful." Whether the experiment would continue was uncertain, Lower maintained in 1927, but what was certain was its tremendous contribution to the world. He concluded his article with the assertion: "Whatever the future may have in store, the world is already the richer for the experience of the British league of nations in its regulation of the relations of its members otherwise than by the sword."[15]

In the 1930s, Lower shifted his focus away from British-Canadian relations to Canada only. Indeed, he became obsessed with the need for a strong Canadian national community. Now he saw the attachment of English Canadians to Britain as detrimental to the growth of this innate Canadian national community. It led the dominant group in Canada – English Canadians – to seek their identity with Britain and its Empire rather than with Canada. This colonial response he saw as immature, and he reserved some of his harshest criticisms for this colonial frame of mind: "I have always felt that we should blush for the unconscionable time it has taken us [English Canadians] to arrive at maturity. While Uruguayans and Peruvians, to say nothing of Guatemalans, have, for these many generations, taken for granted their place as self-determining peoples, Canadians have sat around their parents' house like great lubberly, overgrown boys afraid to learn and face the facts of life."[16] Lower pointed out that this imperial attachment of English Canadians to the motherland not only caused a deep rift between French and English Canadians but also prevented new ethnic Canadians from finding a strong Canadian nationalism with which they could identify. It had contributed as well to Canada getting involved in wars not based on national and rational considerations but on imperial, emotional responses, a kind of knee-jerk reaction. Throughout the 1930s, Lower consistently insisted on Canada having its own foreign policy based solely on Canadian concerns.

But for Lower the attachment of British Canadians to the motherland had another negative effect not normally considered by analysts of British-Canadian relations in the 1930s. Lower believed that large-scale immigration to Canada, even of British immigrants, had a negative impact on the growth of a Canadian nation and the cultivation of a Canadian identity because these immigrants took jobs away from native Canadians, forcing many of them to migrate south to the United States in search of work.[17] The end result was the diluting of the Anglo-Saxon "blood," the weakening of English Canadian "stock," and thus the undermining of a strong Canadian nationalism.

Underhill, like Lower, also continued to praise the British Empire and Commonwealth in the 1920s. Where the two men differed was in their perspective on a Canadian foreign policy. Lower wanted Canada to take a responsible role in the world but one dictated by Canadian interests and formulated by Canadian leaders. Underhill in the 1920s still wanted Canada to take a responsible role in the world through its association with the

Empire and through the formulation of a joint imperial foreign policy that took the Empire as a whole into consideration. In light of Underhill's trenchant anti-imperialist perspective in the 1930s, it is interesting to note his strong pro-British imperial position in the 1920s. In a guest lecture given at the University of Alberta in 1924 on "Canada's National Status," Underhill argued, for example, that the familiar constitutional achievements on the road to nationhood – the formation of the Imperial War Cabinet, the signing of the Versailles Peace Treaty, membership in the League of Nations, the Chanak crisis, and the signing of the Halibut Treaty – were "not really so great as would-be prophets would have us believe." Why? Because they led Canada into two opposing directions that negated one another. Some resulted in closer cooperation with Britain and others moved Canada toward isolationism and autonomy. Canadians had to pursue one of these policies to its logical end. In his concluding remarks he left his audience with little doubt about which policy he favoured: "Are we to raise ourselves to a part worthy of the position which is ours in the British Empire or are we going to be foolish enough to imagine that we alone of all peoples in the world can stand by ourselves in these hard times[?] Are we going to allow these vociferous busy bodies of all our past faiths and loyalties which the dominant school of nationalists is dinning into our ears today to commit us to this will-of-the-wisp of an independent isolated nationality which will lead us dancing into the bogs[?]"[18] He went one step further in an article in the *Canadian Historical Review* in 1929, entitled "Canada's Relations with the Empire as seen by the Toronto *Globe*, 1857-1867," in which he came to realize that nationalism and imperialism were compatible, rather than conflicting or contradictory, forces. As he concluded: The *Globe*'s "fundamental faith that the two seeming opposites, Canadian autonomy and imperial unity, were the most reconcilable things in the world, has been justified by later experience."[19]

In the 1930s both historians took a decisive turn to the left in their thinking that was reflected in a pronounced anti-British imperialist position. But their perspectives were slightly different. Underhill had become a socialist in the 1930s and so saw British imperialism as being first and foremost a form of capitalistic exploitation and, second, an agency of colonialism. From his perspective as an enhanced Canadian nationalist, Lower viewed British imperialism first and foremost as a perpetrator of colonialism and therefore a deterrent to the growth of nationalism in the British dominions and colonies, and only secondarily as a form of capitalistic exploitation. Thus, Underhill focused his attacks on imperialism itself as a root evil that needed to be eradicated, whereas Lower often blamed Canadians for allowing Britain to dominate them, though he was not opposed to blaming the British as well. This explains why Underhill came under attack for his views to a much greater extent than did Lower, which actually led to Underhill's threatened dismissal from the University of Toronto in 1939 to 1941.[20] The attacks came from the Toronto business elite who sat on the university's board of governors and who resented Underhill's attacks on the business class.

Underhill's criticism of British imperialism began shortly after his move from the University of Saskatchewan to the University of Toronto in 1927 and can be attributed in part to his negative reaction to what he perceived as the dour, imperialist, Victorian mentality of the Toronto Establishment. He stepped up his attacks as politicians, university administrators, and the board of governors attempted to silence him. Underhill's views became more vociferous as a second world war seemed imminent, resulting in his efforts to persuade Canadians to be suspicious of the British connection. He argued that British imperialism was only a worse form of the disease of capitalistic nationalism. "The enthusiasts who preach a wider Imperial loyalty as a substitute for our nationalism," he wrote in the *Canadian Forum* in 1932, "are only inoculating us with a worse form of our present disease. Their Empire is a fighting organization in a world at war. Their imperialism is only a more ambitious nationalism."[21] In another article he concluded that "Pax Britannia" really meant "Rule Britannia," and that "peace in our time" meant "peace on our terms."[22] Such opinions revealed just how much Underhill's views on British imperialism had changed since the 1920s.

By the mid-1930s Underhill devoted article after article and speech after speech to persuading Canadians to formulate their own foreign policy independent of Britain. In a memorandum called "Canadian foreign policy in the 1930s," written for the Canadian Institute on International Affairs' eighth international studies conference on collective security in February 1935, he argued that the international situation in the 1930s had reverted to the pre-1914 position: two armed camps ready to attack over any small incident. At that time, he pointed out, Canadians had two choices: pursue a common imperial policy or work toward an independent nationalist position. He noted that former prime minister Wilfrid Laurier had favoured the latter and had diligently worked for Canadian autonomy. Yet when the First World War broke out, Canada became automatically involved owing to its imperial connection. The situation was no different in 1935. Despite William Lyon Mackenzie King's efforts in the 1920s to free Canada from its dependence on Britain, the country was still legally and emotionally tied. Underhill ended his speech with a strongly worded condemnation of those who continued to favour Canada going to the next war at Britain's side:

> We must therefore make it clear to the world, and especially to Great Britain, that the poppies blooming in Flanders fields have no further interest for us. We must fortify ourselves against the allurements of a British war for democracy and freedom and parliamentary institutions, and against the allurements of a League war for peace and international order. And when

overseas propagandists combine the two appeals to us by urging us to join in organizing "the Peace World" to which all the British nations already belong, the simplest answer is to thumb our noses at them. Whatever the pretext on which Canadian armed forces may be lured to Europe again, the actual result would be that Canadian workers and farmers would shoot down German workers and farmers, or be shot down by them, in meaningless slaughter. As the late John S. Ewart remarked, we should close our ears to these European blandishments and, like Ulysses and his men, sail past the European siren, our ears stuffed with tax-bills. All these European troubles are not worth the bones of a Toronto grenadier.[23]

It was speeches like this that led to Underhill's threatened dismissal from the University of Toronto.

When attacked by his opponents as being anti-British, Underhill on one occasion rejoindered: "I am not anti-British. I am anti-Chamberlain and anti-Avery."[24] He agreed that Canada had benefited from the British connection by acquiring "a spirit of political liberalism, the belief in fair play, the conviction that things turn out best when differences are adjusted by free discussion."[25] But he also went on to argue that such liberal values could not be sustained through British imperialism; indeed, imperialism was the very antithesis of this liberal-democratic tradition.

In the 1930s Arthur R.M. Lower also fought against any obstacles that might stand in the way of Canada developing a foreign policy based strictly on Canadian interests and needs. That meant in particular that Canadians divest themselves of their sentimental attachment to the Empire. When attacked by a British critic for taking a hard-line approach to Canadian-British relations in one of his articles in *International Affairs,* Lower responded: "I attempted to present as clearly as I could the realities of this country's position, and in so doing stripped my thought, in so far as I was able, of the sentimentalities which habitually befog us here in Canada. When that is done, one sees that while the two countries have much in common, especially in the realm of the traditional and the ideal, they also diverge widely in the hard matters of self-interest. It is these latter which must be looked straight in the face if common action is to be secured."[26]

Lower was convinced as early as 1933 that another world war was imminent and that Great Britain was bound to be involved. He attributed this involvement to Britain's imperial holdings that she was prepared to protect even at the price of war. Lower had a low opinion of British leaders. As he recalled in his autobiography:

From 1933 on it became plainer and plainer to me that the British government of the time would bring Great Britain to the brink of destruction, that it had no idea of where it was going, and that there were in it elements with which no liberal-minded person would wish to be associated ... I felt that if Canada were not to have to go through the whole bloody mess of 1914-18 over again, she would have to reduce her imperial ties to the minimum and make herself in spirit what she was in the letter, an independent nation. And given the English-Canadian people, there was absolutely no prospect of her doing any such thing.[27]

For Lower, the only way that Canada could pursue a foreign policy independent of Britain was to be isolationist, and neutral in the next European war. He argued that geography made such a policy feasible, being like an island with oceans on three sides and a friendly nation on the fourth that "one comes to think of as almost another ocean, so completely is the wall it interposes between us and the rest of the world."[28] Add to this the diversity of the Canadian population, with fewer and fewer of British descent, and even among them fewer who any longer identified with Britain, and a common Canadian policy of isolationism seemed even more feasible. Lower went so far as to appeal to British Canadians to support a policy of neutrality by pointing out that killing young British Canadians in another war would dilute the "Anglo-Saxon race" in Canada:

Those persons who would wish to get us into another European war are also, by and large, those who are most anxious to keep Canada a British country, that is, a country dominated by British ideals, with British institutions, and predominantly British in population. These are objectives with which I am in hearty agreement. But another European adventure of the magnitude of the last would be the most effective means of bringing the whole structure down, for it would have the same selective effect as the last: our young men would enlist in about the same order [as in the First World War].[29]

Both Lower and Underhill underwent a major shift in perspective during the Second World War. For both historians, the rapid fall of the Low Countries, the Scandinavian countries, and France in the spring of 1940 and the possible defeat of Britain in the Battle of Britain in the summer of 1940 shocked them into realizing the magnitude of the war and the foolhardy nature of their isolationist positions. Lower recalled the agony and guilt he felt: "The emotion of those horrible days in June showed me that things infinitely deep were waking up inside me, things over which I had little control. The spirit of my ancestors, I suppose! I could not cut myself off from my past and my father's past. In the hour of danger I was one with them ... Had I been wrong in trying to get Canadians to shape their own course, to make their own way in the world, to put their allegiance to their own country before and above their traditional ties to Great Britain?"[30] But from his strictly Canadian perspective, Lower welcomed the signing of the Ogdensburg Agreement in August of 1940 that established a common North American defence against a foreign attack in that it provided Canada with the protection that Britain could no longer provide. He also mused on the possibility of the agreement resurrecting the old ideal of the United Empire Loyalists of reuniting the Anglo-Saxon race. "Anglo-Saxondom united," he wrote at the time of the agreement, "could still be the greatest force in the world."[31]

Underhill also felt pangs of guilt for his isolationist policy and his desired neutrality for Canada in another European war after the Nazis' sweep through the Low Countries, the fall of France, and the prospect of a British defeat. Now he saw the war as the military component of a social and intellectual revolution that would decide whether democracy or totalitarianism would be supreme in the world. The battle between socialism and capitalism that had been his focus in the 1930s was insignificant compared to this more fundamental and irreconcilable ideological struggle between democracy and totalitarianism. Underhill realized that he had been so busy fighting British capitalists and imperialists of the last war that he had been blind to the new power struggles in the present war. Now Underhill saw Communism as the number one enemy in the world, and he attacked it with relentlessness comparable to his attacks on British imperialism in the 1930s.

From the late 1940s through to the 1950s, with the threat to Canadian autonomy from British imperialism no longer present, Lower and Underhill were able to adopt a more balanced perspective on British-Canadian relations. Now both emphasized the liberal nature of Britain and the positive attributes in the British connection with Canada. Lower became concerned about the possible loss of British liberal-democratic values in a world in which Communism posed a serious threat. He wrote his book *This Most Famous Stream: The Liberal Democratic Way of Life* (1954) as his contribution to "a restatement of the faith upon which our western world is founded"[32] and that he saw as being under threat from the spread of Communism. He emphasized throughout the book that "liberal democracy worked out first in England, then transferred by colonization to America and the rest of the English-speaking world and by example to a number of associated countries"[33] and was the finest gift Great Britain had given the world. As a true Canadian nationalist, Lower noted the important role Canada played in the development of British liberal democracy in the world:

> The Canadian struggle against privilege in Church and State was conducted in a backwater, but it has turned out to be one of the major factors in securing the ancient institutions. In the first place, its success prevented a second disruption of the English-speaking race. A second disruption would

have meant a splintering such as the former Spanish Empire in America has undergone. Canada kept together the British Empire of the nineteenth century: it made the Commonwealth of the twentieth. It went on to show the compromise of the most stubborn questions was usually possible: not only those of sovereignty but the even more intractable ones of religion and race. It is impossible to imagine compromise of such questions being reached under any other regime than that of self-government. Free discussion is the life blood of tolerance. By its conduct in many such areas as these, Canada injected new elements of vitality into the ancient institutions, extended their ambit and in due course brought its contributions of experience and spirit to the welfare of the nations in the internationalism of the modern world.[34]

Underhill also took a more balanced perspective on British-Canadian relations in his post Second World War writings. He saw Canada's association with Britain in the Commonwealth as a healthy counterbalance to the American pull. He compared Canada's ideal relationship with her two principal associates, Britain and the United States, as being in the form of an isosceles triangle, with the British and the American angles of equal strength. He also emphasized the value of the British Commonwealth as a great liberal organization that recognized the independence of its member nation states while working together to assist other countries to achieve greater autonomy. Underhill gave a series of lectures at Duke University, subsequently published as *The British Commonwealth: An Experiment in Cooperation* (1956), in which he emphasized the role that the dominions, especially Canada, played in shaping this great organization. In his conclusion to the lecture series, Underhill returned to his dualistic perspective of Britain that had emerged from his student days at Oxford and from his stint in the British army during the First World War. Underhill acknowledged the idea put forward by a British analyst, Sir Fred Clarke, in an article entitled "'British' with a Small 'b'" as being appropriate for appreciating the British Commonwealth. Underhill summarized Clarke's point:

Like all his countrymen in the 1930s, Clarke was concerned about the declining power of Britain, her seeming incapacity for decisive action. He suggested, however, that as her power declined, her influence might expand, if she continued to cherish those values which he called British with a small *b*. The purely local tribal institutions, which he called British with a capital *B*, would be such things, I suppose, as the monarchy (or, at any rate, the monarchy that has something mysterious or magical about it), the peerage, the Church of England, the old school tie, the Oxford-B.B.C. accent, "Britannia rules the waves," a certain condescension towards foreigners. British with a small *b*, are the long tradition of the freedom and dignity of the

individual, the habit of reaching decisions by discussion, the spirit of tol-
eration, the flair for compromise, a sense of limits, social solidarity, the
independence of the judiciary, a free press, free political parties, free churches,
free trade unions. But these, as Clarke pointed out, are precisely the features
of British civilization that have a universal appeal. It is the men and women
who are British with a small *b,* whatever their race or color, who have turned
the Empire into the Commonwealth.[35]

Arthur R.M. Lower and Frank Underhill had similar backgrounds and similar ideas about Britain and British-Canadian relations that would classify
them as being Canadian liberal nationalists. Both historians were critical of
British imperialism, seeing it as exploitive and power hungry and as an
ideology that had perpetuated Canada's colonial status. They attacked the
British Empire in the 1930s, in particular as the world prepared for another
war, fearful that Canada's association with the Empire would lead the country into another war without considering the needs of Canada itself. In
essence, both men saw the Second World War as a repeat of the first. When
they came to appreciate the differences and to realize the serious possibility
of a British defeat, both Lower and Underhill realized what would have
been lost in a British defeat: those liberal-democratic values that Britain had
given to Western civilization. Both historians re-emphasized this aspect of
the British-Canadian connection in the post-Second World War era. They
came to appreciate that there were two Britains: the imperial Britain and
the liberal Britain, two Britains that were diametrically opposed in terms of
the values they upheld, and in terms of their impact on Canada.

Notes

1 For biographical sketches of Lower and Underhill, see Carl Berger, *The Writing of Canadian
   History* (Toronto: University of Toronto Press, 1976), 112-36 and 54-84. See also W.H. Heick,
   "The Character and Spirit of an Age: A Study of the Thought of Arthur R.M. Lower," in *His
   Own Man: Essays in Honour of Arthur Reginald Marsden Lower,* ed. W.H. Heick and Roger
   Graham (Montreal and Kingston: McGill-Queen's University Press, 1974), 14-35; and R.
   Douglas Francis, *Frank H. Underhill: Intellectual Provocateur* (Toronto: University of Toronto
   Press, 1986).
2 Arthur R.M. Lower, *My First Seventy-Five Years* (Toronto: Macmillan, 1967), 4.
3 Ibid., 21.
4 Frank H. Underhill, *The Image of Confederation,* Massey Lectures, 1963 (Toronto: Canadian
   Broadcasting Corporation, 1964), 38.
5 Lower, *My First Seventy-Five Years,* 17.
6 Francis, *Frank H. Underhill,* 25.
7 Ibid., 26.
8 Ibid., 38.
9 Frank H. Underhill, *In Search of Canadian Liberalism* (Toronto: Macmillan, 1961), x.
10 Lower, *My First Seventy-Five Years,* 84. Emphasis in original.
11 Ibid., 94.
12 Ibid.
13 Ibid., 139.

14 Arthur R.M. Lower, "The Evolution of the Sentimental Idea of Empire: A Canadian View" (1927), reprinted in Welf H. Heick, ed., *History and Myth: Arthur Lower and the Making of Canadian Nationalism* (Vancouver: UBC Press, 1975), 299.
15 Ibid., 304.
16 Quoted in Heick, "The Character and Spirit of an Age," 24.
17 See Arthur R.M. Lower, "The Case against Immigration," *Queen's Quarterly* 37 (Summer 1930): 557-74.
18 Quoted in Francis, *Frank H. Underhill*, 56.
19 Ibid., 70.
20 For a discussion of the Underhill case, see Francis, *Frank H. Underhill*, chap. 10, "The University Crisis," 109-27.
21 Ibid., 93.
22 Ibid.
23 Quoted in ibid., 107.
24 Ibid., 93.
25 Ibid.
26 Arthur R.M. Lower, "Is There an Empire Foreign Policy?" Letter to the Editor, *International Journal* 13 (September 1934): 746.
27 Lower, *My First Seventy-Five Years*, 189.
28 Arthur R.M. Lower, "The Social and Economic Bases of Canadian Foreign Policy," in *Canada: The Empire and the League* (Toronto: Nelson, 1936), 103.
29 Arthur R.M. Lower, "External Policy and Internal Problems," *University of Toronto Quarterly* 6 (April 1937): 331.
30 Lower, *My First Seventy-Five Years*, 243.
31 Arthur R.M. Lower, "Canada Now Centre of U.S.-Empire Defence," *Financial Post* 34, 35 (31 August 1940), 9.
32 Arthur R.M. Lower, *This Most Famous Stream: The Liberal Democratic Way of Life* (Toronto: Ryerson Press, 1954), vii.
33 Ibid.
34 Ibid., 151-52.
35 Frank H. Underhill, *The British Commonwealth: An Experiment in Co-operation Among Nations* (Durham, NC: Duke University Press, 1956), 100-1.

19

The Monarchy, the Mounties, and Ye Olde English Fayre: Identity at All Saints' Anglican, Edmonton, 1875-1990s

Frances Swyripa

On a Sunday morning in September 1997, a senior citizen in the scarlet tunic of the Royal Canadian Mounted Police attended the sung eucharist at All Saints' Anglican Cathedral in Edmonton, Alberta. Impossible to miss among the well-dressed but sparse older congregation, the retired officer let it be known that he wore his uniform that day because he regretted not wearing it at the Edmonton memorial service for Diana, Princess of Wales, the cathedral had recently hosted.[1] The man's gesture, together with the assumptions and sense of propriety it reflected, speaks volumes about identity at All Saints' – particularly the often blurred boundaries separating Britishness or a diasporic British World, Canadianism, and English ethnicity.

All Saints' Anglican dates its beginnings from 1875,[2] with the arrival at Fort Edmonton of English-born Rev. (later Canon) William Newton, supported by the Society for the Propagation of the Gospel in England, near the end of the fur trade era. Services were held in premises rented from the Hudson's Bay Company and then on Newton's homestead (the "Hermitage"), until the first All Saints' church was built in 1878-79 west of the fort near present 121 Street and Jasper Avenue, on land donated by businessman-settler Malcolm Groat. In 1891, the year the railway from Calgary reached the opposite bank of the North Saskatchewan River, bringing ever more settlers to the area, the building was moved to 106 Street and 99 Avenue, closer to the emerging commercial centre of the growing settlement. A new church constructed on 103 Street south of Jasper Avenue, a site All Saints' still occupies, proclaimed the parish's desired identity as a "downtown" church even more forcefully. At its dedication in 1896, Bishop Pinkham of Saskatchewan and Calgary declared the building "the best belonging to the Church of England in the Territories" outside Regina.[3] After fire destroyed the structure in 1919, consuming almost all the material history of the parish, its brick replacement served the congregation for more than three decades. The current cathedral, dedicated in 1956, was consecrated in 1967. By then fifty-three years had passed since the installation of Henry Allen

Gray as first bishop of the Anglican diocese of Edmonton and the elevation of All Saints' to an acting or a pro-cathedral. By Diana's memorial service, All Saints' had been part of the Edmonton landscape and Anglican worship for over a century. During that time it had embraced a number of interlocking roles and identities – religious and secular, local and (inter)national – that together defined the parish and its members.

Most importantly, the cathedral belonged to a worldwide Anglican communion and ecclesiastical institution led by the archbishop of Canterbury that enjoyed established status in the United Kingdom as the Church of England, with the reigning monarch as its formal head. Possessing privileges and influence unknown to other denominations, the Church of England figured prominently in the official rituals and collective life of the nation, presiding over state occasions and landmark events, providing a focus for communal joy and grief, and acting as both guardian and interpreter of the past. In Canada, following its failure to secure establishment standing in Upper Canada in the nineteenth century,[4] the immigrant Anglican church could not automatically assume pre-eminence by right or tradition and had to readjust its self-image and purpose accordingly. This readjustment was particularly acute in the prairie West. Initially a fluid frontier society without entrenched interests, shared memory, and a consensus as to spiritual authority or ritual leadership, the region became increasingly ethnically diverse as agricultural settlement advanced. Anglicans faced not only the French-dominated Roman Catholic Church, which inherited a comparable sense of entitlement and secular authority from its Quebec and fur trade experiences, but also at least the potential for competition from new immigrant churches that, in their homelands, had also been national institutions. Ultimately, all such churches were transformed, becoming more limited and ethnic (sometimes with an exaggerated sense of their ethnicity), and forced to behave more circumspectly than they had in the homeland.

In post-fur-trade Edmonton, the political contest between the English Anglican and French Roman Catholic churches for recognition as the voice of the community, especially regarding its ritual and memory, was quickly won by the former. Long known as the "English church,"[5] All Saints' thus became much more than an Anglican congregation or a place of worship for Anglican faithful, or even an expression of members' English ethnicity. A comfortable symmetry between "Canadian" and "homeland" privileged the British identity of the cathedral and its flock, obscured the distinction between sacred and secular, and rendered All Saints' Edmonton's established church in all but name. Its role as host for state or semi-official occasions – putting All Saints' at the centre of the corporate ritualistic life of the city and province – was both appropriated by the cathedral and instinctively granted by the Anglo circles that dominated government, business, and the military. This role also identified the cathedral and Anglicanism with the state and state interests, and equated the church's particular agenda and priorities, from imperial (British) and national (Canadian) to narrowly eth- nic (English) and local (Edmonton, Alberta, Prairie), with those of the com- munity at large. The participation of All Saints' in secular affairs gave the latter the added status and authority of God's sanction. It also raised the status and authority of the Anglican Church, its clergy, and its members, reinforcing the traditional dominance of the Anglo-British element in Ca- nadian nation-building. The cathedral never renounced its establishment functions or the notion that it was the logical site for communal celebra- tion and commemoration. But with time, tensions emerged over its secular activities, official identification with a politicized Britishness, and whether, in a pluralistic country, hosting state rituals should be shared with other faiths, Christian and non-Christian. As well, as society became increasingly secular and elite circles increasingly included those who were neither Anglo nor Anglican, there was no longer the same overlap and shared assump- tions among secular influence, religion, and ethnic origin that had ben- efited All Saints'. By the 1970s the cathedral was experimenting with a cultural English ethnic identity that reflected the popular tenets of Cana- dian multiculturalism.

This interaction among Britishness or a diasporic British World, Canadianism, and English ethnicity in articulating identity at All Saints' is explored through three themes. First, All Saints' is a church with deep roots in Edmonton's history and a strong sense of itself as a local institution greatly enriching city life. Augmenting this Edmonton identity is the parish's sense of its own internal landmarks, history, and significance. Second, the cathedral's ceremonial functions and symbolic associations represent both a British imperial (later Commonwealth) influence or connection and emo- tional identification with Canada and the Prairies. Third, the homeland, and especially England, has been a catalyst for supplementary activities in the cathedral that are cultural or ethnic in nature. While identity at All Saints' has always been multi-layered and fluid, the consciousness that the cathedral belongs to an Edmonton community, and that the parish consti- tutes a particular community within Edmonton, is the filter through which all other facets of its life are viewed.

When, in the 1890s, All Saints' elected to relocate closer to the centre of the expanding settlement outside the old fort walls, the pioneer parish was staking its future as part of Edmonton. It would grow with the city; it would put its stamp on it; it would share its leading citizens; it would both incor- porate it into its worship and provide a place for its citizens to collectively gather. What made this ambition realizable was not All Saints' assumption that such a role represented the natural order, but the fact that those in positions of power and influence thought similarly. In the early years in particular, Edmonton's modest political, social, and economic elite was predominantly British in origin, even if often not always Anglican.[6] The city also was home to the provincial government, the provincial university, a handful of military units, and one of the first detachments of the North West Mounted Police (subsequently the Royal Canadian Mounted Police); members of these organizations extended this small circle and strengthened both its general impact and ties to All Saints'. According to historian Lewis G. Thomas, "the years immediately preceding the war were a kind of golden age for the Anglican church in Edmonton ... As Edmonton changed from a small frontier town, isolated at the end of steel, into a provincial capital and regional railway centre, the multiplication of the British and Anglican population markedly affected every aspect of life – from politics to sports and pastimes, from religious exercises to reading habits."[7]

That All Saints' identified with and felt entitled to call upon the larger Edmonton community – and that the latter responded – was already evident at the laying of the cornerstone of the "downtown" church in 1895. Appropriating public space for an Anglican event while opening that event to everyone, a procession led by the Edmonton Fire Brigade wound down the street from the Masonic hall to the site; there, the Masons, who also marched, laid the stone according to the rules of their craft. The eventual structure, they assured the crowd, would be a "noble monument to a pious exercise, a bright ornament to our faith and people, and a just pride to the citizens of Edmonton."[8] For the laying of the cornerstone of the replacement church in 1921 after the fire, besides a general invitation to "the Clergy and laity of the City," special invitations went to the lieutenant-governor of Alberta, the mayor of Edmonton, and the city's commissioners and aldermen, all of whom attended.[9] Reflecting on the occasion, the rector of All Saints' did his part for frontier boosterism, stating that his church did not merely conserve tradition but also engaged in making history. "Placed as we are in the very heart of what will be a great history," he wrote, "we would be derelict in our duty if we failed to be an influence for good – or failed to welcome and attract the new comer and the visitor."[10]

During its heyday, networking between All Saints' and both the Edmonton establishment and the province extended well beyond symbolic attendance by civic dignitaries at church functions, or clergy at civic functions. For instance, in 1957 All Saints' highlighted the secular legacy of the first bishop, Henry Allen Gray, during the dedication of his memorial window in the present cathedral. "Known and beloved by the whole community in Edmonton," Gray (who died in his native England) was not only an important judge and educator, with a public school named after him, but also "the proud possessor of Newsboys' Badge No. 1, [which] he wore ... at all times on the lapel of his coat."[11] Yet it was the mutual reinforcement of church and state that was most visible. When W.F. Barfoot left Edmonton in the 1950s to take up his new appointment in Winnipeg as metropolitan of the ecclesiastical province of Rupert's Land, both the mayor and the premier of Alberta attended the tribute in the cathedral.[12] Civic leaders invited to the public reception for H.H. Clark on his election as primate of all Canada in 1959 included Lieutenant-Governor J.J. Bowlen (who was Catholic), Premier Ernest Manning's representative, Mayor J.F. Mitchell (the dean apologized for failing to recognize him), the president of the University of Alberta, and the RCAF base commander at Namao. The list of religious leaders was more modest: the Roman Catholic archbishop (who sent an alternate), the president of the local Council of Churches, and the president of the United Church's St. Stephen's College on campus.[13]

The consecration of the present cathedral and service of thanksgiving marking its freedom from debt in November 1967 continued this tradition of outreach, although the nature of the targeted religious and secular communities was changing. The guest list again situated All Saints' within a larger Anglican and non-Anglican faith community, with invitations, for example, not only to the primate of the Anglican church in Canada but also to the local Roman Catholic archbishop and head of the Salvation Army (both with personal letters), and, much more formally, the Russian Orthodox archbishop. The guest list also continued to identify All Saints' with the power structures of the secular society. In attendance were Douglas Walker-Brash on behalf of the British government; Grant MacEwan, Alberta's lieutenant-governor; Walter Johns, president of the University of Alberta; and the acting mayor of Edmonton, alderman Morris Weinloss.[14] Premier Manning sent regrets. MacEwan, Johns, and Manning all had British backgrounds, but none was Anglican; Weinloss was Jewish. In the future, although state participation in the internal milestones of All Saints' continued to confer a measure of outside legitimacy and status, both invitation and acceptance became less personal and more political. When All Saints' celebrated its hundredth anniversary in 1975, the list of government dignitaries on the guest list had shrunk to William Yurko, the cabinet minister representing the province, and William Hawrelak, mayor of Edmonton – one Romanian, the other Ukrainian, both Orthodox.[15]

Increasing distance between All Saints' and government circles mirrored the secularization of Canadian society as well as a shift from Anglo-conformity to multiculturalism. Something similar can be seen in the cathedral's relationship with Edmonton. Before the Great War, when city boosters promised unlimited growth, transforming Edmonton from a fur-trading post to a populous and prosperous metropolis serving a thriving agricultural hinterland, All Saints' considered itself an integral player from its location in the downtown core. "The change from the character of a small town congregation to that of a large city church, as well as the changing methods of work," stated a 1911 document, "must be met without delay if we are to keep up with the progress of the place."[16] At its diamond jubilee in 1935, All Saints' looked back on a proud history: part of Edmonton, its booms and busts, and the pioneer West; founder status as the first Anglican church in Alberta.[17] At mid-century, the cathedral celebrated the seventy-fifth anniversary of the arrival of Canon Newton, "first Anglican missionary" in Alberta.[18] It also celebrated the golden jubilee of organist Vernon Barford, again mobilizing its secular establishment ties to secure him recognition within the larger Edmonton musical scene. Although unsuccessful, the most ambitious proposals were to interview the senate of the University of Alberta about a possible honorary degree, "in consideration of [Barford's] long and painstaking efforts on behalf of the Art in the City of Edmonton," and to seek support from Sir Ernest MacMillan, the conductor and composer, for a doctorate from either Alberta or the Toronto Conservatory of Music.[19] When Barford retired six years later and the cathedral decided to purchase a memorial organ, it felt that "sufficient private support among people not members of the congregation" existed to fund-raise in the non-cathedral, non-Anglican community. But All Saints' misjudged its image and influence as a city-wide institution, and by 1959 some two thousand letters to individuals, organizations, and firms had produced disappointing results.[20]

Yet through the 1950s, the cathedral retained its self-image and pride as a downtown church, and, to a large extent, its ability to draw on the larger Edmonton community for support. When the archbishop of Canterbury visited in 1954 and All Saints' approached local businesses to donate items for a mammoth public evensong at Edmonton Gardens, the Hudson's Bay Company provided the decorations, Woodward's department store the organ.[21] In the fundraising pamphlets issued for the construction of the present cathedral, a succession of deans couched their appeal in All Saints' pioneering credentials, the need to keep faith with "the sacrifices of past generations," and the belief of a shared conviction "that the Diocese of Edmonton should have a Cathedral Church whose building is more adequate and more in keeping with a growing city."[22] Over the next two decades the fruits of a downtown mentality, as befitting "a Cathedral situated strategically at the centre of a City," could be seen in All Saints' sense of responsibility to those with whom it shared space, offering a quiet refuge for rushed office workers, holding special Lenten noon services before Easter, and promoting itself as a patron of the arts.[23] But its neighbours also had a duty toward All Saints'. In 1957, for example, businesses such as Woodward's and Northwestern Utilities were asked to help pay for advertising the Lenten noon services, with the suggestion that a printed acknowledgment reading "contributed by a firm believing in spiritual values" would resolve any qualms about supporting a particular denomination.[24]

However, major cracks surfaced between Edmonton businesses and All Saints', and its presumed right to call upon the secular community to fund its sectarian endeavours, over the $100,000 Centennial Appeal launched for the parish's one hundredth anniversary in 1975-76. Two-thirds of the money raised was to go to the cathedral building (replacing rugs, buying a new boiler, and so on), the rest to the cathedral's downtown ministry, including seniors' apartments and an education centre. Describing the projects, All Saints' noted how it had "an historical past which should be maintained as part of our downtown heritage and ... revitalization of the city centre," and how its good works improved the area's quality of life. Portraying the cathedral as an old and valuable member of the Edmonton community, especially its central core, committed to the same social and economic goals as City Hall and local merchants, was politically astute. It implied a unity of purpose that justified asking downtown businesses to donate 40 percent of the total sum, even if, as anticipated, they hesitated to support religious programs per se. Another 10 percent was to come from other outside sources, including government and groups such as the Richard Eaton Singers and the taxpayer-funded RCMP and navy, which used the church. From a list provided by the University of Alberta fundraiser, the cathedral targeted one hundred firms, approaching a select few through personal contacts and an "old boy net," the rest through letters or canvassers bearing gifts of centennial paperweights. In mid-1976, after a concerted blitz had yielded only $575, the campaign was conceded to have failed financially but was praised for raising the cathedral's profile and sending the message that its doors stood open to everyone. Clearly, however, All Saints' self-image as an integral fixture in the life of the inner city, with reciprocal obligations, was out of step with the times. Their clientele increasingly multicultural and multifaith, most of the firms that had declined to participate explained that they simply did not give to churches.[25]

Despite erosion of links between the cathedral and local elites, All Saints' valued its legacy as an Edmonton institution and its place in the city's heritage and landscape. At the time of the consecration of the cathedral in 1967, for example, the dean made a special pilgrimage to the Old Hermitage, symbol of Anglican beginnings in Edmonton, to check on the cairn marking the site at which Canon Newton had held services on his homestead.[26] Physical roots proved to be less important, however, in commemorating the site of the first church building proper. In 1981 the Edmonton Historical Board and the cathedral agreed to install the plaque on the facade of the present church because the original location, blocks to the west, was inconvenient.[27] All Saints' also proclaimed its relationship with the surrounding community within the sacred space of the cathedral, specifically in its stained glass windows. First, nostalgic images below traditional biblical scenes – early model car, log cabin in the bush, Victorians in top hats and fur muffs, Prairie street with false-fronted buildings – celebrate a bygone frontier. Second, the dedications testify to the crossover between prominent Edmontonians and parish membership. After the triptych above the altar in memory of Bishop Gray, the best examples commemorate pioneer merchant Richard Secord and the military Griesbachs. A descendant of Laura Secord, Richard Secord had arrived in Edmonton in 1881, travelling by Red River cart from Winnipeg. He taught school, served as an alderman, represented the region in the Territorial Assembly, and financially supported initiatives like the Misericordia Hospital. He and his wife Annie are also remembered on the memorial doors installed at the dedication of the cathedral in 1956.[28] The two men featured in the Griesbach Memorial Window are Maj. Gen. William Griesbach (CB, CMG, DSO, VD), who founded the 49th Battalion, Edmonton Regiment, in 1915; and Lt. Col. Arthur Griesbach, the first enlisted member of the North West Mounted Police, in 1873.[29]

The Griesbach men make a fitting transition between the self-image of All Saints' as an Edmonton institution and identification of the cathedral, by itself and others, with nation and empire. Here the line between "British" and "Canadian" frequently disappeared in that initially the two were seen as interchangeable and, in fact, overlapped. While All Saints' never totally yielded its privileged position in secular ritual, over time the certainty that such a function naturally fell to the cathedral came under scrutiny. On one hand, it seemed misplaced and exclusionary with acceptance within the larger society of Canada's multicultural reality. On the other hand, the cathedral itself debated whether a religious institution should identify so publicly with the state and secular events, especially if and when the thrust was Britain, not Canada. The official role the cathedral played in state ceremonial life had serious implications for identity at All Saints'. But aside from its own members, it served the people of Edmonton and Alberta in their capacity as citizens of Canada and the British Empire and Commonwealth.

Although Canada has no established church and Anglicans are a minority,[30] the head of state, in the person of the British monarch, both heads and worships in the Church of England, All Saints' mother church. As such, perhaps the least ambiguous role the cathedral played in local ritual and communal life was in its sponsorship of royal events and hosting of visiting royalty. For example, the pioneer church marked Edward VII's accession to the throne in 1902 with a special coronation service, and his death eight years later with a memorial, at which both the mayor of Edmonton and the president of the University of Alberta spoke. The march to the church on the latter occasion, bringing colour and pomp to this outpost of the Empire on the banks of the North Saskatchewan River, reinforced the superiority of Britishness in Edmonton society. The Alberta Mounted Rifles, the Royal North West Mounted Police, and the 101st Fusiliers paraded alongside schoolchildren and city dignitaries, the Royal Society of St. George, the Sons of England, the Caledonian Society, St. Andrew's Society, and the Edmonton Irish Association. When George VI died several decades later, the cathedral responded with not only the customary memorial service on the day of the funeral but also a radio broadcast and noon-day service, the latter in answer to "public demand," on the day of his passing itself.[31] In this context the memorial service at All Saints' for Diana, Princess of Wales, was not simply another version of the unprecedented global emotional response to her death but part of tradition and the cathedral's prerogative in observing royal milestones.

The bond between All Saints' and the Crown became personal when members of the royal family or British aristocracy visited Edmonton and came to the cathedral to worship as fellow Anglicans. It was also important to the cathedral that they did come. For example, the dean wrote to Premier Peter Lougheed about a proposed visit by Elizabeth II to Edmonton in 1974, seeking her attendance at All Saints', "either for ... reasons of historical interest, or for Divine Worship," as part of its centennial celebrations. "All Saints is the first Anglican congregation to be established in the Province of Alberta," the dean stated, naming its more famous clergy before reminding the premier how the cathedral had once been the home church for the local RCMP.[32] That royal visit never materialized, and by 1978, when the Queen and Prince Philip were in Edmonton to open the Commonwealth Games, this intimacy with the monarchy and the world view it reflected were jeopardized by the need for the monarch in Canada to balance personal worship with openness to all her subjects. Although All Saints' extended an invitation to attend a service at the cathedral, it acknowledged that the decision rested with the lieutenant-governor's office, which could choose "a large community service such as took place in Ottawa" instead.[33] A religious event for the general public downplayed the Crown's specific and special Anglican relationship and consciously embraced Canadians of other faiths.

As long as the governor general, as the monarch's representative, was drawn from the British (and Anglican) aristocracy, or even Canada's own leading Anglo families, the symbiotic relationship between All Saints' and the Crown persisted at both personal and ceremonial levels. Thus the transition from the Earl of Bessborough in the 1930s to Vincent Massey, the first Canadian to occupy the vice-regal role, in the 1950s did not involve a revolutionary shift in either thinking or behaviour. When Massey visited Edmonton in October 1952, some nine months after being sworn in, and read the Lessons at All Saints', his attendance at the cathedral and active participation in the service came not only as governor general but also as a practising Anglican.[34] Massey's successor, the French and Catholic Georges Vanier, spoiled this symmetry. How would All Saints' respond to the disjuncture between state and the symbols of state and its own tradition and self-image of identification with them? While Vanier's state funeral in Ottawa in 1967 took place at the Roman Catholic cathedral of Notre-Dame, his official memorial service in Edmonton under the auspices of the Council of Churches was held in the Anglican cathedral. The dean strongly defended the venue, based on the historical role of All Saints' "stand[ing] at the centre both of the diocesan church life and also of the city of Edmonton." He was equally adamant that although "all churches are inevitably representative of a denomination, 'the Cathedral' means something to Christians of many different traditions in Edmonton." Yet his remark that the choice of All Saints' was "thought most fitting by Christians of *many* denominations" (emphasis added) implies that some did not think it fitting,[35] and one could argue that nearby St. Joseph's Roman Catholic cathedral had at least as legitimate a claim to the governor general. Vanier's death was the first challenge to the precedence of All Saints', and in subsequent years, when the governor general was neither British in origin nor Anglican, the tradition of memorial services at the Anglican cathedral disappeared.[36]

If a Canadian governor general increasingly representative of his country's multicultural and multifaith character undermined All Saints' role in viceregal ritual, the cathedral's military associations reflected an evolving relationship with the Empire, the mother country, and Canada. Initially, Britain's wars were Canada's wars, and the present All Saints' church attests to a lengthy, intimate, and proud association with (para)military institutions and activities. Besides articles and furnishings given in memory of men lost in war, or in thanks for their safe return, a handful of plaques pay homage to the courage and sacrifice of the parish's dead. The most impressive are from the Canadian Mounted Rifles to "a brave and gallant comrade" killed trying to save a wounded fellow officer in the Boer War, and the sixty-eight names in gilt lettering engraved in marble that remember "the men of this congregation who gave up their lives in the Great War 1914-1918." The latter plaque substitutes for a "Soldiers' Corner" in the original plans for the building and replaces the honour roll destroyed in the 1919 fire.[37] Significantly, for both commemorated soldiers and their fellow parishioners, no conflict existed between old and new homelands, in whose joint names these men volunteered for service and made the supreme sacrifice. The Boer War plaque, for example, represents solidarity with imperial aims and adventures, and has its counterparts in Australia and New Zealand as well as in Britain itself. After the Great War, All Saints' also inaugurated an annual Armistice (later Remembrance) Day service, primarily for the parish, though related events have reached into and drawn on the larger community. For example, evening concerts by the Richard Eaton Singers in the 1980s were intended for all Edmontonians, while the official presence of the Princess Patricia Canadian Light Infantry at the service itself in the mid-1960s reinforced the bond between All Saints' and British (Canadian) militarism.[38]

In other respects, a secular politicized identity at All Saints' based on the British imperial connection (and the peculiar Canadianness it typified) has been surprisingly muted. The present All Saints' is unusual for an Anglican church in that since the mid-1980s it has had no state flags in the interior, although historically the Union Jack and later also the Maple Leaf were hung, and the issue is a recurring and controversial one.[39] Nor are there any military banners or standards (although the Royal Canadian Navy flag was once displayed), or any reminders of their presence, as there are in All Saints' pioneer contemporaries First Presbyterian and McDougall Methodist (now United).[40] Also strikingly absent, despite discussion in the 1960s, is a memorial to those parishioners who fought in the Second World War.[41] Finally, in the 1980s formal identification with militarism and a politicized British identity was openly questioned, centring on the tradition that had crystallized after the Second World War to commemorate the Battle of the Atlantic on the first Sunday in May. A special service (initially also broadcast on radio) was attended by war veterans, local naval groups, and Silver Cross Mothers, while a military parade with bands, drums, and bagpipes added to the pageantry.[42] But in 1987, the dean cancelled the annual observance, upsetting not only the navy but also many of his parishioners. Although a committee with both navy and cathedral representation was struck for the following year, 1988 was the last time the Battle of the Atlantic formed part of the regular ritual and worship at All Saints'.[43]

But All Saints' had long possessed a second secular politicized identity, rooted within and nurtured by Canada itself. Its finest expression was the cathedral's relationship with the North West Mounted Police, and later the Royal Canadian Mounted Police, which arrived in Alberta in 1874 to facilitate Sir John A. Macdonald's policy of settling and developing the West. Arthur Griesbach, parishioner and first enlisted member, opened All Saints' to one of the grand narratives of Canadian history. He also established a special tie between the cathedral and the force whose heroic trek west and image of manly courage and integrity are so much a part of western myth and identity. Becoming the Mounties' home church cemented the tie, reinforced again in 1974 when the cathedral hosted the local RCMP centennial service.[44] The service itself was ecumenical, acknowledging Canada's many faiths and the evolution of the RCMP away from its Anglo and Anglican roots.[45] The other major expression of a specifically Canadian identity at All Saints' was the Centennial of Confederation in 1967, celebrated by paying off the cathedral's debt. Speaking at the consecration service, the primate of the Anglican Church of Canada applauded All Saints' history and accomplishments while criticizing attitudes in the West toward Quebec and Canada's Natives. "We used to treat ... [Natives] with dignity," he said (unaware of the residential schools issue waiting to engulf his church), "but then the settlers treated them like children. We must treat them like adults." As a gesture to national unity, a prayer was also read in French.[46] A final aspect of All Saints' Canadian identity pertains to its changing role in the rituals of the province of Alberta. In the early 1980s, when All Saints' broached inviting Members of the Legislative Assembly to a special service in conjunction with the opening of the legislature, it was rebuffed.[47]

As All Saints' struggled with its self-image as a partner of Empire and the Canadian state, a more cultural ethnic identity took it in other directions. According to historian Lewis G. Thomas, "nominal Anglicans..., their ecclesiastical allegiance as much cultural as doctrinal," preponderated among immigrants from the United Kingdom during the settlement era, and the "'English church' [acted] as a rallying point and a comforting support for those who saw themselves as inheritors of an English, or perhaps more properly, a British tradition."[48] Even if Thomas' claims as to numbers cannot be substantiated, English ethnicity clearly existed at All Saints'. Initially, cultural Englishness was at least quasi-political in nature, as measured by the parish's sponsorship and accommodation of patriotic organizations such as the Boy Scouts, the Girl Guides, and the Imperial Order Daughters of the Empire. By the 1960s, however, ethnic identity at the cathedral was being expressed most forcefully through the annual Ye Olde English Fayre, popularizing the innocuous symbols favoured by the proponents of multiculturalism as the essence of being Canadian.

Historically, the most important group affiliated with All Saints' was the Boy Scouts, though the Scouts themselves registered some ambivalence about the connection, especially in the mid-1930s when there was pressure to vest control of their organization in the cathedral.[49] The troop, the first in Edmonton, was organized in 1920, twelve years after Baden-Powell's movement reached Canada, and was joined by Cubs, Guides, Rovers, and Brownies.[50] In addition to their own scouting and guiding activities, these groups participated in the rituals and worship of All Saints'. For example, from the 1930s to the 1950s they marched in church parades ranging from the feast of St. George, patron saint of both England and the scouting movement, to the coronation of Edward VIII, the fiftieth anniversary of scouting in Canada, and Baden-Powell's birthday. Visiting royalty and other dignitaries conducted formal inspections: the Earl of Bessborough, governor general and Chief Scout of Canada, of the Scouts in 1932; Princess Alice of the Guides in 1941.[51] The colours of both the Scouts and the Boys Brigade, founded by Gray while still a parish priest and subsequently absorbed by the Scouts, hung in successive churches, and their historical significance, preservation, and placement were recurrent topics of discussion.[52] In 1935 All Saints' accepted for safekeeping the standard of the late Beaver House Chapter (established in 1906) of the Imperial Order Daughters of the Empire to honour the lodge's pioneer work in the city.[53] Other groups associated over the years with All Saints' had an altruistic focus and often an ethnic identity broader than Englishness alone.[54] Before the First World War, for example, the Daughters of the King called on the sick (they also provided flowers for church festivals), while the Brotherhood of St. Andrew visited both hospitals and newcomers to the city at the Immigration Hall.[55] Between the wars, the Northern Star Lodge of the Daughters of England Benevolent Society continued this tradition of philanthropy, and after the Second World War, the newly formed Men's Fellowship welcomed Anglican immigrants to the city arriving under the provincial sponsorship scheme.[56]

While a politicized cultural identity and ethnically tinged outreach had a long history at All Saints', the notion of Englishness as entertainment emerged much later. Ye Olde English Fayre, with its self-conscious name and spelling, was deliberately evocative of the castles, medieval knights, thatched cottages, and village greens beloved of North American tourists. Moreover, its romantic image of rural England and the English heritage was easily incorporated into the dance, foods, and folk artefacts then being cultivated as the ethnic contribution to the Canadian national fabric. Sponsored by the Friendship Guild, the first fair was held in 1966, and proceeds went to the cathedral debt. The last regular event occurred in 1973, though there were still fairs into the mid-1980s. When All Saints' wrote to Woodward's in 1985 asking the department store to donate English foods as prizes (Woodward's obliged with $100 toward their purchase), it explained that the cathedral wanted to "recapture the colour and festivity of 'Ye Old English Fayre' for which All Saints Cathedral was widely known" two decades earlier.[57]

Like Ukrainians evoking Cossack horsemen or Icelanders seafaring Vikings, All Saints' turned to the homeland's distant past to express its English cultural identity, in that the symbols it fostered were far removed from the lived lives of English settlers in western Canada or their descendants. "Long will we remember," read the report of the second annual fair, "our Dean in his gaiters and frock coat, and his 'friend' the balloon-lady greeting false-bearded Major Hosty in his delightful antique Salvation Army suit or our much photographed and very busy Pearly King relaying bids for our Beefeater auctioneer." The following year the organizers added morris dancing and a "Mitre Tavern," the latter subsequently judged a "good start" even if it "did not exactly capture the Saturday weekend atmosphere of a British 'pub.'" By 1969, however, ethnic English was ruled too narrow and the event was recast as Ye Olde English International Fayre, featuring dancers from various ethnic groups. "Representing the coming of the peoples to this country," ethnic dancers returned in 1970 as part of a Canadian theme focusing on the western Native and fur trade legacy, complete with a "Wigwam ... [and] Indian Character to welcome people" and goods lent from the Hudson's Bay Company department store "to create atmosphere."[58] Yet alongside the cultural, at times playful, content of the fair were reminders of other identities at work in the cathedral. The men upon whom the organizers called to open the fair – the lieutenant-governor, the minister of education, a descendant of pioneer businessman Richard Secord, and, in

1985, the British consul general[59] – reaffirmed All Saints' close Establishment ties.

In 1985 a "visioning" questionnaire asked parishioners about important memories in the life of All Saints'. The answers, mingling the secular with the spiritual, reinforced the multi-faceted nature of identity at the cathedral. Some respondents singled out Ye Olde English Fayre, others the royal visits, one individual the visit by the archbishop of Canterbury wearing the robes in which he had crowned "Queen Elizabeth, our present Queen."[60] The church continued, as it had long had, to play a number of interlocking roles: member of a worldwide Anglican communion, figure in Canadian hierarchy, voice of British imperialism, refuge for English emigrants and immigrants and forum for English ethnicity, custodian of a Canadian past and ritual, actor on the Edmonton scene, place of worship and fellowship.

Notes

1 Personal observation, 14 September 1997; pers. comm., Gust Olson, 7 November 1997.
2 Sources include fieldwork, All Saints', September 1997, May 2001, May 2003; Harold Munn (dean) and Gust Olson (warden), pers. comm., 1997; Lewis G. Thomas, "Establishing an Anglican Presence," in *Edmonton: The Life of a City,* ed. Bob Hesketh and Frances Swyripa (Edmonton: NeWest Press, 1995), 21-30; anniversary booklets, *The Cathedral Church of All Saints, 1875-1935,* and Jean Monckton, *All Saints Anglican Cathedral, 1875-1975;* the undated "Walking Tour of the Edmonton Cathedral of All Saints"; Provincial Archives of Alberta, Records of the Anglican Diocese of Edmonton, Ed.15/All Saints' and Acc.95.31.
3 *Edmonton Bulletin,* 13 January 1896.
4 See for example Curtis Fahey, *In His Name: The Anglican Experience in Upper Canada, 1791-1854* (Ottawa: Carleton University Press, 1991), and J.L.H. Henderson, ed., *John Strachan: Documents and Opinions* (Toronto: McClelland and Stewart, 1969).
5 Thomas, "Establishing an Anglican Presence," 28.
6 For example, both Alexander Rutherford, Alberta's first premier, and George Bulyea, the first lieutenant-governor, were Baptist.
7 Thomas, "Establishing an Anglican Presence," 30.
8 See Ed.15/All Saints', files 26, 32, *Edmonton Bulletin,* 29 August 1895. All Saints' retained close ties with the Masons, using their hall for concerts, receptions, plays, and Ye Olde English Fayre.
9 Ed.15/All Saints', file 27, *Parochial Magazine,* September 1921; file 34, order of service, "The Laying of the Cornerstone, All Saints' Pro-Cathedral," 17 September 1921; file 117a, *Parochial Magazine,* September 1921 (date added, handwritten).
10 Ed.15/All Saints', file 61, rector's report for 1921. There is no contemporary record of items placed in the 1921 cornerstone, but the scroll describing the 1895 laying ceremony suggests a parish-based vision contrasting sharply with Holy Trinity across the river in Strathcona. Besides copies of Edmonton's four newspapers, that cornerstone (1913) held the names of luminaries from king to local rector, plus coins and stamps of the realm (Ed.18/Holy Trinity, file 23).
11 Ed.15/All Saints', file 114, order of service, Bishop Gray Memorial Window, 27 January 1957.
12 Acc.95.31, box 7.
13 Ibid., letter, Dean Burch to Lt. Gov. J.J. Bowlen, 25 September 1959.
14 See Ed.15/All Saints', file 49, *The Church Today,* November 1967, souvenir edition; files 110, 203, correspondence.
15 Ed.15/All Saints', file 48, order of service, "100 Years of Worship, Witness and Service," 12 October 1975.

16   Ed.15/All Saints', file 62, *Report to the Parishioners of All Saints' Church,* 1911.

17   Ed.15/All Saints', file 118, sixtieth anniversary booklet, 1935, 9-10, 35-44.

18   Ed.15/All Saints', file 114, order of service of witness and thanksgiving, 1 October 1950.

19   Ed.15/All Saints', file 54, vestry minutes, 12 December 1949, 9 January 1950. *The Church Today* (November 1967) notes that Barford received an honorary degree from the University of Alberta for "services on behalf of music in Edmonton and Alberta" (4-5), but this was an MA in 1924.

20   Ed.15/All Saints', file 56, vestry minutes, 7 January 1957; file 57, vestry minutes, 8 June 1959.

21   Ed.15/All Saints', file 113, order of service for evensong, visit, Archbishop Fisher of Canterbury, 19 September 1954. Whether businesses made similar donations when Archbishops Ramsey (1966) and Runcie (1985) visited Edmonton is unclear.

22   Ed.15/All Saints', files 106-9, Building Fund Committee, fundraising pamphlets, quotes from "e" (1956) and "c" (n.d.).

23   Ed.15/All Saints', file 61, dean's report, 1963.

24   Acc.95.31, box 7, letter, Dean Burch to Woodward's, 19 February 1957.

25   On the Centennial Appeal, see Acc.95.31, box 1, vestry minutes, 17 March, 21 April 1974; 16 June 1975; 23 February, 19 and 27 April, 21 June 1976; letter, G. Staring to Centennial Appeal Committee, 16 June 1975; letter, Centennial Appeal Committee, 30 June 1976; box 10, file "Centennial Appeal." Other projects included souvenir bookmarks and spoons, an anthem by organist Hugh Bancroft, and a parish history, while the province pledged $5,000 for "non-religious" events; Acc.95.31, box 1, vestry minutes, 21 April, 12 November, 16 December 1974; 15 September 1975.

26   Ed.15/All Saints', file 58, vestry minutes, 21 November 1967.

27   Acc.95.31, box 1, letter, Edmonton Historical Board, 29 April 1981; vestry minutes, 19 October 1981. The plaque now hangs on an inside wall of a new extension near the cornerstone laid in 1955 and a photograph of Diana, Princess of Wales, commemorating her memorial service.

28   Ed.15/All Saints', file 36, order of service, "The Dedication of the Cathedral Church of All Saints'," 10 May 1956. Information on Secord from http://www.epl.ca/Elections/Results/EPLBiographies/ST.cfm.

29   Ed.15/All Saints', file 52, vestry minutes, 13 November 1933; file 54, vestry minutes, 13 November 1950; also Acc.95.31, box 1, letter, Office of the Ombudsman, 25 October 1973; letter, Dean Randall Ivany to Premier Peter Lougheed, 15 March 1972; vestry minutes, 11 February 1974.

30   In 1991 only 8.1 percent of Canadians were Anglican, compared to 12.7 percent in 1901). The largest church has always been Roman Catholic (41.5 percent in 1901, 45.2 percent in 1991); among Protestants, Presbyterian/Methodist (after 1925, United) adherents have outnumbered Anglicans. Figures from Statistics Canada.

31   Ed.15/All Saints', file 61, dean's report, 1952; file 112, order of service, memorial (Edward VII), 20 May 1910; file 160, register of services, 1897-1904 (Edward VII coronation). See also file 52, vestry minutes, 2 July 1929 (thanksgiving George V recovery); file 52, vestry minutes, 8 April 1935 (George V jubilee); file 55, vestry minutes, 11 February 1952, and file 61, dean's report, 1952 (George VI death); file 112, order of service, memorial (George VI).

32   Acc.95.31, box 1, letter, Dean Randall Ivany to Premier Peter Lougheed, 15 March 1972 (also Lougheed response, 28 March 1972). The letter also invited Lougheed to join All Saints' if he had not chosen an Edmonton parish following his election victory and move from Calgary.

33   Acc.95.31, box 1, vestry minutes, 23 January 1978. See also Ed.15/All Saints', file 55, annual meeting minutes, 2 February 1954, dean's attendance when Princess Patricia visited Calgary; file 58, vestry minutes, 8 May 1967; file 103, reports, 1967, Princess Alexandra and Earl of Tunis visit to Edmonton.

34   Acc.95.31, box 7; Ed.15/All Saints', file 61, dean's report, 1952.

35   Acc.95.31, box 7, letter, Dean Burch to St. John's Cathedral Boys School, Selkirk, Manitoba, 4 April 1967. Emphasis added.

36   When former governor general Ramon Hnatyshyn died in 2002, All Saints' held no memo-
     rial service. Ironically, his state funeral in Ottawa, following the Ukrainian Orthodox (Byz-
     antine) rite, was held in the Anglican cathedral because of its size.
37   On the honour roll and battalion colours, see Ed.15/All Saints', file 117a, *Edmonton Parish
     Magazine* (handwritten), January 1920, comments by Rector Goulding; on the Soldiers'
     Corner, see Ed.15/All Saints', files 106-9, Building Fund Committee, fundraising pamphlets,
     especially "c," blueprint/Plate B.
38   On Remembrance Day, see for example Ed.15/All Saints', file 58, vestry minutes, 13 Octo-
     ber 1964, 14 October 1965; file 61, dean's report, 1962; file 117a, *Parochial Magazine*, 1925
     (date added, handwritten); and Acc.95.31, boxes 1, 6.
39   On flag acquisition and care, flying and hanging, and etiquette, see Ed.15/All Saints', file
     52, vestry minutes, 9 September 1935; 12 September, 7 November 1938; files 46, 47 (no
     flags in photos); file 54, vestry minutes, 11 February, 10 March 1952 (repairs to pole to fly
     flag at half-mast on George VI's death); file 56, vestry minutes, 12 September 1955; file 116,
     brochure, 1970 (date added, handwritten); file 118, sixtieth anniversary booklet, 1935; file
     58, vestry minutes, 10 March 1964; 9 November 1965, 8 November, 13 December 1966, 13
     March 1967; files 106-9, Building Fund Committee, fundraising pamphlets, especially "d"
     (photo, Union Jack) and "e" (photo, dated 1954, no flag); and Acc.95.31, box 6, 1983 file
     (temporary removal for Banners of the Apocalypse). In 2004 the Canadian Maple Leaf flies
     outside the church.
40   For some thirty years McDougall United has displayed the Canadian Armed Forces flag
     from nearby Namao. In 1918 First Presbyterian received the flags of the local 130th Battal-
     ion for safekeeping; although in 2004 a document on the sanctuary wall says they hang by
     the pulpit, none is present.
41   See Ed.15/All Saints', file 57, vestry minutes, 14 November 1961, regarding a Second World
     War memorial.
42   See Acc.95.31, box 1, vestry minutes, 24 April 1972, 9 April 1973; box 7. Ed.15/All Saints',
     file 57, vestry minutes, 8 May 1962, discusses special services for the Battle of Britain.
43   Gust Olson, pers. comm., 7 November 1997.
44   Acc.95.31, box 1, vestry minutes, 11 February, 9 September, 12 November 1974.
45   On the Mounties and their image, see Michael Dawson, "'That Nice Red Coat Goes to My
     Head Like Champagne': Gender, Antimodernism, and the Mountie Image, 1880-1960,"
     Journal of Canadian Studies (Fall 1997): 119-39; Steve Hewitt, "The Masculine Mountie: The
     Royal Canadian Mounted Police as a Male Institution, 1914-1939," *Journal of the Canadian
     Historical Association* (1996): 153-74; Keith Walden, *Visions of Order: The Canadian Mounties
     in Symbol and Myth* (Toronto: Butterworths, 1982); and R.C. Macleod, *The North West Mounted
     Police, 1873-1919* (Ottawa: Canadian Historical Association, 1978).
46   Ed.15/All Saints', file 43a, order of service, "The Consecration of the Cathedral Church of
     All Saints', and the Centennial Year of Canada's Confederation," 1 November 1967; file 49,
     The Church Today (November 1967), souvenir edition; file 110, correspondence/miscella-
     neous, 1966-67. See also, for example, Ed.15/All Saints', file 58, vestry minutes, 17 April, 12
     December 1967; reports, 1967.
47   Acc.95.31, box 1, vestry minutes, 22 February 1983; box 6, 1983 file.
48   Thomas, "Establishing an Anglican Presence," 28.
49   Ed.15/All Saints', file 52, vestry minutes, 17 October 1932; 10 January, 15 February, 8 March,
     8 May 1933; file 80, Scouts annual report 1936.
50   Ed.15/All Saints', file 52, vestry minutes, 8 July 1931; file 71.
51   Ed.15/All Saints', file 52, vestry minutes, 7 November 1938; file 76, Cubs annual report
     1932, Guides annual report 1936; file 78, annual report 1934; file 81, annual report 1937;
     file 85, annual report 1941; Acc.95.31, box 10, file: "Cathedral 1st Edmonton Boy Scouts,
     Group Committee Meetings," minutes, 1957-59.
52   Ed.15/All Saints', file 52, vestry minutes, 7 July 1930; file 53, vestry minutes, 7 February,
     6 March 1944; file 57, vestry minutes, 16 May, 14 June, 13 December 1960; file 118,
     sixtieth anniversary booklet, 1935. Unlike groups that used such occasions to reaffirm
     their place in All Saints', the First Troop gave no jubilee gift in 1960; the comment that

during Baden-Powell month Scouts were to be sidesmen and ushers, "to bring to the attention of the people in the Cathedral that there is a Scout and Cub Pack," suggests that they had faded from consciousness (file 97, annual report 1960).

53 Ed.15/All Saints', file 52, vestry minutes, 8 April 1935; see also file 111, "listing of memorials with particulars" (n.d.). On the Churchill Society service and Prince Philip as guest speaker, see Acc.95.31, box 1, vestry minutes, 11 February, 8 April, 17 June, 9 September 1974.

54 Thomas, "Establishing an Anglican Presence," 28. In the late 1940s All Saints' acquired a priest from Wales, who was encouraged to hold a weeknight worship that used the Welsh service and hymns; Ed.15/All Saints', file 54, vestry minutes, 19 March 1949.

55 Ed.15/All Saints', file 62, *Report to the Parishioners of All Saints' Church* (1911).

56 Ed.15/All Saints', file 52, letter to vestry, 6 December 1931; Acc.95.31, box 10, file: "Men's Fellowship." See also Acc.95.31, box 7, Imperial Order Daughters of the Empire Service of Intercession, 27 May 1957.

57 See Ed.15/All Saints', file 102, annual meeting minutes, 1967; Acc.95.31, box 1, vestry minutes, 19 January, 23 February 1976. Later fairs discussed sharing profits with organizations like Oxfam; Ed.15/All Saints', file 58, vestry minutes, 16 October, 18 November 1968; file 104a, reports, 1968; and Acc.95.31, box 6, 1984 and 1985 files.

58 Ed.15/All Saints', file 58, vestry minutes, 16 October, 18 November 1968; file 59, vestry minutes, 20 January, 20 May, 8 September 1969; 23 March, 14 April 1970; file 103, reports, 1967; file 104a, reports, 1968; file 105, reports, 1969.

59 See Ed.15/All Saints', file 103, reports, 1967; file 105, reports, 1969; and Acc.95.31, box 1, vestry minutes, 10 September, 10 December 1973; box 6, 1985 file.

60 Acc.95.31, box 6, 1985 file.

Contributors

Marilyn Barber is an associate professor of history at Carleton University in Ottawa. Her teaching and research are in the areas of Canadian immigration and ethnic history and women's history. She has published a number of articles relating to the Fellowship of the Maple Leaf and to immigrant domestic servants.

Phillip Buckner is a professor emeritus of history at the University of New Brunswick and a senior research fellow at the Institute of Commonwealth Studies at the University of London.

Gail G. Campbell is a professor of history at the University of New Brunswick. She has published a number of articles on the role ordinary people played in shaping nineteenth-century New Brunswick politics, and is currently completing a book-length manuscript on the experience of nineteenth-century New Brunswick women as viewed through the prism of their diaries and correspondence.

Serge Courville is a professor emeritus at Université Laval and a fellow of the Royal Society of Canada. He is widely respected for his work on the historical geography of Quebec. As a Killam Fellow (Canada Council for the Arts) he authored *Immigration, colonisation et propagande: Du rêve américain au rêve colonial*.

A professor at Memorial University, Andy A. den Otter is the author of *The Philosophy of Railways: The Transcontinental Railway Idea in British North America*, which was awarded the Humanities and Social Science Federation of Canada's Harold Adams Innis Prize. He also wrote *Civilizing the West: The Galts and the Development of Western Canada* and is the co-author with the late Alex Johnston of *Lethbridge: A Centennial History*. Currently, he is preparing a monograph on the concepts of civilization and wilderness in mid-nineteenth-century British North America.

After completing graduate degrees in history at Queen's University and the University of Toronto, **Patricia Dirks** taught in the history department at Brock University for thirty years before taking early retirement in 2001. Her research focuses on voluntary organizations and citizenship training programming for English Protestant adolescents in late-nineteenth- and early-twentieth-century Canada. This work has included analysis of why Canada's leading Protestant religious educators produced alternative citizenship training programs for boys and girls in the years immediately following the introduction into Canada of Lord Baden-Powell's Boy Scout and Girl Guide movements and of why the British and the Canadian programs both enjoyed support in Canada.

Elizabeth Jane Errington is a professor of colonial and women's history at the Royal Military College of Canada and Queen's University in Kingston, Ontario. She is the author of *The Lion, The Eagle and Upper Canada* and *Wives and Mothers, School Mistresses and Scullery Maids: Working Women in Upper Canada 1790-1840*, and her latest project, an exploration of British migration to Upper Canada in the first half of the nineteenth century, is scheduled for publication early in 2007.

R. Douglas Francis is a professor of history at the University of Calgary, where he specializes in Canadian intellectual and Western Canadian history. He is the author of *Frank H. Underhill: Intellectual Provocateur* and *Images of the West: Changing Perceptions of the Prairies, 1690-1960*, and co-author, along with Richard Jones and Donald B. Smith, of *Origins: Canadian History to Confederation,* 5th ed., *Destinies: Canadian History since Confederation,* 5th ed., and *Journeys: A History of Canada*.

Sarah Katherine Gibson is a PhD candidate in the Department of History, McGill University in Montreal. Ms. Gibson was the Max-Stern McCord Museum Fellow for 2001-4 and studies the formation of identity and cultural exchange in colonial contexts.

Wesley C. Gustavson received his MA in history from the University of Calgary and is a doctoral candidate in history at the University of Western Ontario. He is working on a history of the Imperial War Graves Commission and its role in the commemoration of the world wars.

Marjory Harper is a reader in history at the University of Aberdeen, Scotland. She is the author of four monographs and the editor or co-editor of four collections, most of which deal with aspects of the Scottish diaspora in the nineteenth and twentieth centuries. Her most recent monograph, *Adventurers and Exiles: The Great Scottish Exodus* won the Saltire Prize for the best historical book of the year. She has recently been commissioned by Oxford University Press to co-author (with Stephen Constantine) a study of migrants and settlers in the Empire and Commonwealth, 1815-2000.

Paula Hastings is a doctoral student in the history department at Duke University in Durham, North Carolina. Her research interests include the social and cultural history of nineteenth- and twentieth-century Canada, colonial studies and British imperial history, the social history of modern Britain, cultural geography, and post-emancipation Caribbean history.

David Murray retired as a full-time member of the Department of History at the University of Guelph in 2005. He is the author of *Colonial Justice: Justice, Morality and Crime in the Niagara District, 1791-1849* as well as other works in Canadian and Latin American History.

James Naylor is an associate professor of History at Brandon University in Manitoba. He is assistant editor of *Labour/Le Travail*, and author of *The New Democracy: Challenging the Social Order in Industrial Ontario, 1914-1925*. He is currently writing a history of the non-Communist left in Canada in the 1930s and '40s.

Katie Pickles is a senior lecturer in history at the University of Canterbury. She has published widely on female imperialism and the British World, including *Female Imperialism and National Identity: Imperial Order Daughter of the Empire*. She is co-editor with Myra Rutherdale of *Contact Zones: Aboriginal and Settler Women in Canada's Colonial Past*, and with Lyndon Fraser, *Shifting Centres: Women and Migration in New Zealand History*. Her monograph on the transnational commemoration of the martyrdom of Edith Cavell will be published in 2006 by Palgrave.

Myra Rutherdale is an assistant professor of Canadian History at York University in Toronto. She is the author of *Women and the White Man's God: Gender and Race in the Canadian Mission Field* and co-editor, with Katie Pickles, of *Contact Zones: Aboriginal and Settler Women in Canada's Colonial Past*. She is particularly interested in gender and colonization and has written extensively on Native/Newcomer relations.

Frances Swyripa teaches Canadian history in the Department of History and Classics at the University of Alberta. She is a specialist on immigration/ethnicity and the West, and has written extensively on the Ukrainian experience, including a monograph – *Wedded to the Cause: Ukrainian-Canadian Women and Ethnic Identity* – published by the University of Toronto Press. The book she is currently writing is comparative, using selected European immigrant settler peoples to examine the construction, character, and impact of ethno-religious identity on the Canadian prairies.

Christopher Tait is a PhD candidate in history at the University of Western Ontario. His dissertation examines colonial Canadian attitudes toward the British monarchy between 1760 and 1867. His academic interests include the historical development of Canadian identity and national mythmaking, as well as the history of science and technology.

David E. Torrance received his PhD from Queen's University in Kingston, Ontario in 1987. Since 1989, he has been a professor of history at Mt. Allison University in Sackville, New Brunswick.

Mary Vipond is a professor of history at Concordia University in Montreal. Her recent research has focused on the history of Canadian radio. In addition to articles in Canadian, American, and British journals, she has published *Listening In: The First Decade of Canadian Broadcasting, 1922-1932* and *The Mass Media in Canada*, 3rd ed. She is currently completing a book on the Canadian Radio Broadcasting Commission (1932-36) and commencing a project on censorship and propaganda at the Canadian Broadcasting Corporation during the Second World War.

Index

Note: BLP stands for British Labour Party, CCF, for Co-operative Commonwealth Federation; ILP, for Independent Labour Party; SA, for Salvation Army

Printed and bound in Canada by Friesens
Set in Stone by Artegraphica Design Co. Ltd.
Copy editor: Judy Phillips
Proofreader: Stephanie VanderMeulen
Indexer: Patricia Buchanan